COLLEGE

MATHEMATICS

with

BUSINESS

APPLICATIONS

THIRD EDITION

COLLEGE MATHEMATICS

PRENTICE-HALL, INC., Englewood Cliffs, New Jersey   07632

with BUSINESS APPLICATIONS

JOHN E. FREUND
Arizona State University

THOMAS A. WILLIAMS
Rochester Institute of Technology

Library of Congress Cataloging in Publication Data

Freund, John E.
  College mathematics with business applications.

  Includes bibliographical references and index.
  1. Business mathematics. I. Williams,
Thomas Arthur, (date). II. Title.
HF5691.F7 1983   510'.2465   82-18109
ISBN 0-13-146498-1

COLLEGE MATHEMATICS WITH BUSINESS APPLICATIONS, third edition
John E. Freund / Thomas A. Williams

© 1983, 1975, 1969 by Prentice-Hall, Inc., Englewood Cliffs, N.J.   07632

Editorial/production supervision by Margaret Rizzi
Interior design by Lee Cohen
Cover photograph by Floyd Rollefstad
Cover design by Lee Cohen
Manufacturing buyer: Ed O'Dougherty

Printed in the United States of America
10 9 8 7 6 5 4 3 2

ISBN   0-13-146498-1

Prentice-Hall International, Inc., *London*
Prentice-Hall of Australia Pty. Limited, *Sydney*
Editora Prentice-Hall do Brasil, Ltda., *Rio de Janeiro*
Prentice-Hall Canada Inc., *Toronto*
Prentice-Hall of India Private Limited, *New Delhi*
Prentice-Hall of Japan, Inc., *Tokyo*
Prentice-Hall of Southeast Asia Pte. Ltd., *Singapore*
Whitehall Books Limited, *Wellington, New Zealand*

CONTENTS

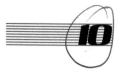

DIFFERENTIAL CALCULUS, 260

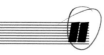

PREFACE

The purpose of this text is to provide students with a general understanding of the role of mathematics in business and economics, and to prepare them in these disciplines for more advanced work in areas such as management science, statistics, production and operations management, and econometrics. The only prerequisite for this book is some high school algebra, namely, some familiarity (and, hopefully, a lack of fear) of dealing with letters and symbols instead of numbers.

The examples used to illustrate the mathematical concept being introduced are illustrative of applied problems in business and economics. Whenever possible, we take an intuitive approach as compared to a formal theorem-proving approach. The result is a text that is not only simpler and more concise, but a text that focuses on the needs of the student.

The text is designed for teaching the subject with maximum flexibility. Our primary objective in selecting topics was to reflect the mathematical background needed to successfully pursue a program of study in business and economics. Conceptually, the text is subdivided into five major parts: Review of basic mathematical concepts; Functions; Systems of equations and inequalities; Calculus; Probability and decision making. Thus, considerable flexibility exists in designing particular courses for specific groups of students.

There have been several changes in organization following the suggestions of colleagues who have used the second edition. The new features in this edition are:

1. Chapter 1 now provides a review of basic concepts in mathematics and elementary algebra. The concept of a set is introduced, followed by a discussion of numbers and number systems, mathematical notation (including exponential notation, subscript notation, and summation notation), polynomials, fractions, and linear equations in one variable.

2. The material relating specifically to functions has been grouped together as a three-chapter sequence. Chapter 2 provides an introduction to functions, Chapter 3 discusses linear and quadratic functions, and Chapter 4 covers exponential and logarithmic functions.

3. A separate chapter on mathematics of finance (Chapter 5) covers the concepts of interest, future value and present value, annuities, and depreciation.

4. The material involving inequalities and systems of inequalities has now been made a separate chapter preceding the chapter on linear programming.

5. The previous edition's two chapters on linear programming have been combined into one chapter.

6. The material on sequences and limits has been revised to provide a more intuitive introduction to the concept of a limit and its use in calculus. As such, this material is now part of the chapter on differential calculus.

7. The material on the basic theory of probability and decision making has been combined into one chapter; however, the introduction to probability (with an emphasis on counting, permutations, and combinations) remains a separate chapter preceding the chapter on probability and decision making.

8. The second edition chapter on periodic functions has been dropped from the third edition, as has the chapter on simulation.

In addition to the above changes in organization, the third edition includes the following new pedagogical features.

1. Each chapter begins with a short introduction that provides an overview of the chapter material.

2. Each chapter concludes with a summary that reviews the concepts introduced in the chapter.

3. An end-of-chapter glossary enables the student to look up key terms and check his or her understanding of the concepts introduced.

4. Each chapter concludes with a set of supplementary exercises.

The authors would like to thank their many friends and colleagues, whose suggestions, criticisms, and comments contributed greatly to the third edition of this book; specifically, we are indebted to Professor Laurence P. Maher, Jr., North Texas State University; Professor Rebecca Klemm, Georgetown University; Professor Subhash C. Narula, Rensselaer Polytechnic Institute; Professor James F. Hurley, University of Connecticut; Professor Thomas A. Carnevale, Virginia Commonwealth University; and Professor L. G. Schilling, University of Texas–Arlington.

We are also indebted to Ms. Margaret Rizzi for her courteous cooperation during the production of the book.

John E. Freund   *Thomas A. Williams*

A REVIEW
OF BASIC
CONCEPTS
IN MATHEMATICS
AND
ELEMENTARY
ALGEBRA

Most applications of mathematics in business and economics involve the development of a **mathematical model**. For example, consider an automobile dealer who receives an end-of-the-year rebate of $200 for every car sold. The annual rebate can be determined by multiplying the per-unit rebate by the number of cars sold during the year. If we let x represent the number of cars sold during the year and R the annual rebate in dollars, the following mathematical model defines the total annual rebate earned by selling x cars.

$$R = 200x$$

This mathematical model, or equation, which we will learn to recognize as an example of a linear equation, is a simple illustration of how symbols and numbers can be used to represent a business situation.

The purpose of this chapter is to review several mathematical concepts that provide the background for studying this and other types of mathematical models. First, we discuss the concept of a set. In subsequent sections of this chapter we consider additional topics involving number systems, mathematical notation, and elementary algebra. In Chapter 2 we show how much of this material forms a base from which we begin our study of functions and their applications in business.

1.1 AN INTRODUCTION TO SETS

In mathematics, the term **set** is used to denote any well-defined collection of objects. In everyday usage, it has many synonyms; for example, we speak of a group of industries, a class of students, a team of athletes, a collection of coins or stamps, and so on. The objects belonging to a set are referred to as its **elements**.

EXAMPLE 1.1   The six students taking an advanced course in accounting constitute a set and each of the students in an element of the set.

Sets are often specified by listing the individual elements between braces. To illustrate this approach, consider the following extension of Example 1.1.

EXAMPLE 1.1   If the six students taking the advanced course in accounting are named
(Continued)   Ames, Cooper, Knight, Leone, Rogers, and Vaughn, we can indicate the corresponding set by writing

{Ames, Cooper, Knight, Leone, Rogers, Vaughn}

Note that when the elements of a set are listed in this way, their order does not matter; the six students taking the advanced course in accounting listed in any order constitute the same set.

EXAMPLE 1.2   A firm has manufacturing facilities in Boston, Dallas, and San Francisco. We can denote the corresponding set by

{Boston, Dallas, San Francisco}

Note that since the order of the elements does not matter, this set can also be written as {Boston, San Francisco, Dallas}, {Dallas, Boston, San Francisco}, {Dallas, San Francisco, Boston}, {San Francisco, Boston, Dallas}, and {San Francisco, Dallas, Boston}.

conventions   Sets are usually denoted by capital letters, $A, B, C, \ldots$, and to indicate
for naming sets   that object a is an element of set A, we use the symbol $\in$ and write $a \in A$. To indicate that a is not an element of set A, we use the same symbol with a line through it and write $a \notin A$. Literally, $a \in A$ is read "a is an element of A," and $a \notin A$ is read "a is not an element of A."

EXAMPLE 1.1   If we denote the set of students in the advanced course in accounting
(Continued)   with the letter A, we can write

$$A = \{\text{Ames, Cooper, Knight, Leone, Rogers, Vaughn}\}$$

Thus Ames $\in A$, Cooper $\in A$, and so on. Note, however, that Smith $\notin A$, whoever Smith may be.

EXAMPLE 1.2
(Continued) Let $M = \{\text{Boston, Dallas, San Francisco}\}$. Then Boston $\in M$, Dallas $\in M$, and San Francisco $\in M$. Note, however, that Atlanta $\notin M$, Miami $\notin M$, and so on.

In Example 1.1, we used an equal sign to indicate that A and {Ames, Cooper, Knight, Leone, Rogers, Vaughn} represent the same set. Similarly, in Example 1.2 an equal sign was used to equate M and {Boston, Dallas, San Francisco}. More generally, when we say that two given sets A and B are equal, we mean that A and B have exactly the same elements. In other words,

two sets A and B are equal and we write A = B if every element of A is also an element of B, and vice versa.

To make it clear that in a given situation our discussion is limited to a particular set, we refer to this set as the **universal set**. Generally speaking,

a universal set is a set containing all of the elements with which we are concerned in a given situation.

Since the answer to a question can well depend upon the choice of the universal set, it is always important to state specifically what universal set we have in mind. For instance, in one problem we may be concerned with the universal set of people who have graduated from business schools, and in another problem we may be concerned with the universal set of all people who hold MBA degrees. We shall denote a universal set by the letter I.

In contrast to the universal set, which comprises all the elements of relevance in a given situation, we define the **null set** (or **empty set**) as the set which has no elements at all. We denote the null set by the symbol $\emptyset$. For example, the set of airline companies that never lose passengers' luggage is the empty set.

The term **subset** is used to denote a set whose elements comprise part or all of the elements of a given set. In general,

set A is a subset of set B if and only if every element of A is also an element of B.

EXAMPLE 1.3 The insurance companies incorporated in Arizona constitute a subset of the set consisting of all the insurance companies incorporated in the United States.

From the above definition of a subset, it follows that every set is a subset of itself and that the null set ($\emptyset$) is a subset of every set. In addition, if a given subset constitutes only part of a set (not the whole set), we refer to it as a **proper subset**. Finally, to indicate that set A is a subset of set B, we write $A \subset B$, which is read "A is a subset of B" or "A is contained in B." Correspondingly, to indicate that set A is not a subset of set B, we write $A \not\subset B$.

EXAMPLE 1.2
(Continued) Let R = {Atlanta, Boston, Cincinnati, Dallas, New York, San Francisco} denote the set of cities in which the firm has a regional sales office. Because every element of M = {Boston, Dallas, San Francisco} is an element of R, M is a subset of R; thus we write $M \subset R$. In words, the set of cities in which the firm has a manufacturing facility is a subset of the set of cities in which the firm has a regional sales office. (Note that since M constitutes only part of R, it is a proper subset of R.)

EXAMPLE 1.4 A manufacturer of sporting goods is considering adding a line of golf equipment to its existing set of products. Let G = {clubs, balls, bags} denote the set of golf products the manufacturer is considering. The possible subsets of G are $\emptyset$, {clubs}, {balls}, {bags}, {clubs, balls}, {clubs, bags}, {balls, bags}, {clubs, balls, bags}. Note that the null set corresponds to a decision not to produce any golf equipment and that only the first seven subsets are proper subsets.

operations
involving sets There are various ways in which we can use sets to form new sets. For example, given a set A, we can form the set consisting of all the elements of the universal set which are not in A. We refer to this new set as the **complement** of A and write it as A'. In general,

if A is a subset of the universal set I, then A', called the complement of A, is the set composed of all the elements of I that are not in A.

EXAMPLE 1.5 If I is the set of all the cars listed for sale in a given newspaper and F is the set of those priced at $1500 or less, then F' consists of those cars listed in the newspaper that are priced at more than $1500.

New sets can also be formed by combining the elements of two or more sets in some fashion. For example, given two sets A and B, we can form the set consisting of all the elements that belong to A as well as B. We call this new set the **intersection** of A and B and denote it by $A \cap B$, which is read "A intersection B," or simply "A and B." Formally,

the intersection of two sets A and B, denoted by A $\cap$ B, is the set consisting of all the elements belonging to both A and B.

In set notation, this can be written as

$$A \cap B = \{x \mid x \in A \text{ and } x \in B\}$$

In this expression the vertical line stands for *such that* and the entire expression in braces is read "the set consisting of the elements x such that x is an element of A and x is an element of B." Note that if $A \cap B = \emptyset$ (that is, there are no elements in the intersection), sets A and B are said to be **disjoint**.

EXAMPLE 1.6   If I is the set of all the students enrolled at a given university and J and K represent those majoring in economics and those who work part time, respectively, then $J \cap K$ is the set of all the students at that university who major in economics *and* work part time. Also, if I is the set of all stocks listed at the American Stock Exchange and D and E represent those which paid a dividend in 1981 and those which currently have a price-earnings ratio of less than 15, respectively, then $D \cap E$ is the set of all the stocks listed at the American Stock Exchange which paid a dividend in 1981 *and* currently have a price-earnings ratio of less than 15.

EXAMPLE 1.7   Let F = {Anderson, Dunton, McConville} denote the set of employees of a consulting firm who are chartered financial analysts and P = {Anderson, DiCarlo, Ebert, McConville, Sullivan} denote the set of employees who are certified public accountants. Then $F \cap P$ = {Anderson, McConville} is the set of employees who are chartered financial analysts *and* certified public accountants.

When we form the intersection of two sets, we do not literally "combine" their elements; instead we take only those contained in both. If we actually want to combine the elements of two sets A and B—that is, take them all together—we form what is called their **union** and denote it by $A \cup B$, which is read "A union B," or simply "A or B." Formally, the union of two sets A and B, denoted by A ∪ B, is the set consisting of all the elements belonging to either A or B, including those which belong to both.

In set notation, this can be written

$$A \cup B = \{x \mid x \in A \text{ or } x \in B\}$$

Note that the expression in braces is read "the set consisting of the elements x such that x is an element of A or x is an element of B."

EXAMPLE 1.6
(Continued)   With J, K, D, and E defined in Example 1.6, $J \cup K$ is the set of all the students at the given university who are majoring in economics, working part time, or both. The set $D \cup E$ consists of all the stocks listed at the American Stock Exchange which paid dividends in 1981, have current price earnings ratios of less than 15, or both.

EXAMPLE 1.7
(Continued)   With F and P as defined in Example 1.7, $F \cup P = \{$Anderson, DiCarlo, Dunton, Ebert, McConville, Sullivan$\}$ is the set of employees that are chartered financial analysts, certified public accountants, or both.

---

venn diagrams   Sets and subsets are often depicted by means of **Venn diagrams** like those of Figure 1.1.* In each case the univeral set I is represented by a

---

*These diagrams are named after the British logician who first used them in 1876.

FIGURE 1.1
Venn Diagrams

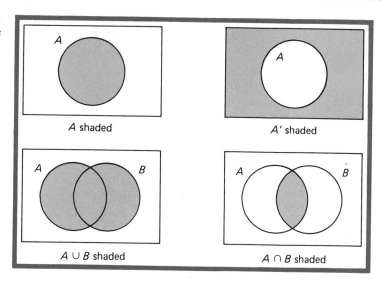

A shaded

A' shaded

A ∪ B shaded

A ∩ B shaded

rectangle, and subsets of *I* are represented by regions within the rectangle, usually by circles or parts of circles. Thus the shaded regions of Figure 1.1 represent the set *A*, the complement of set *A*, the union of sets *A* and *B*, and the intersection of sets *A* and *B*, respectively; the sets *A* and *B* are represented by the respective circles.

EXERCISES

1. The following sets represent the South American countries in which five U.S. manufacturers of office equipment have agencies.

$$A = \{\text{Brazil, Argentina, Colombia, Ecuador}\}$$

$$B = \{\text{Argentina, Peru, Venezuela}\}$$

$$C = \{\text{Brazil, Colombia, Paraguay, Peru}\}$$

$$D = \{\text{Brazil, Argentina, Peru, Venezuela}\}$$

$$E = \{\text{Brazil, Ecuador, Paraguay}\}$$

Determine whether each of the following is true or false.
(a) Argentina $\notin A$ (e) $A \cap B = \{\text{Argentina}\}$
(b) Ecuador $\notin D$ (f) $C \cup E = \{\text{Brazil, Colombia, Ecuador,}$
(c) $E \subset C$ Paraguay, Peru$\}$
(d) $E \not\subset C$ (g) $C \cap E = E$
                    (h) $B \cap D = B$

2. With reference to Exercise 1, determine whether each of the following is true or false.
(a) Brazil $\in B$ (e) $A \cap C = \{\text{Brazil, Colombia, Ecuador}\}$
(b) Colombia $\notin C$ (f) $B \cup D = \{\text{Brazil, Argentina, Paraguay,}$
(c) $C \subset E$ Peru$\}$
(d) $B \not\subset D$ (g) $C \cup E = E$
                    (h) $A \cap C = D \cap E$

3. Let $S = \{a, b, c, d, e, f, g, h\}$ denote the service stations located in Brookville, Indiana. The stations denoted by b, e, and h accept credit cards, and the stations denoted by b, d, e, and h sell diesel fuel as well as gasoline. Let C denote the set of all stations that accept credit cards and D the set of all stations that sell diesel fuel.
(a) Write the elements of C and D in set notation.
(b) Write the set $C \cap D$ and describe the elements of this set in words.

4. The following sets represent the airlines which provide service to four different cities.

$K = \{\text{American, TWA, United}\}$

$L = \{\text{American, Western}\}$

$M = \{\text{Delta, American, TWA, Western, Eastern, United}\}$

$N = \{\text{TWA, Republic, Continental, Western, United}\}$

Determine whether each of the following is true or false.
(a) Western $\in K$ (e) $M \cap N = \{\text{TWA, Western}\}$
(b) United $\notin L$ (f) $K \cup L = \{\text{American, TWA, Western,}$
(c) $M \subset K$ United, Continental$\}$
(d) $K \subset M$ (g) $L \cap M = L$
                         (h) $L \cap N = \emptyset$

5. Use Exercise 4 to determine whether each of the following is true or false.
(a) United $\in M$ (e) $L \cap N = \{\text{American, Western}\}$
(b) Republic $\notin N$ (f) $K \cup N = \{\text{American, TWA, Republic,}$
(c) $L \not\subset N$ Western$\}$
(c) $L \subset M$ (g) $L \cap N = L$
(d) $L \subset M$ (h) $K \cap L = K \cap M$

6. Let C denote the set of all colleges and universities in the United States, B denote the subset of C that grant degrees in business, E the subset that grant degrees in engineering, and P the subset of C that are private colleges or universities. Describe (in words) each set.
(a) $B \cup E$ (c) P'
(b) $B \cap P$ (d) $B \cap P'$

7. In a study of European cars, a consumer testing service considered the universal set

$I = \{\text{Mercedes, Fiat, Renault, Volkswagen, Porsche, Jaguar, Volvo, BMW}\}$

and performed different tests on the sets

$C = \{\text{Mercedes, Volkswagen, BMW}\}$

$D = \{\text{Fiat, Renault, Porsche, Jaguar, Volvo}\}$

$E = \{\text{Fiat, Volkswagen, Jaguar, Volvo}\}$

List the makes of cars included in each set.
(a) C' (e) $C \cap E$
(b) D' (f) $D \cap E$
(c) E' (g) $C \cup D$
(d) $C \cap D$ (h) $D \cup E$

8. Let *A* denote the set of all models produced by an automobile manufacturer with a list price of $8000 or less and let *B* denote the set of all the manufacturer's models that have front-wheel drive. Describe (in words) each set.
   (a) A' (c) $A \cap B$
   (b) B' (d) $A \cup B$

9. Let *I* denote the set of all employees at Jacobs Machine Company, *A* the set of accountants, *C* the set of computer programmers, *E* the set of engineers, and *M* the set of all managers. Describe (in words) each set.
   (a) A' (d) $A \cap E$
   (b) $M \cap C$ (e) $M' \cap A$
   (c) $A \cup E$

10. If *I* is the set of all houses advertised for sale in Chicago (on a given day), within which set *A* contains all those with two or more baths, set *B* contains all those with three bedrooms, set *C* contains all those priced at $45,000 or more, and set *D* contains all those that are at least three years old, describe (in words) each set. (a) A'; (b) B'; (c) C'; (d) D'; (e) $A \cap B$; (f) $A \cap C$.

11. Use Exercise 10 to describe (in words) each set. (a) $B' \cap C$; (b) $C \cup D$; (c) $C' \cap D$; (d) $A \cup B$; (e) $A \cup C$; (f) $C \cap D$.

12. Let C = {Anderson, Sweeney, Peters, Jones, Newton, Haverly, Tyler} denote the set of candidates for a new management position. If M = {Peters, Haverly, Tyler} is the set of candidates that have an MBA degree and E = {Anderson, Peters, Tyler, Sweeney} is the set of candidates with 10 or more years of experience, write the following sets and describe (in words) each set.
   (a) M' (c) $M \cap E$
   (b) E' (d) $M' \cup E$

13. Suppose that *A* is the set of all companies listed on the New York Stock Exchange and *B* is the set of companies with annual sales of less than $25 million. Describe (in words) each set.
   (a) $A \cup B'$ (b) $A \cap B$ (c) $(A \cap B)'$

14. If *I* is the set of all American tourists who traveled to Europe in a given year, within which *A* is the set of all those who visited Rome, *B* is the set of all those who visited Paris, *C* is the set of all those who went both ways by air, and *D* is the set of all those who carried traveler's checks, find a symbolic expression for each set.
    (a) Those who did not go both ways by air.
    (b) Those who did not visit Paris.
    (c) Those who visited Rome and Paris.
    (d) Those who went both ways by air and carried traveler's checks.
    (e) Those who visited Rome but did not go both ways by air.

15. Use Exercise 14 to find a symbolic expression for each set.
    (a) Those who visited either Rome or Paris.
    (b) Those who either visited Paris or did not go both ways by air.
    (c) Those who visited neither Rome nor Paris.
    (d) Those who either did not visit Paris or did not carry traveler's checks.
    (e) Those who carried traveler's checks but visited neither Rome nor Paris.

16. In a group of 150 college students, 83 are enrolled in a course in accounting, 67 are enrolled in a course in statistics, and 45 are enrolled in both. How many of these students are not enrolled in either course?

17. A market research organization claims that among 200 executives interviewed 124 regularly read the *Wall Street Journal*, 106 regularly read the *U.S. News & World Report*, 35 regularly read both, and 23 read neither on a regular basis. Are these figures compatible, or do they involve a contradiction? Explain your answer.

1.2 NUMBERS AND NUMBER SYSTEMS

rational numbers   The whole numbers, 1, 2, 3, 4, 5, 6, 7, . . . , are also called the **natural numbers**. Although it is true that the sum and the product of any two natural numbers are also natural numbers, analogous assertions for differences and quotients are incorrect. For example, we can subtract 3 from 5 and get the natural number 2, but we cannot subtract 5 from 3 as long as we are working only with natural numbers. The situation changes, however, if we consider the set of **integers,** which include the natural numbers 1, 2, 3, 4, 5, 6, 7, . . . , the corresponding negative numbers $-1, -2, -3, -4, -5, -6, -7, . . .$, and the number 0. The difference between any two integers is also an integer; for example, $3 - 5 = -2$ and $8 - 8 = 0$.

   Although there are quite a few things we can do with integers that cannot be done with natural numbers, we still have to be careful when it comes to division. For example, although we can divide 12 by -3 and get -4 or -24 by -4 and get 6, we cannot divide -3 by 12 or -4 by -24 as long as we are working only with integers. To get around this difficulty, we shall have to extend our discussion to the fractions, or the set of **rational numbers**. Working with rational numbers, we can divide -3 by 12 and get $-\frac{1}{4}$, and we can divide -4 by -24 and get $\frac{1}{6}$.

irrational numbers   The idea of associating numbers with distances and, hence, with points on a line dates back to ancient times. Until the fifth century B.C., it was believed that all distances could be measured by means of rational numbers, but this was proved to be wrong when Pythagoras discovered that *there is no rational number whose square equals 2.*

The fact that there were distances that could not be measured by means of rational numbers was quite a blow to Pythagoras and his contemporaries, since a major part of their philosophy was built on the mystical significance they attached to numbers of this kind. Today we look at this problem from an entirely different point of view. If there is no rational number whose square equals 2 and if we want to have such a number, we simply go ahead and define one. We refer to this particular number as the square root of 2 and write it as $\sqrt{2}$; since it is not a rational number, we call it **irrational** (meaning nonrational).

For a long time after Pythagoras, the square root of 2 was the only irrational number known. About a century later, it was shown that the numbers whose squares are 3, 5, 6, 7, 8, 10, 11, 12, 13, 14, 15, and 17 are also irrational; today it can be shown that there are infinitely more irrational numbers than rational numbers. Irrational numbers include such numbers as π, which arises in connection with the circumference and the area of a circle, and the number e, used in connection with logarithms.

real number system The number system which enables us to measure any distance (that is, assign a number to any point on a line) is the set we call the **real numbers**. It consists of the rational numbers as well as the irrational numbers, which—so to speak—fill the gaps. The distinction between rational numbers and irrational numbers is important to the mathematician, but it is of very little significance so far as practical applications are concerned. This is because any irrational number can be approximated to any desired degree of accuracy by means of a rational number. For instance, if we have to perform calculations involving $\sqrt{2}$, we can use the rational number 1.41 instead or, if more accuracy is required, the rational number 1.414, and so on.

To summarize the number systems we have mentioned thus far in this section, consider Figure 1.2. It shows that the real numbers consist

FIGURE 1.2
Systems of Numbers

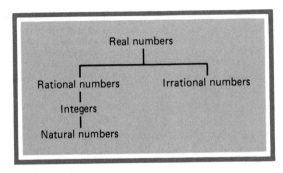

of rational numbers and irrational numbers; the rational numbers include the integers, which in turn include the natural numbers.

algebraic properties of real numbers   Three important properties associated with the use of real numbers are the commutative properties of addition and multiplication, the associative properties of addition and multiplication, and the distributive property of multiplication over addition.

Commutative Property of Addition

$$a + b = b + a$$

Commutative Property of Multiplication

$$ab = ba$$

EXAMPLE 1.8

$$10 + 5 = 5 + 10 = 15$$

$$5 \cdot 8 = 8 \cdot 5 = 40$$

Associative Property of Addition

$$(a + b) + c = a + (b + c)$$

Associative Property of Multiplication

$$(ab)c = a(bc)$$

EXAMPLE 1.9

$$(8 + 6) + 4 = 8 + (6 + 4) = 18$$

$$(4 \cdot 2)5 = 4(2 \cdot 5) = 20$$

Distributive Property of Multiplication over Addition

$$a \cdot (b + c) = ab + ac$$

EXAMPLE 1.10

$$2(7 + 3) = 2 \cdot 7 + 2 \cdot 3 = 20$$

In subsequent sections of this chapter we discuss other properties of real numbers and illustrate the use of these properties in manipulating algebraic expressions.

1.3 COMMON MATHEMATICAL NOTATION

decimal notation   The main feature of **decimal notation** is that it combines the use of symbols for zero, one, two, . . . , and nine with the convention that the position of each digit tells us whether it represents ones, tens, hundreds, thousands, and so on. It is a **positional notation**, a fact which is stressed even in the elementary grades.

EXAMPLE 1.11   In 234 the 2 represents hundreds, the 3 represents tens, and the 4 represents ones; in other words,

$$234 = 2 \cdot 10^2 + 3 \cdot 10^1 + 4 \cdot 10^0$$

where, *by definition*, $10^0 = 1$ (see page 18). Similarly, in 1579 the 1 represents thousands, the 5 represents hundreds, the 7 represents tens, and the 9 represents ones; namely,

$$1579 = 1 \cdot 10^3 + 5 \cdot 10^2 + 7 \cdot 10^1 + 9 \cdot 10^0$$

Once the significance of the positional notation is understood, it is easy to follow the logic behind the various tricks that are taught in elementary arithmetic.

EXAMPLE 1.12   To multiply 87 by 35, for instance, we write (more or less automatically)

$$
\begin{array}{r}
87 \\
\times \quad 35 \\
\hline
435 \\
261 \\
\hline
3045
\end{array}
$$

First we multiply 87 by 5 and then we multiply it by 3, moving the second product one place to the left (because we are really multiplying by 30 rather than 3). Note that this result is just an application of the distributive property of real numbers. That is, $87 \cdot 35 = 87(30 + 5) = 87 \cdot 30 + 87 \cdot 5$.

In order to adapt decimal notation to work with fractions, observe that when a digit is moved *one place to the right*, the number it represents is *divided by* 10; similarly, when a digit is moved *two places to the right,* the number it represents is *divided by 100;* and so on. With this argument we can divide 7 by 10 by moving the 7 one place to the right, and to indicate that this has been done we write the result as 0.7. The *decimal point* (which was introduced early in the seventeenth century) is the key to this notation, as it indicates the "place value" of each digit. It enables us to write 0.1 for 1/10, 0.07 for 7/100, 0.003 for 3/1000, and so on. (The purpose of the 0 to the left of the decimal point is mainly to make sure that the decimal point does not get lost; it is also correct to write the above fractions as .1, .07, and .003, respectively.)

The great advantage of decimal notation for work with fractions is that we can add, subtract, multiply, and divide fractions using the same rules and the same methods as for whole numbers. The problem of adding 3.42 and 1.89 is essentially the same as that of adding 342 and 189, and the problem of multiplying 3.56 by 2.14 is essentially the same as that of multiplying 356 by 214. The only difference is that in each case the decimal point will be in a different place in the final answer.

scientific notation A minor (though annoying) disadvantage of the decimal notation is that the decimal point often manages to get lost or misplaced during the course of calculations. Somehow 34.687 becomes 34,687, 0.000981 becomes 0.0000981, and so forth. In order to avoid mistakes of this kind and to make it easier to work with very large or very small numbers, it has become common practice to use what is called **scientific notation**. In this notation each number is written as a *product* of a number between 1 and 10 and an appropriate power of 10.

EXAMPLE 1.13 In scientific notation 346.87 is written as $3.4687 \cdot 10^2$ and 0.000981 is written as $9.81 \cdot 10^{-4}$.

In case you are not familiar with *negative exponents,* let us point out that $10^{-1} = 1/10$, $10^{-2} = 1/100$, $10^{-3} = 1/1000$, and, in general, $10^{-k} = 1/10^k$ for any positive integer k; also $10^0 = 1$ by definition (see page 18). Further work with negative exponents may be found in the next part of this section.

It requires some practice to convert numbers from ordinary decimal notation to scientific notation, and vice versa, but it is not really difficult. All we have to do is count how many places the decimal point has to be moved to the left or to the right so that we get a number between 1 and 10. If the decimal point has to be moved n places to the left, where n is a positive integer or zero, the exponent of 10 is n; if the decimal point has to be moved n places to the right, the exponent of 10 is $-n$.

EXAMPLE 1.13
(Continued) For 346.87 the decimal point has to be moved two places to the left (to yield a number between 1 and 10), and we write it as $3.4687 \cdot 10^2$; for 0.000981 the decimal point has to be moved *four* places to the right (to yield a number between 1 and 10), and we write it as $9.81 \cdot 10^{-4}$.

There are several modifications of scientific notation which make it easier to keep track of decimal points in work with high-speed electronic computers; they involve what we call **floating-point decimals**. To convert a number from an ordinary decimal to a floating-point decimal, we write it first as the *product* of a number between 0.1 and 1 and an appropriate power of 10; in other words, we move the decimal point to the left of the first nonzero digit and account for this by multiplying by an appropriate power of 10. In contrast to scientific notation, we then *code* the exponent in some fashion and "incorporate" it into the number. For instance, 2553.6 is written as $2.5536 \cdot 10^3$ in scientific notation, but it is written as 25536E4 in the *E*-**notation** of floating-point arithmetic. Actually, this means $0.25536 \cdot 10^4$, and it should be observed that the letter *E* separates the magnitude, or "mantissa," of the number from the exponent of 10.

*exponential
notation* **Exponential notation** is a mathematical kind of shorthand that dates back to the early part of the seventeenth century; it saves space and time, and it makes it easy, or at least easier, to write otherwise unwieldy expressions. Formally,

if n is a positive integer, we write

$$b^n = \underbrace{b \cdot b \cdot b \cdot \ldots \cdot b}_{n \ factors}$$

for any real number b.

Here n is called the **exponent** of b and b is called the **base**, and we read b^n as "the nth power of b" or "b raised to the power n." The exponential notation immediately found wide acceptance among mathematicians, who soon discovered that there are certain rules about the manipulation of exponents which provide extraordinary simplifications. There are rules for adding exponents, multiplying exponents, subtracting exponents, and so on.

If m and n are positive integers, then

Rule 1

$$b^m \cdot b^n = b^{m+n}$$

and

Rule 2

$$(b^m)^n = b^{m \cdot n}$$

for any real number b; also,

Rule 3

$$(ab)^n = a^n b^n$$

for any real numbers a and b, and

Rule 4

$$\left(\frac{a}{b}\right)^n = \frac{a^n}{b^n}$$

provided that b is not zero; finally, if m is greater than n, then

Rule 5

$$\frac{b^m}{b^n} = b^{m-n}$$

for any nonzero real number b.

EXAMPLE 1.14

(a) $2^2 2^3 = 2^{2+3} = 2^5 = 32$ (Rule 1)

(b) $(2^2)^3 = 2^{2 \cdot 3} = 2^6 = 64$ (Rule 2)

(c) $(2 \cdot 3)^2 = 2^2 3^2 = 4 \cdot 9 = 36$ (Rule 3)

(d) $\left(\dfrac{6}{3}\right)^2 = \dfrac{6^2}{3^2} = \dfrac{36}{9} = 4$ (Rule 4)

(e) $\dfrac{2^5}{2^2} = 2^{5-2} = 2^3 = 8$ (Rule 5)

EXAMPLE 1.15 To illustrate some of the simplifications that are brought about by the use of exponents, let us evaluate the quantity $(8 \cdot 256)/(32 \cdot 4)$.

Expressing each number as a power of 2, we get

$$\frac{8 \cdot 256}{32 \cdot 4} = \frac{2^3 \cdot 2^8}{2^5 \cdot 2^2} = \frac{2^{11}}{2^7} = 2^{11-7} = 2^4 = 16$$

Now let us suppose that we tried to apply the rule according to which we subtract exponents to simplify $3^5/3^5$ and $3^4/3^6$. In the first case we would get

$$\frac{3^5}{3^5} = 3^{5-5} = 3^0$$

and in the second case we would get

$$\frac{3^4}{3^6} = 3^{4-6} = 3^{-2}$$

These results are meaningless as long as we limit ourselves to our definition in which the exponent has to be a positive integer. Note, however, that these results suggest that if we want the rule $b^m/b^n = b^{m-n}$ to apply regardless of whether m is greater than, equal to, or less than n, we have only to define zero and negative exponents so that

$$3^0 = 1 \quad \text{and} \quad 3^{-2} = \frac{1}{3^2}$$

These are the results we should actually have obtained for $3^5/3^5$ and $3^4/3^6$. Thus let us make the following definition.

If b is a nonzero real number, then $b^0 = 1$, and furthermore, if k is a positive integer, then

$$b^{-k} = \frac{1}{b^k}$$

We now have extended the concept of an exponent to the set of all integers, and it is easy to verify that the various rules for adding, multiplying, and subtracting exponents still hold.

Actually, our main objective in this section is to generalize the concept of an exponent so that it can be *any real number*, not merely a positive integer or an integer. Keeping this goal in mind, let us now investigate what meaning we might assign to expressions such as $4^{1/2}$, $7^{3/4}$, or $5^{13/11}$, where the exponent in each case is a fraction. Let us see, for example, whether there is any reason for assigning a particular meaning to $4^{1/2}$, keeping in mind, of course, that we do not want to violate any of the rules of exponents that we have already discussed. If the rule which tells us to *multiply exponents* is to apply to fractional exponents of this kind, we must be able to write

$$(4^{\frac{1}{2}})^2 = 4^{\frac{1}{2} \cdot 2} = 4^1 = 4$$

and we find that $4^{1/2}$ is a number whose square equals 4—in other words, $4^{1/2}$ is *a square root* of 4. We said *a* square root rather than *the* square root because there are two square roots of 4, $+2$ and -2, and either one would do the trick. Having to make a choice, though, we shall say that $4^{1/2}$ denotes $+2$ rather than -2. More generally, this argument suggests the following definition.*

> *If b is a positive real number and n is a positive integer, then $b^{1/n}$ is the positive nth root of b, which is ordinarily written $\sqrt[n]{b}$.*

Thus $64^{1/2} = 8$, $125^{1/3} = 5$, $81^{1/4} = 3$, and $1024^{1/10} = 2$. (Incidentally, in case you are not familiar with the terminology used in this definition, the positive nth root of b is *the positive number x which is such that* $x^n = b$. In our four examples, 8, 5, 3, and 2 are all positive numbers and $8^2 = 64$, $5^3 = 125$, $3^4 = 81$, and $2^{10} = 1024$.)

We are now ready to consider expressions of the form $b^{p/q}$, where b is a positive real number and p and q are positive integers. If the rule according to which we *multiply exponents* is to apply to exponents of this kind, we must be able to write

$$b^{p/q} = (b^p)^{1/q} \quad \text{and} \quad b^{p/q} = (b^{1/q})^p$$

and we thus have *two* interpretations of $b^{p/q}$—it can be looked upon as the qth root of b^p or as the pth power of the qth root of b. Actually, these two interpretations are equivalent, and we can use whichever is the most convenient in any given situation.

To complete our definition of **rational exponents**, we still have to take care of expressions such as $125^{-1/3}$ or $32^{-3/5}$, where the exponent is a *negative fraction*. However, if we extend the definition of negative exponents so that it applies also when k is a fraction, we can write

$$125^{-1/3} = \frac{1}{125^{1/3}} = \frac{1}{5} \quad \text{and} \quad 32^{-3/5} = \frac{1}{32^{3/5}} = \frac{1}{2^3} = \frac{1}{8}$$

---

*This definition can be extended to the case where b is negative provided that n is odd, but we shall not have the occasion to use it in this text.

It can easily be checked that with this definition of negative fractional exponents all the special rules of exponents will still apply.

subscript notation For many of the mathematical models we will develop later there are too many variables involved to make it practical to select a unique letter or symbol to associate with each variable. For example, assume that the marketing director of a firm employing 100 salespeople wants to select a unique identifier for the number of units sold by each salesperson. Then, 100 different symbols are required. A simple way around this difficulty involves selecting one letter (or symbol) to refer to the general variable of interest (in this case, the number of units sold) and attaching to this letter an identifier (in this case, a number that refers to a specific salesperson), which is called a **subscript**. For example, let

$$x_1 = \text{number of units sold by salesperson 1}$$

$$x_2 = \text{number of units sold by salesperson 2}$$

.

.

.

$$x_{100} = \text{number of units sold by salesperson 100}$$

In general, we can refer to the number of units sold by the ith salesperson as x_i (x-sub-i). Thus we see that the subscript itself can be a letter or symbol. There is nothing special about using the letter i for the subscript in this illustration. We can use any letter or symbol. In subsequent chapters we will see how the use of subscripts can simplify the selection of symbols for the problem variables.

EXAMPLE 1.16 An automobile manufacturer keeps track of the number of cars produced each week at a particular assembly plant by letting x_i denote the number of cars produced in week i. For example, x_1 = number of cars produced in week 1, x_2 = number of cars produced in week 2, and so on.

---

summation notation Let us now consider a mathematical kind of shorthand that will enable us to form the sum of a series of variables that involve subscripts. For example, suppose the marketing director in the preceding illustration involving salespeople wanted to determine the total number of units sold by all 100 salespeople. Clearly, this total is equal to

$$x_1 + x_2 + \cdots + x_{100}$$

Although this is a fairly common way of writing the sum of a series of terms, mathematicians use the Greek letter Σ (sigma) to develop an even more abbreviated way of writing this type of expression. Using this symbol we can write the above sum as

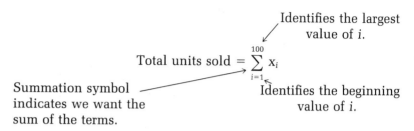

Thus we see that

$$\sum_{i=1}^{100} x_i = x_1 + x_2 + \cdots + x_{100}$$

We will discuss more complex examples involving subscripts and summations in subsequent chapters.

EXAMPLE 1.16
(Continued)

The number of cars produced during weeks 1–10 is $x_1 + x_2 + \cdots + x_{10}$. Using summation notation this can be written as

$$\sum_{i=1}^{10} x_i$$

Also, the average number of cars produced over this 10-week period is

$$\begin{array}{c} \text{Average number} \\ \text{produced per week} \\ \text{(weeks 1–10)} \end{array} = \dfrac{\displaystyle\sum_{i=1}^{10} x_i}{10}$$

---

1. Convert each decimal into scientific notation.
   (a) 12.89   (b) 0.000138   (c) 12,689.4
2. Convert each decimal into scientific notation.
   (a) 0.0000017   (b) 13,250,499   (c) 0.003694

3. Convert each number from scientific notation to ordinary decimal notation.
   (a) $3.1667 \cdot 10^3$ (b) $1.72 \cdot 10^{-2}$ (c) $2.5773 \cdot 10^4$

4. Convert each number from scientific notation to ordinary decimal notation.
   (a) $2.9948 \cdot 10^{-5}$ (b) $6.285 \cdot 10^7$ (c) $8.99931 \cdot 10^{-6}$

5. Convert each number in Exercise 1 into the E-notation of floating-point arithmetic.

6. Convert each number of Exercise 2 into the E-notation of floating-point arithmetic.

7. Convert each number from the E-notation of floating-point arithmetic to an ordinary decimal.
   (a) $147E{-}2$ (b) $33157E4$ (c) $-91582E{-}6$

8. Convert each number from the E-notation of floating-point arithmetic to an ordinary decimal.
   (a) $18582E6$ (b) $-1129E2$ (c) $373E{-}4$

9. Evaluate each expression.
   (a) $\dfrac{5^5 \cdot 5^6}{(5^2)^5}$ (b) $\dfrac{2^4(2^3)^5}{(2^6)^3}$ (c) $\left(\dfrac{5}{3}\right)^4 \cdot \left(\dfrac{6}{5}\right)^3$

10. Evaluate each expression.
    (a) $\dfrac{(7^4)^2}{7^5 7^3}$ (b) $\dfrac{6^4}{2^3 \cdot 3^5}$ (c) $\dfrac{(22)^4}{2^3(11^2)^2}$

11. Simplify each expression.
    (a) $\dfrac{x^4 \cdot x^5}{x^2 \cdot x^3}$ (c) $\dfrac{(x^2)^5(y^3)^4}{(x^3)^4(y^5)^2}$

    (b) $\dfrac{x^2 \cdot y^3}{(3xy)^4}$ (d) $\dfrac{(x/y)^2 \cdot y^3}{x}$

12. Write each expression without negative or zero exponents and simplify.
    (a) $\dfrac{3^{-2}}{5^{-1}}$ (b) $\dfrac{6^{-2} \cdot 4^0}{6^{-4}}$ (c) $\dfrac{3^3 \cdot 3^{-6}}{(3^{-4})^2}$

13. Write each expression without negative or zero exponents and simplify.
    (a) $\dfrac{2^{-2}}{\frac{1}{2}}$ (b) $\dfrac{2^4 \cdot 7^5}{14^6}$ (c) $\left(\dfrac{15^{-4}}{7^{-3}}\right)^0$

14. Evaluate each quantity.
    (a) $9^{3/2}$ (b) $625^{-3/4}$ (c) $\dfrac{49^{-2}(1/7)^4}{343^3(49^{-2})^4}$ (d) $\sqrt[4]{\dfrac{81}{256}}$

15. Evaluate each quantity.
    (a) $(1/5)^{-3}$ (b) $64^{5/6}$ (c) $\sqrt[3]{\dfrac{125}{8}}$ (d) $\sqrt[2]{\dfrac{49 \cdot 81}{16 \cdot 5^4}}$

16. A grocery store sells eight different brands of laundry detergent. If we let x_1 denote the number of boxes of brand 1 sold per week, x_2 denote the number of boxes of brand 2 sold per week, and so on, use summation notation to write an expression for the total number of boxes of laundry detergent sold per week.

17. A national chain of pizza parlors has 500 company restaurants. If x_i is used to denote the weekly sales volume (in dollars) for a restaurant, use subscripted variables and summation notation to write an expression for the total weekly sales volume for the entire chain.

18. A university with 15,000 alumni is conducting a fund raising drive. Assume the university has a list of the alumni numbered from 1 to 15,000. Use subscripted variables and summation notation to write an expression for the total amount contributed.

1.4 POLYNOMIALS

A **polynomial** in one variable x is an algebraic expression of the form

$$a_0 + a_1 x + a_2 x^2 + a_3 x^3 + \cdots + a_k x^k$$

where $a_0, a_1, a_2, a_3, \ldots,$ and a_k are numerical constants* with a_k not equal to zero. In this expression k is a positive integer called the **degree** of the polynomial. For $k = 0$ we get the polynomial a_0 (of degree zero), so that the polynomials include ordinary numbers.

EXAMPLE 1.17 $3x + 1$ is a polynomial of degree 1 and $4x^2 + \frac{1}{2}x - 1$ is a polynomial of degree 2.

---

addition and subtraction of polynomials   In order to add or subtract two polynomials, we first combine like terms and then simplify. Note that the concept of *like terms* refers to those terms which differ only by their numerical constant. For example, $3x^2$ and $4x^2$ are like terms, as are $2x$ and $-6x$. Examples 1.18 and 1.19 illustrate this approach.

EXAMPLE 1.18   To add $3x^3 + 4x^2 - 6x + 8$ and $2x^3 + 6x^2 + 10x - 2$, we first collect like terms. Thus we obtain

---

*In this text the terms *numerical constant* and *real number* are used interchangeably.

$$(3x^3 + 2x^3) + (4x^2 + 6x^2) + (-6x + 10x) + (8 - 2)$$

After simplifying, we obtain the result $5x^3 + 10x^2 + 4x + 6$.

EXAMPLE 1.19   To subtract $5x^2 + 6x - 8$ from $8x^2 + 12x + 20$, we proceed as follows.

$$(8x^2 + 12x + 20) - (5x^2 + 6x - 8)$$
$$= (8x^2 - 5x^2) + (12x - 6x) + [20 - (-8)]$$

After simplifying, we obtain the result $3x^2 + 6x + 28$.

multiplication of polynomials   To multiply two polynomials, we multiply each term of the first polynomial times each term of the second polynomial and combine like terms. For example, to multiply $2x + 3$ times $4x + 5$ we proceed as follows

$$(2x + 3)(4x + 5) = (2x + 3)4x + (2x + 3)5$$
$$= 8x^2 + 12x + 10x + 15$$
$$= 8x^2 + 22x + 15$$

With a little practice the product of two polynomials such as this can be written directly. Nonetheless, for more complex problems, it is best to take a little more time to write each product before collecting like terms such as $12x$ and $10x$.

EXAMPLE 1.20   To multiply $3x + 2$ times $8x^2 + 4x + 5$, we multiply each term of $3x + 2$ times each term of $8x^2 + 4x + 5$ and combine like terms.

$$(3x + 2)(8x^2 + 4x + 5) = (3x + 2)8x^2 + (3x + 2)4x + (3x + 2)5$$
$$= 24x^3 + 16x^2 + 12x^2 + 8x + 15x + 10$$
$$= 24x^3 + 28x^2 + 23x + 10$$

In cases where more than two polynomials must be multiplied, we apply the above procedure as many times as necessary in order to obtain the desired product.

EXAMPLE 1.21   To multiply $(x + 1)(x + 2)(x + 3)$, we first form the product of $x + 1$ and $x + 2$; we then multiply this result times $x + 3$ to yield the desired product.

Step 1
$$(x + 1)(x + 2) = (x + 1)x + (x + 1)2$$
$$= x^2 + x + 2x + 2$$
$$= x^2 + 3x + 2$$

Step 2
$$(x^2 + 3x + 2)(x + 3) = (x^2 + 3x + 2)x + (x^2 + 3x + 2)3$$
$$= x^3 + 3x^2 + 2x + 3x^2 + 9x + 6$$
$$= x^3 + 6x^2 + 11x + 6$$

Thus $(x + 1)(x + 2)(x + 3) = x^3 + 6x^2 + 11x + 6$.

Although the general procedure described above can always be used to multiply two or more polynomials, we frequently encounter special cases for which formulas exist that show the product directly. One special case involves the multiplication of two polynomials such as $x + 4$ and $x - 4$, the product of which is equal to $x^2 - 16$. To generalize this case, let us consider the product of $x + a$ and $x - a$, where a is some numerical constant.

$$(x + a)(x - a) = (x + a)x + (x + a)(-a)$$
$$= x^2 + ax - ax - a^2$$
$$= x^2 - a^2$$

Thus the product of $x + a$ and $x - a$ is equal to $x^2 - a^2$.

Another special case involves the multiplication of two polynomials such as $x + 2$ and $x + 3$. For this example we obtain the result

$$(x + 2)(x + 3) = (x + 2)x + (x + 2)3$$
$$= x^2 + 2x + 3x + 6$$
$$= x^2 + 5x + 6$$

To generalize this case, consider the product of $x + a$ and $x + b$, where a and b are arbitrary constants.

$$(x + a)(x + b) = (x + a)x + (x + a)b$$
$$= x^2 + ax + bx + ab$$
$$= x^2 + (a + b)x + ab$$

Thus for this special case the product is equal to $x^2 + (a + b)x + ab$.

EXAMPLE 1.22

$$(x + 6)(x - 6) = x^2 - 6^2 = x^2 - 36$$

$$(x + 4)(x + 6) = x^2 + (4 + 6)x + 4 \cdot 6 = x^2 + 10x + 24$$

Special cases such as those shown above provide an easy way to identify the factors of a polynomial.

factoring polynomials
In elementary mathematics the concept of **factoring** refers to writing a number as the product of two or more numbers, each of which is called a **factor** of the original number. For example, $10 = 2 \cdot 5$ and thus 2 and 5 are factors of 10; $30 = 2 \cdot 3 \cdot 5$ and thus 2, 3, and 5 are factors of 30; and so on. A similar concept applies for polynomials. Specifically, the expression *to factor a polynomial* means to write the polynomial as the product of two or more polynomials, each of which is called a *factor* of the original polynomial. For example, consider the polynomial $x^2 - 16$. In the preceding discussion we showed that a special case of multiplication involved a product of the form $(x + a)(x - a)$, the result of which is $x^2 - a^2$. Recognizing that $x^2 - 16$ is this special case with $a = 4$ enables us to identify the two factors of $x^2 - 16$ as $x + 4$ and $x - 4$. In other words, $x^2 - 16$ is factored as $(x + 4)(x - 4)$. Similarly, to factor $x^2 + 5x + 4$ we recognize that with $a + b = 5$ and $ab = 4$, this polynomial fits the special case of multiplication where $(x + a)(x + b) = x^2 + (a + b)x + ab$. Since $a + b = 5$ and $ab = 4$ has the solution $a = 4$ and $b = 1$, we get $x^2 + 5x + 4 = (x + 4)(x + 1)$; consequently $x + 4$ and $x + 1$ are factors of $x^2 + 5x + 4$.

EXAMPLE 1.23
To factor $x^2 - 25$, we recognize that $(x + 5)(x - 5)$ is equal to $x^2 - 25$; thus the two factors of $x^2 - 25$ are $x + 5$ and $x - 5$. Similarly, to factor $x^2 + 9x + 20$, we note that $a + b = 9$ and $ab = 20$, so $a = 4$ and $b = 5$; therefore this polynomial can be factored as the product of $x + a$ and $x + b$; that is, $x^2 + 9x + 20 = (x + 4)(x + 5)$.

For more complex problems it often helps to factor out a common term, as shown in the following example.

EXAMPLE 1.24
To factor $x^3 + 8x^2 + 16x$, we first factor out the x common to each term. That is,

$$x^3 + 8x^2 + 16x = x(x^2 + 8x + 16)$$

Then, by recognizing that $x^2 + 8x + 16$ can be factored as $(x + 4)(x + 4)$, we can write the result as

$$x^3 + 8x^2 + 16x = x(x + 4)(x + 4)$$

The common term we factor out is often a numerical constant. For example, to factor $5x^2 - 20$ we first recognize that $5x^2 - 20 = 5(x^2 - 4)$. Then, by recognizing that $x^2 - 4$ can be factored as $(x + 2)(x - 2)$, we can write the final result as

$$5x^2 - 20 = 5(x + 2)(x - 2)$$

EXERCISES

In **Exercises 1–9,** multiply the polynomials.

1. $(2x + 6)(4x + 7)$
2. $(3x^2 + x + 4)(x + 2)$
3. $(4x^2 + 2x)(3x + 4)$
4. $(x + 8)(x - 8)$
5. $(x + 7)(x + 6)$
6. $x^2(x + 10)(x - 10)$
7. $(x - 2)(x - 2)$
8. $x(x + 2)(x + 4)$
9. $x(x + 7)(x - 7)$

In **Exercises 10–18,** factor each polynomial.

10. $x^2 + 12x + 36$
11. $x^2 + 10x + 24$
12. $x^2 - 64$
13. $x^2 + 6x + 9$
14. $x^3 - 25x$
15. $4x^2 - 36$
16. $x^3 + 10x^2 + 25x$
17. $x^2 + 2x$
18. $3x^2 + 33x + 84$

Many business and economic applications involve equations that contain fractions. The purpose of this section is to briefly review the operations on such algebraic fractions.

reducing fractions to lowest terms To reduce a fraction to lowest terms, we must factor both the numerator and denominator and then cancel common terms. For example, the fraction $\frac{10}{14}$ can be reduced to lowest terms by first factoring the numerator and denominator to obtain

$$\frac{2 \cdot 5}{2 \cdot 7}$$

By canceling the 2 common to both the numerator and denominator, we obtain $\frac{5}{7}$, which is $\frac{10}{14}$ reduced to lowest terms.

When the fraction is expressed as the ratio of two polynomials, we use the same basic approach. For example,

$$\frac{x^2 - 9}{x^2 + 5x + 6}$$

can be reduced to lowest terms by recognizing that the numerator can be factored as $(x + 3)(x - 3)$ and the denominator as $(x + 2)(x + 3)$.
Thus we obtain

$$\frac{x^2 - 9}{x^2 + 5x + 6} = \frac{(x + 3)(x - 3)}{(x + 2)(x + 3)}$$

$$= \frac{x - 3}{x + 2} \qquad \text{(provided } x \neq -3)$$

EXAMPLE 1.25

$$\frac{64}{80} = \frac{\cancel{8} \cdot 8}{\cancel{8} \cdot 10} = \frac{\cancel{2} \cdot 4}{\cancel{2} \cdot 5} = \frac{4}{5}$$

$$\frac{x^2 + 6x + 8}{x^2 - 16} = \frac{(x + 2)(x + 4)}{(x + 4)(x - 4)}$$

$$= \frac{x + 2}{x - 4} \qquad \text{(provided } x \neq -4)$$

---

addition and subtraction of fractions Let a, b, and c represent polynomials. Then

$$\frac{a}{b} + \frac{c}{b} = \frac{a+c}{b}$$

and

$$\frac{a}{b} - \frac{c}{b} = \frac{a-c}{b}$$

providing b is not equal to zero. In words this says that we can add or subtract fractions with the same denominator by adding or subtracting their numerators.

If the denominators of the two fractions are not the same, we must write equivalent fractions with a common denominator. For example,

$$\frac{1}{5} + \frac{1}{2} = \frac{2}{10} + \frac{5}{10} = \frac{7}{10}$$

In general, if a, b, c, and d are polynomials (b and d not equal to zero), then

$$\frac{a}{b} + \frac{c}{d} = \frac{ad}{bd} + \frac{bc}{bd} = \frac{ad+bc}{bd}$$

and

$$\frac{a}{b} - \frac{c}{d} = \frac{ad}{bd} - \frac{bc}{bd} = \frac{ad-bc}{bd}$$

EXAMPLE 1.26 To add $(2x)/(x-2)$ and $(3x)/(x-3)$ we use the general formula shown above with $a = 2x$, $b = x - 2$, $c = 3x$ and $d = x - 3$ and write

$$\frac{2x}{x-2} + \frac{3x}{x-3} = \frac{2x(x-3) + (x-2)3x}{(x-2)(x-3)}$$

$$= \frac{2x^2 - 6x + 3x^2 - 6x}{(x-2)(x-3)}$$

$$= \frac{5x^2 - 12x}{(x-2)(x-3)}$$

Let a, b, c, and d represent polynomials. Then

$$\frac{a}{b} \cdot \frac{c}{d} = \frac{ac}{bd}$$

and

$$\frac{a}{b} \div \frac{c}{d} = \frac{a}{b} \cdot \frac{d}{c}$$

excluding any division by zero. In words, to multiply two fractions we simply multiply their respective numerators and denominators. For division, we convert the problem to an equivalent multiplication problem.

EXAMPLE 1.27

$$\frac{x + 2}{x^2 + 5x + 6} \cdot \frac{x + 3}{x^2 - 4} = \frac{(x + 2)(x + 3)}{(x^2 + 5x + 6)(x^2 - 4)}$$

$$= \frac{(x + 2)(x + 3)}{[(x + 3)(x + 2)][(x + 2)(x - 2)]}$$

$$= \frac{1}{(x + 2)(x - 2)} \qquad \text{(provided } x \neq -2 \text{ and } x \neq -3\text{)}$$

$$\frac{x + 4}{x^2 - 9} \div \frac{x + 4}{x - 3} = \frac{x + 4}{x^2 - 9} \cdot \frac{x - 3}{x + 4}$$

$$= \frac{(x + 4)(x - 3)}{[(x + 3)(x - 3)](x + 4)}$$

$$= \frac{1}{x + 3} \qquad \text{(provided } x \neq 3 \text{ and } x \neq -4\text{)}$$

EXERCISES

In **Exercises 1–6,** reduce each fraction to lowest terms.

1. $\dfrac{18}{24}$

2. $\dfrac{240}{500}$

3. $\dfrac{64}{120}$

4. $\dfrac{x^2 - 25}{x^2 + 7x + 10}$

5. $\dfrac{x^2 + 6x + 9}{x^2 - 9}$

6. $\dfrac{x^2 - 16}{x^2 - 8x + 16}$

In **Exercises 7–15,** perform the indicated operation.

7. $\dfrac{2}{8} + \dfrac{3}{4}$

8. $\dfrac{5}{32} - \dfrac{12}{160}$

9. $\dfrac{x + 2}{x - 4} + \dfrac{2x}{x + 3}$

10. $\dfrac{4x}{x + 5} + \dfrac{2x}{x - 5}$

11. $\dfrac{2}{3} \cdot \dfrac{1}{8}$

12. $\dfrac{5}{18} \cdot \dfrac{4}{7}$

13. $\dfrac{x + 1}{x + 4} \cdot \dfrac{x - 1}{x - 4}$

14. $\dfrac{1}{4} \div \dfrac{5}{4}$

15. $\dfrac{x + 5}{x^2 - 16} \div \dfrac{2x}{x + 4}$

1.6 *LINEAR EQUATIONS IN ONE VARIABLE*

A **linear equation in one variable** x is an algebraic equation of the form

$$ax + b = c$$

where a, b, and c are real numbers and $a \neq 0$. For example, $2x + 4 = 10$

and $3x - 5 = 10$ are both linear equations. A **solution** of a linear equation is a number which, when substituted for the variable, makes the equation true. Thus, since $2(3) + 4 = 10$, we see that $x = 3$ is a solution to the linear equation $2x + 4 = 10$; similarly, since $3(5) - 5 = 10$, $x = 5$ is a solution to the linear equation $3x - 5 = 10$. However, since $3(6) - 5 \neq 10$, $x = 6$ is *not* a solution of the linear equation $3x - 5 = 10$.

solving linear equations in one variable

In order to solve a linear equation (that is, to find a solution of a linear equation) we can perform a number of elementary operations on the original equation that result in a new equation with an obvious solution. For example, if a, b, and c are real numbers, we can perform the following elementary operations.

Addition Property

We can add the same value on both sides of the equal sign. That is,

$$\text{if } a = b \quad \text{then} \quad a + c = b + c.$$

EXAMPLE 1.28   To solve the linear equation $x - 5 = 10$, we simply add 5 on both sides of the equation.

$$x - \underbrace{5 + 5}_{0} = 10 + 5$$

$$\therefore x = 15$$

The three triangular dots form the mathematical symbol standing for *therefore*. Thus we read $\therefore x = 5$ as "therefore x equals 5."

Subtraction Property

We can subtract the same value on both sides of the equal sign. That is,

$$\text{if } a = b \quad \text{then} \quad a - c = b - c.$$

EXAMPLE 1.29   To solve the linear equation $x + 4 = 10$, we simply subtract 4 on both sides of the equation.

$$x + 4 - 4 = 10 - 4$$

$$\underbrace{}_{0}$$

$$\therefore x = 6$$

Multiplication Property

We can multiply on both sides of an equation by a nonzero number. That is,

$$\text{if } a = b, \quad \text{then} \quad ac = bc.$$

EXAMPLE 1.30   To solve the linear equation $\frac{1}{3}x = 8$, we multiply on both sides of the equation by 3.

$$\left(\frac{1}{3}x\right)3 = 8(3)$$

$$\therefore x = 24$$

Division Property

We can divide on both sides of an equation by a nonzero number. That is,

$$\text{if } a = b \quad \text{then} \quad \frac{a}{c} = \frac{b}{c}.$$

EXAMPLE 1.31   To solve the linear equation $8x = 48$, we divide on both sides of the equation by 8.

$$\frac{8x}{8} = \frac{48}{8}$$

$$\therefore x = 6$$

In most cases several of these operations must be performed in order to solve a linear equation. Example 1.32 illustrates the type of approach used.

EXAMPLE 1.32   To find a solution to the linear equation $2x - 8 = 7x + 12$, we first use the subtraction property to get both terms involving x on the left-hand side of the equation. We obtain

$$(2x - 8) - 7x = (7x + 12) - 7x$$

or

$$-5x - 8 = 12$$

Then by adding 8 on both sides of $-5x - 8 = 12$, we obtain

$$(-5x - 8) + 8 = (12) + 8$$

or

$$-5x = 20$$

Finally, by dividing on both sides of $-5x = 20$ by -5, we obtain

$$\frac{-5x}{-5} = \frac{20}{-5}$$

and hence $x = -4$. Substituting this value back into the original equation provides a check of the solution process.

$$2(-4) - 8 = 7(-4) + 12$$
$$-8 - 8 = -28 + 12$$
$$-16 = -16$$

forming linear   The ability to solve a linear equation is an important part of your
equations   mathematical skills. Nonetheless, the most important part of problem solving is to be able to develop the equation that accurately describes the situation being studied. In the next example we provide an illustration of how these two skills must be combined to solve a problem. In Chapters 2 and 3 we will provide additional practice in forming algebraic equations.

EXAMPLE 1.33   A car-rental firm charges a daily rate of $20 plus $0.20 per mile. If the total bill for one customer for one day's rental is $120, how many miles were driven?

To solve this problem let x denote the number of miles driven.

Thus
$$\text{Total cost} = 20 + 0.20x$$
or
$$120 = 20 + 0.20x$$
Solving this equation for x we obtain

$$0.20x = 100$$
$$\therefore x = 500 \text{ miles}$$

Note that in economic terms, $20 is referred to as the *fixed cost* and $0.20 is called the *variable cost*.

EXAMPLE 1.33
(Continued)

If the rental rate at another firm is $12 per day and $0.25 per mile, how many miles would a customer have to drive in one day in order for the total cost at both firms to be equal?

If we let y denote the number of miles for which total daily costs are equal, we know that, at this mileage, the total costs for both firms are

Firm 1   total cost = 20 + 0.20y

Firm 2   total cost = 12 + 0.25y

The value of y for which these costs are equal can be obtained by setting the two total costs equal to one another and solving for y. Thus we obtain

$$20 + 0.20y = 12 + 0.25y$$
$$0.05y = 8$$
$$\therefore y = 160$$

Hence if a customer drives 160 miles in one day, the cost for both firms is the same. Note that if a customer drives less than 160 miles in one day, the total cost is less for firm 1, while if a customer drives more than 160 miles the total cost is less for firm 2. In economics this type of problem is referred to as *break-even analysis*.

EXERCISES

For **Exercises 1–16,** solve each linear equation.

1. $5x = 25$
2. $2x + 6 = 18$

3. $\dfrac{1}{3}x + 4 = 6$

4. $2(x - 4) = 7$

5. $y - 2(y + 4) = 0$

6. $2x + \dfrac{1}{4}(x - 8) = 4(x + 3)$

7. $\dfrac{x + 1}{4} = 2x - 5$

8. $\dfrac{1}{2}\left(y + \dfrac{2}{3} \right) = 12$

9. $\dfrac{2}{3}y = 7$

10. $12x - 20 = 8$

11. $0.4y - 0.2 = 1.8$

12. $8(x + 3) = 24$

13. $3x + 2 = 10$

14. $18y - 13.6 = 21.4$

15. $3\frac{1}{3}x = 30$

16. $5\left(\dfrac{x + 1}{4} \right) = 2x$

17. An investor buys and sells stock for which the sales commission is $25 per transaction (buying or selling). If the investor purchases 100 shares of a stock at $52 per share, write a linear equation that can be used to determine how much the value of the stock (per share) would have to increase to cover the cost of buying and selling. Solve this equation to determine the breakeven point.

18. A manufacturer of lawn mower engines has estimated that the cost to set up the production equipment needed to produce oil filter caps is $100. Once set up, the cost to produce each cap is $0.25. Write an equation that shows the cost of producing x units. If the manufacturer can purchase 1000 of the caps for $325, should the caps be purchased or manufactured?

19. A salesperson is paid a base salary of $200 per week plus a commission of $25 for each unit sold. Write an equation that shows the weekly salary if x units are sold.

20. A builder estimates that the cost to build a two-story house is $40 per square foot. If the builder wants to make a profit of $10,000 per house, write an expression that shows the selling price for a house of x square feet that gives the desired profit.

SUMMARY

In this chapter we introduced several basic mathematical concepts that are needed in order to study the applications of mathematics in business. First, we showed how the concept of a *set* can be used to denote any well-defined collection of objects. We saw that sets are often specified by listing the individual elements between braces and that $a \in A$ indicates that object a is an element of set A. We introduced the term *subset* to denote a set whose elements comprise part or all of the elements of another set and discussed several ways in which we can use sets to form new sets (for example, the complement, intersection, and union).

In Section 1.2 we presented an overview of numbers and number systems. We showed that the *real number system* consists of the *rational numbers* and the *irrational numbers* and that the rational numbers include the *integers* (1, 2, 3, . . . , 0, −1, −2, −3 . . .) which in turn include the *natural*, or *whole*, *numbers* (1, 2, 3, . . .). We discussed three important algebraic properties of the operations on real numbers—the *commutative properties of addition and multiplication,* the *associate properties of addition and multiplication,* and the *distributive property of multiplication over addition*—which provide a means for manipulating algebraic expressions.

To be able to read and understand the applications of mathematics, you must be familiar with common mathematical notation. Thus we reviewed the concept of *decimal notation* and then showed how *scientific notation* can be used to write each number as a product of a number between 1 and 10 and an appropriate power of 10. We then provided an introduction to the use of *exponential notation,* including a discussion of rules for adding, multiplying, and subtracting exponents. Our introduction to common mathematical notation concluded with a brief discussion of *subscript* and *summation notation.*

In the remaining sections of the chapter we provided a review of the basic concepts of elementary algebra. First, we introduced the concept of a *polynomial.* Then we discussed operations involving the addition and subtraction of polynomials, multiplication and division of polynomials, and factoring polynomials. Finally, in Section 1.6, we provided a review of *linear equations* involving one variable, with an emphasis on forming and solving such equations.

GLOSSARY

1. **Mathematical Model** Mathematical symbols and expressions used to represent a situation.
2. **Set** Any well-defined collection of objects.
3. **Universal Set** A set containing all of the elements with which we are concerned in a given situation.

4. **Null Set**   The set with no elements.
5. **Subset**   A set whose elements are also elements of a given set.
6. **Complement**   The set, denoted by A', composed of all elements of I not in A, where A is a subset of the universal set I.
7. **Intersection**   The intersection of two sets A and B, denoted by $A \cap B$, is the set consisting of all the elements belonging to both A and B.
8. **Union**   The union of two sets A and B, denoted by $A \cup B$, is the set consisting of all the elements belonging to either A or B, including those belonging to both.
9. **Venn Diagram**   A graphical method of representing sets and operations involving sets. In each case the universal set I is represented by a rectangle, and subsets of I are represented by regions (usually circles or parts of circles) within the rectangle.
10. **Natural Numbers**   The set of numbers consisting of the whole numbers 1, 2, 3, 4, 5, 6, 7, ...
11. **Integers**   The set of numbers consisting of the natural numbers, the corresponding negative numbers $(-1, -2, -3, . . .)$, and the number 0.
12. **Rational Numbers**   The set of numbers of the form a/b, where a and b are integers and $b \neq 0$.
13. **Irrational Numbers**   The set of numbers measuring distances which are not represented by rational numbers.
14. **Real Numbers**   The set consisting of all rational and irrational numbers.
15. **Commutative Properties of Addition and Multiplication**   If a and b are real numbers, then $a + b = b + a$ and $ab = ba$.
16. **Associative Properties of Addition and Multiplication**   If a, b, and c are real numbers, then $(a + b) + c = a + (b + c)$ and $(ab)c = a(bc)$.
17. **Distributive Property of Multiplication over Addition**   If a, b, and c are real numbers then $a(b + c) = ab + ac$.
18. **Decimal Notation**   A system of notation that combines the use of symbols for zero, one, two, . . . , and nine with the convention that the position of each digit tells us whether it represents ones, tens, hundreds, thousands, and so on.
19. **Scientific Notation**   A system of notation in which each number is written as a product of a number between 1 and 10 and an appropriate power of 10.
20. **Exponential Notation**   A mathematical kind of shorthand in which if n is a positive integer, we write

$$\underbrace{b^n = b \cdot b \cdot b \cdots b}$$

n factors

for any real number b. Also, $b^{-n} = 1/b^n$ and $b^0 = 1$.

21. **Subscript Notation** A method of identifying problem variables where it is impractical to select a unique letter or symbol to associate with each variable.
22. **Summation Notation** A mathematical shorthand that enables us to form the sum of a series of variables involving subscripts.
23. **Polynomial** A polynomial in one variable x is an algebraic expression of the form

$$a_0 + a_1x + a_2x^2 + a_3x^3 + \cdots + a_kx^k$$

where $a_0, a_1, a_2, a_3, \ldots, a_k$ are numerical constants with a_k not equal to zero.
24. **Degree of a Polynomial** In the algebraic expression showing the form of a polynomial, k is called the degree of the polynomial.
25. **Factor a Polynomial** Writing a polynomial as the product of two (or more) polynomials.
26. **Linear Equation in One Variable** An algebraic equation of the form $ax + b = c$ where a, b, and c are real numbers and $a \neq 0$.

SUPPLEMENTARY
EXERCISES

1. Let A be the set of all courses that require financial accounting as a prerequisite, E the set of all courses that require economics, and S the set of all courses that require statistics. Describe (in words) each set.
   (a) $A \cup E$ (b) $E \cap S$ (c) S'
2. A regional trucking firm has offices in Cleveland, Cincinnati, Louisville, Lexington, and Pittsburgh. The firm has terminal facilities in Cincinnati, Dayton, and Pittsburgh. If O is the set of office locations and T is the set of terminal locations, write the elements of O and T in set notation. Write the set $O \cap T$. Describe (in words) $O \cup T$.
3. Anderson Heating is an authorized dealer for the following brands of wood stoves: North Country Products, Advanced Heating, Modern Heating, Alaskan Stoves, and North Bay. Bender Heating, a competitor of Anderson Heating, is an authorized dealer for Lake Country Stoves, Modern Heating, North Country Products, and Vermont Stoves. Let A denote the set of brands of wood stoves carried by Anderson and B the set of brands of wood stoves carried by Bender.
   (a) Write the elements of A and B in set notation.
   (b) Write the elements of $A \cup B$.
   (c) Describe (in words) $A \cap B$.

4. Finger Lakes Boats manufactures three different lengths of sail-boats and five powerboats. The sailboat model numbers are S-14, S-17, and S-20. The powerboat model numbers are P-11, P-13, P-15, P-17, and P-20. Let S denote the set of all sailboats manufactured by Finger Lakes Boats and P denote the set of all power-boats.

   (a) Write the sets S and P in set notation.
   (b) If A = {S-17, S-20, P-17, P-20} denotes the set of models that have a list price of $5000 or more, write the set A' and describe (in words) A'.

5. The following sets represent the states in which five different life insurance companies are licensed to sell their policies.

$$A = \{\text{Arizona, California, Nevada, Texas}\}$$

$$B = \{\text{California, Washington, Oregon}\}$$

$$C = \{\text{Arizona, Nevada, Utah, Washington}\}$$

$$D = \{\text{Arizona, California, Washington, Oregon}\}$$

$$E = \{\text{Arizona, Texas, Utah}\}$$

Determine whether each of the following is true or false.

(a) California $\in A$
(b) Arizona $\in B$
(c) Texas $\notin D$
(d) Nevada $\notin C$
(e) $E \subset C$
(f) $C \subseteq E$
(g) $E \not\subset A$
(h) $B \not\subseteq D$
(i) $A \cap B = \{\text{California}\}$
(j) $A \cap C = \{\text{Arizona, Nevada, Texas}\}$

(k) $C \cup E = \{\text{Arizona, Nevada, Texas, Utah, Washington}\}$
(l) $B \cup D = \{\text{Arizona, California, Utah, Washington}\}$
(m) $C \cap E = E$
(n) $C \cup E = E$
(o) $B \cap D \ne E$
(p) $A \cap C = D \cap E$

6. In a study of magazine circulation and advertising, a research worker considered the universal set

$$I = \{\textit{Reader's Digest, TV Guide, Life, Look, McCall's, Time, Newsweek, Ladies' Home Journal}\}$$

and the subsets

$$C = \{\textit{Reader's Digest, McCall's, Ladies' Home Journal}\}$$

$$D = \{\textit{TV Guide, Life, Look, Time, Newsweek}\}$$

$$E = \{\textit{TV Guide, McCall's, Time, Newsweek}\}$$

List the magazines contained in each set.

(a) C' (c) E' (e) $C \cap D$ (g) $D \cup E$
(b) D' (d) $C \cap E$ (f) $D \cap E$ (h) $C \cup D$

7. A company plans to build a research laboratory somewhere in Connecticut and it asks four different consulting firms to recommend two of the state's eight counties, which are Fairfield, Hartford, Litchfield, Middlesex, New Haven, New London, Tolland, and Windham counties. If their recommendations are given by the sets T = {Hartford, New Haven}, U = {Hartford, Litchfield}, V = {New Haven, New London}, and W = {Fairfield, New Haven}, list the elements of each set.

(a) T' (c) $V \cap W$ (e) $U \cup V$ (g) $V \cup W$
(b) W' (d) $U \cap V$ (f) $T \cup U$ (h) $(U \cup V)'$

8. A company has 420 employees of which 240 got a raise, 115 got a promotion, and 60 got both. How many of the employees got neither a raise nor a promotion?

9. Among 60 visitors to a resort hotel, 37 stayed at least for a week, 43 spent at least $100 a day, 32 were completely satisfied with their accommodations, 30 stayed at least for a week and spent at least $100 a day, 26 stayed at least for a week and were completely satisfied with their accommodations, 27 spent at least $100 a day and were completely satisfied with their accommodations, and 24 stayed at least for a week, spent at least $100 a day, and were completely satisfied with their accommodations.

(a) How many of the visitors stayed at least for a week, spent at least $100 a day, but were not completely satisfied with their accommodations?

(b) How many of the visitors were completely satisfied with their accommodations, but stayed less than a week and spent less than $100 a day?

(c) How many of the visitors stayed less than a week, spent less than $100 a day, and were not completely satisfied with their accommodations?

10. Evaluate each expression.

(a) $\dfrac{4^5}{4^3}$ (c) $27^{1/3}$ (e) $\dfrac{7^3 6^7}{(21)^3 3^2}$

(b) $\dfrac{2^4}{2^7}$ (d) $\dfrac{4^3 \cdot 4^5}{(4^2)^5}$ (f) $27^{-2/3}$

11. Evaluate each expression.

(a) $\dfrac{3^4 3^7}{(3^3)^2}$ (c) $\dfrac{2^3 (2^5)^2}{(2^4)^3}$ (e) $\left(\dfrac{3}{2}\right)^4 \left(\dfrac{4}{3}\right)^2$

(b) $\dfrac{(5^4)^2}{5^5 5^3}$ (d) $\dfrac{6^5}{2^3 3^4}$ (f) $\dfrac{(21)^4}{3^3 (7^2)^2}$

12. Simplify each expression.

(a) $\dfrac{x^3 x^5}{x^2 x^4}$ (c) $\dfrac{(x^3)^5 (y^2)^4}{(x^2)^6 (y^3)^2}$

(b) $\dfrac{x^4 x^5}{(2xy)^3}$ (d) $\dfrac{(x/y)^3 y^4}{x^2}$

13. Write each expression without negative or zero exponents and simplify.

(a) $2^{-3}/5^{-2}$ (c) $\dfrac{7^{-3} 5^0}{7^7}$ (e) $\dfrac{2^3 2^{-4}}{2^{-5} 2^{12}}$

(b) $\dfrac{3^{-2}}{\frac{1}{3}}$ (d) $\dfrac{2^5 3^4}{6^6}$ (f) $\left(\dfrac{28^{-4}}{15^2}\right)^0$

14. Evaluate each quantity.

(a) $4^{3/2}$ (c) $625^{-3/4}$ (e) $\dfrac{9^{-2}(\frac{1}{3})^4}{27^3(9^{-2})^3}$ (g) $\sqrt[4]{\dfrac{625}{16}}$

(b) $\left(\dfrac{1}{3}\right)^{-2}$ (d) $16^{5/4}$ (f) $\sqrt[3]{\dfrac{27}{8}}$ (h) $\sqrt[2]{\dfrac{49}{16}}$

15. Convert each decimal into specific notation.
(a) 13.45   (d) 0.00000034
(b) 0.00271   (e) 2,348,500
(c) 1,785.4   (f) 0.035846

16. Convert each number from scientific notation to ordinary decimal notation.
(a) $2.1466 \cdot 10^4$ (d) $3.5552 \cdot 10^{-6}$
(b) $1.81 \cdot 10^{-2}$ (e) $7.269 \cdot 10^6$
(c) $1.4763 \cdot 10^5$ (f) $9.9934 \cdot 10^{-5}$

17. Convert each number of Exercise 15 into the E-notation of floating-point arithmetic.

18. Convert each number from the E-notation of floating-point arithmetic to an ordinary decimal.
(a) 258E−2   (d) 53536E7
(b) 26463E5   (e) −5316E1
(c) −75589E−5   (f) 646E−4

19. A brokerage firm keeps track of the daily closing price of a particular stock by letting p_i denote the closing price on day i. Using summation notation write an expression for the average closing price for the next 10 trading days.

20. Let r_i denote the number of inches of rain recorded during day i for a particular community. Using summation notation write an expression for the total rainfall during a 20-day period. Write an expression for the average daily rainfall over this period.

21. If x_i denotes the number of employees at a particular plant that are absent on the ith day of operation, use summation notation to

write an expression for the average number of employees absent during the next 10-day period.

In **Exercises 22–27**, multiply the polynomials.

22. $(2x^2 + 3x + 2)(x + 3)$
23. $(x - 10)(x + 10)$
24. $x(x + 2)(x + 3)$
25. $(x + 6)(x^2 + 2x)$
26. $(x^2 + 2x + 4)(2x^2 + 4x + 5)$
27. $(x - 4)(x - 4)$

In **Exercises 28–32**, factor the polynomials.

28. $x^2 - 81$
29. $x^2 + 12x + 27$
30. $2x^3 - 18x$
31. $3x^2 + 24x + 48$
32. $x^2 + 10x + 25$

In **Exercises 33–37**, reduce the fractions to lowest terms.

33. $\dfrac{81}{405}$

34. $\dfrac{66}{110}$

35. $\dfrac{x^2 - 49}{x^2 + 5x - 14}$

36. $\dfrac{2x^2 - 2x - 12}{x^2 - 9}$

37. $\dfrac{5x^3 - 10x^2 + 10x}{10(x^2 - 1)}$

In **Exercises 38–45**, perform the indicated operation.

38. $\dfrac{1}{7} + \dfrac{4}{21}$

39. $\dfrac{8}{15} + \dfrac{6}{45}$

40. $\dfrac{1}{6} + \dfrac{1}{7}$

41. $\dfrac{2x}{x - 2} + \dfrac{3(x + 1)}{x + 2}$

42. $\dfrac{4}{7} \cdot \dfrac{5}{9}$

43. $\dfrac{5}{8} \div \dfrac{5}{32}$

44. $\dfrac{x^2 - 1}{2x} \cdot \dfrac{x + 4}{(x + 1)}$

45. $\dfrac{x^2 + 5x + 6}{x + 1} \div \dfrac{4(x + 2)}{x^2 + 2x + 1}$

In **Exercises 46–51** solve each linear equation.

46. $4x = 24$

47. $\dfrac{1}{3}x + 2 = 14$

48. $\dfrac{1}{4}(y + 2) = 1.5$

49. $6(x + 4) = 18$

50. $4\left(\dfrac{x + 2}{5}\right) = 10$

51. $1.3z + 5 = 11.5$

52. A manufacturer of 14-foot fiberglass sailboats must decide how many boats to produce during the next production run. If the cost to set up the mold and prepare for production is $2500 and the manufacturing cost per boat is $1400, write an equation for the total cost to produce x boats.

53. In Exercise 52 assume the manufacturer sells each boat to dealers for $2000. Write an equation that shows the profit corresponding to producing and selling x boats.

54. The average price of new homes in an area is expected to increase by 12% during the next year. If the increase brings the price to $72,800, what would be the average price of this year's homes?

55. Two trucks leave a terminal in Buffalo, New York, at the same time. One truck travels at 55 miles per hour and the other at 60 miles per hour. Write an equation that shows the number of miles the slower truck will be behind the faster truck at the end of x hours.

56. A wholesaler purchases color television monitors directly from the manufacturer for $285 per monitor. The wholesaler pays a finance charge of approximately 1.7 percent of the purchase price for each month a monitor stays in inventory. If the wholesaler sells the monitors to retailers at a price of $325 per set, write an expression that shows the profit for a monitor that has been in inventory for x months.

AN INTRODUCTION TO FUNCTIONS

One of the most important concepts of mathematics concerns the relationships, or correspondence, between the elements of two sets. In this book we shall deal mainly with relationships between two sets of numbers—sets of numbers representing supply and demand, sets of numbers representing the age and the value of different pieces of property, sets of numbers representing the unit cost of a product and the number of items produced, and so on. Furthermore, we shall limit our discussion to relationships in which each element of the first set corresponds to one and only one element of the second set. Relationships such as these are called **functions**, and—to distinguish between the two sets (whose elements they relate)—we refer to the first as the **domain** of the function and to the second as its **range**. More formally,

a function is a correspondence which assigns to each element of a set, called its domain, *exactly one element of a set, called its* range.

EXAMPLE 2.1 Among the following tables, in which the elements of the domain are always listed on the left, (a) and (b) represent functions, but (c) does not.

(a)		(b)		(c)	
Year	Sales	Time	Temperature	Age (years)	Height (inches)
1978	$365,043	8 A.M.	66°	27	70
1979	$285,957	9 A.M.	73°	31	72
1980	$567,481	10 A.M.	76°	28	66
1981	$950,325	11 A.M.	78°	31	69
1982	$1,668,694	12 noon	78°	30	68
		1 P.M.	73°	30	71

In (c) the relationship between the ages and the heights of a group of six persons is not a function; there is more than one height corresponding to two of the ages (30 and 31).

So far we have displayed functions by means of tables. The tables indicate how the elements of the range are matched to those of the domain, and this shows that a function is actually a set of pairs—a set of ordered pairs, to be exact. They are ordered in the sense that we must always specify which number belongs to the domain and which belongs to the range.

EXAMPLE 2.1
(Continued)

The function represented by Table (b) of Example 2.1 may, thus, be given as

$$\{(8, 66), (9, 73), (10, 76), (11, 78), (12, 78), (1, 73)\}$$

where the elements of the domain, the time, always come first.

This process of listing all possible pairs is easy when the number of pairs is small, but it can be quite cumbersome when the number of pairs is large and impossible when there are infinitely many. This is why we often turn to alternative methods of expressing functional relationships; in Section 2.1 we express them by means of mathematical equations, and in Section 2.2 we express them geometrically by means of graphs.

2.1 FUNCTIONS AND EQUATIONS

If set X is the domain of a function, set Y is its range, and x and y denote their respective elements, then exactly one value of y must be associated with each x. In the examples given so far, we actually listed the y that corresponds to each x, but in most situations it is easier (and preferable) to express functions by means of equations.

EXAMPLE 2.2

A plant has the capacity to produce anywhere from one to six electric power generators per day; the daily overhead is $900 and the direct cost (materials and labor) of producing one generator is $185. On the basis of all this information, the production manager wants to know *how the unit cost (namely, the cost per generator) is related to the number of generators produced on any given day*. To express this relationship by means of an equation, we have only to argue that if x generators are produced, the total cost is $900 + 185x$, namely, the overhead *plus* the direct cost of producing x generators. Since this is the cost of x generators, we then divide the total cost by x and find that the cost per generator, the *unit cost*, is given by

$$y = \frac{900 + 185x}{x}$$

This equation and the fact that the domain is the set $X = \{1, 2, 3, 4, 5, 6\}$ specifies the function which relates the unit cost of these generators to the number produced on any given day. Note that this particular relationship *is* a function—there is a unique value of y for each value of x. To find the y which corresponds to any particular x, we have only to substitute into the above equation; for $x = 3$, for example, we get

$$y = \frac{900 + 185 \cdot 3}{3} = \$485$$

You should verify that the values corresponding to $x = 1, 2, 4, 5,$ and 6 are $y = 1{,}085, 635, 410, 365,$ and 335, respectively.

EXAMPLE 2.3   A new-car dealer sells a certain model car with anywhere from zero to eight extras (such as power steering, radio, air-conditioning, special bumpers, and so on). If x is the number of extras he puts on these cars, the dealer knows from past experience that the expected sales during the model year are

$$y = 40 + 8x - x^2$$

cars. This equation expresses the functional relationship between x, the number of extras, and y, the number of cars expected to sell during the model year. The domain of the function is the set

$$X = \{0, 1, 2, 3, 4, 5, 6, 7, 8\}$$

and if we calculate y for different values of x, it will soon become apparent that more than one value of x has the same value of y. For example, for $x = 2$ and $x = 6$ we get the same value of y, namely,

$$y = 40 + 8(2) - 2^2 = 52$$

and

$$y = 40 + 8(6) - 6^2 = 52$$

Observe that the number of cars the dealer can expect to sell during the model year increases from $y = 40$ (corresponding to zero extras) to $y = 56$ (corresponding to four extras) and then it decreases again to $y = 40$ (corresponding to eight extras). Perhaps, this relationship can be explained by the fact that although most persons like the extras, too many extras will put the prices of the cars beyond their budgets.

When we work with functions, we generally refer to x (the symbol that denotes the elements of the domain) as the **independent variable**, and to y (the symbol that denotes the elements of the range) as the **dependent variable**. To justify this terminology, we have only to point out that in Example 2.2 the unit cost, y, *depends* on the number of generators produced, x; and in Example 2.3 the numbers of cars the dealer can expect to sell, y, *depends* on the number of extras, x. Since this kind of dependence can easily be misunderstood, let us point out that it does not necessarily imply a *cause-effect* relationship. This is demonstrated by the fact that in Example 2.2 we can solve for x, the number of generators produced, and make this variable the one which depends on the unit cost. Originally, it was the unit cost which depended on the number of generators produced.

To emphasize this kind of dependence of y on x, we often use the symbol $f(x)$, which is read "f of x" or more explicitly "the value of the function at x," for y. The advantage of this notation, called **functional notation**, is that it leads to considerable simplifications; its only disadvantage is that $f(x)$ might be mistaken for the product of two separate quantities, f and x.

EXAMPLE 2.2
(Continued) To illustrate the advantages of functional notation, let us now write the equation relating the unit cost of the generators to the number produced as

$$f(x) = \frac{900 + 185x}{x}$$

If we wanted to know what value of y corresponds to x = 3, we simply ask for $f(3)$, and if we want to know what values of y correspond to x = 1 and x = 5, we simply ask for $f(1)$ and $f(5)$. The answers are

$$f(3) = \frac{900 + 185 \cdot 3}{3} = 485$$

$$f(1) = \frac{900 + 185 \cdot 1}{1} = 1085$$

and

$$f(5) = \frac{900 + 185 \cdot 5}{5} = 365$$

and this agrees with the results previously shown. Of course, nothing has been changed except the notation.

EXAMPLE 2.3
(Continued)

In this case let us substitute for *y* the symbol *g*(x) rather than *f*(x) to make it clear that we are dealing with a different function. We would thus write the equation as

$$g(x) = 40 + 8x - x^2$$

and *g*(2), for example, would stand for the number of cars *with two extras* the dealer can expect to sell during the model year. Similarly, *g*(0) would stand for the number of cars *without any extras* the dealer can expect to sell during the model year. Referring to the results on page 49, we can write *g*(2) = 52 and *g*(0) = 40.

Generally speaking, it does not matter whether we write the value of a function as *f*(x), *g*(x), *F*(x), *h*(x), and so on, so long as we do not use the *same* symbol for two *different* functions in one and the same problem. Also, there is no reason why the independent variable has to be referred to as *x*. For instance, if it represents the number of items produced, sold, or consumed, we often use the letter *n*, and if it represents a price we often use the letter *p*. Thus the production cost of *n* radios might be denoted *C*(n), and the demand for milk might be denoted *D*(p), where *p* is the price per quart.

2.2 THE GRAPH OF A FUNCTION

In Example 2.2 we had no difficulty in finding the equation which related the unit cost to the number of generators produced; it was simply the total cost divided by the number produced. In Example 2.3 we claimed that the equation (which related the dealer's expected sales to the number of extras on the cars) was based on *past experience*. We did not say *how* it was based on past experience, but the usual procedure is to plot whatever data are available on a piece of graph paper and look for patterns which justify the use of a particular equation. Since the problem of determining an equation by inspecting a graph is difficult, to say the least, let us first investigate the inverse problem, namely, that of plotting a graph which represents a given function.

To represent a function graphically, we use two perpendicular lines called the **coordinate axes**; along one of these lines (usually the horizontal line) we measure *x* and along the other line we measure *y*, starting in each case from the point at which the two lines intersect. This point is called the **origin**, and the two coordinate axes are appropriately called the **x-axis** and the **y-axis**. To complete the picture, we

FIGURE 2.1
Coordinate Axes

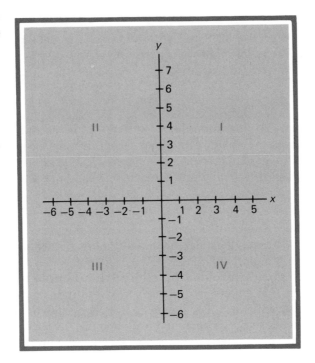

indicate units of length on the two axes (not necessarily the same for each one) as shown in Figure 2.1. Observe that if x is *positive* we go to the *right*, and if it is *negative* we go to the *left*; if y is *positive* we go up and if it is *negative* we go *down*.

We are now ready to establish a one-to-one correspondence between pairs of numbers and the points of the plane. The two numbers we shall assign to a point tell us how far we have to go first in the direction of the x-axis and then in the direction of the y-axis until the point is reached.

EXAMPLE 2.4   For x = 3 and y = 4 we get the point P of Figure 2.2, and for x = −1 and y = −2 we get the point Q.

It is customary to refer to the two numbers which are thus assigned to a point as its **coordinates**.* Specifically, we refer to them as the **x**-

---

*The idea of employing coordinates to label points is widely used even in everyday life. For instance, we may visit a friend who lives on 325 Fourteenth Avenue, or we may be watching a hockey game from Seat 12 in Row 5. Although these numbers may not refer to *all* the points of a plane, the desired location can in each case be found on the basis of *two* numbers.

FIGURE 2.2
The Coordinates
of Points

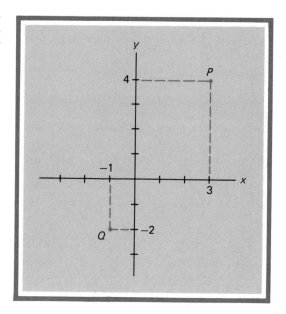

coordinate and the y-coordinate (or the abscissa and the ordinate). To simplify our notation, we let (x, y) represent the point whose coordinates are the numbers x and y; the x-coordinate always comes first.

EXAMPLE 2.4
(Continued)
The points P and Q of Figure 2.2 are represented by (3, 4) and (−1, −2); similarly, (5, −4) stands for the point whose x-coordinate is 5 and whose y-coordinate is −4, (−1, 3) stands for the point whose x-coordinate is −1 and whose y-coordinate is 3, and (0, 0) stands for the origin.

The coordinate axes divide the plane into four parts called **quadrants**, which are numbered as in Figure 2.1. In the first quadrant x and y are both positive, in the second quadrant x is negative and y is positive, in the third quadrant x and y are both negative, and in the fourth quadrant x is positive and y is negative. Since most business problems deal with positive quantities, we shall be concerned mainly with points in the first quadrant, but if we regard losses as negative profits, deductions as negative additions, deficits as negative income, and soon, we shall also have the occasion to work with points in the other three quadrants.

According to our definition, a function assigns one value of y to each value of x within its domain, and it establishes a set of ordered pairs which we write as (x, y). Each of these pairs corresponds to a

FIGURE 2.3
The Graph
of a Function

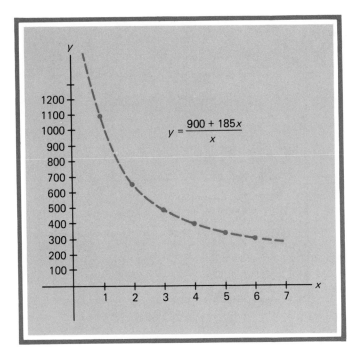

point, and if we plotted all these points we would obtain what is called
the **graph** of the given function.

EXAMPLE 2.2
(Continued) We previously used the equation

$$y = \frac{900 + 185x}{x}$$

to calculate the values of y for $x = 1, 2, 3, 4, 5,$ and 6, getting the six
pairs $(1, 1085)$, $(2, 635)$, $(3, 485)$, $(4, 410)$, $(5, 365)$, and $(6, 335)$, where
x is always listed first. Now, if we plot the corresponding points as in
Figure 2.3, we obtain the graph of the given function. It may be tempting
to draw a curve through these six points (like the dashed curve of Figure
2.3), but this would be meaningless unless we change the domain. So
long as the domain of the function is the set $\{1, 2, 3, 4, 5, 6\}$—the number
of electric power generators that can actually be produced—it is meaningless to plot points corresponding to, for example, $x = \frac{1}{2}$, $x = 2\frac{3}{4}$, or
$x = 5\frac{7}{10}$. However, if we changed the domain of the function, say, to the
set of all real numbers on the interval from $\frac{1}{2}$ to $6\frac{1}{2}$ (and forgot about the
physical meaning which we attached to x and y), the dashed curve
would, indeed, be the corresponding graph.

FIGURE 2.4
The Graph
of a Function

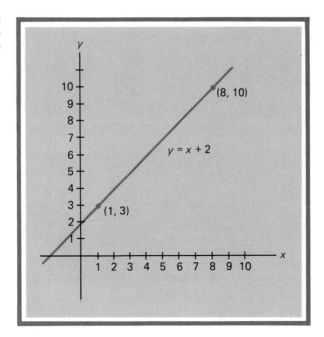

If the domain of a function consists of very many points, perhaps infinitely many, it may be impractical or even impossible to plot each individual point. In that case we can only hope that a general picture of the overall pattern can be obtained by plotting some of the points.

EXAMPLE 2.5   If we tried to plot the graph of the function given by the equation

$$y = 2 + x$$

over the domain X of the real numbers, it would not take very many points to discover that they all fall on a straight line. If we know for sure that this is the case, it suffices to find the coordinates of, and plot, two points, and through them draw a straight line. Calculating the values of y which correspond to, for instance, $x = 1$ and $x = 8$, we obtain $y = 2 + 1 = 3$ and $y = 2 + 8 = 10$, the points $(1, 3)$ and $(8, 10)$, and, hence, the straight-line graph shown in Figure 2.4.

EXAMPLE 2.6   Suppose that we want to plot the graph of the function given by the equation

$$y = x^3 - 9x^2 + 24x$$

FIGURE 2.5
Attempt to Find
the Graph
of a Function

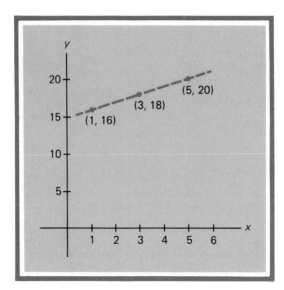

for all real values of x. Starting with the points corresponding to x = 1, x = 3, and x = 5, we find (by substitution) that the corresponding values of the function are y = 16, y = 18, and y = 20. Plotting the points (1, 16), (3, 18), and (5, 20) as in Figure 2.5, we discover that they fall on a straight line, and we may be tempted to conclude that the whole graph of the function is, in fact, given by this line. However, the error of this conclusion becomes apparent as soon as we try to plot more points. For x = 2 and x = 4, for example, we obtain

$$y = 2^3 - 9 \cdot 2^2 + 24 \cdot 2 = 20$$
$$y = 4^3 - 9 \cdot 4^2 + 24 \cdot 4 = 16$$

and, hence, the points (2, 20) and (4, 16), which are shown in Figure 2.6 together with three points of Figure 2.5. Whether the smooth curve we have drawn through the five points of Figure 2.5 actually represents the function given by $y = x^3 - 9x^2 + 24x$ is difficult to decide. It is conceivable that the actual graph of the function oscillates wildly between the points or beyond the range of the five points for which we have determined the value of y.

For the time being, we shall avoid the question raised in the last example by limiting our work to functions whose graphs are smooth curves which can be drawn on the basis of relatively few points—you will have to take our word for that. In Chapter 11 we discuss a method

FIGURE 2.6
The Graph
of a Function

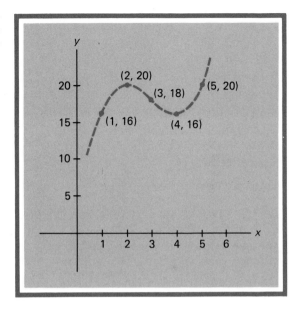

which enables us to answer the question we raised about the curve of Figure 2.6.

EXERCISES

1. The demand for a certain kind of cracker is such that the *product* of the demand (in thousands of boxes) and the price per box (in cents) is always equal to 240,000, so long as the price is not less than 20¢ or more than 60¢ per box.
   (a) Find the equation which expresses the demand for these crackers in terms of their price, and give the domain as well as the range of the corresponding function.
   (b) Use the equation of part (a) to calculate the demand for prices of 20, 25, 30, 40, 50, and 60 cents.

2. An office machine is supposed to be checked once a month. If this is not done (but the machine is checked at least once a year), the expected cost of repairs is $12 *plus* three times the *square* of the number of months the machine has gone without being checked. Express this relationship between the number of months the machine has gone without being checked and the expected cost of repairs by means of an equation, and use it to calculate the expected cost of repairs when the machine has not been checked for (a) 2 months, (b) 4 months, (c) 6 months, (d) 8 months, and (e) 12 months.

3. If $f(x) = 3x + 4$ for any real number x, find (a) $f(0)$, (b) $f(1)$, (c) $f(-2)$, (d) $f(7)$, (e) $f(-3)$, and (f) the value of x for which $f(x) = 0$.

4. If the demand for a product is given by $d(p) = p^2 - 20p + 125$ thousand cartons for p = 2, 3, 4, 5, 6, 7, 8, 9, or 10 cents, calculate (a) $d(2)$, (b) $d(5)$, (c) $d(8)$, and (d) $d(10)$.

5. If the values of a function are given by $G(x) = 3 + 2^x$ for x = 1, 2, 3, and 4, find each of the following.
   (a) Its range.
   (b) The value of $\dfrac{G(4) - G(1)}{G(3) + G(2)}$.

6. If $F(x) = (x + 3)/(x - 3)$ for any real value of x greater than 3, find each of the following.
   (a) The values of $F(4)$, $F(6)$, and $F(15)$.
   (b) The value of x for which $F(x) = 4$.

7. Draw a coordinate system like the one in Figure 2.1 and plot the following points.
   (a) (2, 5)   (d) (−3, −5)   (g) (−6, 1)
   (b) (4, −5)   (e) (−1, 4)   (h) (−4, −4)
   (c) (0, 6)   (f) (−4, 0)   (i) (0, −5)

8. Use the results of Exercise 3 to plot the graph of the function given by the equation $y = 3x + 4$ for any real number x. What kind of graph do we seem to get?

9. Use the results of Exercise 4 to plot the graph of the function given by the equation $d(p) = p^2 - 20p + 125$ for integral values of p from 2 through 10. Also draw a smooth curve through these points, but be careful not to extend it beyond p = 10. Why? (Hint: Label the coordinate axes p and $d(p)$ instead of x and y.)

10. Use the results of Exercise 6 to plot the graph of the function which is given by $y = (x + 3)/(x - 3)$ for all real values of x greater than 3. What happens to y when we substitute greater and greater values of x?

11. Use the results of Exercise 1 to plot the graph of the function which relates the demand for the given kind of cracker to its price. Draw a smooth curve through the six points.

12. Use the results of Exercise 2 to plot the graph of the function which relates the expected cost of repairs to the number of months the office machine has gone without being checked. Draw a smooth curve through the five points.

13. The following are the amounts of meat (in thousands of pounds) sold by the two supermarkets of a suburb in five consecutive months.

Jim's Market	Tom's Market
x	y
57	58
64	56
88	34
99	20
72	50

(a) Display this information graphically by drawing coordinate axes with suitable scales and plotting the five points (57, 58), (64, 56), . . . , (72, 50).

(b) Check visually whether the function given by $y = 120 - x$ can be used to approximate the relationship between the monthly sale of meat in the two markets by calculating y for each of the given values of x, plotting the corresponding points on the diagram constructed in part (a), and joining them by means of a smooth curve. What kind of curve do we seem to get?

14. The manager of a chain of grocery stores has the following data on the supply, $f(p)$, of certain fresh vegetables and their price, p, in dollars per crate.

Price (dollars) p	4	6	8	10	14
Supply (thousand crates) $f(p)$	2	14	23	27	29

(a) Display this information graphically by drawing coordinate axes with suitable scales and plotting the five points (4, 2), (6, 14), . . . , (14, 29). The coordinate axes will have to be labeled p and $f(p)$ instead of x and y.

(b) Check *visually* whether the function given by

$$f(p) = 32 - \frac{60}{p - 2}$$

can be used to approximate the above data by calculating $f(p)$ for each of the given values of p, plotting the corresponding points on the diagram constructed in part (a), and joining them by means of a smooth curve.

(c) Use the equation of part (b) to calculate $f(62)$ and $f(122)$ and discuss the *practical* significance of the results.

2.3 FUNCTIONS RELATING MORE THAN TWO VARIABLES

Although many situations can be described with the use of functions that involve one independent variable and one dependent variable, there are also problems in which we must consider *more than one independent variable*. For instance, the cost of a product may depend on the price of raw materials as well as the cost of labor; the supply of a product may depend on the size of its potential market, its retail price, and also the prices of competing products; and the profits of a resort hotel may well depend on the state of the economy in general, prices charged by competing hotels, the weather, and numerous other factors.

EXAMPLE 2.7   Consider, for example, the equation

$$z = 130 + 12x + 27y$$

which relates z, the cost of a certain product in dollars, to x, the cost of raw materials in dollars per pound, and y, the cost of labor in dollars per hour. Observe that corresponding to any pair of values of x and y there is one and only one value of z. In fact, if we specify the domains of x and y, we refer to the relationship as a *function of two independent variables*—in our example, the two independent variables are x and y, while the dependent variable is z.

If we generalize the functional notation introduced previously, we can replace z with the symbol $f(x, y)$, which is read "f of x and y," and for x = \$1.20 and y = \$4.60, for example, we get

$$f(1.20, 4.60) = 130 + 12(1.20) + 27(4.60) = \$268.60$$

This means that the product will cost \$268.60 when raw materials cost \$1.20 per pound and labor costs \$4.60 an hour.

The example we have given here involves two independent variables, but it is easy to see how our argument (the definition of a function and the notation) can be generalized to accommodate situations where the number of independent variables is greater than two.

To draw the graph of a function that involves the variables x, y, and z, we have to use a three-dimensional coordinate system such as the one shown in Figure 2.7. It consists of three mutually perpendicular axes, the x-axis going from *left to right*, the y-axis going from *front to back*, and the z-axis going *up and down*. The point at which the three axes meet (and from which we begin to measure along each of the axes)

FIGURE 2.7
Three-dimensional
Coordinate System

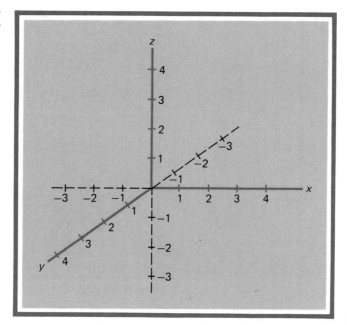

is again called the *origin*. With reference to this kind of axes, any point in space can be located by means of three numbers called its x-, y-, and z-*coordinates*. The x-coordinate tells us how far we must go in the direction of the x-axis (starting at the origin), the y-coordinate tells us how far we must then go in the direction of the y-axis, and the z-coordinate tells us how far we must finally go up or down. We shall let (x, y, z) denote the point whose respective coordinates are the numbers x, y, and z. Thus the point (2, −3, 5) is reached by first going 2 units to the right (starting at the origin), then 3 units "toward the back," and then 5 units up, as shown in Figure 2.8. In case you find it difficult to picture three-dimensional coordinate systems like those of Figures 2.7 and 2.8, it may help to think of the positive parts of the x- and y-axes as the lines in which two walls meet the floor of the room, and to think of the positive part of the z-axis as the line in which these two walls meet.

EXAMPLE 2.7
(Continued)

In the same way in which we showed that z = 268.60 corresponds to x = 1.20 and y = 4.60, namely, that (1.20, 4.60, 268.60) is a point on the graph of the given function, it can be shown that the points (1, 6, 304), (2, 5, 289), (3, 4, 274), (5, 3, 271), and (4, 2, 232) are also parts of this graph. If we actually plotted all these points, we would find that they lie on a plane, and this is true for the graph of any function which is given by an equation of the form z = a + bx + cy (where a, b, and c are numerical constants). This is discussed further in Chapter 3.

FIGURE 2.8
The Coordinates
of a Point in Three
Dimensions

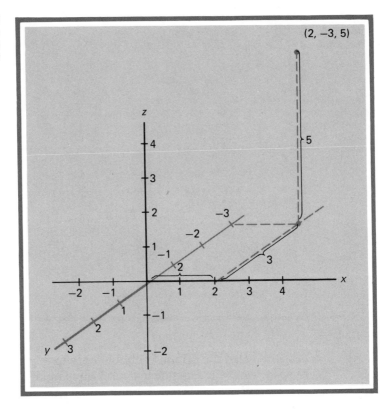

In conclusion, let us point out that when there are *more than two* independent variables we cannot very well picture the graph of a function since this would require a space of more than three dimensions.

EXERCISES

1. If the prices of two given commodities are x and y (cents per dozen), then the demand for the first commodity (in 1000 dozens) is given by

$$z = 120 - 3x + 5y$$

where x and y are both positive integers less than 40.

(a) What will be the demand for the first commodity when it sells for 20¢ a dozen while the second commodity sells for 18¢ a dozen?

(b) What will be the demand for the first commodity when it sells for 15¢ a dozen while the second commodity sells for 22¢ a dozen?

2. If a company spends x dollars on research and development and y dollars on advertising, its profits (in dollars) is given by

$$f(x, y) = 36{,}000 + 40x + 30y + \frac{xy}{100}$$

for all positive integers x and y less than 20,000.
   (a) What will be the company's profit if it spends $2000 on research and development and $5000 on advertising?
   (b) What will be the company's profit if it spends $10,000 on research and development and $8000 on advertising?
   (c) If the company is planning to spend $4000 on research and development and hopes to make a profit of $546,000, how much should they spend on advertising?

3. If $h(x, y) = x^2 + 2y^2 - 1$ for all real values of x and y, find each value.
   (a) $h(1, -2)$ (c) $h(0, 5)$ (e) $h(1, 1)$
   (b) $h(-1, 0)$ (d) $h(-1, -1)$ (f) $h(-4, -3)$

4. If $f(x, y, z) = 2 + x - 2y + 3z$ for all real values of x, y, and z, find each value.
   (a) $f(1, 0, 3)$ (c) $f(-2, 4, -3)$
   (b) $f(2, 0, 2)$ (d) $f(4, 6, 3)$

5. Draw a three-dimensional system of coordinates like that of Figure 2.7 and plot the following points.
   (a) $(2, 3, 4)$ (d) $(4\frac{1}{2}, 0, 0)$ (g) $(0, 0, -3\frac{1}{3})$
   (b) $(-1, 3, 5)$ (e) $(0, -2, 0)$ (h) $(-2, -5, 4)$
   (c) $(0, 2, -4)$ (f) $(-2, -1, -3)$ (i) $(-3, -3, 3)$

6. Using a three-dimensional system of coordinate axes like that of Figure 2.7, plot the points $(3, 0, 0)$, $(0, 4, 0)$, and $(0, 0, 5)$, and connect them with straight lines to indicate the plane on which they all lie. Judging from this diagram, does this plane also contain the point $(0, 0, 1)$? Does it seem to contain the point $(1\frac{1}{2}, 0, 2\frac{1}{2})$?

7. (Continuation of Exercise 6) By substituting the coordinates of the original three points, verify that the plane of Exercise 6 has the equation

$$z = 5 - \frac{5}{3}x - \frac{5}{4}y$$

and then check whether it also contains the points $(0, 0, 1)$, $(1\frac{1}{2}, 0, 2\frac{1}{2})$, and $(3, 4, -5)$.

A major part of your studies in business and economics will deal with relationships between two sets of numbers—sets of numbers representing supply and demand, sets of numbers representing the unit cost of a product and the number of items produced, and so on. As we showed in this chapter, relationships such as these, where each element of the first set corresponds to one and only one element of the second set, are called *functions*.

We showed that functional relationships can be expressed by means of tables, mathematical equations, and graphs. In doing so, we introduced the terms *independent variable* and *dependent variable*. For example, if the cost of a product (y) depends upon the number of items produced (x), then x is called an independent variable and y a dependent variable. To emphasize this kind of dependence of y on x, we indicated that for y we often use the symbol $f(x)$, which is read "f of x," or more explicitly, "the value of the function at x."

The chapter concluded with a brief introduction to problems involving more than one independent variable, including a discussion of how a three-dimensional coordinate system can be used to draw the graph of a function that involves three variables.

GLOSSARY

1. **Function**   A correspondence which assigns to each element of a set, called its *domain*, exactly one element of a set, called its *range*.
2. **Domain**   See the definition of function.
3. **Range**   See the definition of function.
4. **Independent Variable**   The symbol (usually x) which denotes the elements of the domain.
5. **Dependent Variable**   The symbol (usually y) which denotes the elements of the range.
6. **Functional Notation**   A notation used to emphasize the dependence of y (the dependent variable) on x (the independent variable). In this notation we often use the symbol $f(x)$, which is read "the value of the function at x," for y.
7. **Coordinate Axes**   Two perpendicular lines used to represent a function graphically.
8. **Origin**   The point where the coordinate axes intersect.
9. **x-axis**   One of the coordinate axes (usually the horizontal line) along which we measure the independent variable x.
10. **y-axis**   One of the coordinate axes (usually the vertical line) along which we measure the dependent variable y.

11. **Coordinates** The two numbers we assign to a point that tells us how far to go in the direction of the x-axis and then in the direction of the y-axis until the point is reached.

1. Draw a coordinate system like the one in Figure 2.1 and plot the following points.
   (a) $(3, 6)$ (c) $(0, 2)$ (e) $(-2, 5)$ (g) $(6, 0)$
   (b) $(2, -3)$ (d) $(0, -4)$ (f) $(-2, -3)$

2. Construct a coordinate system like the one of Figure 2.1 and plot the following points.
   (a) $(2, 4)$ (d) $(-5, -2)$ (g) $(-3, 1)$
   (b) $(3, -2)$ (e) $(-1, 6)$ (h) $(-3, -3)$
   (c) $(0, -4)$ (f) $(3, 0)$ (i) $(0, 0)$

3. If $f(x) = 2x + 6$ for any real number x, find each value.
   (a) $f(0)$ (b) $f(-1)$ (c) $f(2)$ (d) $f(4)$ (e) $f(-3)$

4. If $f(x) = 2x + 7$ for any real number x, find (a) $f(0)$, (b) $f(2)$, (c) $f(5)$, (d) $f(-1)$, (e) $f(-3)$, and (f) $f(-10)$.

5. Use the results of Exercise 4 to plot the graph of the function whose values are given by the equation $y = 2x + 7$ for all real values of x. What kind of curve do we seem to get?

6. If the values of a function $P(x)$ are given by $P(x) = x - 0.1x^2$ for integral values of x from 6 through 10, calculate each value.
   (a) $P(6)$ (b) $P(7)$ (c) $P(8)$ (d) $P(9)$ (e) $P(10)$

7. Use the results of Exercise 6 to plot the graph of the function relating P and x. Draw a smooth curve through the five points.

8. If $F(x) = (x + 2)/(x - 2)$ for any real value of x greater than 2, find (a) $F(3)$, (b) $F(4)$, (c) $F(6)$, (d) $F(7)$, (e) $F(10)$, and (f) $F(27)$.

9. Using the result of Exercise 8, plot the graph of the function which is given by $y = (x + 2)/(x - 2)$ for all real values of x greater than 2. What happens to y when we substitute greater and greater values of x?

10. The demand for a certain kind of candy bar is such that the product of the demand (in thousands of cartons) and the price per carton (in cents) is always equal to 150,000, so long as the price is not less than $1.00 or more than $2.50. Express this relationship between the price and the demand by means of an equation, and use it to calculate the demand when the price is (a) $1.00, (b) $1.25, (c) $1.50, (d) $2.00, (e) $2.40, and (f) $2.50. Also find the domain of this function.

11. Use the results of Exercise 10 to plot the graph of the function which relates the demand for the given kind of candy to its price. Draw a smooth curve through the six points.

12. The cost (in hundreds of dollars) of producing x units of a product is given by

$$y = \frac{1}{4}x^2 + 2x + 4$$

(a) Calculate the cost for producing 1, 2, 3, 4, and 5 units.
(b) Use the results of part a to plot the graph of the function which relates the cost of production to the number of units produced. Draw a smooth curve through the five points.

13. An automobile leasing company estimates that the annual maintenance cost (y) of a leased vehicle is related to the number of miles driven (x) by the equation.

$$y = 200 + 0.01x$$

(a) Which variable in the above equation is the dependent variable? Why?
(b) Calculate the estimated maintenance cost for a leased vehicle that is driven 5000 miles, 10,000 miles, 15,000 miles, and 20,000 miles.

14. Use the results of Exercise 13 to plot the graph of the function relating y and x. Draw a smooth curve through the four points. How many points are really necessary to draw the graph of this function? Explain.

15. A furniture manufacturer has the following data on the total cost y of filling an order for x custom-made chairs.

Number of chairs x	1	2	5	8	10	15
Total cost (dollars) y	100	250	400	700	850	1300

(a) Display this information graphically by drawing coordinate axes with suitable scales and plotting the six points (1, 100) (2, 250), . . . , and (15, 1300).
(b) Check *visually* whether the function given by y = 50 + 80x can be used to approximate the above data by calculating y for each of the given values of x, plotting the corresponding points on the diagram constructed in part a, and joining them by means of a smooth curve. What kind of curve do you seem to get?

16. If $f(x, y) = 2x^2 + 3y^2 + 2$ for all real values of x and y, find each value.

 (a) $f(0, 0)$ (d) $f(0, -1)$
 (b) $f(2, 3)$ (e) $f(-2, -3)$
 (c) $f(-1, 0)$

17. Verify that the points $(1, 6, 304)$, $(2, 5, 289)$, $(3, 4, 274)$, $(5, 3, 271)$, and $(4, 2, 232)$ must lie on the graph of the function given by the equation

$$z = 130 + 12x + 27y$$

18. If $g(x, y) = x^2 + y^2 + 3$ for all real values of x and y, find each value.

 (a) $g(1, -3)$ (c) $g(0, 6)$ (e) $g(1, 1)$
 (b) $g(-2, 5)$ (d) $g(-2, -2)$ (f) $g(-4, 0)$

19. Draw a three-dimensional system of coordinates like that of Figure 2.7 and plot the points $(3, 2, 4)$, $(-2, 4, 6)$, $(0, 3, -1)$, $(5, 0, 0)$, $(0, 4, 0)$, $(-1, -2, -1)$, $(0, 0, -1)$, and $(-4, -3, 5)$.

20. A hardware store has determined that $R(x, y)$, its annual revenue (thousands of dollars) from the sale of lawn and garden equipment, is related to x, its average inventory value (thousands of dollars), and y, its annual advertising expenditure (thousands of dollars). That is,

$$R(x, y) = \frac{x^2}{100} + \frac{y^2}{20} + \frac{xy}{50} + 10$$

(*Note:* This equation is appropriate for values of at most $100,000 for average inventory and $20,000 for annual advertising.)

 (a) What will the store's annual revenue be if the average inventory value is $100,000, and the store spends $10,000 on advertising?

 (b) What will the store's annual revenue be if it keeps the average inventory at $100,000 but increases advertising to $20,000? Is it worth spending the additional $10,000 on advertising? Explain.

LINEAR
AND
QUADRATIC
FUNCTIONS

In this chapter we study two general classes of functions which provide important models for many situations that arise in business and economics. We begin our study with **linear functions**, a special type of function whose graphs are straight lines. Our main reason for doing this is that linear functions are the easiest to handle mathematically. However, in spite of their simplicity, they have many important applications. The chapter concludes with a discussion of functions whose graphs are not straight lines, but instead are described by means of curves. Specifically, we will study a special class of such functions called **quadratic functions**. The chapter concludes with a brief introduction to polynomial functions.

3.1 LINEAR FUNCTIONS

In Chapter 2 we claimed that the graph of the function given by $y = 2 + x$ is a straight line. Actually, we plotted only two points, which does not prove anything, but if we had plotted more points, we would have found that all the points do, in fact, lie on a straight line. It is for this reason that we refer to the given function (and to any function whose graph is a straight line) as linear. As we shall demonstrate later in this section, any equation of the form

$$y = mx + b$$

is the equation of a straight line.* Here m and b are numerical constants called the **slope** and the **y-intercept**, respectively.

---

*The line, itself, is the totality of points (x, y) which are such that $y = mx + b$, or in set notation it is the set

$$\{(x, y) \mid y = mx + b\}$$

EXAMPLE 3.1 $y = 3 - 5x$, $y = 7x + 6$, and $y = 12.4 + 0.9x$ are all equations of straight lines, and so are $u = 1 - 3v$, $z = 10t + 5$, and $F = 35 - 2G$, where we used letters other than x and y to denote the two variables.

To begin our study of linear functions, let us demonstrate first that the graph of any function given by an equation of the form $y = mx + b$ is, in fact, a straight line. Since this is by no means obvious, let us begin by explaining what we mean by the **slope** of a line segment connecting two points. Then we shall use this concept to give a formal definition of what we mean by a line, and finally we shall complete the proof by showing that the graph of any function given by an equation of the form $y = mx + b$ is a line.

The idea of a *slope* is of great importance in business and economics because it measures the *rate* at which changes are taking place—how rapidly a company's sales are growing, how fast the value of the dollar is dwindling, how quickly or how slowly the Consumer Price Index is going up or down, and so forth.

EXAMPLE 3.2   Consider the following data on the annual sales of three companies in two different years.

	1975	1980
Sales of Company X	500,000	600,000
Sales of Company Y	500,000	1,200,000
Sales of Company Z	500,000	300,000

As can be seen from this table, all three companies originally had sales of $500,000 in 1975, but while the sales of the first company showed a modest increase in 1980, those of the second company showed a very substantial increase, and those of the third company decreased. More specifically, the sales of Company X increased by $100,000 over a period of 5 years or on the average by $100,000/5 = \$20,000$ per year; those of Company Y increased by $700,000 or on the average by $700,000/5 = \$140,000$ per year; while those of Company Z decreased by $200,000 or on the average by $200,000/5 = \$40,000$ per year.

Graphically, this information about the three companies' sales can be displayed as in Figure 3.1, where we "coded" the years so that 1973 corresponds to $x = 0$, 1974 corresponds to $x = 1$, 1975 corresponds to $x = 2, \ldots$, and where we gave the sales in units of $100,000 on the

FIGURE 3.1
Slopes of Line
Segments

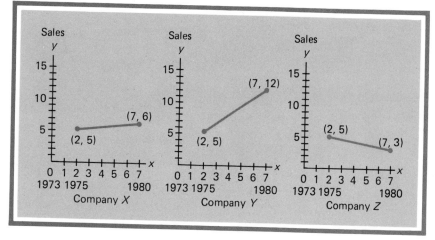

y-axes. The points corresponding to the given data were then plotted and connected by means of straight lines. For Company X the line segment has a slight *upward slope* (going from left to right), for Company Y *the slope is much steeper*, and for Company Z the line segment actually *slopes downward*.

The way in which we used the word *slope* in this example is the way it is normally used, for instance, by railroads to measure the inclination of a track; if a train has to climb 4 feet while traveling through a horizontal distance of 1000 feet, the track is said to have an upward slope of "four in a thousand," or simply a slope of 0.004. Referring to a horizontal x-axis and a vertical y-axis, we might thus say that

$$\text{slope} = \frac{\text{change in y}}{\text{change in x}}$$

More specifically, if we consider the line segment which joins the points P and Q of Figure 3.2, namely, the points (x_1, y_1) and (x_2, y_2), we find that the change in y is given by the difference $y_2 - y_1$, that the change in x is given by the difference $x_2 - x_1$, and hence, that *the slope of the line segment PQ is given by*

$$\text{slope} = \frac{y_2 - y_1}{x_2 - x_1}$$

The use of subscripts, as in x_1, y_1, x_2, and y_2, is a common and very convenient way of distinguishing between the coordinates of different points.

71 *LINEAR AND QUADRATIC FUNCTIONS*

FIGURE 3.2
The Slope of a Line
Segment

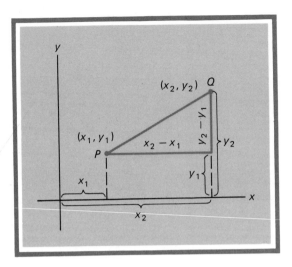

FIGURE 3.2
The Slope of a Line
Segment

EXAMPLE 3.2
(Continued)

For Company X we find that the slope of the line segment connecting the points (2,5) and (7,6) is

$$\frac{600,000 - 500,000}{7 - 2} = \frac{100,000}{5} = 20,000$$

which represents an average annual increase in sales of $20,000. Similarly, for Company Y the slope of the line segment connecting the points (2,5) and (7,12) is

$$\frac{1,200,000 - 500,000}{7 - 2} = \frac{700,000}{5} = 140,000$$

which represents an average annual increase in sales of $140,000; and for Company Z the slope of the line segment connecting the points (2,5) and (7,3) is

$$\frac{300,000 - 500,000}{7 - 2} = \frac{-200,000}{5} = -40,000$$

Note that the negative value represents an average annual decrease of $40,000.

This example has shown that if there is an increase (going from left to right), the slope is *positive*; and the greater the increase, the greater is the slope. Also, if there is a *decrease* (going from left to right), the

FIGURE 3.3
Line Segments
with a Negative Slope

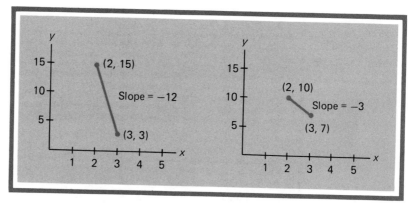

slope is negative. In the next example we show that the greater the decrease, the greater numerically is the slope.

EXAMPLE 3.3 Consider the straight line depicted in Figure 3.3. The slope of the line segment connecting the points (2, 15) and (3, 3) is

$$\frac{3 - 15}{3 - 2} = \frac{-12}{1} = -12$$

and that of the line segment connecting the points (2, 10) and (3, 7) is

$$\frac{7 - 10}{3 - 2} = \frac{-3}{1} = -3$$

As can be seen from Figure 3.3, the steeper line segment has the numerically greater negative slope.

If the y-coordinates of two points are the same (as in the first diagram of Figure 3.4), the line segment is horizontal and has zero slope; on the other hand, if the line segment is vertical (as in the second diagram of Figure 3.4), the slope (involving division by zero) is undefined.

Making use of the following definition of a line, we are now ready to show that $y = mx + b$ is the equation of a straight line.

A line is a set of points which is such that the line segments connecting any two of the points must all have the same slope. *

---

*This definition does not include *vertical* lines, but we can take care of this by replacing the last six words with the phrase "must all have the same slope or their slopes must all be undefined."

FIGURE 3.4
Horizontal and Vertical
Line Segments

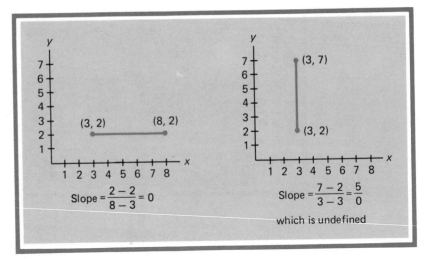

Suppose now that a function has the equation $y = mx + b$ and that x_1 and x_2 are the x-coordinates of two arbitrary points which lie on its graph. This means that the y-coordinates of these points must be $y_1 = mx_1 + b$ and $y_2 = mx_2 + b$, and we find that the slope of the line segment which connects them is

$$\frac{y_2 - y_1}{x_2 - x_1} = \frac{(mx_2 + b) - (mx_1 + b)}{x_2 - x_1}$$

$$= \frac{mx_2 - mx_1}{x_2 - x_1}$$

$$= \frac{m(x_2 - x_1)}{x_2 - x_1}$$

$$= m$$

Thus, any line segment connecting two points on the graph of $y = mx + b$ has the constant slope m and we conclude that *the graph must be a straight line.* Not only that, but we can also conclude that m is the slope of the line.

EXAMPLE 3.4   Given the equations $y = 6x + 2$ and $y = 15 - 9x$, we can now say that they represent lines having slopes of 6 and -9.

So far as the constant b is concerned, it is simply the value of y which corresponds to $x = 0$; geometrically speaking, $(0, b)$ is the point at which the line $y = mx + b$ cuts the y-axis; we call it the *y-intercept.*

Combining all this terminology, we refer to $y = mx + b$ as the **slope-intercept form** of the equation of a straight line.

We also say that $y = mx + b$ is the equation of a line given in *explicit form*, solved for y. This distinction is important because there are situations in which we may want to change the equation so that x is expressed in terms of y. To take care of this, we have only to subtract b from the expressions on both sides of the equation $y = mx + b$ and divide by m. This gives us

$$x = -\frac{b}{m} + \frac{y}{m}$$

and we say that the equation of the line is now in *explicit form*, solved for x. If the equation of the line is changed to $y - mx = b$ or $b + mx - y = 0$, we say that it is in **implicit form**, which means that it is not solved for either x or y. To complete our terminology, if A, B, and C are numerical constants, then

$$Ax + By = C$$

is said to be the **standard form** of the equation of a straight line; this form has the advantage that it can easily be generalized to situations in which there are more than two variables.

EXAMPLE 3.5   To convert the equation of a line from one form to another requires but very simple algebra. For instance, to change $3x - 2y = 5$ from the standard form to the slope-intercept form, we have only to solve for y, getting first $2y = 3x - 5$ and, hence,

$$y = \frac{3}{2}x - \frac{5}{2}$$

This tells us immediately that the slope of the line is $\frac{3}{2}$ and that it cuts the y-axis at the point $(0, -5/2)$.

EXERCISES

1.   Find the slope of the line segment connecting each pair of points.
     (a) $(1, 1)$ and $(2, 4)$ (d) $(2, -1)$ and $(4, 7)$
     (b) $(-1, -2)$ and $(1, 6)$ (e) $(-2, -2)$ and $(3, -10)$
     (c) $(-1, 3)$ and $(8, 0)$ (f) $(-6, 0)$ and $(0, 18)$
2.   Check whether the points $(-3, -8)$, $(2, 2)$, and $(4, 6)$ lie on a straight line.

3. Verify that the points $(2, 1)$, $(5, 4)$, and $(8, 9)$ do not lie on a straight line.

4. Two line segments are said to be **parallel** if they have the same slope. Which of the line segments of Exercise 1 are parallel?

5. Find the slope of each line.
   (a) $y = -13 + 7x$ (c) $4x + 3y = 12$
   (b) $x = 5 + \frac{2}{3}y$ (d) $5x - 3y - 15 = 0$

6. Find the equation of the line which has the slope $m = 4$ and which cuts the y-axis at the point $(0, -3)$. Does this line contain the point $(6, 3)$? Does it contain the point $(-1, -7)$?

7. Change the equation $5x - 2y = 6$ into the slope-intercept form; give its slope and its y-intercept.

8. If the demand for a certain kind of breakfast food (in thousands of boxes) is given by

$$d = 12{,}000 - 1{,}500p$$

where p is the proposed change in price (in cents per box), what is the significance of the slope of the corresponding line?

9. If an insurance salesperson's estimated cost of operating a car (in dollars) is $C = 1{,}500 + 0.14m$ per year, where m is the total mileage, what is the significance of the slope of the corresponding line? Should the salesperson's figures be questioned by the Internal Revenue Service, if the insurance salesperson reports driving 12,000 miles and claims a deduction of $3,650?

10. If the demand for a certain kind of ice cream (in thousands of pints) is given by

$$d = 20 - \frac{1}{8}p$$

where p is the proposed change in price (in cents per pint), what is the significance of the slope of the corresponding line? Be careful about the units.

3.2 DETERMINING THE EQUATION OF A LINE

If we are given the slope of a line and its y-intercept, we can immediately write down its equation as $y = mx + b$. Given *other information*, the process of finding the equation of a line is usually not quite so simple. Suppose, for instance, that we are given m, the slope of a line, and the additional information that it passes through a given point P with the coordinates (x_1, y_1). To find its equation, let us refer to Figure 3.5, which shows the point P, the line, and an arbitrary point Q on the

FIGURE 3.5
Diagram for Derivation
of Point-Slope Formula

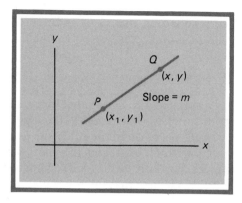

line with the unknown coordinates (x, y). We can write the slope of the line segment PQ as

$$\frac{y - y_1}{x - x_1}$$

and since this quantity is known to equal m, we get

$$\frac{y - y_1}{x - x_1} = m$$

This is the **point-slope formula** for the equation of a straight line. By multiplying left- and right-hand sides of this equation by $x - x_1$, we see that

$$y - y_1 = m(x - x_1)$$

or

$$y = y_1 + m(x - x_1)$$

For many practical applications the third form is the most convenient.

EXAMPLE 3.6 Find the equation of the line which passes through the point $(3, -2)$ and has the slope $m = 4$. Substituting into the third of the above equations, we get $y = -2 + 4(x - 3)$, which simplifies to

$$y = -14 + 4x$$

A characterizing feature of linear functions is that *the values of the function increase (or decrease) at a constant rate*, which is, in fact, the slope of the corresponding line. This is important, because there are many situations in which constant rates enable us to *recognize* that functional relationships are actually linear.

EXAMPLE 3.7   The manager of a variety store knows that in the summer she can expect to sell 16 pairs of sunglasses per week at the regular price of $4.95, and that for each 10-cent decrease in the price she can sell an extra 4 pairs. To find an equation which expresses this store's sales of sunglasses in terms of their price, we observe that sales change at the constant rate of $4/-10 = -0.40$; this means that the relationship is linear and that the slope of the line is -0.40. Then, making use of the fact $y = 16$ when $x = 495$ (where x is the price in cents and y represents the corresponding sales), we find by substitution into the third of the above formulas that $y = 16 - 0.40(x - 495)$, which simplifies to

$$y = 214 - 0.40x$$

Using this result, we can find, for example, that when the manager of the variety store charges $4.80 for the sunglasses, she can expect to sell

$$y = 214 - 0.40(480) = 22$$

pairs per week.

Another important formula for the equation of a straight line is the **two-point formula**, which enables us to write the equation of a line in terms of the coordinates of two of its points. Referring to Figure 3.6, suppose that we want to find the equation of the line which passes through points P and R, whose coordinates are (x_1, y_1) and (x_2, y_2). Now, if we take any other point on this line, such as the point Q of Figure 3.6

FIGURE 3.6
Diagram for Derivation
of Two-Point Formula

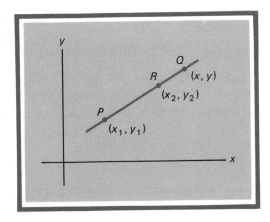

with the unknown coordinates (x, y), we know from the definition of a line that the slope of line segment PQ must equal that of line segment PR, namely, that

$$\frac{y - y_1}{x - x_1} = \frac{y_2 - y_1}{x_2 - x_1}$$

This is the *two-point formula* for the equation of a straight line, and if we multiply the expressions on both sides by $x - x_1$, we find that the equation can also be written as

$$y - y_1 = \frac{y_2 - y_1}{x_2 - x_1}(x - x_1)$$

EXAMPLE 3.8   To illustrate the use of this formula, suppose that the number of restaurants for a particular fast-food franchise grows at a constant rate. In 1974 there were 572 company restaurants and in 1980 there were 641 restaurants. Let us find the equation of the trend line which passes through these two points and use it to predict the number of restaurants that will be operating in 1988. Coding the years so that 1974 corresponds to $x = 0$ and subsequent years correspond to $x = 1, 2, 3, \ldots$, we shall have to find the equation of the line which passes through the points $(0, 572)$ and $(6, 641)$ of Figure 3.7. Substituting $x_1 = 0$, $y_1 = 572$, $x_2 = 6$, and $y_2 = 641$ into the two-point formula for the equation of a straight line, we get

$$y - 572 = \frac{641 - 572}{6 - 0}(x - 0)$$

$$y - 572 = \frac{69}{6} \cdot x$$

$$y - 572 = 11.5x$$

and, hence

$$y = 572 + 11.5x$$

This is the equation of the trend line of Figure 3.7, where the years are coded as indicated and the y-units are the number of company restaurants. Now, if we substitute $x = 14$ (corresponding to 1988), we can predict that the number of company restaurants in 1988 will be

$$y = 572 + 11.5(14)$$

$$= 733$$

FIGURE 3.7
Total Number
of Company
Restaurants

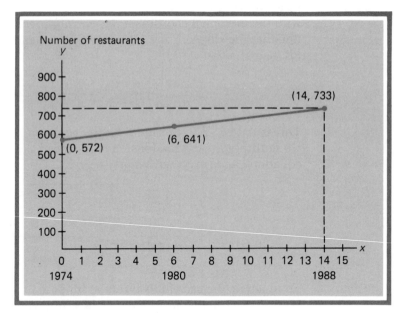

Of course, this prediction is based on the assumption that the growth pattern will continue unchanged, namely, that the line can be extended to the right.

When we write the formula for the slope of a line segment, it does not matter which point is called (x_1, y_1) and which point called (x_2, y_2). It is important, however, to be careful to take the differences of the y-coordinates and the differences of the x-coordinates *the same way*. It is also important to observe that the two-point formula cannot be used when the x-coordinates of the two points are equal, namely, when we are dealing with a *vertical* line. The equation of the vertical line which passes through the point (x_1, y_1) is simply $x = x_1$, which expresses the fact that each point on this line has the same x-coordinate x_1 (see also Figure 3.4). For *horizontal* lines we can use any one of the formulas which we have discussed; since the slope of a horizontal line is *zero*, the slope-intercept formula leads to $y = b$ and the two-point formula leads to $y = y_1$, where y_1 (or, for that matter, the b in $y = b$) is the common y-coordinate of any point on the horizontal line.

EXAMPLE 3.9 The three dashed vertical lines of Figure 3.8 have the equations $x = -7$, $x = 3$, and $x = 12$, while the three dashed horizontal lines have the equations $y = -4$, $y = 2$, and $y = 15$. Note also that the equation of the x-axis is $y = 0$ and the equation of the y-axis is $x = 0$.

FIGURE 3.8
Horizontal and Vertical
Lines

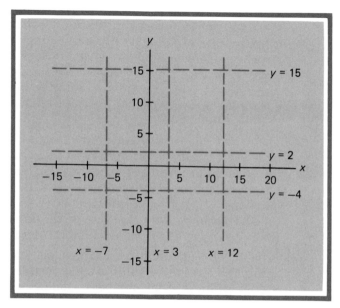

EXERCISES

1. Find the equation of each line.
   (a) Passing through the point (2, 3) and with slope $m = 6$.
   (b) Passing through the point (1, 8) and with slope $m = -1$.
   (c) Passing through the point $(-2, 7)$ and with slope $m = 0$.
   (d) Passing through the points $(-2, 3)$ and (3, 8).
   (e) Passing through the points $(-1, 4)$ and (1, 13).
   (f) Passing through the points $(-2, 3)$ and $(-2, 8)$.

2. Find the equation of each line.
   (a) Passing through the point (1, 2) and with slope $m = 3$.
   (b) Passing through the point (2, -7) and with slope $m = -2$.
   (c) Passing through the points (3, 2) and (5, 3).
   (d) Passing through the points $(-1, 2)$ and (3, 8).

3. In 1979 a company earned $3.18 per share and it expects this figure to increase by 29¢ a year. Coding the years so that 1975 corresponds to $x = 0$ and successive years correspond to $x = 1, 2, 3, \ldots$, use the point-slope formula to find the equation that will enable us to predict the company's earnings per share for future years. What should be the company's earnings per share in 1985? What is the significance of the value we would get if we substituted $x = -3$ into the formula?

4. The sales manager of a local television station claims that a company's sales will increase by $30 for every additional dollar

spent on television commercials. If a furniture store has averaged monthly sales of $165,000 while spending $100 a month on television commercials, find the equation which relates the company's expected average monthly sales to the amount spent on television commercials. What can we say about the store's average monthly sales if its manager decides to spend $400 a month on television commercials?

5. The import value of a certain product to the United States increased from $21.4 billion in 1975 to $45.4 billion in 1981. Assuming that the trend is linear and coding the years so that 1970 corresponds to $x = 0$ and subsequent years to $x = 1, 2, 3, \ldots$, find each of the following.
   (a) The equation of the line that passes through these two points.
   (b) The expected 1985 value of imports for this product.

6. A paint company produces a commercial brand of water-resistant paint. The cost to step up the equipment to produce the paint is $500, regardless of the number of gallons produced. If the cost to produce each gallon is $2 (assuming the equipment has been set up), write a linear equation that shows the total cost of producing x gallons of paint.

7. A company specializing in special-promotion record albums sold only through television advertising is considering a new record promotion. Advertising costs for the promotion are $25,000. If x denotes the number of albums sold and if the company makes a profit of $1.50 per album, write a linear equation that shows total profit as a function of the number of albums sold.

8. A promoter has estimated that total expenses for a rock concert are $50,000. If x is the number of seats sold and the ticket price is $10, write a linear equation for total revenue. How would your equation change if the sale of special-promotion items such as albums and posters would result in additional revenue of $18,000?

9. A manufacturer of floor tiles can expect to sell 25,000 vinyl asbestos tiles if the tiles cost 15¢ each, but only 8000 if the tiles cost 17¢ each. Assuming that the relationship is linear, use the two-point formula to find the equation of the line that relates the number of vinyl asbestos tiles the manufacturer can expect to sell to their price. How many of these tiles can the manufacturer expect to sell if the tiles cost 17.5¢ each?

3.3 QUADRATIC FUNCTIONS

Since we devoted the beginning of this chapter to linear functions, you may have gotten the impression that linear functions are the only ones that really matter. This is far from true. Although there are many equa-

FIGURE 3.9
Demand for a Frozen
Dessert

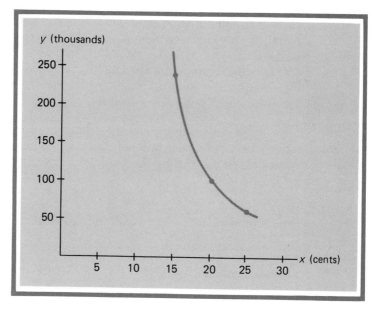

tions that can be described by means of linear equations, we often encounter situations where the points do not all lie on a straight line or a straight line cannot be used to describe the overall pattern. For example, Figure 3.9 depicts the relationship between the weekly demand for a new frozen dessert and the price at which it is sold. Actually, a market-research study showed that 240,000 of the desserts were sold when they were priced at 15¢, 100,000 we sold when they were priced at 20¢, and 60,000 were sold when they were priced at 24¢. The information conveyed through these three points makes it clear that the relationship between the price and the demand for this new frozen dessert is definitely not linear.

In the above example, the relationship can be described by means of a slightly bent curve which raises the question about what kinds of equations might be appropriate to describe the underlying physical situation. Sometimes, the choice of a particular equation is dictated by the nature of the situation itself; this is the case, for example, in the illustration of Example 2.2, which related the unit cost of specific generators to the number of generators produced. Most of the time, though, we have no choice but to try various kinds of equations and decide more or less subjectively which one provides the best fit. (This may sound like a "hit-and-miss" procedure, but it can be done in a fairly systematic fashion, especially with the use of high-speed computers.)

For relationships such as the one shown in Figure 3.9 we often choose a **quadratic function**, a function given by an equation of the form

$$y = ax^2 + bx + c$$

where a, b, and c are numerical constants and c is not equal to zero. Note that if a were zero, we would be left with the equation of a linear function.

Quadratic functions are sometimes referred to as **parabolic functions**, and their graphs are called **parabolas**.

quadratic equations In Example 2.3 we described the relationship between the number of extras a new car dealer puts on cars and the number of cars the dealer can expect to sell during the model year by means of the equation

$$y = 40 + 8x - x^2$$

Thus the relationship is a quadratic function.

EXAMPLE 3.10 Suppose now that the dealer has 52 cars in stock and that the dealer wants to know *how many extras to put on each of these cars so that all the cars can be sold without having to turn any customers away.* One way of obtaining an answer to this question is to look at the graph reproduced in Figure 3.10. Judging from this graph, it seems that $x = 2$ and $x = 6$ are the values of x that correspond to $y = 52$, and we conclude that he should put either 2 or 6 extras on each car. To handle this problem *algebraically,* we must solve the equation

$$52 = 40 + 8x - x^2$$

which can also be written as

FIGURE 3.10
Graph
for Example 3.10

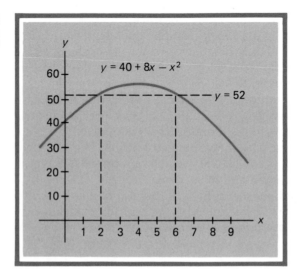

$$12 - 8x + x^2 = 0$$

after we add x^2 on both sides of the equation, subtract 8x, and then subtract 40 (getting the constant term $52 - 40 = 12$).

This equation is called a **quadratic equation** (in *one unknown*), a term which applies to any equation which can be put in the form

$$ax^2 + bx + c = 0$$

where a, b, and c are numerical constants and a is not equal to zero. A *solution* of a quadratic equation is a value of x that "satisfies" the equation, namely, a value of x that makes $ax^2 + bx + c = 0$ a *true* statement.

EXAMPLE 3.10
(Continued)   We see that $x = 2$ is a solution of the quadratic equation $12 - 8x + x^2 = 0$ since $12 - 8(2) + 2^2 = 0$, and so is $x = 6$ since $12 - 8(6) + 6^2 = 0$; on the other hand, $x = 3$ is *not* a solution since $12 - 8(3) + 3^2 = -3$ and *not* 0.

Quadratic equations can be solved in various ways. One way is to plot the graph of $y = ax^2 + bx + c$ and read the value or values of x that correspond to $y = 0$, namely, the value or values of x at which the curve cuts the x-axis. This graphical method will work nicely if the solutions happen to be whole numbers, if we are good at plotting graphs, or if we are interested only in *approximate solutions*.

EXAMPLE 3.11   To solve the quadratic equation $3 - x^2 = 0$, we might plot the graph of $y = 3 - x^2$, as in Figure 3.11, and read the answers (the x-coordinates of the points where the graph cuts the x-axis) as approximately $x = -1.7$ and $x = 1.7$. If this approximation is too crude, we might observe that the equation can be written as $x^2 = 3$, so that the solutions are given by $x = \sqrt{3}$ and $x = -\sqrt{3}$. Thus we find from a square root table or calculator that the solutions are $x = -1.732$ and $x = 1.732$ (to three decimal places).

The solution of a quadratic equation can cometimes be facilitated by factoring and making use of the fact that *if the product of two real numbers is zero, then one or the other must be zero.*

FIGURE 3.11
Graph
for Example 3.11

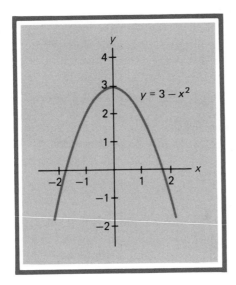

$y = 3 - x^2$

EXAMPLE 3.10
(Continued)

We could write $12 - 8x + x^2 = 0$ as

$$(x - 2)(x - 6) = 0$$

and conclude that either $x - 2 = 0$ or $x - 6 = 0$; hence, either $x = 2$ or $x = 6$.

The methods we have described so far are of no use whatsoever unless $y = ax^2 + bx + c$ is easily graphed, unless we are satisfied with approximations, or unless $ax^2 + bx + c$ is easily factored. A general method of much wider use is that in which the quadratic equation $ax^2 + bx + c = 0$ is actually *solved symbolically*, so that the solutions of any given quadratic equation can be obtained by substituting the values of a, b, and c into an appropriate formula. It can be shown that the two solutions of $ax^2 + bx + c = 0$ are given by

$$x = \frac{-b + \sqrt{b^2 - 4ac}}{2a} \quad \text{and} \quad x = \frac{-b - \sqrt{b^2 - 4ac}}{2a}$$

which is usually condensed to

$$x = \frac{-b \pm \sqrt{b^2 - 4ac}}{2a}$$

This formula is usually called the **quadratic formula**.

EXAMPLE 3.10
(Continued) If we use the quadratic formula to solve $x^2 - 8x + 12 = 0$, we find that substitution of $a = 1$, $b = -8$, and $c = 12$ yields

$$x = \frac{-(-8) \pm \sqrt{(-8)^2 - 4(1)(12)}}{2(1)} = \frac{8 \pm \sqrt{64 - 48}}{2} = \frac{8 \pm 4}{2}$$

Thus the two solutions of the quadratic equation $x^2 - 8x + 12 = 0$ are

$$x = \frac{8 + 4}{2} = 6 \text{ and } x = \frac{8 - 4}{2} = 2$$

which agrees, of course, with the results we obtained before.

When we gave the formula for the solutions of a quadratic equation, we indicated that there are always two solutions. This was true in our example, where the solutions were unequal real numbers. It would be a mistake, however, to conclude that the two solutions must necessarily be unequal, or for that matter, that they must necessarily be real numbers.

EXAMPLE 3.12 If we look at Figure 3.12, which shows the graph of $y = 4x^2 - 12x + 9$, we find that there is only one point on the curve which corresponds to $y = 0$, the point $(\frac{3}{2}, 0)$. This suggests that the quadratic equation $4x^2 - 12x + 9 = 0$ has only the one solution $x = \frac{3}{2}$. If we substitute $a = 4$, $b = -12$, and $c = 9$ into the quadratic formula, we get

$$x = \frac{-(-12) \pm \sqrt{(-12)^2 - 4(4)(9)}}{2(4)} = \frac{12 \pm 0}{8} = \frac{3}{2}$$

and we see that the two solutions are equal.

In Example 3.12 the two solutions were actually equal, and to avoid ambiguities we say that the given quadratic equation has the double solution $x = \frac{3}{2}$. Observe that, in general, the quadratic equation $ax^2 + bx + c = 0$ has a double solution whenever $b^2 - 4ac$ (the quantity which appears under the radical sign) is equal to zero. Although we do not do so, an example can also be constructed where neither solution of the quadratic equation is a real number.*

---

*For example, one simple illustration of a quadratic equation for which neither solution is given by a real number is $x^2 + 1 = 0$.

FIGURE 3.12
Graph
for Example 3.12

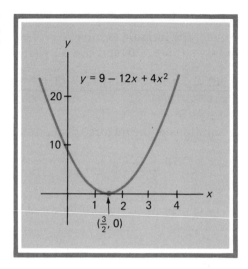

$$y = 9 - 12x + 4x^2$$

$\left(\frac{3}{2}, 0\right)$

EXERCISES

1. To solve the quadratic equation $2 + 2x - x^2 = 0$ graphically, calculate the values of $y = 2 + 2x - x^2$ for $x = -3, -2, -1, 0, 1, 2, 3,$ and 4; plot the corresponding points; join them with a smooth curve; and read the x-coordinates of the points at which this curve cuts the x-axis. (See also part (d) of Exercise 5 below.)

2. To solve the quadratic equation $7 - 8x + 2x^2 = 0$ graphically, calculate the values of $y = 7 - 8x + 2x^2$ for $x = -1, 0, 1, 2, 3, 4,$ and 5; plot the corresponding points; join them with a smooth curve; and read the x-coordinates of the points at which this curve cuts the x-axis. (See also Exercise 6 below.)

3. Use the quadratic formula to solve each quadratic equation.
   (a) $14 - 9x + x^2 = 0$ (d) $x^2 - 5x = 24$
   (b) $x^2 = 7x - 10$ (e) $x^2 + 4x = 12$
   (c) $20 + 9x + x^2 = 0$ (f) $x^2 + x - 30 = 0$

4. Use the quadratic formula to solve each quadratic equation.
   (a) $3 + 4x - 4x^2 = 0$ (c) $1 - 2x - 3x^2 = 0$
   (b) $6 + 5x - 4x^2 = 0$ (d) $1 - 4x - 5x^2 = 0$

5. Use the quadratic formula to solve each quadratic equation.
   (a) $3 - 2x - x^2 = 0$ (c) $x^2 - 2x - 8 = 0$
   (b) $x^2 + 6x + 5 = 0$ (d) $2 + 2x - x^2 = 0$

6. Use the quadratic formula to solve the quadratic equation of Exercise 2.

7. Solve each quadratic equation by factoring:
   (a) $x^2 - 2x = 24$

(b) $-8 + 2x + x^2 = 0$

(c) $x^2 + 2x - 35 = 0$

8. The expected cost of repairs for a machine (y) is related to the number of months since it was previously serviced (x) as follows:

$$y = x^2 - 4x + 20$$

In order to maintain an expected cost of repairs of $32 per machine, how often should the machines be serviced?

9. The cost (in thousands of dollars) of producing x units of a product is given by

$$y = \frac{1}{4}x^2 + x - 18$$

where x is measured in hundreds of units produced. If the firm has $6000 to spend on the production of this product during the next production period, how many units can be produced?

3.4 POLYNOMIAL FUNCTIONS

Linear and quadratic functions belong to a general type of functions referred to as **polynomial functions**. They are given by equations of the form

$$y = a_0 + a_1x + a_2x^2 + a_3x^3 + \cdots + a_kx^k$$

where $a_0, a_1, a_2, a_3, \ldots,$ and a_k are numerical constants with a_k not equal to zero. Also, k is a positive integer which we call the *degree* of the polynomial function. Note that for $k = 1$ and $k = 2$ we get

$$y = a_0 + a_1x$$

and

$$y = a_0 + a_1x + a_2x^2$$

which means that in these special cases the polynomial functions are linear and quadratic, respectively.

In contrast to linear and quadratic functions, polynomial functions of degree higher than two have graphs which can turn up and down several times; Figure 3.13 for example, shows the graph of

$$y = 5 + 24x - 50x^2 + 35x^3 - 10x^4 + x^5$$

FIGURE 3.13
Graph of Polynomial
Function

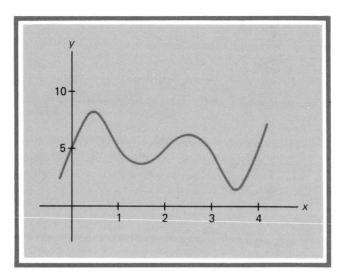

and it can be seen that the graph turns (changes from going up to going down, or vice versa) four times.

Polynomial functions of degree higher than two or three do not arise in many business applications, and we shall not study them here in any detail. However, in later chapters we shall use them to illustrate some of the basic techniques of differentiation and integration.

SUMMARY

Linear and quadratic functions provide important models for many situations in business and economics. In this chapter we provided an introduction to these two important classes of functions.

First, we showed that *linear functions* are a general class of functions given by an equation of the form $y = mx + b$. For such functions we discussed the practical importance of the slope (m) in business and economics, showed the difference between *explicit* and *implicit* form, and defined a general method for writing the equation of a straight line as $Ax + By = C$, a form called the *standard form*. Our introduction to linear functions concluded with a detailed discussion of the process of finding the equation of a straight line.

The remainder of the chapter provided an introduction to *quadratic functions*, which are functions given by an equation of the form $y = ax^2 + bx + c$. We presented several solution procedures for *quadratic equations*, a term which applies to any equation which can be put in the form $ax^2 + bx + c = 0$. The chapter concluded with a brief introduction to *polynomial functions*.

1. **Linear Function** Any function whose graph is a straight line. In general, $y = mx + b$ is the equation of a function whose graph is a straight line; thus, we refer to the function as linear.

2. **Slope (m)** The slope of the equation $y = mx + b$ measures the rate of change in y per unit change in x.

3. **y-intercept (b)** The y-intercept of the equation $y = mx + b$ is the value of y that corresponds to $x = 0$.

4. **Slope-intercept Form** We refer to $y = mx + b$ as the slope-intercept form of the equation of a straight line.

5. **Standard Form** If A, B, and C are numerical constants, then $Ax + By = C$ is the standard form of the equation of a straight line.

6. **Quadratic Function** A function given by an equation of the form $y = ax^2 + bx + c$ where a, b, and c are numerical constants.

7. **Quadratic Equation** Any equation that can be put in the form $ax^2 + bx + c = 0$.

8. **Quadratic Formula** A formula that can be used to find the solution to any quadratic equation. Specifically, it can be shown that the two solutions of $ax^2 + bx + c = 0$ are given by

$$x = \frac{-b \pm \sqrt{b^2 - 4ac}}{2a}$$

9. **Polynomial Function** A function whose equation is of the form

$$y = a_0 + a_1 x + a_2 x^2 + a_3 x^3 + \cdots + a_k x^k$$

where $a_0, a_1, a_2, a_3, \ldots, a_k$ are numerical constants with $a_k \neq 0$.

1. Find the slope of the line segment connecting each pair of points.
   (a) (2, 2) and (4, 6)   (d) (3, −1) and (5, 7)
   (b) (−2, −1) and (1, 5)   (e) (−1, −1) and (4, −9)
   (c) (−1, 4) and (7, 0)   (f) (−5, 0) and (1, 12)

2. Verify that the points (−1, −11), (2, 1), and (4, 9) lie on a straight line.

3. Verify that the points (1, 2), (4, 5), and (6, 8) do *not* lie on a straight line.

4. Determine whether the points (0, 4), (3, 19), and (−2, −6) lie on a straight line.

5. Find the slope of each line.
   (a) $y = -10 + 5x$ (c) $3x + 4y = 16$

   (b) $x = 6 + \frac{3}{4}y$ (d) $2x + 6y - 18 = 0$

6. Find an equation of the line with slope $m = -2$ and which cuts the x-axis at the point $(2, 0)$.

7. Find the slope of each line.
   (a) $y = -12 + 8x$
   (c) $3x - 4y = 12$
   (b) $x = 4 + \frac{1}{2}y$
   (d) $3x + 8y + 24 = 0$

8. Find an equation of the line with slope $m = 5$ and which cuts the y-axis at the point $(0, 2)$. Does this line contain the point $(2, 12)$? Does it contain the point $(-1, -4)$?

9. Change $4x - 2y = 5$ into slope-intercept form and read the slope as well as the y-intercept of the line.

10. Find an equation of the line that passes through the point $(6, 8)$ and has the slope $m = 2$.

11. If the total cost to produce and market a personal computer is $C(x) = 100,000 + 200x$, where x is the number of units manufactured and $C(x)$ is the total cost in dollars, what is the significance of the slope and the y-intercept of the corresponding line?

12. The growth in sales for a company has been increasing in a linear fashion over the past 5 years. If 100,000 units were sold in the first year and 180,000 units were sold in the fifth year, find each of the following.
    (a) The equation of the line that describes this relationship.
    (b) The expected number of units sold for the sixth year.

13. A manufacturer of calculators estimates that the cost to set up the production line to produce a new model is $5000, regardless of the number of units produced. If the cost to manufacture each unit is $8 (assuming the production equipment is set up) write a linear equation that shows the total cost of manufacturing x units.

14. In 1978 a company earned $3.17 per share and it expects this figure to increase by 24 cents a year. Coding the years so that 1975 corresponds to $x = 0$ and successive years correspond to $x = 1, 2, 3, \ldots$, use the point-slope formula to find the equation which will enable us to predict the company's earnings per share for future years. What should be the company's earnings per share in 1985? What is the significance of the value we would get if we substituted $x = -1$ into the formula?

15. The manager of a furniture store claims that the store's sales will increase by $25 for every additional dollar spent on advertising. If the store has averaged monthly sales of $148,000 while spending $100 a month on advertising, find the equation that relates the store's expected average monthly sales to the amount spent on advertising.

16. The total numbers of chicken dinners served by a well-known restaurant in Southern California on Mother's Day 1973 through 1981 were 13,600, 14,000, 14,200, 14,600, 14,800, 15,000, 15,200, 15,900, and 16,200.
    (a) Plot these data on a piece of graph paper, with the years *coded* so that 1973 corresponds to x = −4 and successive years correspond to x = −3, −2, −1, 0, 1, . . .
    (b) To check a statistician's claim that the line y = 14,800 + 300x pretty well describes the overall trend, plot it on the diagram constructed in part (a) and judge by eye how well it fits the given data. (*Hint: it* takes the coordinates of two points to plot the line. Why would it be better to choose those corresponding to x = −4 and x = 4 rather than those corresponding to x = 0 and x = 1?)

17. To solve the quadratic equation $1 + 2x - x^2 = 0$ graphically, calculate the values of $y = 1 + 2x - x^2$ for x = −2, −1, 0, 1, 2, 3, and 4; plot the corresponding points; join them with a smooth curve; and read the x-coordinates of the points where this curve cuts the x-axis.

18. To solve the quadratic equation $11 - 16x + 4x^2 = 0$ graphically, calculate the values of $y = 11 - 16x + 4x^2$ for x = −1, 0, 1, 2, 3, 4, and 5; plot the corresponding points; join them with a smooth curve; and read the x-coordinates of the points where this curve cuts the x-axis.

19. Solve each quadratic equation by factoring
    (a) $6 - 5x + x^2 = 0$
    (b) $x^2 = 6 + x$
    (c) $15 + 8x + x^2 = 0$

20. Solve the quadratic equation $x^2 - 2x - 8 = 0$ graphically.

21. Solve the quadratic equation $x^2 - 2x - 8 = 0$ by factoring.

22. Solve the quadratic equation $x^2 - 2x - 8 = 0$ by using the quadratic formula.

23. Use the quadratic formula to solve each quadratic equation.
    (a) $2x^2 - 6x - 4 = 0$
    (b) $x^2 - 36 = 0$
    (c) $x^2 - 7x - 8 = 0$

24. A corporation estimates that its annual earnings are given by the equation

$$f(t) = \frac{1}{5}t^2 + 3t + 20$$

where $f(t)$ is in millions of dollars and t is in years (coded so that $t = 0$ corresponds to 1980, $t = 1$ corresponds to 1981, and so on).

Use this equation to estimate sales for 1984. Could a simpler linear relationship provide a reasonable approximation?

25. Assume that the demand for a product (in thousands of units) is given by

$$D(p) = p^2 - 8p - 80$$

where p is the price of the product in dollars. To maintain a demand of 100,000 units, what price should be charged?

EXPONENTIAL AND LOGARITHMIC FUNCTIONS

In this chapter we shall study **exponential functions** and their inverses, the corresponding **logarithmic functions.** Exponential functions provide important models for the description of economic growth. Logarithmic functions, in addition to their use in numerical computations, also provide a method for deciding whether an exponential function is the appropriate model for the relationship between two variables.

4.1   EXPONENTIAL FUNCTIONS

Any function which is given by an equation of the form $y = a \cdot b^x$ is referred to as an **exponential function**; it owes its name to the fact that the independent variable appears as the exponent of the constant b, which is called the **base** of the exponential function. In this kind of equation, a and b must be real numbers, a must not equal 0, b must not equal 0 or 1 (because this would give the linear functions $y = 0$ or $y = a$) and—in most practical applications—a and b are both positive. The domain of an exponential function can be the set of all real numbers or a subset consisting of, for example, the positive real numbers, an interval on the x-axis, or a set of integers. If the base b of an exponential function is greater than 1 and a is positive, the graph of $y = a \cdot b^x$ has the general shape of the graph of Figure 4.1, where we plotted $y = 3 \cdot 2^x$. The values of this kind of exponential function are never negative and they increase as x increases; in fact, as x increases, the values of the function increase more and more rapidly, and this is why exponential functions like that of Figure 4.1 are often used as models for economic growth. It is customary to refer to such exponential curves as **growth curves.**

If the base b of an exponential function is positive but less than 1 and a is positive, the graph of $y = a \cdot b^x$ has the general shape of the graph of Figure 4.2, where we plotted $y = 3(\frac{1}{2})^x$. The values of such an exponential function are never negative, and they *decrease* as x increases, getting closer and closer to zero. At the same time, the *rate* at

FIGURE 4.1
Graph of Exponential
Function

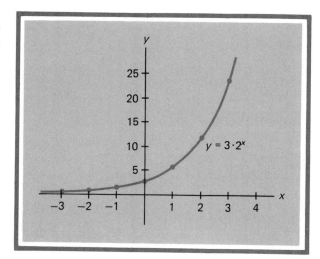

which they decrease gets slower and slower, and this is why exponential functions like that of Figure 4.2 are often used as models for *economic decay*. The corresponding curves are also called *growth curves*, although they describe growth in an *inverse* sense, namely, in the sense of depreciation, wear and tear, wasting away, or decay.

EXAMPLE 4.1   Consider, for example, the demand curve given by the equation

$$D = 1280(0.93)^p$$

where D is the demand (in thousands) for a new product and p is the

FIGURE 4.2
Graph
of an Exponential
Function

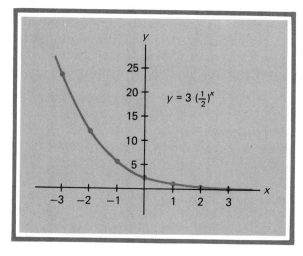

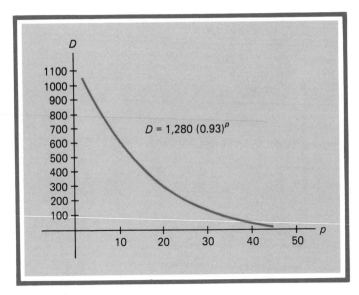

FIGURE 4.3
Exponential Demand
Curve

price in dollars. The graph of this function is shown in Figure 4.3. To calculate the demand for the new product when it is priced at $40, for example, we substitute $p = 40$ and get

$$D = 1280(0.93)^{40}$$

Using a calculator with an exponentiation key (a key such as y^x that is used to raise the number y to the power x), we find that $(0.93)^{40} = 0.0549$ (to four decimal places), and hence the demand for the new product is approximately $D = 1280(0.0549) = 70,272$ units.

When we deal with growth curves describing depreciation or decay (namely, when the base b of an exponential function is less than 1), it is common practice to change the base to $1/b$ and thus make it greater than 1. Thus, the equation of the function whose graph is shown in Figure 4.2 can be modified by writing

$$y = 3(\tfrac{1}{2})^x \quad \text{as} \quad y = 3 \cdot 2^{-x}$$

since $\tfrac{1}{2}$ can be written as 2^{-1} and $(\tfrac{1}{2})^x = (2^{-1})^x = 2^{-x}$. Note that *when we make this change, the exponent becomes negative.*

EXAMPLE 4.1
(Continued)

Similarly, the demand curve of Figure 4.3 can be changed from

$$D = 1280(0.93)^p \quad \text{to} \quad D = 1280 \left(\frac{1}{0.93} \right)^{-p}$$

and then to

$$D = 1280(1.075)^{-p}$$

since $1/0.93$ is approximately 1.075.

Another modification which is often applied to the equations of exponential functions, regardless of whether they describe growth or decay, is to change the base to the irrational number $e = 2.71828\ldots$. With this change the equation of an exponential function can be written as

$$y = a \cdot e^{cx}$$

instead of $y = a \cdot b^x$, where a and c are real numbers and e is approximately 2.71828. This kind of conversion to the base e is not very difficult, and on page 112 we shall demonstrate how it is actually done.

modified exponential functions
The growth curves mentioned so far in this section apply to situations where the values of a function increase faster and faster (as in Figure 4.1) or where they decrease, slowly approaching zero (as in Figure 4.2). This does not take care of growth problems where the values of a function increase rapidly and then level off, as might happen, for example, when the demand for a new product increases rapidly at first and then stabilizes. It also does not take care of growth problems where the values of a function decrease rapidly at first and then level off at a value greater than zero, as might happen, for example, when the demand for a novelty item starts out high, but decreases and then remains more or less constant. Situations like these can often be described by means of **modified exponential functions** given by equations of the form

$$y = k - a \cdot b^{-x} \quad \text{or} \quad y = k - a \cdot e^{-cx}$$

where a, b, c, and k are real numbers, k is positive, and either c is positive or b is greater than 1. If a is also positive, the graph of the function will be like that of the first diagram of Figure 4.4; and if a is negative, it will be like that of the second.

EXAMPLE 4.2
To give a numerical example, consider the curve of Figure 4.5 which shows how the demand (y) for a new meat tenderizer (in thousands of packages) might change with the course of time (in years). Note that the years are coded such that the first year corresponds to $x = 0$, 1 year later

FIGURE 4.4
Modified Exponential
Functions

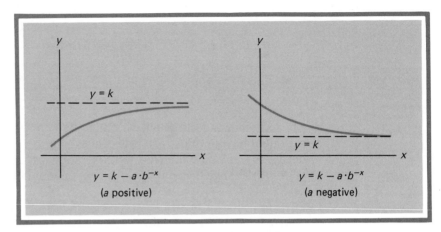

$y = k$

$y = k - a \cdot b^{-x}$
(a positive)

$y = k$

$y = k - a \cdot b^{-x}$
(a negative)

corresponds to x = 1, and so on. The pattern of the graph of Figure 4.5 reflects the fact that at first it takes time for the product to become established, after which the demand more or less levels off. Supposing that the equation of this modified exponential function is

$$y = 100 - 94e^{-x}$$

we can obtain the values of the function for x = 0, 1, 5, and 8, for example, by substituting the corresponding values of e^{-x} obtained from Table III in the appendix or using a calculator with an e^x key. Thus for x = 0, we obtain $e^0 = 1$ and y = 100 − 94 = 6; for x = 1 we obtain

FIGURE 4.5
Demand Curve

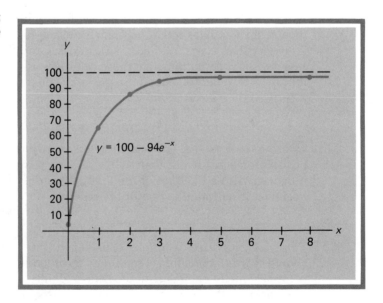

$y = 100 - 94e^{-x}$

$e^{-1} = 0.368$ and $y = 100 - 94(0.368) = 65.4$; for $x = 5$ we obtain $e^{-5} = 0.0067$ and $y = 100 - 94(0.0067) = 99.4$; and for $x = 8$ we obtain $e^{-8} = 0.00034$ and $y = 100 - 94(0.00034) = 99.97$. After plotting these points as in Figure 4.5, we were able to draw the curve actually shown in that diagram. Observe that the values of this function approach 100 (although they always remain slightly less); in the language of mathematics we say that the line $y = 100$ is an *asymptote*, which is approached by this modified exponential curve.

EXERCISES

1. Calculate the values of $y = 3 \cdot 4^x$ for $x = -2, -1, 0, 1, 2,$ and 3, plot the corresponding points, and through them draw the graph of the given exponential function.

2. Calculate the values of $y = \frac{1}{5}(0.2)^x$ for $x = -2, -1, 0, 1, 2,$ and 3, plot the corresponding points, and through them draw the graph of the given exponential function.

3. Comparing Figures 4.1 and 4.2, we find that if we viewed the graph of Figure 4.1 through the back of the paper, we would obtain the graph of Figure 4.2. What is the equation of the function whose graph we would see if we viewed the graph drawn in Exercise 1 through the back of the paper?

4. Rewrite the equation of Exercise 2 in the form $y = a \cdot b^{-x}$.

5. Rewrite each equation in the form $y = a \cdot b^{-x}$.
    (a) $y = 15(0.125)^x$
    (b) $y = 1,200(0.60)^x$
    (c) $y = 900(0.04)^x$

6. During its first 5 years of operation, a company grossed $95,000, $170,000, $240,000, $450,000, and $720,000.
    (a) Plot these values at $x = 1, 2, 3, 4,$ and 5 on a diagram with suitable scales, draw a smooth curve which (more or less) represents the company's gross earnings, and use it to predict what the company's gross earnings should be in the sixth year (to the nearest $100,000).
    (b) Calculate the values of $y = 60,000e^{0.5x}$ for $x = 1, 2, 3, 4,$ and 5 and compare these figures with the company's actual earnings by plotting the corresponding points on the diagram of part (a).
    (c) Use the equation of part (b) to predict what the company's gross earnings should be in the sixth year, and compare this prediction with the one of part (a).

7. A study of radial automobile tires made by one company showed that the percentage of tires still usable after having been driven for x miles is given by the equation $y = 100e^{-0.000025x}$.
   (a) Determine what percentage of the tires should still be usable after having been driven for 20,000 miles, for 40,000 miles, for 60,000 miles, for 80,000 miles, and for 100,000 miles.
   (b) Use the results of part (a) to plot the graph of this exponential function.

8. The planning committee of a city determines the projected population of the city x years hence by means of the equation $y = 75,000e^{x/10}$.
   (a) Determine the projected population of this city for the next 10 years.
   (b) Use the results of part (a) to plot the graph of this exponential function.

9. A certain machine heats up when it is in continuous use, and when it heats up its output is reduced. More specifically, during the xth hour that it is in continuous use, its output is

$$y = 3000e^{-0.15x}$$

units. Find the machine's output during the second, fourth, sixth, eighth, and tenth hour of continuous use, and use these figures to plot the graph of this exponential function.

10. Suppose that a survey shows that the proportion of television viewers who remember what product is regularly advertised during the evening news program is given by $y = 1 - 0.96e^{-0.4x}$, where x is the number of times they have seen the program.
    (a) Calculate the proportion which corresponds to x = 1, 3, 5, 10, and 20.
    (b) Use the results of part (a) to plot the graph of this modified exponential function.

11. A manufacturer's annual profit from the sales of a certain toy is given by

$$y = 12,000 + 30,000e^{-0.3x}$$

where y is in dollars and x denotes the number of years the toy has been on the market.
    (a) Calculate the manufacturer's profit for x = 1, 2, 3, 5, 10, and 20.
    (b) Use the results of part (a) to plot the graph of this modified exponential function.

Consider the correspondence shown in the following table; it tells us how a sales manager assigns three salespeople (Smith, Brown, and Jones) to eight states.

State	Salesperson
Montana	Smith
Idaho	Smith
Wyoming	Smith
Colorado	Brown
New Mexico	Jones
Arizona	Jones
Utah	Jones
Nevada	Jones

However, if we assign states to salespeople instead of salespeople to states, we get

Salesperson	Sales Territory
Smith	Montana, Idaho, Wyoming
Brown	Colorado
Jones	New Mexico, Arizona, Utah, Nevada

With reference to this example, we say that the relationship which assigns territories to salespeople is the **inverse** of the relationship which assigns salespeople to territories. Similarly, the relationship which assigns debtors to creditors is the *inverse* of the relationship which assigns creditors to debtors, the relationship which assigns students to teachers is the *inverse* of the relationship which assigns teachers to students, and in general

the relationship which assigns the elements of set A to the elements of set B is the inverse of the relationship which establishes the same correspondence by assigning the elements of set B to the elements of set A.

Consider the graph of the exponential function $y = 3 \cdot 2^x$, which is shown in Figure 4.1. The general shape of this graph was obtained by finding a set of points satisfying the function and then drawing a smooth curve through these points. Specifically, we determined the corresponding value of y for a variety of values of x, as shown below.

x	$y = 3 \cdot 2^x$
-3	$\dfrac{3}{8}$
-2	$\dfrac{3}{4}$
-1	$1\dfrac{1}{2}$
0	3
1	6
2	12
3	24

Consider developing a new graph by plotting these same points, but with y on the horizontal axis and x on the vertical axis. After drawing a smooth curve through these points, we would have the general shape of a graph whose corresponding function is the inverse of the exponential function $y = 3 \cdot 2^x$. This graph is shown in Figure 4.6. All

FIGURE 4.6
Graph of the Inverse
of $y = 3 \cdot 2^x$

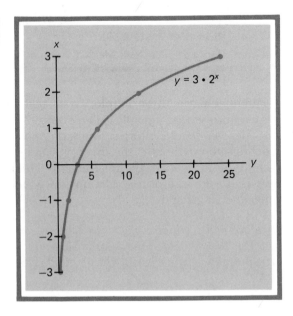

we really did was to express x in terms of y instead of expressing y in terms of x. In the next section we will study in detail the relationship between exponential functions of the form $y = b^x$ (that is, exponential functions of the form $y = ab^x$ with $a = 1$) and their corresponding inverses.

1. Consider the exponential function $y = 2^x$.
    (a) Calculate the values of y for $x = 0, 1, 2, 3, 4,$ and 5, and through them draw the graph of the given function.
    (b) Draw the graph of the corresponding inverse.
2. Consider the exponential function $y = 3(\frac{1}{2})^x$ depicted in Figure 4.2. Draw the graph of the corresponding inverse function.
3. The demand curve for Example 4.1 is given by the equation

$$D = 1280(0.93)^p$$

where D is the demand (in thousands) for a new product and p is the price in dollars. Draw the graph of the inverse function.
4. Draw the graph of the inverse of $y = 3 \cdot 4^x$ (see Exercise 1 of Section 4.1).
5. Draw the graph of the inverse function of $y = \frac{1}{5}(0.2)^x$ (see Exercise 2 of Section 4.1).
6. Consider the exponential function $y = 10^x$.
    (a) Calculate the values of y for $x = 0, 1, 2,$ and 3, and through them draw the graph of the given function.
    (b) Draw the graph of the inverse of this function.
7. Consider the exponential function $y = e^x$.
    (a) Calculate the values of y for $x = 0, 1, 2, 3,$ and 4, and through them draw the graph of the given function.
    (b) Draw the graph of the inverse function.

4.3 LOGARITHMIC FUNCTIONS

The inverse of the exponential function $y = a \cdot b^x$ is also a function—it assigns a unique value of x to each positive real value of y. In the special case where $a = 1$ and, hence, the equation of the function is $y = b^x$, the inverse of the function is so important that we give it a special name. We call it a **logarithmic function** and write its values (namely, $y = b^x$ solved for x) as

$$x = \log_b y$$

This is read "x is the logarithm of y to the base b," and in case you are confused by this notation, let us point out that $x = \log_b y$ is merely another way of writing $y = b^x$. In fact, it is customary to refer to $y = b^x$ as the **exponential form** and to $x = \log_b y$ as the **logarithmic form** of one and the same relationship between x and y. If we had to explain in words what we mean by $\log_b y$, we could say that it is *the power to which we have to raise b to get y.*

EXAMPLE 4.3   To familiarize ourselves with this notation, let us find the values of $\log_2 4$ and $\log_3 \frac{1}{27}$. If we let the first of these two quantities equal x, we find that $x = \log_2 4$ changed into the exponential form becomes $4 = 2^x$, and—since $4 = 2^2$—it follows that $x = 2$, namely, that

$$\log_2 4 = 2$$

Similarly, to find $\log_3 \frac{1}{27}$, we change $x = \log_3 \frac{1}{27}$ into the exponential form $\frac{1}{27} = 3^x$. Since $\frac{1}{27} = 3^{-3}$, it follows that $x = -3$, namely, that

$$\log_3 \tfrac{1}{27} = -3$$

What we have shown here amounts to the fact that 2 has to be raised to the power 2 to get 4, and 3 has to be raised to the power -3 to get $\frac{1}{27}$.

It is important to remember that *any question concerning a logarithmic function, its values or its graph, can always be answered by referring to the corresponding exponential function, and vice versa.*

In Chapter 1 we studied rules that simplified our work with exponents. In view of the close relationship between exponents and logarithms, it should not be surprising that there are corresponding rules that simplify work with logarithms. Corresponding to the first rule for exponents, $b^m \cdot b^n = b^{m+n}$, we now have

(1)

$$\log_b M \cdot N = \log_b M + \log_b N$$

for any positive real numbers b, M, and N. In words, *the logarithm of the product of two numbers equals the sum of their logarithms.* For instance, if we knew the values of $\log_b 17{,}382$ and $\log_b 184{,}665$ to some base b, we could multiply these two numbers, or at least find the logarithm of their product, by writing

$$\log_b 17{,}382 \cdot 184{,}665 = \log_b 17{,}382 + \log_b 184{,}665$$

Thus a lengthy multiplication can be replaced with a much simpler addition. Let us make it clear, though, that the above rule applies only to the logarithm of a product; some people make the mistake of applying it to sums, but, unfortunately, there is no general rule for simplifying $\log_b (M + N)$.

Corresponding to the rule for dividing terms involving exponents $b^m/b^n = b^{m-n}$, we now have

(2)
$$\log_b \frac{M}{N} = \log_b M - \log_b N$$

for any positive real numbers b, M, and N. In words, *the logarithm of a quotient of two numbers equals the difference of their logarithms.* For instance, if we knew the values of $\log_b 32{,}559{,}113$ and $\log_b 6{,}385{,}007$, we could divide the first of these two numbers by the second, or at least find the logarithm of their quotient, by writing

$$\log_b \frac{32{,}559{,}113}{6{,}385{,}007} = \log_b 32{,}559{,}113 - \log_b 6{,}385{,}007$$

Finally, corresponding to the third rule for exponents, $(b^m)^n = b^{m \cdot n}$, we now have

(3)
$$\log_b N^k = k \cdot \log_b N$$

for any positive real numbers b and N and any real number k. In words, *the logarithm of the kth power of a number equals k times the logarithm of the number.* It can also be shown that

$$\log_b b = 1 \quad \text{and} \quad \log_b 1 = 0$$

for any positive number b. In words, the logarithm of any number to the same base ($\log_b b$) is equal to 1, and the logarithm of 1 is always equal to 0.

To illustrate how the three basic rules are used, suppose that we are given $\log_{10} 2 = 0.3010$, $\log_{10} 3 = 0.4771$, and $\log_{10} 7 = 0.8451$, and that we are asked to evaluate $\log_{10} (\sqrt{2}/21)$. Substituting $2^{1/2}$ for $\sqrt{2}$ and

3·7 for 21, we get

$$\log_{10} \frac{\sqrt{2}}{21} = \log_{10} \frac{2^{1/2}}{3\cdot7}$$

$$= \log_{10} 2^{1/2} - \log_{10} 3\cdot7$$

$$= \frac{1}{2}\,(\log_{10} 2) - (\log_{10} 3 + \log_{10} 7)$$

$$= \frac{1}{2}\,(0.3010) - (0.4771 + 0.8451)$$

$$= -1.1717$$

It will be left to you to judge which rule (or rules) were used in each step.

common
logarithms
and natural
logarithms
In the preceding discussion we defined $\log_b y$ as the logarithm of y to the base b. The values of b most widely used in this context are 10 and the irrational number $e = 2.71828 \ldots$. Logarithms to the base 10 are called **common logarithms** and logarithms to the base e are called **natural logarithms**. When using common logarithms, the usual practice is to drop the subscript of 10 and write $\log_{10} N$ simply as $\log N$. When using natural logarithms it is customary to abbreviate $\log_e N$ to $\ln N$, which is read "the natural logarithm of N."

In the appendix to this chapter we show how a table can be used to determine the common logarithm of a number. In recent years, however, the availability of low-cost calculators with logarithm keys has resulted in a significant decline in the use of such tables. Thus we shall assume you have access to a calculator that has either a common logarithm or a natural logarithm key.

EXAMPLE 4.4
If your calculator has a common logarithm key (usually identified by LOG) verify that $\log 10 = 1$, $\log 100 = 2$, $\log 0.1 = -1$, $\log 0.01 = -2$, $\log 356 = 2.5514$, and $\log 1280 = 3.1072$. If your calculator has a natural logarithm key (usually identified by LN) verify that $\ln e = \ln 2.7183 = 1.0000$, $\ln 10 = 2.3026$, $\ln 100 = 4.6052$, $\ln 0.1 = -2.3026$, $\ln 0.01 = -4.6052$, $\ln 356 = 5.8749$, and $\ln 1280 = 7.1546$. (Note that e is only approximately 2.7183.)

If your calculator only has one of these keys, the following formulas can be used to convert from one form to another.

---

*Converting from a Common Logarithm
to a Natural Logarithm*

$$\ln N = \frac{\log N}{0.4343} \quad \text{(approximately)}$$

For example,

$$\ln 10 = \frac{\log 10}{0.4343} = \frac{1}{0.4343} = 2.3036$$

*Converting from a Natural Logarithm
to a Common Logarithm*

$$\log N = 0.4343 \cdot \ln N \quad \text{(approximately)}$$

For example,

$$\log 10 = 0.4343 \cdot \ln 10 = 0.4343 \cdot 2.3026 = 1$$

To prove the above relationship between $\log N$ and $\ln N$, we begin with the equation $x = \ln N$. Recall that the exponential form of this equation is $N = e^x$, since

$$\ln N = \ln e^x = x \cdot \ln e = x$$

If we take the logarithm of both sides of $N = e^x$ to the base 10, we get

$$\log N = \log e^x = x \log e$$

Upon dividing by $\log e$, we obtain

$$x = \frac{\log N}{\log e}.$$

Since x equals $\ln N$ and $\log e$ is approximately equal to 0.4343, this completes the proof that

$$\ln N = \frac{\log N}{0.4343}$$

In addition, by solving this equation for $\log N$, we also prove that

$$\log N = 0.4343 \cdot \ln N$$

It is often advantageous to change the equation of an exponential function from the exponential form $y = a \cdot b^x$ into the logarithmic form

$$\log y = \log a + x \cdot \log b$$

To make this change, we have only to write

$$\log y = \log (a \cdot b^x)$$
$$= \log a + \log b^x$$
$$= \log a + x \cdot \log b$$

A very important feature of this logarithmic form of the equation of an exponential function is that it expresses a linear relationship between x and log y. (Clearly, if we substitute Y for log y, A for log a, and B for log b, we get the *linear equation* $Y = A + Bx$.) Thus an *exponential relationship between x and y is equivalent to a linear relationship between x and log y.* This makes it easy to calculate the values of an exponential function (as in the above example), and it also provides a means of deciding whether an exponential function is the appropriate model for the relationship between two variables displayed by a set of data.

EXAMPLE 4.5   Consider the following data, which show the average amount of life insurance coverage (in thousands of dollars) of families in the United States for selected years from 1940 to 1970.

Year x	Life Insurance Coverage (in $1000) y	log y
1940	2.7	0.4314
1945	3.2	0.5051
1950	4.6	0.6628
1955	6.9	0.8388
1960	10.2	1.0086
1965	14.7	1.1673
1970	20.9	1.3201

Now, if we plot the values of log y (given in the right-hand column of this table) at the corresponding values of x, we get the pattern displayed in Figure 4.7, and it can be seen that the points fall very close to a straight line. This is looked upon as supporting evidence for the conten-

FIGURE 4.7
Logarithms
of Insurance Data
Plotted on Ordinary
Graph Paper

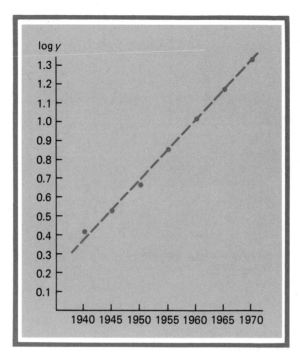

tion that the growth of family coverage of life insurance in the United States can be described by means of an exponential equation. In other words, it justifies the use of an exponential model.

In actual practice, the work we have just described can be simplified greatly by using **semilogarithmic graph paper,** a special kind of graph paper which has ordinary (equal) subdivisions along one scale, while the subdivisions along the other scale are such that we automatically plot the logarithm of a number instead of the number itself.

EXAMPLE 4.6   In Figure 4.8 we plotted the original insurance data (shown in the y-column of the above table) on this kind of graph paper, and it can be seen that the pattern we got is identical with that of Figure 4.7.

Thus there really is no need to calculate the logarithms of the y's; we can judge directly whether an exponential fraction provides the appropriate model in a given situation by plotting the data on semi-logarithmic graph paper (which is commercially available) and checking whether the points fall close to a straight line.

FIGURE 4.8
Insurance Data Plotted
on Semi-logarithmic
Graph Paper

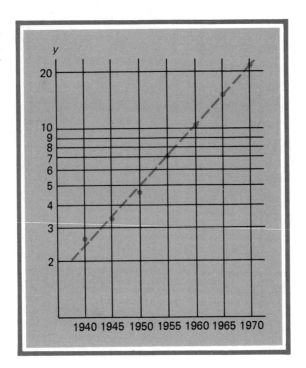

**changing
the base
of an
exponential
function**

Since exponential functions are often given with the base e, let us indicate briefly how to change $y = a \cdot b^x$ so that the base of the exponential function becomes e. All we really have to do is change b^x so that it equals e raised to some power, such as e^z. Thus $b^x = e^z$, and if we make use of the fact that the logarithms of two equal numbers are equal, we can write

$$\ln b^x = \ln e^z \quad \text{and, hence,} \quad x(\ln b) = z(\ln e) = z$$

since $\ln e = 1$. Thus $b^x = e^z = e^{x(\ln b)}$, and we can write

$$y = a \cdot e^{x(\ln b)} \quad \text{instead of} \quad y = a \cdot b^x$$

EXAMPLE 4.1
(Continued)

To illustrate this technique, let us refer back to Example 4.1 on page 97, where the relationship between the price and the demand for a new product was given by the equation

$$D = 1280(0.93)^p$$

Performing the change suggested above, we can now write

$$D = 1280 \, e^{p(\ln 0.93)}$$

Using a calculator with a natural logarithm key (or a calculator with a common logarithm key and the formula for converting from common logarithms to natural logarithms) we get ln 0.93 = −0.0726. Thus the equation of this price-demand relationship can be written as

$$D = 1280e^{-0.0726p}$$

1. Change each equation from exponential form to logarithmic form.
   (a) $9 = 7^x$ (c) $15 = b^4$ (e) $y = 12^{1/3}$
   (b) $y = 5^{1/3}$ (d) $112 = 3^x$ (f) $200 = b^7$

2. Change each from logarithmic form to exponential form.
   (a) $x = \log_5 12$ (c) $15 = \log_b 7$ (e) $17 = \log_9 y$
   (b) $2 = \log_3 y$ (d) $x = \log_{10} 14$ (f) $24 = \log_b 7$

3. Evaluate each logarithm by letting it equal x and changing the equation thus obtained into exponential form.

   (a) $\log_2 64$ (c) $\log_7 49$ (e) $\log_4 \dfrac{1}{2}$

   (b) $\log_{11} 11$ (d) $\log_{1/3} 9$ (f) $\log_7 1$

4. Rework parts (a), (c), and (e) of Exercise 3 by making use of the rules $\log_b N^k = k \cdot \log_b N$ and $\log_b b = 1$.

5. Given $\log_{10} 2 = 0.3010$, $\log_{10} 3 = 0.4771$, and $\log_{10} 7 = 0.8451$, evaluate each logarithm.

   (a) $\log_{10} 6$ (c) $\log_{10} \dfrac{7}{2}$ (e) $\log_{10} 5$

   (b) $\log_{10} \sqrt{14}$ (d) $\log_{10} \sqrt[3]{3}$ (f) $\log_{10} 882$

6. Calculate the values of $y = \log_3 x$ for $x = \frac{1}{9}, \frac{1}{3}, 1, 3, 9$, and 27, plot the corresponding points, and through them draw the graph of this logarithmic function.

7. Calculate the values of $y = \log_4 x$ for $x = \frac{1}{64}, \frac{1}{16}, \frac{1}{4}, 1, 4$, and 16, plot the corresponding points, and through them draw the graph of this logarithmic function.

8. The demand for a certain product is given by

$$D = 28.2p^{-0.52}$$

   where p is its price in cents and D is the demand in units of 1000.
   (a) Express log D in terms of log p, and use this equation to find the demand which corresponds to $p = 5, 10, 15, 20$, and 25. Also plot the graph of this price-demand function for values of p falling within the range for which points have been obtained.

(b) Suppose that the supply of this product is given by $S = p$, where S is also in units of 1000. Plot the graph of $S = p$ on the diagram obtained in part (a) and find the value of p at which the market for the product is in *equilibrium*, namely, the value of p at which the two curves intersect.

(c) Verify the result of part (b) by equating supply to demand, namely, by solving the equation $p = 28.2p^{-0.52}$. (*Hint:* Take the logarithm of the expressions on both sides of the equation, and solve for log p.)

9. Rewrite each equation in the form $y = a \cdot e^{cx}$.
   (a) $y = 75(1.22)^x$ **(c)** $y = 124(2.35)^{-x}$
   (b) $y = 183(3.75)^x$ **(d)** $y = 1020(0.45)^x$

10. During the first year of sales for a new product (coded $x = 0$) a company sold 100 units of the product ($y = 100$). For the next 4 years of operation ($x = 1, 2, 3, 4$), the sales were 200, 400, 800, and 1600 units.
    (a) Plot the data corresponding to the first 5 years of operation. Does an exponential relationship appear to be appropriate?
    (b) Take the common logarithm of each sales' value and plot the log of sales versus the year. What type of relationship does this indicate between y and x? Why?
    (c) Write an equation that describes the relationship between x (year) and y (sales) for this problem.

11. Consider the following data, which show freshman enrollment at a particular university for the past 4 years, where $x = 3$ corresponds to the most recent year.

Year (x)	Enrollment (y)
0	674
1	795
2	938
3	1107

(a) Plot the common logarithm of y versus x. What type of relationship does this indicate between y and x? Explain.
(b) Develop a forecast of next year's enrollment.

12. The registrar of a college predicts future enrollment by means of the formula

$$y = 674(1.18)^x$$

where the years are coded so that $x = 0$ corresponds to 1965, $x = 1$

corresponds to 1966, x = 2 corresponds to 1967, and so on. What are the registrar's predictions for the enrollment at this college during 1985 and 1986? Use logarithms to determine the requested numerical solutions and check your computations using a calculator with an exponentiation key.

SUMMARY

In this chapter we showed that *exponential functions* are a general class of functions given by an equation of the form $y = a \cdot b^x$, where a and b must not equal 0 or 1. We gave several examples of different exponential functions to show their importance in modeling situations involving economic growth, as well as economic decay. In addition, we introduced *modified exponential functions* to provide a model for situations where the values of a function increase rapidly at first and then stabilize, or decrease rapidly at first and then level off at a value greater than zero.

We then discussed the concept of the *inverse of a function* in order to illustrate the relationship between exponential and *logarithmic functions*. Specifically, we showed that the inverse of the exponential function $y = b^x$ is a logarithmic function.

The chapter concluded with a discussion of common and natural logarithms, a method for converting from exponential to logarithmic form, and a procedure for changing the base of an exponential function. An appendix describing the use of tables to determine the common logarithm of a number is also provided at the end of this chapter.

GLOSSARY

1. **Exponential Function**   Any function given by an equation of the form $y = a \cdot b^x$, where a and b are real numbers; a must not equal 0 and b must not equal 0 or 1 (because this would give the linear functions $y = 0$ or $y = a$).
2. **Logarithmic Function**   A function that is the inverse of the exponential function $y = b^x$. We write its values ($y = b^x$ solved for x) as $x = \log_b y$.
3. **Common Logarithms**   Logarithms to the base 10, written $\log_{10} N$, or simply $\log N$.
4. **Natural Logarithms**   Logarithms to the base $e = 2.71828 \ldots$, written $\log_e N$, or simply $\ln N$.

1. Calculate the values of $y = 4 \cdot 2^x$ for $x = -2, -1, 0, 1, 2$, and 3, plot the corresponding points, and through them draw the graph of the given exponential function.

2. Calculate the values of $y = 4 \cdot (\frac{1}{2})^x$ for $x = -3, -2, 0, 1, 2$, and 3, plot the corresponding points, and through them draw the graph of the given exponential function.

3. Rewrite the equation of Exercise 2 in the form $y = a \cdot b^{-x}$.

4. Rewrite the equation $y = 12(0.80)^x$ in the form $y = a \cdot b^{-x}$.

5. The demand y for a product having a price of x dollars per unit is thought to be represented by $y = 1000 \,(0.7)^x$ for values of x between \$1.00 and \$1.50. Plot the corresponding points for $x = \$1.00, \$1.10, \$1.20, \$1.30, \$1.40$, and \$1.50 and through them draw the graph of the given exponential function. Would a "simpler" function appear to be appropriate in this situation? Explain.

6. Suppose that a study of the efficiency of workers on an assembly line shows that after x hours of work without a break the efficiency of a worker (measured as a percent) is approximately equal to $y = 100e^{-x/5}$.

   (a) Calculate the efficiency after $\frac{1}{2}$ hour, 1 hour, $1\frac{1}{2}$ hours, and 2 hours of work.

   (b) Use the results of part (a) to plot the graph of this exponential function.

   (c) To the nearest half hour, after what amount of time should workers be provided with a break if management does not want the efficiency to fall below 70 percent?

7. During the next x years the total earnings for a recent college graduate will be $y = 150,000(1.12)^x - 150,000$ dollars.

   (a) Compute the graduate's earnings during the first year, during the first 5 years, during the first 10 years, and during the first 20 years.

   (b) Use the results of part (a) to plot the graph of this function.

8. During its first five years of operation, a company grossed \$80,000, \$140,000, \$200,000, \$375,000, and \$600,000.

   (a) Plot these values at $x = 1, 2, 3, 4$, and 5, draw a smooth curve which (more or less) represents the company's gross earnings, and use it to predict the amount which the company should gross during the seventh year (to the nearest \$100,000).

   (b) Calculate the values of $y = 50,000e^{0.5x}$ for $x = 1, 2, 3, 4$, and 5, and compare these figures with the company's actual gross earnings during the first five years by plotting the corresponding points on the diagram of part (a).

(c) Use the equation of part (b) to predict the amount which the company should gross during the seventh year and compare this prediction with the one of part (a).

9. A manufacturer's annual profit from the sales of a product is given by

$$y = 8,000 + 30,000e^{-0.4x}$$

where y is in dollars and x denotes the number of years the product has been on the market.
(a) Calculate the manufacturer's annual profit for $x = 1, 2, 3, 5, 10$, and 15.
(b) Use the results of part (a) to plot the graph of this modified exponential function.

10. Change each of the following equations from exponential form to logarithmic form.
(a) $10^x = 81$
(b) $e^x = 15$
(c) $2^x = 40$
(d) $8^x = 125$

11. Based upon a marketing research study, a firm believes that the demand for a new product is given by

$$D = 10,000p^{-0.6}$$

What is the demand for the product for prices (p) of $1.00 and $1.25? What price corresponds to a demand of 9196 units?

12. A special promotion record album developed for sale through television advertising is believed to have a weekly demand of $y = 2000 + 32,000(\frac{1}{2})^x$, where x is the number of weeks the special promotion has been running. For $x = 1, 2, 3, 4$, and 5, plot the corresponding points and through them draw the graph of the given exponential function.

13. At a particular firm the number of days an employee is late for work appears to be a function of how long the employee has worked for the firm. Based upon an analysis of company records, the personnel department has determined that employees with 1 year of seniority ($x = 1$) are late an average of 13.4 days per year ($y = 13.4$); employees with 2, 3, 4, and 5 years of seniority average 8.8, 6.0, 4.0, and 2.6 late days per year, respectively.
(a) Plot the given data. What type of function appears to describe the relationship between average number of days late and years of employment?
(b) Take the log of the number of days late and plot the data again, using log y instead of y. What type of relationship does this indicate between y and x. Why?

(c) Write an equation that describes the relationship between x and y for this problem.

In **Exercises 14** and **15** use logarithms to determine the numerical solutions requested. Then, using a calculator with an exponentiation key, check your results obtained using logarithms.

14. It is expected that in a certain city the number of families with incomes of x dollars or more in 1985 will be given by

$$y = 6{,}000{,}000x^{-0.7}$$

(a) How many families in this city should have incomes of $10,000 or more in 1985?
(b) How many families in this city should have incomes of $50,000 or more in 1985?
(c) How many families in this city should have incomes of $100,000 or more in 1985?

15. An economist estimates the monthly demand for soap in a certain country by means of the formula

$$D = 27p^{-0.68}q^{0.42}r^{0.26}$$

where p is the average retail price per bar (in cents), q is the average monthly family income (in dollars), and r is the expected average value of the country's Consumer Price Index for that month; the demand is in units of 1000 bars of soap. What estimate will the economist get for $p = 15¢$, $q = \$1200$, and $r = 129.0$?

THE USE
OF TABLES
TO DETERMINE
THE LOGARITHM
OF A NUMBER

APPENDIX

Common, or Briggsian, logarithms are named after the English mathematician Henry Briggs, who published the first table of logarithms to the base 10 early in the seventeenth century. In this appendix we show how such a table can be used to determine the common logarithm of a number. The natural logarithm can then be computed by using the conversion formula presented in Section 4.3.

$$\ln N = \frac{\log N}{0.4343} \quad \text{(approximately)}$$

Alternatively, a table of natural logarithms can be found in most handbooks of mathematical tables.

An important concept in using a table to determine the common logarithm of a number involves the fact that the common logarithms of integral powers of the base 10 can be easily determined using the definition of the logarithm of a number. That is, the logarithm of a number is the power to which the base has to be raised so that it will equal the given number. Consequently, since $10 = 10^1$, $100 = 10^2$, and $1000 = 10^3$, $\log 10 = 1$, $\log 100 = 2$, and $\log 1000 = 3$. Similarly, since $0.1 = 10^{-1}$, $0.01 = 10^{-2}$, and $0.001 = 10^{-3}$, $\log 0.1 = -1$, $\log 0.01 = -2$, and $\log 0.001 = -3$.

The overall size of a table of common logarithms can be held down considerably by making use of *scientific notation* (see page 15), in which any positive real number is written as the product of a number between 1 and 10 and an integral power of 10. For example, we write 33.5 as $3.35 \cdot 10^1$, 0.024 as $2.4 \cdot 10^{-2}$, and 67,200 as $6.72 \cdot 10^4$. Thus all we need is a table which gives the approximate values of the common logarithms of the numbers between 1 and 10 (rounded, for instance, to two decimals), and we will be able to determine the approximate value of $\log N$ for any positive real number N (suitably rounded, if necessary).

EXAMPLE 4.7 To find log 356, for instance, we write

$$\log 356 = \log 3.56(10^2) = \log 3.56 + \log 10^2 = \log 3.56 + 2$$

and to find log 0.0000471 we write

$$\log 0.0000471 = \log 4.71(10^{-5}) = \log 4.71 + \log 10^{-5}$$
$$= \log 4.71 - 5$$

Proceeding this way, we can express the common logarithm of any positive real number as the logarithm of a number between 1 and 10, called the **mantissa**, plus or minus a whole number called the **characteristic**. The mantissa can be found in a table (such as Table IV in the appendix), and the characteristic is simply the exponent of 10 when the number whose logarithm we are trying to find is converted into the scientific notation.

EXAMPLE 4.7
(Continued)
With reference to Table IV (in which all decimal points are omitted and the third digit is given by the headings of the respective columns), we find that log 3.56 = 0.5514 and, hence, that

$$\log 356 = 0.5514 + 2 = 2.5514$$

Similarly, we find that log 4.71 = 0.6730 and, hence, that

$$\log 0.0000471 = 0.6730 - 5$$

In Example 4.7, the answer could be written as 0.6730 − 5 = −4.3270, but *it is generally preferred to leave the fractional part of logarithms positive, so that they will represent the corresponding mantissas.*
Having explained how to find the common logarithm of any positive real number (suitably rounded, if necessary), let us now investigate the *inverse problem* of finding the number which has a given logarithm to the base 10.

EXAMPLE 4.8
Let us look for the number whose common logarithm is 3.8722. Since the characteristic is 3, we know that the number must be between $10^3 = 1000$ and $10^4 = 10,000$, and since Table IV shows that a mantissa of 0.8722 corresponds to 7.45, we find that the answer is $7.45(10^3) = 7450$. Similarly, to find the number whose common logarithm is 0.8142 − 2, we use Table IV, in which a mantissa of 0.8142 corresponds to 6.52; hence, the answer is $6.52(10^{-2}) = 0.0652$.

MATHEMATICS
OF
FINANCE

In this chapter we present several applications of mathematics that involve financial analysis and problem solving. Specifically, we investigate the relationships between time and the value of money in order to show how an individual or an organization can determine the value of an investment which promises to return a sum of money at some time in the future. In order to be an intelligent consumer in today's society and to function in a business world based upon financial analysis, it is essential to have a knowledge of mathematics of finance.

5.1 INTEREST

Interest is a charge for the use of money. For example, if you lend someone $200 for one year at an annual interest rate of 15%, the interest at the end of the year is 15% of $200, or 0.15(200) = $30. This $30 represents the charge you have set for the use of your money. Note the terminology in use here: We speak of 15% as the **interest rate** and $30 as the **interest**. In any problem situation the interest depends upon (1) the interest rate, (2) the amount of money borrowed or saved, and (3) the length of time involved. In order to fully understand the relationships among these three items, we need to distinguish between the concepts of simple and compound interest.

simple interest   Suppose we borrow $100 at the **simple interest rate** of 12 percent. At the end of one year the interest on the loan is $100(0.12) = $12. Thus if we pay the loan off at the end of the first year, the amount we owe is $100 + $100(0.12) = $112. If the loan were for 2 years, we should pay an additional $12 of interest, so the amount that we should owe at the end of 2 years is $100 + [$100(0.12)](2) = $124. Thus we see that *with simple interest the interest rate applies only to the amount we borrow.* In general, then, if we borrow P dollars (called the **principal**) at the simple interest rate i, the annual interest is $P \cdot i$ and the amount A that we owe at the end of n years is given by

$$A = P + (P \cdot i)n$$

This simple interest formula is usually written as

$$\boxed{A = P(1 + i \cdot n)}$$

which is obtained by factoring out P; we wrote the formula the other way mainly to emphasize the point that there is a linear relationship between n and A.

EXAMPLE 5.1   If we borrow \$12,000 at the simple interest rate $i = 0.09$ (9 percent), the amount we owe after n years is

$$A = 12{,}000(1 + 0.09n)$$
$$= 12{,}000 + 1080n$$

Here the independent variable is n, the dependent variable is A, and the relationship is obviously linear; the slope of the corresponding line is the *constant* interest of \$1080 (9 percent of \$12,000), which is added each year. Note that the domain of this function is not limited to whole numbers—the amount we owe after one month is obtained by substituting $n = \frac{1}{12}$, and the amount we owe after a year and a half is obtained by substituting $n = \frac{3}{2}$.

Although we described the situation for simple interest in terms of borrowing a specific sum of money, the situation corresponding to depositing a sum of money P at the simple interest rate i for n years is analogous. That is, the amount owed to us at the end of n years is $A = P + (P \cdot i)n$, or $A = P(1 + i \cdot n)$.

compound interest   In actual practice, simple interest is used only for short-term transactions; for long-term transactions, the interest is added to the principal at regular intervals of time, and thereafter the interest itself earns interest. This is called **compounding**, and if the interval of time between successive calculations and additions of the interest is 1 year, we say that the interest is **compounded annually**. For example, assume that we deposit \$100 in a savings account where interest is compounded annually at the rate of 8 percent. At the end of the first year, the amount of interest earned is \$100(0.08) = \$8. Hence, our initial deposit of \$100 will be worth \$108 at the end of the first year. For the second year we shall earn interest on the amount of savings available at the end of the first year. Thus we not only earn interest on our original deposit of $100, but also on the $8 of interest earned the first year. Therefore the amount of interest earned the second year is $108(0.08) = $8.64, and our savings at the end of the second year are $108 + $8.64 = $116.64. For the third year we earn interest on $116.64, the amount available at the end of the second year. Thus our savings at the end of the third year will be $116.64 + $116.64(0.08) = $125.97. Based upon these 3 years of computation, let us see if we can identify how the amount of savings can be computed for any length of time.

Savings Available at the End of Year 1

$$\text{Amount} = \$100 + \underbrace{\$100(0.08)}$$

Initial deposit   Interest

$$\boxed{\text{Amount} = \$100\,(1 + 0.08)}$$

Savings Available at the End of Year 2

$$\text{Amount} = \underbrace{\text{savings available at the end of year 1}} + \underbrace{\text{interest}}$$

$$= \$100(1 + 0.08) \quad\quad + [\$100(1 + 0.08)]0.08$$

$$= [\$100(1 + 0.08)^2](1 + 0.08)$$

$$\boxed{\text{Amount} = \$100(1 + 0.08)^2}$$

Savings Available at the End of Year 3

$$\text{Amount} = \underbrace{\text{savings available at the end of year 2}} + \underbrace{\text{interest}}$$

$$= \$100(1 + 0.08)^2 \quad\quad + [\$100(1 + 0.08)^2]0.08$$

$$= [\$100(1 + 0.08)](1 + 0.08)$$

$$\boxed{\text{Amount} = \$100(1 + 0.08)^3}$$

Based upon the above analysis it can be shown that the amount of savings available at the end of n years is $\$100(1 + 0.08)^n$. Thus, in general, if we invest (or borrow) a sum of money P at the interest rate i, the amount of money we have coming (or owe) at the end of n years, denoted by A, is given by

$$A = P(1 + i)^n$$

EXAMPLE 5.2   If we borrow $10,000 at 14 percent interest compounded annually, we use $i = 0.14$ and find that the amount we owe after n years is given by

$$A = 10,000(1 + 0.14)^n$$

Thus after 1 year we owe $10,000(1 + 0.14)^1 = \$11,400$, after 2 years we owe $10,000(1 + 0.14)^2 = \$12,996$, after 3 years we owe $10,000 \times (1 + 0.14)^3 = \$14,815.44$, and so on.

In Example 5.2 we used a calculator with an exponentiation key (y^x) to compute the value of $(1 + 0.14)^2$ and $(1 + 0.14)^3$. As an alternative, we could look up these values in Table I of the appendix. Table I is a **compound interest table** and gives the values of $(1 + i)^n$ for selected values of i and n. For example, using Table I to determine the value of $(1.14)^2$, we find the value in the row corresponding to $n = 2$ and the column corresponding to $i = 0.14$: $(1.14)^2 = 1.299600$.

multiple   Even though interest rates are usually quoted on an annual basis, most
compounding   interest is compounded quarterly, monthly, weekly, or daily. Thus if we are told that a bank pays 6 percent interest (on savings accounts) compounded quarterly, this does not mean that the bank pays 6 percent every 3 months or that it actually pays 6 percent a year, but that it pays a fourth of 6 percent, or 1.5 percent, every 3 months. Similarly, if a mortgage company charges 9 percent compounded monthly, this means that it charges a twelfth of 9 percent, namely, $\frac{3}{4}$ of 1 percent, each month.

The formula which we use to calculate A when interest is compounded m times a year is

$$A = P\left(1 + \frac{i}{m}\right)^{n \cdot m}$$

where $n \cdot m$ is the number of times interest is compounded over the n years. Note that when $m = 1$ this formula simplifies to our previous formula for annual compounding.

EXAMPLE 5.3   If we invest $5000 at 8 percent compounded quarterly, after 3 years this investment will have grown to

$$A = 5000\left(1 + \frac{0.08}{4}\right)^{12} = 5000(1.268242) = \$6341.21$$

and after 5 years it will have grown to

$$A = 5000\left(1 + \frac{0.08}{4}\right)^{20} = 5000(1.485947) = \$7429.74$$

In case you are curious to know where we got the values of $(1.02)^{12}$ and $(1.02)^{20}$ in the preceding example, rest assured that we did not calculate these quantities directly, but looked them up in Table I of the appendix. As we previously pointed out, this table gives the values of $(1 + i)^n$ for selected values of i and n. In our current problem, we need to determine the values of $(1 + i/m)^{n \cdot m}$. However, by simply locating the value of i in the table corresponding to i/m and the value of n in the table corresponding to $n \cdot m$, we can also use the compound interest table to solve problems where interest is compounded m times a year. Thus to determine the value of $(1 + 0.08/4)^{3 \cdot 4} = (1 + 0.02)^{12}$, we looked up the value in Table I corresponding to $i = 0.02$ and $n = 12$. A calculator with an exponentiation key can be used to obtain the same result.

As we pointed out above, if money is invested at 6 percent compounded quarterly, this does not mean that it will actually yield 6 percent. This is only what we called the **nominal interest rate** and to determine the actual rate, or **effective rate**, we have to investigate *what happens to $1 in 1 year*. Clearly, at 6 percent compounded quarterly, $1 becomes

$$A = 1\left(1 + \frac{0.06}{4}\right)^4 = (1.015)^4 = \$1.0614$$

rounded to four decimal places, and we find that the effective rate is approximately 6.14 percent—this is what the money *actually* earns. By use of the same kind of argument, it can be shown in general that *if an investment pays i percent compounded m times a year, the corresponding effective rate is given by*

$$\boxed{i' = \left(1 + \frac{i}{m}\right)^m - 1}$$

EXAMPLE 5.3
(Continued)

Thus if an investment pays 8 percent compounded quarterly, the effective rate is

$$i' = \left(1 + \frac{0.08}{4}\right)^4 - 1 = (1.02)^4 - 1 = 0.082432$$

or approximately 8.24 percent. As before, the value of $(1.02)^4$ was obtained from Table I, although it could have been calculated quite easily using a calculator.

As a result of this discussion and Example 5.3, you may wonder whether *we can make the effective rate as large as we want by compounding a sufficient number of times.* The answer is no—there is a limit. In fact, it can be shown that when m (the number of compoundings per year) gets larger and larger, the effective rate comes closer and closer to the quantity $e^i - 1$. This is referred to as **continuous compounding**.

EXAMPLE 5.3
(Continued)
If an investment pays 8 percent compounded continuously, the effective interest rate is $e^i - 1 = 2.71828^{0.08} - 1 = 0.083287$, or approximately 8.33 percent.

EXERCISES

1. If $9,000 is invested at 7 percent compounded annually, find the value of this investment in each case.
    (a) After 1 year.
    (b) After 5 years.
    (c) After 20 years.

2. If someone borrows $2000 at 15 percent compounded annually, how much does the individual owe in each case?
    (a) At the end of the first year.
    (b) At the end of the second year.
    (c) At the end of the third year.

3. If $6500 is invested at 6% compounded annually, what is the value of this investment in each case?
    (a) After 2 years.
    (b) After 5 years.
    (c) After 10 years.
    (d) After 20 years.

4. If $4000 is invested at i percent compounded annually, what is i in each case?

(a) This investment is worth $5360.38 after 6 years.

(b) This investment is worth $15,478.74 after 20 years.

(c) This investment is worth $8635.70 after 10 years.

5. In Section 5.1 we showed that the formula $A = P(1 + i)^n$ holds for $n = 1$, $n = 2$, and $n = 3$. Continue the argument to show that it also holds for $n = 4$.

6. Assuming that interest is 15 percent compounded annually, how long does it take for a sum of money to double?

7. If $1200 is borrowed at 8 percent compounded quarterly and $1000 is repaid after 2 years, how much is still owed at that time?

8. If a department store charges 1.5 percent per month on amounts owed on its budget accounts, what interest rate does a person actually pay per year?

9. What effective rate corresponds to each nominal rate?
(a) 6 percent compounded quarterly.
(b) 8 percent compounded semiannually.
(c) 12 percent compounded monthly.

10. If $6000 is invested at 12 percent, what is the value of this investment after 4 years in each case?
(a) Interest is compounded annually.
(b) Interest is compounded semiannually.
(c) Interest is compounded quarterly.
(d) Interest is compounded monthly.

11. Assuming that interest is 10 percent compounded annually, which amount is worth more: $5000 today or $8000 at the end of 6 years?

12. An individual borrows $10,000 at 10 percent compounded quarterly. At the end of 2 years how much does the individual owe?

13. With reference to Exercise 12, how much would the individual owe if the interest rate is 12 percent compounded quarterly?

14. In Exercise 13, how much would the individual owe if the interest rate is 15 percent compounded quarterly?

15. Solve Exercise 12 assuming interest is compounded monthly.

16. Solve Exercise 13 assuming interest is compounded monthly.

17. Solve Exercise 14 assuming interest is compounded monthly.

5.2 FUTURE VALUE AND PRESENT VALUE

In the previous section we showed how to calculate the amount of money we earn (or owe) if we invest (or borrow) a sum of money P at the interest rate i. The amount, denoted by A, is referred to in financial analysis as the **future value**, **compound value**, or **terminal value** of the principal P. In this text we shall always use the term *future value* to refer to this concept. Thus when interest is compounded annually, we can compute the future value of a sum of money P using the general formula for compound interest. That is,

$$
\begin{array}{l}
\text{Future value of } P \qquad = A = P(1 + i)^n \\
\text{(annual compounding)}
\end{array}
\tag{5.1}
$$

If compounding is done m times a year, we compute the future values as

$$
\begin{array}{l}
\text{Future value of } P \qquad = A = P\left(1 + \dfrac{i}{m}\right)^{n \cdot m} \\
\text{(compounding } m \text{ times} \\
\text{each year)}
\end{array}
\tag{5.2}
$$

EXAMPLE 5.4   To finance the purchase of new equipment, a small business has obtained $50,000 through private financing. The terms of the loan call for the loan amount plus interest to be paid at the end of 2 years. What is the amount that will be due, assuming the interest rate is 12 percent compounded quarterly?

To compute the future value for this example, we use Equation 5.2 with $m = 4$, $i = 0.12$, $n = 2$, and $P = \$50,000$. Thus we obtain

$$
\text{Future value of } P = P\left(1 + \frac{i}{m}\right)^{n \cdot m}
$$

$$
= 50,000\left(1 + \frac{0.12}{4}\right)^{2 \cdot 4}
$$

$$
= 50,000(1 + 0.03)^8
$$

$$
= 50,000(1.26677)
$$

$$
= \$63,338.50
$$

Let us consider a financial concept that is really the inverse of the concept of future value. To begin with, we shall assume that interest is compounded annually. To introduce the concept, consider the following question: How much money would we have to invest at the present time in order to get $100 at the end of one year if the nominal interest rate is 10 percent? The amount needed is referred to as the **present value** of the $100 we shall receive at the end of the year. To determine the present value for this illustration, we need to solve the compound interest formula for P. Thus, since $A = P(1 + i)^n$, dividing both sides of this equation by $(1 + i)^n$ gives

$$\text{Present value of } A \atop \text{(annual compounding)} = P = \frac{A}{(1 + i)^n} = A(1 + i)^{-n} \qquad (5.3)$$

Equation 5.3 represents the present value, or the discounted value, of the amount A. That is, to compute the present value of a sum of money that is to be received in the future, the sum of money is subjected to "compound discounting" at the interest rate i for n years. Thus for our simple illustration above, where $A = \$100$, $n = 1$, and $i = 0.10$, we obtain

$$\text{Present value of } \$100 = \frac{100}{(1 + 0.10)^1} = \frac{100}{1.10} = \$90.91$$

In other words, if we invested $90.91 for one year at an interest rate of 10 percent, our investment would grow to $100 at the end of the year.

Note that if compounding is done m times per year, we would need to solve Equation 5.2 for the present value. Doing so we obtain

$$\text{Present value of } A = P = \frac{A}{(1 + i/m)^{n \cdot m}} = A\left(1 + \frac{i}{m}\right)^{-n \cdot m} \qquad (5.4)$$
$$\text{(compounding } m \text{ times each year)}$$

To simplify the computation of present value, Table II in the appendix gives the values of $(1 + i)^{-n}$ for selected values of i and n. When using this table for a situation in which compounding is done m times per year, we simply locate the value of i in the table corresponding to i/m and the value of n in the table corresponding to $n \cdot m$.

EXAMPLE 5.5 The terms of a short-term loan require that a company pay a lump sum payment of $25,000 at the end of 2 years. If interest is 18 percent compounded monthly, what is the present value of the $25,000?

Using Table II and Equation 5.4 with $A = 25{,}000$, $i = 0.18$, $n = 2$, and $m = 12$, we obtain

$$\text{Present value of } A = \frac{A}{(1 + i/m)^{n \cdot m}}$$

$$= \frac{25,000}{(1 + 0.18/12)^{2 \cdot 12}}$$

$$= \frac{25,000}{(1 + 0.015)^{24}}$$

$$= 25,000(1 + 0.015)^{-24}$$

$$= 25,000(0.699544)$$

$$= \$17,488.60$$

EXERCISES

1. Find the present value of a note for $7500 due 5 years hence in each case.
   (a) 6 percent compounded semiannually.
   (b) 6 percent compounded monthly.
   (c) 8 percent compounded quarterly.

2. Two years from now, a school needs $2,000,000 for an expansion of its facilities. What sum should be set aside now and invested at 8 percent compounded quarterly so that the $2,000,000 will be available when needed?

3. If the discount rate is 8 percent (annual compounding), find the present value of $1500 due at the end of 2 years.

4. If someone is willing to pay us $5464 now for a promissory note for $8000 due in 4 years, at what rate (annual compounding) is the individual discounting the note?

5. Tom Comte wants to borrow $3200 and pay it back in a lump sum after 4 years. How much will he have to pay after 4 years in each case?
   (a) If he is being charged 8 percent simple interest.
   (b) If he is being charged 10 percent simple interest.

6. Mrs. Adams wants to borrow $4000 to buy a new car and pay off the loan with monthly payments stretched over a period of 3 years. If the dealer charges her 18 percent simple interest and computes the monthly payments by dividing the total amount due in 3 years by 36, how much will Mrs. Adams have to pay each month?

7. The construction of the facilities for a new business can be financed either with an immediate payment of $500,000 or with an

immediate payment of $300,000 and another payment of $300,000 in 6 years. If the future payment is discounted at 12 percent compounded quarterly, which of the two alternatives has a smaller present value?

8. To clear up a debt, a person agrees to pay $1000 now, another $1000 a year from now, and another $1000 in 2 years. If the future payments are discounted at 8 percent compounded quarterly, what is the present value of these three payments?

9. An individual planning for retirement wants to invest a sum of money in long-term savings certificates. Assuming that interest is 12 percent compounded quarterly, what sum should be invested now in order to provide a $100,000 retirement fund at the end of 8 years?

10. The terms of a promissory note call for a lump-sum payment of $20,000 in 5 years. If interest is compounded annually at the rate of 18 percent, what is the present value of the $20,000 payment?

11. What final payment must be made in order to pay off a $50,000 loan in 10 years if interest is 16 percent compounded annually?

5.3 ANNUITY

Consider a situation in which an individual (for example, the owner of an office building) receives a series of equal amounts (for example, rent) for some specified period of time. Determining the present value of the future series of equal amounts is referred to as determining the **present value of the annuity**. In this type of situation, the word *annuity* simply refers to the fact that an equal amount is received each period for two or more periods. Note the similarity of this type of problem and the usual present value problem, in which we determine the present value of some amount to be received in the future. The essential difference is that now a series of future payments is to be received.

We will also investigate how to determine the **future value of an annuity**. For example, suppose an individual deposits $1000 in a savings account at the end of each year and interest is compounded annually at the rate of 8 percent. At the end of 20 years, what is the balance in the savings account? Basically, determining the future value of an annuity is similar to an ordinary future-value problem. The difference is that instead of receiving or paying one initial amount, we receive or pay an equal amount for two or more periods of time.

In this text we shall discuss annuity problems for which the interval between successive payments coincides with the interval of time between successive calculations and additions of interest. In order to understand how these types of problems are solved, we introduce the concept of a **progression**.

progressions When we studied *simple interest*, we learned that if P dollars are borrowed at the simple interest rate i, the amount owed at the end of the first year is $P + (P \cdot i)$, the amount owed at the end of the second year is $P + 2(P \cdot i)$, the amount owed at the end of the third year is $P + 3(P \cdot i)$, the amount owed at the end of the fourth year is $P + 4(P \cdot i)$, and so forth. What is characteristic about these amounts is that each one is obtained from the preceding amount by adding $P \cdot i$, which makes them an **arithmetic progression**. In general,

> *if we begin with the number a and repeatedly add the number d (called the* **common difference***), then the numbers a, a + d, a + 2d, a + 3d, a + 4d, . . . are said to constitute an arithmetic progression.*

In contrast, if we look at the *compound interest* formula on page 126, we find that if P dollars are borrowed at the interest rate i compounded annually, the amount owed at the end of the first year is $P(1 + i)$, the amount owed at the end of the second year is $P(1 + i)^2$, the amount owed at the end of the third year is $P(1 + i)^3$, the amount owed at the end of the fourth year is $P(1 + i)^4$, and so forth. What is characteristic about these amounts is that each one is obtained from the preceding amount by multiplying by $(1 + i)$, which makes them a **geometric progression**. In general,

> *if we begin with the number a and repeatedly multiply by the same number r (called the* **common ratio***), then the numbers a, ar, ar^2, ar^3, ar^4, . . . are said to constitute a geometric progression.*

In many of the applications of mathematics in finance, we must deal with the sum of several terms of a geometric progression. Therefore we need a formula for the sum, S_n, of the first n terms of a geometric progression whose first term is a and whose common ratio is r. Note that this sum is written as

$$S_n = a + ar + ar^2 + ar^3 + \cdots + ar^{n-1}$$

If we multiply the expressions on both sides of this equation by r, we get

$$r \cdot S_n = r(a + ar^2 + ar^3 + \cdots + ar^{n-2} + ar^{n-1})$$
$$= ar + ar^2 + ar^3 + ar^4 + \cdots + ar^{n-1} + ar^n$$

and if we then subtract the expressions on both sides of the equation for $r \cdot S_n$ from those of the equation for S_n, we get

$$S_n - r \cdot S_n = (a + ar + ar^2 + ar^3 + \cdots + ar^{n-2} + ar^{n-1})$$
$$- (ar + ar^2 + ar^3 + ar^4 + \cdots + ar^{n-1} + ar^n)$$

Since each term except a and ar^n is *added as well as subtracted* on the right-hand side of this last equation, we are left with

$$S_n - r \cdot S_n = a - ar^n$$

which can also be written as

$$S_n(1 - r) = a(1 - r^n)$$

Finally, dividing by $1 - r$, we get

$$S_n = a \cdot \frac{1 - r^n}{1 - r} \qquad (5.5)$$

which is the desired formula for the *sum of the first n terms of a geometric progression* provided that r does not equal 1. (If r equals 1, the terms of the progressions are all equal to a and the above formula for S_n cannot be used, but the sum of the first n terms is simply $n \cdot a$.)

future value of an annuity Now that we know how to compute the sum of a geometric progression, let us see how we can use this result to compute the **future value of an annuity**. For example, assume that an individual deposits $1000 in a savings account at the end of the year for 5 successive years. If the interest is compounded annually at the rate of 8 percent, how much money is available in the account at the end of 4 years? Figure 5.1 depicts the time sequence of deposits for this illustration. Note that we refer to the current time (whatever it is) as $t = 0$, 1 year later as $t = 1$, 2 years later as $t = 2$, and so forth. In addition, we follow the common practice in finance which assumes that the first deposit occurs at $t = 1$, the second at $t = 2$, and so on.* Looking at Figure 5.1 we see that the initial deposit of $1000 will earn interest for 4 years. Thus we can use Equation 5.1 to compute the amount of money to which this $1000 will grow when interest is compounded annually at the rate of 8 percent. That is,

$$\begin{aligned}\text{Future value of} \ &= P(1 + i)^n \\ \text{the first deposit} \ &= \$1000(1 + 0.08)^4\end{aligned}$$

---

*The annuity to which we refer in this text, where payments are made at the end of each year, is called a *regular annuity*. If payments are made at the beginning of each year, each payment would simply be shifted back 1 year. We discuss regular annuities in order to be consistent with the approach taken in most introductory textbooks in finance.

FIGURE 5.1
Time Sequence
for Future Value
Illustration

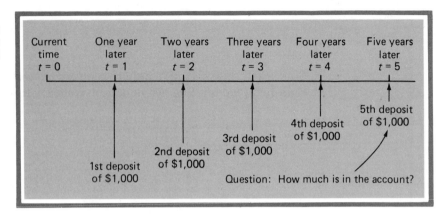

Similarly, since the second deposit of $1000 will earn interest for 3 years, the future value of the second deposit is

$$\text{Future value of the second deposit} = \$1000(1 + 0.08)^3$$

Continuing this process, we can show that the future value of the third deposit is $\$1000(1 + 0.08)^2$ and the future value of the fourth deposit is $\$1000(1 + 0.08)^1$. Finally, the future value of the last deposit is $1000, since no interest will be earned. Thus the amount to which the $1000 annuity for five successive years will grow can be computed by adding the future values associated with each deposit.

Deposit	Future Value
1	$\$1000(1.08)^4 = \$1360.49$
2	$\$1000(1.08)^3 = \$1259.71$
3	$\$1000(1.08)^2 = \$1166.40$
4	$\$1000(1.08)^1 = \$1080.00$
5	Value of deposit $= \$1000.00$
	Future value of the annuity $\rightarrow \$5866.60$

Now, let us see if we can compute the future value of an annuity without first having to evaluate the future value corresponding to each deposit. For our current illustration note that if we write the sum of the four individual terms beginning with the last term, we obtain

$$\text{Future value of the annuity} = 1000 + 1000(1.08)^1 + 1000(1.08)^2 + 1000(1.08)^3 + 1000(1.08)^4$$

Thus the expression for the future value of the annuity is just the sum of a geometric progression whose first term is 1000 and whose common ratio is 1.08. Hence, using Equation 5.5, the sum of this geometric progression is

$$S_5 = 1000\left[\frac{1 - (1.08)^5}{1 - 1.08}\right]$$

$$= 1000\left(\frac{1 - 1.469328}{1 - 1.08}\right)$$

$$= 1000(5.86660)$$

$$= \$5866.60$$

By using the formula for the sum of a geometric progression, we see that the future value of the annuity is $5866.60.

Based upon the above analysis, it can be shown that if we have an annuity where a constant amount A is deposited at the end of each year for n years and where interest is compounded annually at the nominal interest rate i, the future value of the annuity is equal to

$$\text{Future value of the annuity}^* = A \cdot \frac{1 - (1 + i)^n}{1 - (1 + i)} \qquad (5.6)$$

Although we described the computation of the future value of an annuity in terms of payments made on an annual basis and interest compounded annually, the same general formula can be used for other payment situations. For example, if instead of depositing $1000 at the end of each year for 4 years, as in our previous illustration, suppose $250 were deposited at the end of every quarter. There would then be four payments per year for each of the 4 years, so $n = 16$, which corresponds to the total number of periods for which a payment is made. The per-period interest rate is now $i = 0.08/4 = 0.02$, and the amount contributed each period is $250. Thus we can use Equation 5.6 with $n = 16$, $i = 0.02$, and $A = \$250$ to compute the future value for this type of situation. In doing so, Table I of the appendix can be used to determine the value of $(1 + i)^n$.

---

*This formula assumes that deposits are made at the end of each year (period). If deposits are made at the beginning of each year (period), the formula for computing the future value is

$$A \cdot (1 + i) \cdot \left[\frac{1 - (1 + i)^n}{1 - (1 + i)}\right]$$

$$\text{Future value of the annuity} = 250\left[\frac{1 - (1 + 0.02)^{16}}{1 - (1 + 0.02)}\right]$$
(quarterly payments)

$$= 250(18.6393)$$

$$= \$4659.83$$

EXAMPLE 5.6 Jim Evans has won a magazine sweepstakes that provides an annual payment of \$5000 for 5 years. If interest is compounded annually at 12 percent, the future value of this annuity can be computed using Equation 5.6 with $A = \$5000$, $i = 0.12$, and $n = 5$. We obtain

$$\text{Future value of the annuity} = A \cdot \frac{1 - (1 + i)^n}{1 - (1 + i)}$$

$$= 5000\frac{1 - (1 + 0.12)^5}{1 - (1.12)}$$

$$= 5000\frac{1 - 1.762342}{-0.12}$$

$$= 5000(6.352850)$$

$$= \$31,764.25$$

present value of an annuity

Suppose an individual wants to begin withdrawing \$1000 each year from a savings account for a period of 4 successive years. If the interest rate is 8 percent compounded annually, how much money would have to be in the account initially if after the last withdrawal no money is left in the account? Figure 5.2 depicts the time sequence of withdrawals for this illustration.

To determine the present value of the four consecutive withdrawals of \$1000, we need to compute the sum of the present values

*FIGURE 5.2
Time Sequence
for Present Value
Illustration*

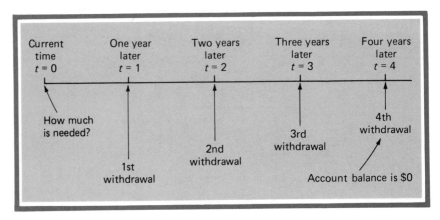

corresponding to each withdrawal. Thus using Equation 5.3, the general formula for computing the present value of an amount assuming annual compounding, we obtain the following results.

Withdrawal	Present value $= \dfrac{\text{amount}}{(1 + i)^n}$
4	$\dfrac{\$1000}{(1 + 0.08)^4} = \$735.03$
3	$\dfrac{\$1000}{(1 + 0.08)^3} = \$793.83$
2	$\dfrac{\$1000}{(1 + 0.08)^2} = \$857.34$
1	$\dfrac{\$1000}{(1 + 0.08)^1} = \$925.93$

Present value of the annuity → $3312.13

Note that the present value of the annuity is just the sum of the present value of each term. That is,

$$\text{Present value of the annuity} = \frac{\$1000}{1.08} + \frac{\$1000}{(1.08)^2} + \frac{\$1000}{(1.08)^3} + \frac{\$1000}{(1.08)^4}$$

Note that the expression on the right-hand side of this equation is the sum of a geometric progression whose first term is 1000/1.08 and whose common ratio is 1/1.08. Hence, using Equation 5.5 and Table II of the appendix, the sum of this geometric progression is

$$S_4 = \frac{1000}{1.08} \cdot \frac{1 - \dfrac{1}{(1.08)^4}}{1 - \dfrac{1}{1.08}}$$

$$= 1000 \left[\frac{1 - \dfrac{1}{(1.08)^4}}{1.08 - 1} \right]$$

$$= 1000 \left[\frac{1 - (1.08)^{-4}}{0.08} \right]$$

$$= 1000 \left(\frac{1 - 0.735030}{0.08} \right)$$

$$= 1000(3.31213)$$

$$= \$3312.13$$

In general, then, if the amount received each year for n years is A and if interest is compounded annually at the nominal interest rate i, the **present value of the annuity** is

$$\text{Present value of the annuity} = A\left[\frac{1 - \dfrac{1}{(1+i)^n}}{i}\right] \qquad (5.7)$$
$$\text{(annual compounding)}$$

A generalization of the above formula for the present value similar to that of the formula for the future value of an annuity is also possible. For example, if the individual discussed earlier wanted to withdraw $500 every 6 months instead of $1000 per year, we could also use Equation 5.7 to determine the amount of money that would be required. Since there would be two withdrawals per year for 4 years, $n = 4(2) = 8$, corresponding to 8 payment periods. The interest rate for a 6-month period would be $i = 0.08/2 = 0.04$. Using Equation 5.7 with $n = 8$, $i = 0.04$, and $A = \$500$, we have

$$\text{Present value of the annuity} = 500\left[\frac{1 - \dfrac{1}{(1 + 0.04)^8}}{0.04}\right]$$
$$\text{(6-month payments)}$$

$$= 500\left[\frac{1 - (1 + 0.04)^{-8}}{0.04}\right]$$

$$= 500\left(\frac{1 - 0.730690}{0.04}\right)$$

$$= \$3366.38$$

EXAMPLE 5.6
(Continued) How much would the magazine have to have set aside in order to pay Jim Evans the $5000 annuity for 5 years? That is, what is the present value of this annuity? Using Equation 5.7 with $A = \$5000$, $i = 0.12$, and $n = 5$, we obtain

$$\text{Present value of the annuity} = A\left[\frac{1 - \dfrac{1}{(1+i)^n}}{i}\right]$$

$$= 5000\left[\frac{1 - \dfrac{1}{(1 + 0.12)^5}}{0.12}\right]$$

$$= 5000\left[\frac{1 - (1 + 0.12)^{-5}}{0.12}\right]$$

$$= 5000\left(\frac{1 - 0.567427}{0.12}\right)$$

$$= 5000(3.604775)$$

$$= \$18,023.88$$

amortization The word **amortization** refers to the process of paying off a debt or obligation by periodic payments. For example, assume an individual borrows $10,000 at an annual interest rate of 12 percent. The terms of the loan call for the $10,000 to be repaid in five annual installments, the first one due at the end of the first year. What should the annual payment be in order to pay off the loan with five equal payments?

An amortization problem is really just the inverse of a problem in which we find the present value of an annuity. The difference between the two problems is that in amortization problems we must compute the value of the payment to be made each period instead of the present value. Thus, a formula for determining the payment per period is obtained by solving Equation 5.7 for A after setting the present value equal to the loan amount. Doing so, we obtain the following formula.

$$\text{Payment per period} = (\text{amount of loan})\left[\frac{i}{1 - (1 + i)^{-n}}\right] \qquad (5.8)$$

For our current illustration, $n = 5$, $i = 0.12$, and the loan amount is $10,000. Thus

$$\text{Payment per period} = (10,000)\left[\frac{0.12}{1 - (1.12)^{-5}}\right]$$

$$= 10,000\left(\frac{0.12}{1 - 0.567427}\right)$$

$$= 10,000(0.277410)$$

$$= \$2774.10$$

Thus we see that five payments of $2774.10 will amortize the $10,000 loan.

EXAMPLE 5.7 A $25,000 loan calls for payment to be made in 10 annual installments. If the interest rate is 14 percent compounded annually, what annual payment must be made?

Using Equation 5.8 with $i = 0.14$ and $n = 10$, we obtain

$$\text{Payment per period} = (\text{amount of loan})\left[\frac{i}{1 - (1 + i)^{-n}}\right]$$

$$= 25{,}000\left[\frac{0.14}{1 - (1 + 0.14)^{-10}}\right]$$

$$= 25{,}000\left(\frac{0.14}{1 - 0.269744}\right)$$

$$= 25{,}000(0.191714)$$

$$= \$4792.84$$

EXERCISES

1. If someone invests $60 at the end of each month at 12 percent compounded monthly, what is the balance of his or her account at the end of three years?

2. If someone invests $250 at the end of every three months at 8 percent compounded quarterly, what is the balance of his or her account at the end of 10 years?

3. If we deposit $80 in a savings account at the end of every 6 months and the bank pays 6 percent compounded semiannually, what will be our balance at the end of 5 years?

4. Find the present value of an annuity paying $2000 at the end of each year for 5 years, if the interest rate is 7 percent compounded annually.

5. Find the present value of an annuity paying $150 at the end of each month for 4 years, if the interest rate is 6 percent compounded monthly.

6. What equal monthly payments would someone have to make for 3 years to repay $4000 borrowed from a bank at 9 percent compounded monthly?

7. Determine the monthly payment required to pay off an $800 loan at the end of 1 year if the annual interest rate is 8 percent.

8. The owner of a four-unit apartment building receives monthly rentals totaling $1000. If the annual interest rate is 9 percent, compute the present value of monthly receipts for 1 year.

9. To finance the cost of a college education an individual wants to accumulate a fund of $25,000 over a 10-year period. Assuming that interest is compounded annually at the rate of 10 percent, how much money would have to be deposited each year?

10. An individual borrowed $5000 and the total amount is to be paid back in 12 monthly installments. What is the difference in monthly payments between an interest rate of 12 percent annually and one of 18 percent?

11. A real estate investment company offers to make you a limited partner in a new office building complex. To become a limited partner you must invest $50,000 now and pay an additional $100,000 over the next 5 years.
    (a) Assuming that you can earn 8 percent compounded annually by investing in municipal bonds, to what amount would your $50,000 grow if you invested the money in municipal bonds?
    (b) If the remaining $100,000 were to be paid off in five equal installments of $20,000 each, what is the future value of a 5-year annuity of $20,000, assuming you purchased municipal bonds each year that returned 8 percent compounded annually?
    (c) At the end of 5 years, what amount would the limited partnership have to be worth in order to match the value of the alternate investment in municipal bonds?

12. Assuming that interest is 16 percent compounded quarterly, which amount is worth more: $10,000 today or a 5-year annuity of $1000 each quarter?

13. Assume that you are considering purchasing an apartment building for $200,000. The sales contract requires you to pay a downpayment of $25,000, with the remaining balance of $175,000 to be paid in 10 annual installments. What would your annual payments be if the interest rate is 14 percent compounded annually?

14. A truck costs $4200, and it has a scrap value of $800 at the end of 5 years. What equal amounts will have to be paid into a fund at the end of each year to provide for the replacement of the truck, if the fund earns 7 percent compounded annually?

15. The manager of a company wishes to accumulate a sinking fund to provide for the replacement of a $15,000 machine (with no scrap value) at the end of 9 years. What equal deposits should be made at the end of each 6 months in a fund which earns 6 percent compounded semiannually?

16. What annual payment must be made in order to pay off a $50,000 loan in 10 years if the interest rate is 16 percent compounded annually?

linear
depreciation

Linear or **straight-line depreciation** is one of several methods approved by the Internal Revenue Service for depreciating business property. If the original cost of the property is C dollars and it is depreciated linearly over N years, its *value* (undepreciated balance) V at the end of n years is given by

$$V = C - \left(\frac{C}{N}\right) \cdot n$$

which can also be written as

$$V = C\left(1 - \frac{n}{N}\right)$$

by factoring out C. Here the independent variable is n, the domain is usually the set of integers 0, 1, 2, 3, . . . , n, and the dependent variable is V.

EXAMPLE 5.8 If office furniture worth $6000 is depreciated linearly over 10 years, the undepreciated balance after n years is given by

$$V = 6000\left(1 - \frac{n}{10}\right)$$
$$= 6000 - 600n$$

Note that after 10 years (that is, for $n = 10$) we get

$$V = 6000 - 600(10) = 0$$

which means that the property is completely depreciated.

---

compound
depreciation

If a property valued at C dollars is to be depreciated by the **double-declining-balance** method over a period of N years, it is depreciated each year by $2/N \cdot 100$ percent of its value at the beginning of that year. (This makes it different from *linear depreciation*, where the property is depreciated each year by the same percentage of the original cost.) Thus the undepreciated balance, or **book value**, is multiplied by $(1 - 2/N)$ each year, and it follows that after n years its value is

$$V = C\left(1 - \frac{2}{N}\right)^n$$

EXAMPLE 5.9 If office furniture worth $4000 is to be depreciated by the double-declining-balance method over 10 years, the undepreciated balance after n years is given by

$$V = 4000\left(1 - \frac{2}{10}\right)^n$$

Thus the undepreciated balance after the first year $(n = 1)$ is

$$V = 4000\left(1 - \frac{2}{10}\right)^1 = \$3200$$

At the end of the second year $(n = 2)$, it is

$$V = 4000\left(1 - \frac{2}{10}\right)^2 = \$2560$$

and so on.

If we subtract the undepreciated balance at the end of n years from that at the end of $n - 1$ years, we find that the amount by which the property is depreciated *during the nth year* is given by

$$D = C\left(1 - \frac{2}{N}\right)^{n-1} - C\left(1 - \frac{2}{N}\right)^n = C\left(1 - \frac{2}{N}\right)^{n-1}\left[1 - \left(1 - \frac{2}{N}\right)\right]$$

$$= \frac{2C}{N}\left(1 - \frac{2}{N}\right)^{n-1}$$

EXAMPLE 5.9
(Continued) For the office furniture worth $4000 that is to be depreciated by the double-declining balance method over 10 years, the amount by which the furniture is depreciated during the nth year is given by

$$D = \frac{2(4000)}{10}\left(1 - \frac{2}{10}\right)^{n-1}$$

Thus the amount depreciated during the first year $(n = 1)$ is

$$D = \frac{2(4000)}{10}\left(1 - \frac{2}{10}\right)^0 = \$800$$

The amount depreciated during the second year ($n = 2$) is

$$D = \frac{2(4000)}{10}\left(1 - \frac{2}{10}\right)^1 = \$640$$

and so on.

---

1. An office building worth $400,000 was built in 1975 and is being depreciated linearly over 40 years. What is its undepreciated value in each year?
   (a) 1985
   (b) 2000

2. A manufacturer bought $160,000 worth of new tools in 1979. If these tools are being depreciated linearly over a period of 8 years, what is their value in each year?
   (a) 1982
   (b) 1985

3. If an office building worth $800,000 was built in 1980 and is being depreciated by the double-declining-balance method over a period of 25 years, what is its book value (a) in 1983, and (b) in 1985?

4. If school buses worth $120,000 are depreciated by the double-declining-balance method over $N = 9$ years, by how much are they depreciated in each of the first 4 years? If it is desirable to have high income-tax deductions for depreciation during these 4 years, is the double-declining-balance method preferable to the straight-line method, according to which the annual depreciation would be $120,000/8 = \$15,000$?

5. An apartment building worth $600,000 was built in 1980 and is being depreciated linearly over 25 years. What is the undepreciated value in 1985? If the apartment building is depreciated by the double-declining-balance method, what is its book value in 1985? Which of the two methods would be preferred by most investors? Why?

6. A company specializing in sailboat charters bought five new sailboats in 1981. If each of these boats was purchased for $200,000 and is being depreciated linearly over 10 years, what is the undepreciated value of each boat after 2 years? What would the value be if the double-declining-balance method were used?

7. Assume that $500,000 of new equipment was purchased. Develop a table that would compare the undepreciated value of linear depre-

ciation with the undepreciated value for the double-declining-balance method, assuming that the equipment can be depreciated over 5 years.

SUMMARY

This chapter presented an introduction to mathematical applications involving financial analysis. First, we introduced the concepts of *simple interest*, *compound interest*, and *multiple compounding*. You should now understand the difference between the nominal interest rate and the effective rate of an investment. Moreover, you should be able to calculate the amount of money coming (or owed) if a sum of money is invested (or borrowed) at a stated interest rate; this amount is referred to as the *future value* of the sum of money originally invested or borrowed.

In Section 5.2 we showed how to compute the *present value* of a sum of money that is to be received in the future, a concept that is really the inverse of determining the future value of a sum of money. Then in Section 5.3 we showed how to compute the *present value* and *future value* of an annuity, a situation in which a series of equal amounts is received for some specified period of time.

We discussed how to solve *amortization problems*, that is, problems in which we must compute the value of the payment to be made each period in order to pay off a debt or obligation. We saw that an amortization problem is really just the inverse of a problem where we find the present value of an annuity.

The chapter concluded with a discussion of methods for depreciating business property. Specifically, we showed how to use both *linear*, or *straight-line*, depreciation and *compound depreciation*.

GLOSSARY

1. **Interest** A charge for the use of money, expressed in terms of dollars received or paid.
2. **Interest Rate** A charge for the use of money, expressed in terms of a percentage of the amount borrowed or saved.
3. **Principal** The amount borrowed or saved.
4. **Simple Interest** Interest determined when the interest rate applies only to the amount borrowed or saved.
5. **Compound Interest** Interest determined when the interest is added to the principal at regular intervals of time and thereafter the interest itself earns interest.

6. **Nominal Interest Rate** The interest rate which would be received without compounding.
7. **Effective Rate** The actual rate of interest when the effect of compounding is taken into account.
8. **Continuous Compounding** A situation where the number of times interest is compounded is allowed to get larger and larger, resulting in the effective rate coming closer and closer to the quantity $e^i - 1$ (where e is approximately 2.71828).
9. **Future Value** The amount of money coming (or owed) if a sum of money P is invested (or borrowed) at the interest rate i (other terms for future value are *compound value* and *terminal value*).
10. **Present Value** The inverse of the concept of future value; that is, the amount that must be invested in order to grow (with compounding) to some specific value at a later point in time.
11. **Annuity** An amount of money that is payable at stated invervals for a fixed period of time.
12. **Present Value of an Annuity** The present value of a series of fixed payments that are made at stated intervals for a specified period of time.
13. **Future Value of an Annuity** The future value of a series of fixed payments that are made at stated intervals for a specified period of time.
14. **Amortization** The process of paying off a debt or obligation by periodic payments.
15. **Linear Depreciation** A method for depreciating business property where the property is depreciated each year by the same percentage of the original cost.
16. **Compound Depreciation** A method for depreciating business property that permits a "faster" depreciation than when using linear depreciation.

SUPPLEMENTARY
EXERCISES

1. An individual borrows $1000 from a relative at the simple interest rate of 10 percent. At the end of 2 years what is the amount owed? At the end of 5 years?

2. With reference to the preceding exercise, compute the amount owed in each case assuming that interest is compounded annually.

3. In Exercise 1 assume that interest is compounded quarterly. What is the amount owed at the end of 2 years and at the end of 5 years?

4. An individual invests $10,000 in a savings certificate that pays 16 percent compounded quarterly. What is the value of the investment at the end of 2 years?

5. If a sum of money is invested at 10 percent compounded monthly, what is the effective annual rate?

6. With reference to the preceding exercise, what is the effective annual rate if the money is compounded daily, or 365 times each year?

7. The banking industry uses a 360-day year to compute effective rates for daily compounding. Using a 360-day basis, compute the effective rate for Exercise 5.

8. Rework Exercise 5 assuming that interest is compounded continuously.

9. To finance a new business an individual has obtained $100,000 through private financing. The terms of the loan call for the loan amount plus interest to be paid at the end of 4 years. What is the amount that will be due assuming the interest rate is 18 percent compounded monthly?

10. How much money would you have to invest at the present time in order to get $1000 at the end of 1 year if the nominal rate is 12 percent?

11. With reference to the preceding exercise, how much would you have to invest if interest is compounded quarterly?

12. What is the present value of a $10,000 payment that is to be received at the end of 2 years? Assume the interest rate is 18 percent compounded monthly.

13. Find the present value of a note for $5000 due 3 years from now if money is worth 18 percent compounded monthly.

14. Through the sale of real estate, an individual is to receive an annual payment of $25,000 for 5 years. If interest is compounded annually at 12 percent, determine the future value of this annuity.

15. How much would an individual have to set aside in order to provide a $10,000 annuity for 10 years? Assume that interest is compounded annually at 15 percent.

16. To finance the cost of a new car Bill Johnson needs to obtain a 3-year automobile loan for $8000. If the bank's rate is 18 percent compounded monthly, determine the monthly payments Bill will have to make.

17. In Exercise 16, how much interest will Bill pay over the lifetime of the loan?

18. A $10,000 loan calls for payment to be made in five annual installments. If the interest rate is 16 percent compounded annually, what annual payment must be made?

19. A small business computer system worth $15,000 is depreciated linearly over 5 years. What is the undepreciated balance at the end of 3 years?

20. In Exercise 20, assume that the computer system is to be depreciated by the double-declining-balance method. What is the undepreciated balance after 3 years?

21. The value of an apartment building (excluding land) is $150,000. If the building can be depreciated over 30 years, compare the difference between straight-line depreciation and compound depreciation over the first 5 years.

SYSTEMS
OF
EQUATIONS

In Chapter 3 we referred to $Ax + By = C$ as the standard form of the equation of a straight line. This form can be easily generalized to handle situations where there are more than two variables. For example, we refer to

$$2x + 4y + 3z = 8 \quad \text{and} \quad 12p + 9q - 5r = 30$$

as **linear equations in three variables**, we refer to

$$x - y + z - u = 6 \quad \text{and} \quad x_1 + 3x_2 - 2x_3 + 5x_4 = -1$$

as **linear equations in four variables**, and we refer to

$$2x_1 - 3x_2 + x_3 + 5x_4 - 2x_5 = 15$$

and

$$r - 2s + 4t - u + 5v - w = 26$$

as **linear equations in five and six variables**, respectively. In two of these examples we used *subscripts* to distinguish between the variables, and it should be apparent that this is a very good idea, particularly when the number of variables is large.

Even though we refer to all the equations above as linear equations, it should be understood that when there are more than two variables, they do not represent straight lines. For three variables they represent **planes**; when there are more than three variables, we refer to their graphs, which cannot be visualized, as **hyperplanes**.

In Sections 6.1 and 6.2 we study a very elementary method of *solving* systems of linear equations, namely, a method of finding the values of the variables which *at the same time* satisfy (are the solutions of) several linear equations. (Later, in Chapter 7, we shall treat the same kind of problem by more advanced techniques involving *matrices* and *determinants*, and it should not come as a surprise that all this work is referred to under the general heading of *linear mathematics*.) Finally, in Section 6.3, we briefly discuss problem situations in which at least one of the equations is quadratic.

6.1 SOLVING A SYSTEM OF LINEAR EQUATIONS: INTRODUCTORY CONCEPTS

Many situations in business and economics require that we study *several functions* of one and the same independent variable, or the same *set* of independent variables. For instance, if a company produces x television sets per week (where x changes from week to week), it may be of interest to express their total cost in terms of x, to express the profit on their sales in terms of x, to express the hours of labor required to produce them in terms of x, and so on. Similarly, if the same company produces u color sets and v black-and-white sets per week (where u and v change from week to week), it may be of interest to express their total cost in terms of u *and* v, to express the profit on their sales in terms of u and v, to express the hours of labor required to produce them in terms of u and v, and so on.

EXAMPLE 6.1 A typical situation in which two quantities depend on the same variable arises in what is often called **break-even analysis**. Suppose, for example, that a company's cost of producing x television sets is given by

$$\text{Cost of producing } x \text{ sets} = C = \$12{,}000 + \$80x$$

where \$12,000 is the fixed cost, or overhead, and \$80 is the direct cost (materials and labor) of producing one set. If the company receives \$120 per set, the total revenue for producing x sets is given by

$$\text{Total revenue} = R = \$120x$$

and we find that cost and revenue are both linear functions of x; in fact, their graphs are shown together in Figure 6.1.

As its name implies, the basic problem of break-even analysis is to determine how many units the company will have to produce in order to break even. In other words, the problem is to find the value (or values) of x for which both functions—cost and revenue—have the same value. Geometrically, we can take care of this by finding the point (or points) at which the two graphs intersect; algebraically, we simply equate the expressions which represent C and R, and in our example we get

$$12{,}000 + 80x = 120x$$

Solving this equation for x, we get $12{,}000 = 120x - 80x = 40x$, so $x = 12{,}000/40 = 300$. This means that the company will break even (cost and revenue will both equal $120 \cdot 300 = \$36{,}000$) if it produces and sells 300 sets. As we can see from Figure 6.1, the cost will exceed the revenue if they produce and sell fewer than 300 sets, and the revenue will exceed the cost if they produce and sell more than 300 sets.

FIGURE 6.1
Break-Even Analysis

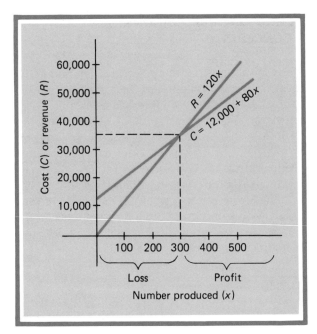

The two functions which we considered in Example 6.1 were both linear, and this made the analysis relatively easy; examples in which either or both of the functions are nonlinear will be taken up in Section 6.3.

The solution to Example 6.1 was especially easy because both equations were given in **explicit form** (that is, solved for the dependent variables). Thus all we had to do was to equate the two expressions representing cost and revenue and solve for x. In general, the situation is not quite so easy when the equations are given in **implicit form**, namely, solved for neither the independent nor dependent variable.

EXAMPLE 6.2 Suppose that we are given the two linear equations

$$2x + 3y = 5$$

$$-5x - 2y = 4$$

and are asked to find the values of x and y which satisfy (are a solution of) both equations. Geometrically speaking, we are asked to find the coordinates of the point in which the corresponding lines intersect (see Figure 6.2). If we wanted to proceed as in Example 6.1, we could first solve each equation for y, getting

$$y = \frac{5 - 2x}{3} \quad \text{and} \quad y = \frac{4 + 5x}{-2}$$

FIGURE 6.2
Diagram
for Example 6.2

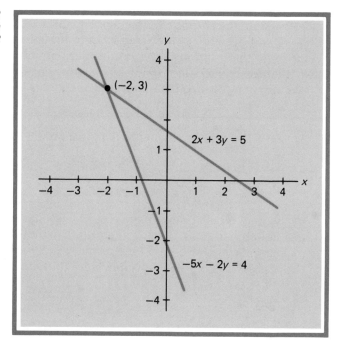

Then if we equate these two expressions for y, we get

$$\frac{5 - 2x}{3} = \frac{4 + 5x}{-2}$$

which leads to $-2(5 - 2x) = 3(4 + 5x)$ and, ultimately, $x = -2$. The corresponding value of y is $y = \dfrac{4 + 5(-2)}{-2} = 3$, and we can now say that the given equations have the solution $x = -2$ and $y = 3$; in other words, the corresponding lines intersect at the point $(-2, 3)$.

6.2 SOLVING A SYSTEM OF LINEAR EQUATIONS: THE METHOD OF ELIMINATION

The method of Section 6.1 is only one of many methods that can be used to solve a system of linear equations. The calculations would have been even simpler if we had used the **method of elimination**, which is based on the fact that we can multiply equals by equals, add equals to equals, and subtract equals from equals. For example, consider the equation $2x = 36$. The solution to this equation is $x = 18$. Clearly, if we multiply on both sides of this equation by 10 and hence create the equation

20x = 360, the solution to the new equation is still x = 18. Similarly, if we add or subtract the same amount on both sides of the equation 2x = 36, the solution to the resulting equation would still be x = 18. With these remarks in mind, let us now reconsider our previous example involving two equations in two unknowns.

EXAMPLE 6.2
(Continued)

To solve the system of equations of Example 6.2,

$$2x + 3y = 5$$

$$-5x - 2y = 4$$

by the method of elimination, we could *eliminate* y by multiplying the expressions on both sides of the first equation by 2, multiplying the expressions on both sides of the second equation by 3, and then adding the expressions on the respective sides of the two equations.

Step 1   Multiply both sides of the first equation by 2 (multiply equals by equals).

$$4x + 6y = 10$$

$$-5x - 2y = 4$$

Step 2   Multiply both sides of the second equation by 3 (multiply equals by equals).

$$4x + 6y = 10$$

$$-15x - 6y = 12$$

Step 3   Add the expressions on the respective sides of the two equations (add equals to equals).

$$-11x = 22$$

Since $-11x = 22$, we see that $x = 22/(-11) = -2$. The value of y can then be obtained by substituting $x = -2$ into either of the *original* equations; substituting $x = -2$ into the first equation we get $2(-2) + 3y = 5$, and this leads to $3y = 9$ and $y = 3$. (To check this result, we substitute $x = -2$ and $y = 3$ into the second original equation, getting $-5(-2) - 2(3) = 10 - 6 = 4$, which checks.)

Had we wanted to *eliminate* x instead of y in this example, we could have multiplied the expressions on both sides of the first equation by 5 and those on both sides of the second equation by 2 and then added the expressions on the respective sides of the two equations. This would have given us

$$10x + 15y = 25$$
$$-10x - 4y = 8$$

and then $11y = 33$ and $y = 3$.

Before we apply the method of elimination to the solution of a system of linear equations involving more than two variables, let us first introduce a general *symbolic notation* for any system of two linear equations in the two variables x_1 and x_2, namely,

$$a_{11}x_1 + a_{12}x_2 = b_1$$
$$a_{21}x_1 + a_{22}x_2 = b_2$$

The reason we refer to the two variables as x_1 and x_2 (instead of x and y) is that we can easily generalize this notation; if there are more than two variables, we denote the others x_3, x_4, x_5, ... Observe also that each x-coefficient has *two subscripts;* the first subscript is 1 or 2 depending on whether the coefficient is in the first equation or in the second, and the second subscript is 1 or 2 depending on whether the coefficient goes with x_1 or x_2. The subscript of the *constant terms* on the right-hand side is 1 or 2 depending on the equation. An obvious advantage of this whole notation is that it can easily be generalized to handle more than two linear equations in more than two variables.

Note that *the method of elimination will not work when the x_1- and x_2-coefficients are proportional.* Geometrically, this means that *the method of elimination will not work when the two lines have the same slope.* This whole argument certainly stands to reason—we shall not get a unique solution (one value for x_1 and one value for x_2) unless the two lines intersect—as in Figure 6.2—and this means that they cannot possibly have the same slope.

When two lines do have the same slope, there are two possibilities: *either the lines are parallel and do not intersect,* in which case they are said to be **inconsistent**, or *they coincide and have infinitely many points in common,* in which case they are said to be **equivalent**.

EXAMPLE 6.3   To illustrate the first possibility, consider the system of equations

$$2x_1 - 3x_2 = 6$$
$$4x_1 - 6x_2 = -18$$

where the x_1- and x_2-coefficients are evidently proportional. If we tried to use the method of elimination and multiplied both sides of the first equation by 2, we would get

$$4x_1 - 6x_2 = 12$$

$$4x_1 - 6x_2 = -18$$

and subtracting we get $0 = 30$, which obviously cannot be correct. Thus the system of equations has no solution and we say that the equations are *inconsistent*; as we can see from Figure 6.3 the two lines are parallel and have no points in common.

EXAMPLE 6.4   To illustrate the other possibility, consider the system of equations

$$2x_1 - 3x_2 = 6$$

$$10x_1 - 15x_2 = 30$$

where the x_1- and x_2-coefficients are again proportional. This time, however, the equations are *not inconsistent*; in fact, if we multiply the expressions on both sides of the first equation by 5, we get $10x_1 - 15x_2 = 30$, and it can be seen that the two equations are actually *equivalent*. They represent the same line, or to put it differently, the two lines coincide. In this case they are infinitely many solutions and the coordinates of any point on the line $2x_1 - 3x_2 = 6$ also satisfy the equation $10x_1 - 15x_2 = 30$. As can be seen from Figure 6.4, where we have plotted the graph of the line $2x_1 - 3x_2 = 6$ (or $10x_1 - 15x_2 = 30$), the

FIGURE 6.3
Diagram
for Example 6.3

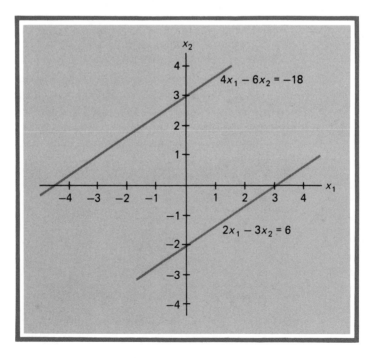

infinite set of solutions includes $x_1 = 3$ and $x_2 = 0$, $x_1 = 0$ and $x_2 = -2$, and $x_1 = 6$ and $x_2 = 2$.

The method of elimination can also be used to solve a system of three linear equations in three variables, a system of four linear equations in four variables, and so on. We simply eliminate one variable at a time, and in each step we *reduce by one* the number of variables as well as the number of equations.

EXAMPLE 6.5 To illustrate how this is done, let us consider the following system of three linear equations in three variables.

$$x_1 - 2x_2 + x_3 = 8$$
$$3x_1 + 5x_2 + 7x_3 = 6$$
$$2x_1 - 3x_2 - 5x_3 = 7$$

The first step is to eliminate one of the variables, thus reducing the problem to that of having to solve a system of two linear equations in the other two variables. To this end we choose *two pairs* of equations (including each equation at least once) and eliminate the chosen variable from each pair. For instance, to eliminate x_1 and thus obtain a system of two linear equations in x_2 and x_3, let us eliminate x_1 from the first two equations and also from the first and third. Multiplying the expressions on both sides of the first equation by 3 and leaving the

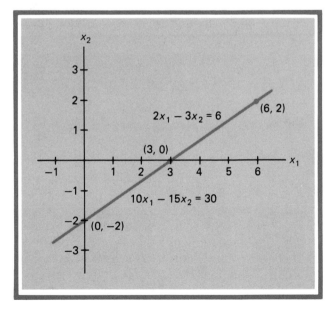

FIGURE 6.4
Diagram
for Example 6.4

second equation as is, we get

$$3x_1 - 6x_2 + 3x_3 = 24$$
$$3x_1 + 5x_2 + 7x_3 = 6$$

and then, by subtraction,

$$-11x_2 - 4x_3 = 18$$

Similarly, to eliminate x_1 from the first and third equations, we multiply the expressions on both sides of the first equation by 2, leave the third equation as is, and get

$$2x_1 - 4x_2 + 2x_3 = 16$$
$$2x_1 - 3x_2 - 5x_3 = 7$$

Then subtracting, we obtain

$$-x_2 + 7x_3 = 9$$

This leaves us with the following system of two linear equations in x_2 and x_3.

$$-11x_2 - 4x_3 = 18$$
$$-x_2 + 7x_3 = 9$$

Now we are on familiar grounds, and we can continue the method of elimination, for instance, by multiplying the expressions on both sides of the second equation by 11, leaving the first equation as is, and then subtracting. This gives

$$-11x_2 - 4x_3 = 18$$
$$-11x_2 + 77x_3 = 99$$

and

$$-81x_3 = -81$$

Hence $x_3 = 1$, and if we substitute this result into the equation $-x_2 + 7x_3 = 9$, we get $-x_2 + 7(1) = 9$ and $x_2 = -2$. Finally, substituting $x_2 = -2$ and $x_3 = 1$ into any one of the original equations we get $x_1 = 3$, and we have thus shown that the given system of equations has the unique solution $x_1 = 3$, $x_2 = -2$, and $x_3 = 1$. It is a sound practice to check results like this by substituting the values obtained into the original equations. For our example we get

$$(3) - 2(-2) + (1) = 3 + 4 + 1 = 8$$

$$3(3) + 5(-2) + 7(1) = 9 - 10 + 7 = 6$$

$$2(3) - 3(-2) - 5(1) = 6 + 6 - 5 = 7$$

which checks.

When we deal with a system of three linear equations in three variables, it can also happen that there are no solutions or that there are infinitely many. Geometrically speaking, we are now dealing with three *planes*, and there are all sorts of possibilities: the three planes may have only one point in common as in our example, and there is a unique solution; the three planes may have infinitely many points in common, which happens when they all intersect in a line or when they all coincide; or they may be *inconsistent* and have no points in common, which happens when all three planes are parallel or when the line in which two of the planes intersect is parallel to (does not intersect) the third plane.

When we apply the method of elimination to the solution of a system of linear equations, we usually begin by eliminating the variable whose coefficients are the smallest numbers (or, at least, the numbers that are easiest to work with). This is why we began by eliminating x_1 in our last illustration, although we could just as well have begun by eliminating x_2 or x_3.

If we had to solve a system of four linear equations in four variables, we could begin by eliminating one of the variables from three different pairs of the equations. This would leave us with a system of three linear equations in three variables, which could be solved by the method of elimination (as in Example 6.5). Generally speaking, though, the method of elimination becomes rather tedious when there are more than three variables, and it is preferable in that case to use one of the alternative techniques discussed in Chapter 7. As we shall see, these methods have the added advantage that they can be more readily programmed for use by computers.

EXERCISES

1. Use the method of elimination to solve each system of linear equations:

   (a) $x + y = 9$
   $\ x - y = 1$

   (b) $3x - y = 2$
   $\ x + 3y = 5$

   (c) $2u - 5v = 16$
   $\ 3u + 3v = 3$

2. Use the method of elimination to solve each system of linear equations.

(a) $x_1 - x_2 = 4$
$3x_1 - 8x_2 = -3$

(b) $x + 2y + 3z = 9$
$2x + y - z = 0$
$3x - 4y - 2z = 4$

(c) $2x_1 + 5x_2 + 7x_3 = 2$
$4x_1 - 4x_2 - 3x_3 = 7$
$3x_1 - 3x_2 - 2x_3 = 5$

3. Write each system of equations in symbolic form.
(a) Three linear equations in x_1, x_2, and x_3.
(b) Four linear equations in x_1, x_2, x_3, and x_4.

4. Check whether the following pairs of lines have the same slope. If they do have the same slope, check also whether the lines are *parallel* (namely, whether the equations are *inconsistent* and have no common solutions) or whether they *coincide* (namely, whether the equations are *equivalent* and have infinitely many common solutions); if the lines do not have the same slope, find their point of intersection.

(a) $3x - 2y = 7$
$6x - 9y = 12$

(b) $2x + 5y = 7$
$8x + 20y = 28$

(c) $3x + 5y = 15$
$3x - 5y = 2$

(d) $2x + 8y = 6$
$3x + 12y = 12$

(e) $2x - 3y = 4$
$4x - 6y = 8$

(f) $3x - 6y = 6$
$-5x + 10y = 9$

5. Verify each of the assertions, which concern the respective systems of three linear equations in three variables and the planes they represent.

(a) The planes represented by $x - 2y + 3z = 5$, $2x - 4y + 6z = 7$, and $-3x + 6y - 9z = 13$ are *all parallel*; that is, all possible pairs of equations are *inconsistent*.

(b) The planes represented by $4x - 6y + 10z = 8$, $8x - 12y + 20z = 16$, and $-6x + 9y - 15z = -12$ coincide; the system of equations has infinitely many solutions, including $x = 1$, $y = 1$, $z = 1$, and also $x = 5$, $y = 2$, $z = 0$, and $x = 5$, $y = -3$, and $z = -3$, as can be checked by substitution.

(c) The equations $x - 2y + z = 5$, $x + 3y - 3z = 1$, and $2x + y - 2z = 3$ are *inconsistent*, but the planes which they represent are not all parallel. (*Hint:* To show that the equations are inconsistent, add the expressions on the respective sides of the first two equations and compare the result with the third equation; to show that they are not all parallel, verify that the point (4, 0, 1) lies on the first two planes, that the point (4, 1, 3) lies on the first and the third, and that the point (1, -1, -1) lies on the second and the third.)

6. A company manufactures two models—standard and deluxe—of a vacuum cleaner, the essential parts of which are produced by

two different machines, A and B. The production of these parts for one standard model requires 5 minutes on machine A and 10 minutes on machine B, while the production of these parts for one deluxe model requires 9 minutes on machine A and 15 minutes on machine B. If, on a given day, machine A is available for 4 hours and machine B is available for 7 hours, how many vacuum cleaners of each type should they schedule for that day's production so that the time on both machines will be fully utilized?

7. A baker sells two kinds of cake for which he charges p_1 dollars and p_2 dollars, respectively. If the daily supply and the demand for the first kind of cake are given by

$$S_1 = 52 + 20p_1 - 4p_2 \quad \text{and} \quad D_1 = 94 - 10p_1 + 4p_2$$

while the supply and the demand for the second kind of cake are given by

$$S_2 = 160 - 15p_1 + 32p_2 \quad \text{and} \quad D_2 = 208 + 5p_1 - 24p_2$$

how should the two kinds of cake be priced so that the market for both will be in *equilibrium*, namely, so that for each kind of cake supply will equal demand?

8. A company makes two kinds of machine parts. The first requires 4 hours of labor and 3.5 pounds of raw material and can be produced at a cost of $22.80; the second requires 3 hours of labor and 4 pounds of raw material and can be produced at a cost of $20.40. What is the cost of labor per hour and the cost of the raw material per pound?

9. An office with three employees, Mr. A, Ms. B, and Ms. C, has a weekly payroll of $544, provided each of the employees works 40 hours. If Mr. A works 40 hours, Ms. B works 24 hours, and Ms. C works 32 hours, the weekly payroll is 433.60; and if Mr. A works 32 hours, Ms. B works 40 hours, and Ms. C works 32 hours, the weekly payroll is $473.60. What are the hourly wages received by Mr. A, Ms. B, and Ms. C?

10. A company sells gift boxes consisting of 6-ounce packages of assorted cheeses. Gift A, which consists of two packages of Swiss cheese and one package each of Cheddar and Edam, costs $3.00; Gift B, which consists of one package of Swiss cheese, three packages of Cheddar, and two packages of Edam, costs $4.35; and Gift C, which consists of three packages of Swiss cheese, four packages of Cheddar, and four packages of Edam, costs $8.15. How much do they charge for each kind of cheese?

6.3 SYSTEMS OF LINEAR AND QUADRATIC EQUATIONS

In Section 6.1 we pointed out that there are many situations in business and economics in which we have to consider *several* functions of one and the same independent variable. At the time, we considered only linear functions, but now let us study a problem in which at least one of the functions is quadratic.

EXAMPLE 6.6   The supply of a commodity generally increases with its price, the demand decreases, and the market for the commodity is said to be in *equilibrium* when supply equals demand. To illustrate how we determine the price at which the market for a commodity is in equilibrium, suppose that the supply for one type of small ceramic insulator is a quadratic function given by the equation

$$S(p) = 2p + 4p^2$$

where p is the price per insulator in cents and the supply is in units of 100 insulators. Suppose, furthermore, that the demand for the insulators is a linear function given by the equation

$$D(p) = 231 - 18p$$

where the units are the same as for $S(p)$. The graphs of these two

FIGURE 6.5
Diagram
for Example 6.6

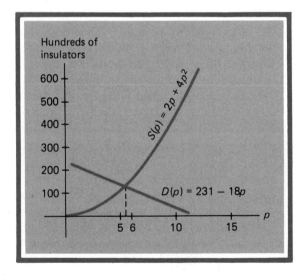

164   CHAPTER 6

functions are shown in Figure 6.5, and it is apparent that the two curves intersect somewhere between $p = 5$ and $p = 6$. To obtain the exact answer, we have only to equate supply to demand, namely, let $S(p) = D(p)$, and solve for p. Thus we get

$$2p + 4p^2 = 231 - 18p$$

and after collecting terms we obtain the quadratic equation

$$231 - 20p - 4p^2 = 0$$

When we solve this equation by means of the quadratic formula, we get $p = 5.5$ and $p = -10.5$, but we can obviously rule out $p = -10.5$ since this value does not lie within the proper domain; the price charged for a product cannot very well be negative. We have thus shown that supply will equal demand when the price charged for the ceramic insulators is 5.5¢, or $5.50 per hundred; the corresponding demand is $D(5.5) = 231 - 18(5.5) = 132$, which means that at that price there is a demand (and a supply) for 13,200 of the insulators.

In the preceding example one function was linear and the other quadratic, but in the exercises which follow there will also be problems in which both functions are quadratic.

EXERCISES

1. A manufacturer knows that if a production run is scheduled for x hours, the total cost of the operation, in dollars, is given by

$$C = 6000 + 500x$$

and the total value of the merchandise produced, also in dollars, is given by

$$V = 1200x + 200x^2$$

(a) For how many hours would the production run have to be scheduled so that the total cost would equal the value of the merchandise produced?

(b) Would V exceed C or C exceed V if the production run were scheduled for longer than that?

2. In Example 6.1 we gave a company's total cost of producing x television sets, which sell for $120 each, as $C = 12{,}000 + 80x$ dollars. If these sets are sold at a discount of 1 percent for 100 sets, at a discount of 2 percent for 200 sets, and in general at a discount of $x/100$ percent for x sets, up to a maximum discount of 8 percent, it can be shown that the company's total receipts, in dollars, for x sets are given by

$$R = 120x\left(1 - \frac{x}{10000}\right)$$

$$= 120x - 0.012x^2$$

(a) Show that with this discount the production cost will equal the receipts for $x = 333\frac{1}{3}$. Explain why the other solution of the quadratic equation which had to be solved does not provide an answer.

(b) At least how many sets would they have to produce to make a profit?

3. A manufacturer of Christmas tree ornaments knows that the total cost of making x *thousand* ornaments of a given kind, but not more than 25,000, is given by

$$C = 300 + 30x$$

where C is in dollars, and that the corresponding sales revenue is given by

$$R = 100x - 2x^2$$

which is also in dollars. (This equation for R implies that the price per ornament is reduced when a greater number is put on the market.) How many thousand ornaments will the manufacturer have to produce to break even?

4. The supply and the demand for a product are given by

$$S = 32p + p^2 \quad \text{and} \quad D = 160 - p^2$$

where p is the price in dollars per carton and the units for S and D are both 1000 cartons. For what value of p will supply equal demand?

5. The supply and the demand for a product are given by

$$S = 6p + p^2 \quad \text{and} \quad D = 36 - p^2$$

where p is the price of the product in dollars while supply and demand are both in units of 1000.

(a) Plot the graphs of these two parabolas on one diagram and read the values of p for which supply equals demand. Which of these values is "impossible"?

(b) Equate supply and demand and solve the resulting quadratic equation for p. What is the corresponding supply?

6. The supply and the demand for a product are given by

$$S = 2p + 20 \quad \text{and} \quad D = \frac{1200}{p}$$

where p is the price charged for the product in cents while the units for S and D are both 100 dozens.

(a) Plot the graphs of these two functions on one diagram and read the value of p for which supply equals demand.

(b) Equating demand and supply (that is, putting $1200/p$ equal to $2p + 20$), solve for the value of p for which the market for the given product will be in equilibrium. What is the corresponding supply?

SUMMARY

In this chapter we provided an introduction to elementary methods for solving a system of linear equations. The primary emphasis was placed on using the method of elimination to solve a system of linear equations. *Break-even analysis* was discussed as a typical problem situation. The chapter concluded with a brief discussion of solving a system of equations in which at least one of the equations is quadratic.

GLOSSARY

1. **Solving a System of Linear Equations** Finding the values of the variables which satisfy several linear equations.
2. **Break-even Analysis** Determining how many units must be produced so the revenue generated from sales will equal the cost of production, and hence the firm will break even.
3. **Method of Elimination** An algebraic procedure for solving a system of linear equations.
4. **Inconsistent Pair of Lines** A pair of lines that are parallel and hence have no points in common.
5. **Equivalent Pair of Lines** A pair of lines that coincide and hence have infinitely many points in common.

1. Consider the linear equations

$$x - 2y = 2$$
$$x + y = 5$$

By graphing both equations find the values of x and y that satisfy both equations.

2. With reference to Exercise 1, use the method of elimination to find the values of x and y that satisfy both equations.

3. Use the method of elimination to solve each system of linear equations.

(a) $x + y = 7$
    $x - y = 1$

(b) $2x - y = 3$
    $x + 2y = 5$

(c) $3u - 2v = 21$
    $4u + 5v = 5$

(d) $x_1 - 2x_2 = 2$
    $6x_1 + 8x_2 = 5$

(e) $x + 3y - 2z = 7$
    $3x - y - 2z = 7$
    $2x + 2y + z = 5$

(f) $2x_1 + 5x_2 + 8x_3 = 1$
    $3x_1 - 4x_2 - 3x_3 = 5$
    $4x_1 - 6x_2 - 2x_3 = 4$

4. Use the method of elimination to solve each system of linear equations.

(a) $2x_1 - 4x_2 = 4$
    $4x_1 - 6x_2 = 10$

(b) $x_1 - 3x_2 = 5$
    $2x_1 - 3x_2 = 7$

(c) $x_1 + x_2 - x_3 = -3$
    $2x_1 + x_2 + 3x_3 = 7$
    $3x_1 + 3x_2 + x_3 = -1$

5. Check whether the following pairs of lines have the same slope. If they do have the same slope, check also whether the lines are *parallel* (namely, whether the equations are *inconsistent* and have no common solutions) or whether they *coincide* (namely, whether the equations are *equivalent* and have infinitely many common solutions); if the lines do not have the same slope, find their point of intersection.

(a) $4x - 2y = -8$
    $3x - \dfrac{3}{2}y = 6$

(b) $3x + y = 5$
    $x - y = -1$

(c) $x + 2y = 4$
    $4x + 8y = 16$

6. A manufacturer of electric pencil sharpeners has determined that the cost of producing x pencil sharpeners is given by

$$C(x) = 3x + 10,000$$

where $C(x)$ is in dollars. If the manufacturer sells the product to wholesalers for $5 per unit, determine how many units the firm will have to produce in order to break even.

7. A manufacturer of office equipment finds that the total cost of making 10 filing cabinets is $380, while the total cost of making 25 is $710.

   (a) Given that the total cost is linearly related to the number of filing cabinets produced, find the equation of the corresponding line.

   (b) If the manufacturer can sell the filing cabinets at $30 apiece, how many will he have to make to break even?

   (c) How many would be have to produce to make a profit of $400? (*Hint:* Equate the receipts minus the profit, namely, $30x - 400$, to the cost of producing x filing cabinets, and solve for x.)

8. A manufacturer knows that the total cost of making x thousand units of a certain product is given by

$$C = 600 + 60x$$

where C is in dollars, and that the corresponding sales revenue is given by

$$R = 200x - 4x^2$$

which is also in dollars. (This implies that the price per unit is reduced when a greater number is put on the market.) How many thousands of units will the manufacturer have to produce and sell to break even?

9. A manufacturer produces two types of water heaters, which sell for p_1 and p_2 dollars, respectively. The annual supply and demand for each type of product are as follows.

Product 1

$$\text{Supply:} \quad S_1 = 50 + \frac{1}{2}p_1 + \frac{1}{3}p_2$$

$$\text{Demand:} \quad D_1 = 100 - \frac{1}{4}p_1 + \frac{2}{3}p_2$$

Product 2

$$\text{Supply:} \quad S_1 = 100 + \frac{1}{4}p_1 + \frac{1}{3}p_2$$

$$\text{Demand:} \quad D_1 = 150 + \frac{3}{4}p_1 - \frac{1}{6}p_2$$

What price should the manufacturer charge for each product so that for each product supply and demand will be equal?

10. The supply and demand for a product are given by

$$S = 80p + 2p^2 \quad \text{and} \quad D = 384 - 2p^2$$

where p is the price of the product in dollars per unit and where the units of S and D are in 100 units. For what value of p will supply equal demand?

11. The supply and the demand for a product are given by

$$S = 56p + p^2 \quad \text{and} \quad D = 120 - p^2$$

where p is the price in dollars per carton and the units for S and D are both 1000 cartons. For what value of p will supply equal demand?

12. The supply and the demand for a product are given by

$$S = 2p + p^2 \quad \text{and} \quad D = 40 - p^2$$

where p is the price of the product in dollars while supply and demand are both in units of 1000.
(a) Plot the graphs of these two parabolas on one diagram and read the values of p for which supply equals demand. Which of these values is "impossible"?
(b) Equate supply and demand and solve the resulting quadratic equation for p. What is the corresponding supply?

13. Because of economies of scale, the cost of producing x units of a product is given by

$$C(x) = 20,000 + 8x - \frac{x^2}{100}$$

If the manufacturer receives $12 per unit, determine how many units he must produce in order to break even.

14. A company sells two kinds of products, for which it charges p_1 dollars apiece and p_2 dollars apiece, respectively. If the supply and the demand for the first kind of product are given by

$$S_1 = 58 + 20p_1 - 5p_2 \quad \text{and} \quad D_1 = 100 - 10p_1 + 5p_2$$

while the supply and the demand for the second kind of product are given by

$$S_2 = 152 - 15p_1 + 40p_2 \quad \text{and} \quad D_2 = 200 + 5p_1 - 30p_2$$

how should they price the two kinds of products so that the market for both kinds of products will be in equilibrium, namely, so that for each kind of product supply equals demand? (*Hint:* Equate S_1 to D_1 and S_2 to D_2, and solve the resulting system of equations for p_1 and p_2.)

MATRIX ALGEBRA

7

Very often a single number is all that matters in the description of a given situation. For example, consider the situation in which an economist is studying income levels in a given city. The economist may be interested only in the fact that the incomes of 12,588 families in the city are below the poverty level. Things would be quite different, however, if the economist also had to know how many wage earners there are in the families with incomes below the poverty level. In that case, the economist might report that among all families with incomes below the poverty level, there are 2859 with no wage earner, 5534 with one wage earner, 3721 with two wage earners, and 474 with three or more wage earners. In abbreviated form, the figures reported by the economist might be written as

$$(2859 \quad 5534 \quad 3721 \quad 474)$$

In mathematics, we refer to arrays of numbers like this as **row vectors**, or simply as **vectors**. The individual numbers are referred to as the **components**, or the **elements**, of the vector, and their significance—which will differ from problem to problem—must be clearly understood. Obviously, the vector $(2859 \quad 5534 \quad 3721 \quad 474)$ will be of no value unless we know exactly what each component represents.

As another illustration consider a department store that has 138 television sets in stock. This inventory consists of 14 deluxe color consoles, 16 standard color consoles, 56 color table models, 33 color portables, and 19 black-and-white portables. In vector notation, the information that describes the department store's inventory of television sets might be written as

$$(14 \quad 16 \quad 56 \quad 33 \quad 19)$$

Again, this vector would be of no value to those associated with the department store unless they know precisely what type of television set each figure represents.

If the components of a vector are written one beneath the other, we refer to it as a **column vector**. Thus in the above illustrations, we could have represented the information by means of the column vectors

$$\begin{pmatrix} 2859 \\ 5534 \\ 3721 \\ 474 \end{pmatrix} \quad \text{and} \quad \begin{pmatrix} 14 \\ 16 \\ 56 \\ 33 \\ 19 \end{pmatrix}$$

where the numbers are again enclosed by parentheses. Whether we use a row vector or the corresponding column vector in a given problem will depend on what we intend to do with the vector.

It may have occurred to you that if the department store in our illustration had carried several brands of television sets, the inventory vector (14 16 56 33 19) would not provide an adequate description. Suppose that the store carries two brands, X and Y. The store could give a separate inventory vector for each brand, for instance (8 10 21 18 19) for brand X and (6 6 35 15 0) for brand Y. This means that the inventory consists of 8 deluxe color consoles of brand X and 6 of brand Y, 10 standard color consoles of brand X and 6 of brand Y, 21 color table models of brand X and 35 of brand Y, and so forth. The store could also have conveyed this information by means of the following array, called a **matrix**.

$$\begin{pmatrix} 8 & 10 & 21 & 18 & 19 \\ 6 & 6 & 35 & 15 & 0 \end{pmatrix}$$

Here the numbers in the first row pertain to brand X, those in the second row pertain to brand Y, and (as before) the first number in each row is the number of deluxe color consoles, the second number is the number of standard color consoles, and so on; the fifth number is the number of black-and-white portables.

With reference to the family-income illustration, we might similarly use a matrix to represent, for instance, the figures for four cities. Letting the original data pertain to the first of these four cities, such a matrix might look as follows.

$$\begin{pmatrix} 2859 & 5534 & 3721 & 474 \\ 1455 & 3286 & 2850 & 379 \\ 4001 & 6883 & 4266 & 1057 \\ 3952 & 7575 & 3994 & 1158 \end{pmatrix}$$

The four cities are represented by the four rows, below-poverty-level families with no wage earner by the first column, below-poverty-level families with one wage earner by the second column, below-poverty-level families with two wage earners by the third column, and below-poverty-level families with three or more wage earners by the fourth column.

In general, a *matrix* is a rectangular (or square) array of numbers arranged in rows and columns. If a matrix has m rows and n columns, it is said to be of **order** $m \times n$ (which is read "m by n" and where the number of rows always comes first); the order of a matrix is also referred to as its **dimensions**. To distinguish matrices from other kinds of mathematical objects (real numbers or lines, for example), we denote them by capital letters in boldface type. Thus, we might refer to the 2×5 matrix of the television-inventory example as matrix **R**, and to the 4×4 matrix of the family-income example as matrix **D**. Note that the second of these two matrices has as many rows as columns, which makes it a **square matrix**.

The individual entries of a matrix are referred to as its **elements**, and in both our examples the elements of the respective matrices are numbers. (In more advanced work in mathematics, the elements of a matrix can also be functions or other kinds of mathematical objects; in fact, the elements of a matrix can, themselves, be matrices. So far as the work in this book is concerned, we shall consider only matrices whose elements are real numbers). As we have already pointed out in connection with vectors, the position of each element within a matrix attaches to it a special significance (in any given problem), and it should be noted that

$$\begin{pmatrix} -3 & 5 \\ 7 & 1 \end{pmatrix} \quad \text{and} \quad \begin{pmatrix} 5 & -3 \\ 1 & 7 \end{pmatrix}$$

are *different* matrices, even though they contain the same numbers.

It is customary to denote the elements of a matrix with the same letter as the matrix, though in lower case and in ordinary (lightface) type. Furthermore, we use **double subscripts** to designate the position of each element within a matrix, with the first subscript designating the row and the second subscript designating the column. Thus, a_{11} is the element in the first row and the first column of matrix **A**, a_{23} is the element in its second row and third column, a_{74} is the element in its seventh row and fourth column, and so on. Similarly, b_{45} is the element in the fourth row and the fifth column of matrix **B**, and c_{36} is the element in the third row and sixth column of matrix **C**.* In general, if **A** is an $m \times n$ matrix, we write

$$\mathbf{A} = \begin{pmatrix} a_{11} & a_{12} & \cdots & a_{1n} \\ a_{21} & a_{22} & \cdots & a_{2n} \\ \cdots\cdots\cdots\cdots\cdots\cdots \\ a_{m1} & a_{m2} & \cdots & a_{mn} \end{pmatrix}$$

---

*If a matrix has more than nine rows or columns, the two subscripts are separated by a comma to avoid confusion; for instance, $a_{12,3}$ is the element in the twelfth row and the third column of matrix **A**.

and if we want to talk about an element of this matrix without being specific, we refer to it as a_{ij}, where i can be 1, 2, 3, . . . , m and j can be 1, 2, 3, . . . , n.

Having defined vectors and matrices, let us point out that there is really no need to treat them separately. After all, a row vector with k components is a $1 \times k$ matrix, and a column vector with k components is a $k \times 1$ matrix.

The next few sections of this chapter will be devoted to **matrix algebra**; namely, to the rules according to which matrices are combined. As we shall see, matrices of the same order can be added and subtracted, some matrices can be multiplied, and some can even be divided. Matrix algebra has many important applications; above all, it is used to deal with large systems of linear equations in many variables. Since this is generally the case when the *Simplex method* is used in linear programming, we shall devote Sections 9.3 and 9.4 to this important application.

7.2 AN INTRODUCTION TO MATRIX OPERATIONS

matrix addition and subtraction   To begin our study of matrix algebra, let us state formally what we mean by the equality of two matrices; two $m \times n$ matrices **A** and **B** are equal, and we write **A** = **B**, if and only if all their corresponding elements are equal. More formally,

> two m $\times$ n matrices **A** and **B** with the elements a_{ij} and b_{ij} are equal, and we write **A** = **B**, if and only if $a_{ij} = b_{ij}$ for each possible pair of subscripts i and j.

EXAMPLE 7.1   Given the four 2×3 matrices

$$\mathbf{A} = \begin{pmatrix} 3 & -7 & 4 \\ 0 & 1 & 5 \end{pmatrix} \quad \mathbf{B} = \begin{pmatrix} 3 & 4 & -7 \\ 0 & 5 & 1 \end{pmatrix}$$

$$\mathbf{C} = \begin{pmatrix} 3 & -7 & 4 \\ 0 & 1 & 5 \end{pmatrix} \quad \mathbf{D} = \begin{pmatrix} 0 & 1 & 5 \\ 3 & -7 & 4 \end{pmatrix}$$

we find that **A** is equal to **C**, but neither **A** nor **C** nor **D** is equal to **B**, and neither **A** nor **B** nor **C** is equal to **D**.

As might, perhaps, be expected, we add two matrices *which are of the same order* by simply adding their corresponding elements. More formally, if **A** and **B** are m × n matrices with the elements a_{ij} and b_{ij}, then **A** + **B** is the m × n matrix which has the elements $a_{ij} + b_{ij}$.

EXAMPLE 7.2 Given the two 3 × 3 matrices

$$\mathbf{A} = \begin{pmatrix} 2 & 1 & 5 \\ 7 & 4 & -1 \\ 1 & 6 & 8 \end{pmatrix} \text{ and } \mathbf{B} = \begin{pmatrix} -3 & 2 & 4 \\ 0 & 7 & 1 \\ -4 & -2 & 3 \end{pmatrix}$$

we find that

$$\mathbf{A} + \mathbf{B} = \begin{pmatrix} 2+(-3) & 1+2 & 5+4 \\ 7+0 & 4+7 & -1+1 \\ 1+(-4) & 6+(-2) & 8+3 \end{pmatrix} = \begin{pmatrix} -1 & 3 & 9 \\ 7 & 11 & 0 \\ -3 & 4 & 11 \end{pmatrix}$$

where we simply added each element of **B** to the corresponding element of **A**.

As should be apparent from the above definition, *two matrices can be added only if they are of the same order.*

EXAMPLE 7.3 We can use the television-inventory illustration to give an applied example in which it is meaningful to speak of a matrix sum. Recall that the department store's inventory was given by the matrix

$$\mathbf{R} = \begin{pmatrix} 8 & 10 & 21 & 18 & 19 \\ 6 & 6 & 35 & 15 & 0 \end{pmatrix}$$

Suppose now that the store places an order with a regional distributor, and that this order is represented by the matrix

$$\mathbf{S} = \begin{pmatrix} 3 & 4 & 15 & 10 & 0 \\ 5 & 12 & 0 & 4 & 10 \end{pmatrix}$$

where the rows and columns have the same significance as before; in other words, the store orders 3 deluxe color consoles of brand X and 5 of brand Y, 4 standard color consoles of brand X and 12 of brand Y, 15 color table models of brand X and none of brand Y, and so on. If this order is filled before the store sells any of the sets in stock, the new inventory matrix is given by the matrix sum

$$\mathbf{R} + \mathbf{S} = \begin{pmatrix} 8+3 & 10+4 & 21+15 & 18+10 & 19+0 \\ 6+5 & 6+12 & 35+0 & 15+4 & 0+10 \end{pmatrix}$$

$$= \begin{pmatrix} 11 & 14 & 36 & 28 & 19 \\ 11 & 18 & 35 & 19 & 10 \end{pmatrix}$$

To continue, suppose that after the store's inventory has been replenished, it holds a special 2-week sale, for which the sales of television sets are given by the matrix

$$\mathbf{T} = \begin{pmatrix} 3 & 10 & 15 & 13 & 12 \\ 9 & 12 & 21 & 16 & 3 \end{pmatrix}$$

Thus at the end of this sale, their inventory is reduced to

$$\begin{pmatrix} 11-3 & 14-10 & 36-15 & 28-13 & 19-12 \\ 11-9 & 18-12 & 35-21 & 19-16 & 10-3 \end{pmatrix} = \begin{pmatrix} 8 & 4 & 21 & 15 & 7 \\ 2 & 6 & 14 & 3 & 7 \end{pmatrix}$$

and it would seem only reasonable to refer to this matrix as the *difference* between **R** + **S** and **T** and write it as (**R** + **S**) − **T**.

Indeed, the difference between two matrices is defined as in the last example; we simply subtract the corresponding elements. More formally,

if **A** *and* **B** *are* m × n *matrices with the elements* a_{ij} *and* b_{ij}, *then* **A** − **B** *is the* m × n *matrix which has the elements* $a_{ij} - b_{ij}$.

As in the case of addition, we can speak of the difference between two matrices only if they are of the same order.

If we subtract an m × n matrix **A** from itself, we obtain the m × n matrix **A** − **A**, whose elements are all zeros. Such a matrix is referred to as a **zero matrix**, or **null matrix**, and it serves the same function as the number zero in "ordinary" arithmetic—as can easily be verified, **A** + **O** = **O** + **A** = **A** for any m × n matrix **A** and the corresponding zero matrix of order m × n. As this discussion suggests, there is more than one zero matrix; in fact, there is one for each possible order. The following are some examples—the zero matrices of order 2 × 2, 4 × 1, and 3 × 5.

$$\begin{pmatrix} 0 & 0 \\ 0 & 0 \end{pmatrix}, \quad \begin{pmatrix} 0 \\ 0 \\ 0 \\ 0 \end{pmatrix} \quad \text{and} \quad \begin{pmatrix} 0 & 0 & 0 & 0 & 0 \\ 0 & 0 & 0 & 0 & 0 \\ 0 & 0 & 0 & 0 & 0 \end{pmatrix}$$

the transpose of a matrix   The **transpose** of matrix **A**, written **A**′, is the matrix whose first row is the same as the first column of **A**, whose second row is the same as the second column of **A**, and so on. More formally,

if **A** *is an* m × n *matrix with elements* a_{ij}, *then* **A**′, *the transpose of* **A**, *is an* n × m *matrix with the elements* $a'_{ij} = a_{ji}$.

EXAMPLE 7.4 Given the 2×3 matrix

$$\mathbf{A} = \begin{pmatrix} 10 & 6 & -2 \\ 4 & 3 & 8 \end{pmatrix}$$

we find that

$$\mathbf{A}' = \begin{pmatrix} 10 & 4 \\ 6 & 3 \\ -2 & 8 \end{pmatrix}$$

---

scalar
multiplication   In matrix algebra, real numbers are referred to as **scalars**. When we multiply a matrix by a scalar, each element of the matrix is multiplied by that scalar. More formally,

> if **A** *is an* m × n *matrix with elements* a_{ij} *and* c *is any constant (scalar), then* c**A** *is an* m × n *matrix with the elements* ca_{ij}.

EXAMPLE 7.5 Given the 3×2 matrix

$$\mathbf{A} = \begin{pmatrix} 5 & 10 \\ -4 & 15 \\ 8 & 2 \end{pmatrix}$$

and $c = 10$,

$$c \cdot \mathbf{A} = 10 \cdot \mathbf{A} = 10 \begin{pmatrix} 5 & 10 \\ -4 & 15 \\ 8 & 2 \end{pmatrix} = \begin{pmatrix} 10(5) & 10(10) \\ 10(-4) & 10(15) \\ 10(8) & 10(2) \end{pmatrix} = \begin{pmatrix} 50 & 100 \\ -40 & 150 \\ 80 & 20 \end{pmatrix}$$

EXERCISES

1. Give the order of each matrix and also state whether it is a row vector, a column vector, a square matrix, or none of these.

   (a) $\begin{pmatrix} 3 \\ -1 \end{pmatrix}$ (c) $(2 \quad -2 \quad 0 \quad 3 \quad 4 \quad 8)$

   (b) $\begin{pmatrix} 0 & 3 & -1 & -5 \\ 2 & -3 & 4 & 1 \\ 1 & 2 & 0 & -3 \\ -6 & 1 & 1 & 2 \end{pmatrix}$ (d) $\begin{pmatrix} 3 \\ 2 \\ -4 \end{pmatrix}$.

(e) $\begin{pmatrix} 2 & 5 & -3 \\ 4 & 0 & 1 \end{pmatrix}$ (g) $\begin{pmatrix} -1 & 2 \\ -3 & 1 \\ 2 & 4 \end{pmatrix}$

(f) $\begin{pmatrix} -5 & 0 & 3 \\ 1 & 0 & 2 \\ -2 & 0 & 0 \end{pmatrix}$ (h) $\begin{pmatrix} -1 & 2 & -4 & 0 & 3 & 8 \\ 5 & -3 & 0 & 1 & -2 & 4 \end{pmatrix}$

2. Given

$$\begin{pmatrix} x & 2 & -3 \\ 0 & -1 & 4 \\ 2 & y & z \\ 3 & -5 & -6 \end{pmatrix} = \begin{pmatrix} 4 & 2 & v \\ 0 & u & 4 \\ 2 & 7 & -3 \\ w & -5 & -6 \end{pmatrix}$$

find the values of u, v, w, x, y, and z.

3. Given

$$\begin{pmatrix} 2 & a & -3 & 0 \\ 1 & -2 & b & 2 \end{pmatrix} = \begin{pmatrix} 2 & -5 & c & 0 \\ d & -2 & 4 & 2 \end{pmatrix}$$

find the values of a, b, c, and d.

4. Find **A** + **B** and **A** − **B** for each part of this exercise, provided, of course, that these quantities exist.

(a) $\mathbf{A} = \begin{pmatrix} -3 & 2 \\ 2 & 1 \end{pmatrix}$, $\mathbf{B} = \begin{pmatrix} 3 & -2 \\ -4 & 0 \end{pmatrix}$

(b) $\mathbf{A} = (1 \quad 3 \quad -4 \quad 5 \quad 2)$, $\mathbf{B} = (-1 \quad 1 \quad 5 \quad -4 \quad 3)$

(c) $\mathbf{A} = \begin{pmatrix} 2 & 0 & -2 \\ -1 & 2 & 0 \end{pmatrix}$, $\mathbf{B} = \begin{pmatrix} 3 & -1 & -3 \\ -2 & 2 & 4 \end{pmatrix}$

(d) $\mathbf{A} = \begin{pmatrix} 3 \\ 3 \\ -1 \end{pmatrix}$, $\mathbf{B} = \begin{pmatrix} -1 \\ 2 \\ 2 \\ 2 \end{pmatrix}$

(e) $\mathbf{A} = \begin{pmatrix} 1 & 0 & 1 \\ 0 & 3 & 4 \\ 4 & -1 & -3 \\ 1 & -4 & 2 \end{pmatrix}$, $\mathbf{B} = \begin{pmatrix} 2 & 1 & -3 \\ -1 & -4 & 1 \\ 2 & 1 & 2 \\ -1 & 4 & -3 \end{pmatrix}$

5. If

$$\begin{pmatrix} 3 \\ -2 \\ 1 \end{pmatrix} + \begin{pmatrix} x \\ y \\ z \end{pmatrix} = \begin{pmatrix} -4 \\ 2 \\ 5 \end{pmatrix}$$

find x, y, and z.

6. Find the transpose of each matrix in Exercise 1.

7. Find the transpose of each matrix in Exercise 4.

8. With reference to Exercise 4, compute 2**A** and 10**B**.

9. Like addition of real numbers, matrix addition is *commutative* and *associative*. Verify this for the matrices

$$\mathbf{A} = \begin{pmatrix} -3 & 2 \\ 4 & 1 \end{pmatrix}, \quad \mathbf{B} = \begin{pmatrix} 2 & -2 \\ 3 & -1 \end{pmatrix}, \quad \mathbf{C} = \begin{pmatrix} 1 & 2 \\ 1 & 3 \end{pmatrix}$$

by showing that $\mathbf{A} + \mathbf{B} = \mathbf{B} + \mathbf{A}$ and $\mathbf{A} + (\mathbf{B} + \mathbf{C}) = (\mathbf{A} + \mathbf{B}) + \mathbf{C}$.

10. An airline reports the number of seats occupied on its flights by means of a 1×4 row vector—the first component represents the number of seats occupied by first-class passengers, the second component represents those occupied by coach passengers, the third component represents those occupied by students traveling at reduced rates, and the fourth component represents those occupied by nonpaying passengers. If (21   65   14   3) represents the seats occupied on a flight as it leaves Denver for Seattle via Reno, (8   22   3   1) represents the persons who get off in Reno, and (6   19   8   0) represents the persons who get on in Reno, find the 1×4 vector which represents the seats occupied on this flight as it arrives in Seattle.

11. In the following matrices, the elements a_{ij} of matrix $\mathbf{A}$ are the daily number of flights from city i to city j, the elements b_{ij} of matrix $\mathbf{B}$ are the daily number of trains from city i to city j, and the elements of c_{ij} of matrix $\mathbf{C}$ are the daily number of buses from city i to city j:

$$\mathbf{A} = \begin{pmatrix} 0 & 4 & 3 \\ 4 & 0 & 5 \\ 3 & 5 & 0 \end{pmatrix}, \quad \mathbf{B} = \begin{pmatrix} 0 & 1 & 2 \\ 1 & 0 & 0 \\ 2 & 0 & 0 \end{pmatrix}, \quad \mathbf{C} = \begin{pmatrix} 0 & 3 & 5 \\ 3 & 0 & 4 \\ 5 & 4 & 0 \end{pmatrix}$$

   (a) Find $\mathbf{A} + \mathbf{B}$ and read the number of daily flights or trains from city 1 to city 3 and from city 2 to city 1.
   (b) Find $\mathbf{A} + \mathbf{B} + \mathbf{C}$ and read the number of flights, trains, or buses each day from city 3 to city 2 and from city 1 to city 2.

7.3 MATRIX MULTIPLICATION

Continuing the line of reasoning of Section 7.2, we might be led to define the *product* of two $m \times n$ matrices as the matrix which would be obtained by pairwise multiplying their respective elements. This could be done, or course, but when mathematicians talk about the product of two matrices, they are actually referring to a different and much more useful concept. Since this definition is fairly complicated, let us illustrate it first in connection with a $1 \times k$ matrix and a $k \times 1$ matrix, namely, in connection with a row vector and a column vector having the same number of components (or elements). Returning to the department-store illustration, where we represented the store's inventory of television sets by means of the vector

$$(14 \quad 16 \quad 56 \quad 33 \quad 19)$$

let us suppose now that we are interested in the total retail value of these sets. If the deluxe color consoles sell for $899, the regular color consoles for $645, the color table models for $449, the color portables for $395, and the black-and-white portables for $149, we can represent this information by means of the column vector

$$\begin{pmatrix} 899 \\ 645 \\ 449 \\ 395 \\ 149 \end{pmatrix}$$

Since the retail values of the deluxe color consoles, regular color consoles, color table models, color portables, and black-and-white portables, are, respectively, 14($899), 16($645), 56($449), 33($395), and 19($149), their total retail value is

$$14(899) + 16(645) + 56(449) + 33(395) + 19(149) = \$63,916$$

Note that this total is the sum of the products obtained by multiplying the *first* element of the row vector by the *first* element of the column vector, the *second* element of the row vector by the *second* element of the column vector, the *third* element of the row vector by the *third* element of the column vector, the *fourth* element of the row vector by the *fourth* element of the column vector, and the *fifth* element of the row vector by the *fifth* element of the column vector.

Since sums of products like this arise in many applications, we shall let it *define* the product of a row vector and a column vector having the same dimension. Aside from the fact that this kind of vector product has important applications, it also serves to define the product of two matrices in the following way.

*If **A** is an m × n matrix and **B** is an n × r matrix, then their product* **C** = **A** · **B** *is the m × r matrix whose elements are*

$$c_{ij} = (a_{i1}, a_{i2}, \ldots, a_{in}) \begin{pmatrix} b_{1j} \\ b_{2j} \\ \vdots \\ b_{nj} \end{pmatrix}$$
$$= a_{i1}b_{1j} + a_{i2}b_{2j} + \cdots + a_{in}b_{nj}$$

where the a's and the b's are the respective elements of matrices **A** and **B**. In words, the element c_{ij} in the ith row and the jth column of the product matrix **C** is obtained by multiplying the ith row of **A** (looked upon as a row vector) by the jth column of **B** (looked upon as a column vector). Before we give any numerical examples, let us make it very clear that with this definition we can speak of $\mathbf{A} \cdot \mathbf{B}$, the product of two matrices **A** and **B**, if and only if *the number of columns in* **A** *equals the number of rows in* **B**.

EXAMPLE 7.6   In this example we shall multiply a 2 × 3 matrix by a 3 × 2 matrix, which is possible because the first matrix has three columns and the second has three rows. Given

$$\mathbf{A} = \begin{pmatrix} 2 & 3 & -1 \\ 4 & 1 & 5 \end{pmatrix} \quad \text{and} \quad \mathbf{B} = \begin{pmatrix} 1 & -2 \\ 3 & -3 \\ 2 & 6 \end{pmatrix}$$

we can write

$$\mathbf{A} \cdot \mathbf{B} = \begin{pmatrix} 2 & 3 & -1 \\ 4 & 1 & 5 \end{pmatrix} \begin{pmatrix} 1 & -2 \\ 3 & -3 \\ 2 & 6 \end{pmatrix} = \begin{pmatrix} c_{11} & c_{12} \\ c_{21} & c_{22} \end{pmatrix} = \mathbf{C}$$

and, multiplying the *first* row of **A** by the *first* column of **B**, we get

$$c_{11} = 2 \cdot 1 + 3 \cdot 3 + (-1)2 = 9$$

Similarly, multiplying the *first* row of **A** by the *second* column **B**, the *second* row of **A** by the *first* column of **B**, and the *second* row of **A** by the *second* column of **B**, we obtain

$$c_{12} = 2(-2) + 3(-3) + (-1)6 = -19$$
$$c_{21} = 4 \cdot 1 + 1 \cdot 3 + 5 \cdot 2 = 17$$
$$c_{22} = 4(-2) + 1(-3) + 5 \cdot 6 = 19$$

Hence,

$$\mathbf{A} \cdot \mathbf{B} = \begin{pmatrix} 2 & 3 & -1 \\ 4 & 1 & 5 \end{pmatrix} \begin{pmatrix} 1 & -2 \\ 3 & -3 \\ 2 & 6 \end{pmatrix} = \begin{pmatrix} 9 & -19 \\ 17 & 19 \end{pmatrix} = \mathbf{C}$$

EXAMPLE 7.7   Consider the following 3 × 3 matrix **D** in which the elements of the first column represent a refreshment stand's sales of hot dogs on three summer days, those of the second column represent the refreshment stand's sales of hamburgers on these days, and those of the third column represent the number of portions of French fries sold on these days.

$$\mathbf{D} = \begin{pmatrix} 435 & 1413 & 891 \\ 512 & 1357 & 914 \\ 386 & 996 & 612 \end{pmatrix}$$

If the hot dogs sell for 65¢, the hamburgers for 75¢, and the French fries for 45¢, we can represent this information by means of the column vector

$$\mathbf{E} = \begin{pmatrix} 65 \\ 75 \\ 45 \end{pmatrix}$$

The total amounts of money received for these food items on the three days by the refreshment stand are given by the elements of the product matrix

$$\mathbf{D \cdot E} = \begin{pmatrix} 435 & 1413 & 891 \\ 512 & 1357 & 914 \\ 386 & 996 & 612 \end{pmatrix} \begin{pmatrix} 65 \\ 75 \\ 45 \end{pmatrix}$$

$$= \begin{pmatrix} 174,345 \\ 176,185 \\ 127,330 \end{pmatrix}$$

namely, \$1743.45, \$1761.85, and \$1273.30. To continue with this example, suppose that we are also interested in the total sales of these items on the three days. These figures are given by the elements of the product matrix

$$(1 \quad 1 \quad 1)\begin{pmatrix} 435 & 1413 & 891 \\ 512 & 1357 & 914 \\ 386 & 996 & 612 \end{pmatrix} = (1333 \quad 3766 \quad 2417)$$

It is true in general that *if an* m × n *matrix* **A** *is multiplied on the left by the* 1 × m *row vector whose elements are all 1's, the result is a* 1 × n *row vector whose elements are the sums of the elements in the corresponding columns of matrix* **A**. As we pointed out previously, two matrices can be multiplied only when the first matrix has as many columns as the second matrix has rows. Thus, if **A** is a 2 × 3 matrix and **B** is a 3 × 5 matrix, then **A · B** is a 2 × 5 matrix, but **B · A** is not defined since **B** has 5 columns while **A** has only 2 rows. Even if both products exist, however, they need not be equal, as is shown in Example 7.8.

EXAMPLE 7.8   Given the two matrices

$$\mathbf{A} = \begin{pmatrix} -2 & 1 \\ 3 & -1 \end{pmatrix} \quad \text{and} \quad \mathbf{B} = \begin{pmatrix} 0 & -1 \\ 3 & 2 \end{pmatrix}$$

we find that

$$\mathbf{A} \cdot \mathbf{B} = \begin{pmatrix} -2 & 1 \\ 3 & -1 \end{pmatrix}\begin{pmatrix} 0 & -1 \\ 3 & 2 \end{pmatrix} = \begin{pmatrix} 3 & 4 \\ -3 & -5 \end{pmatrix}$$

and

$$\mathbf{B} \cdot \mathbf{A} = \begin{pmatrix} 0 & -1 \\ 3 & 2 \end{pmatrix}\begin{pmatrix} -2 & 1 \\ 3 & -1 \end{pmatrix} = \begin{pmatrix} -3 & 1 \\ 0 & 1 \end{pmatrix}$$

and, hence, that $\mathbf{A} \cdot \mathbf{B}$ does *not* equal $\mathbf{B} \cdot \mathbf{A}$.

At the end of Section 7.2 we defined *zero matrices,* or *null matrices,* whose elements are all zeros; such matrices play the same role as the number zero in ordinary arithmetic. Correspondingly, let us now define **identity matrices**, which, for matrix multiplication, play the role of the number 1. An identity matrix is a *square matrix* for which the elements on the diagonal from upper left to lower right are 1's and all other elements are 0's. The following are some examples: the identity matrices of order 2×2, 3×3, and 4×4.

$$\begin{pmatrix} 1 & 0 \\ 0 & 1 \end{pmatrix}, \quad \begin{pmatrix} 1 & 0 & 0 \\ 0 & 1 & 0 \\ 0 & 0 & 1 \end{pmatrix}, \quad \text{and} \quad \begin{pmatrix} 1 & 0 & 0 & 0 \\ 0 & 1 & 0 & 0 \\ 0 & 0 & 1 & 0 \\ 0 & 0 & 0 & 1 \end{pmatrix}$$

It is easy to verify that if $\mathbf{A}$ is an $n \times n$ matrix and $\mathbf{I}$ is the identity matrix of order $n \times n$, then $\mathbf{A} \cdot \mathbf{I} = \mathbf{I} \cdot \mathbf{A} = \mathbf{A}$; this is the property which characterizes the number 1 in arithmetic, where $a \cdot 1 = 1 \cdot a = a$ for any real number a. For instance, for a 2×2 matrix,

$$\mathbf{I} \cdot \mathbf{A} = \begin{pmatrix} 1 & 0 \\ 0 & 1 \end{pmatrix}\begin{pmatrix} a_{11} & a_{12} \\ a_{21} & a_{22} \end{pmatrix} = \begin{pmatrix} 1 \cdot a_{11} + 0 \cdot a_{21} & 1 \cdot a_{12} + 0 \cdot a_{22} \\ 0 \cdot a_{11} + 1 \cdot a_{21} & 0 \cdot a_{12} + 1 \cdot a_{22} \end{pmatrix}$$

$$= \begin{pmatrix} a_{11} & a_{12} \\ a_{21} & a_{22} \end{pmatrix}$$

$$= \mathbf{A}$$

Finally, let us consider an interesting result that occurs whenever we multiply an $m \times 1$ row vector $\mathbf{A}$ by its transpose $\mathbf{A}'$. The result is a scalar that is the sum of squares of the elements of $\mathbf{A}$.

EXAMPLE 7.9 Given the row vector

$$\mathbf{A} = \begin{pmatrix} 2 \\ 5 \\ 10 \end{pmatrix}$$

we find that

$$\mathbf{A}' \cdot \mathbf{A} = (2 \quad 5 \quad 10) \begin{pmatrix} 2 \\ 5 \\ 10 \end{pmatrix}$$

$$= 2^2 + 5^2 + 10^2$$

$$= 129$$

EXERCISES

1. For each pair of matrices, check whether it is possible to calculate $\mathbf{A} \cdot \mathbf{B}$, $\mathbf{B} \cdot \mathbf{A}$, both, or neither.
   (a) $\mathbf{A}$ is a 2×5 matrix and $\mathbf{B}$ is a 5×2 matrix.
   (b) $\mathbf{A}$ is a 5×2 matrix and $\mathbf{B}$ is a 2×5 matrix.
   (c) $\mathbf{A}$ is a 2×5 matrix and $\mathbf{B}$ is a 2×5 matrix.
   (d) $\mathbf{A}$ is a 4×3 matrix and $\mathbf{B}$ is a 2×4 matrix.
   (e) $\mathbf{A}$ is a 3×5 matrix and $\mathbf{B}$ is a 5×6 matrix.
   (f) $\mathbf{A}$ is a 3×4 matrix and $\mathbf{B}$ is a 2×3 matrix.

2. Evaluate each matrix product.
   (a) $(1 \quad -1 \quad 0) \begin{pmatrix} 2 \\ 4 \\ -1 \end{pmatrix}$

   (b) $\begin{pmatrix} 2 & -2 \\ 5 & 1 \end{pmatrix} \begin{pmatrix} 2 & 3 \\ -3 & 4 \end{pmatrix}$

   (c) $\begin{pmatrix} 1 & 0 & -1 & 2 \\ 3 & -2 & 2 & 3 \end{pmatrix} \begin{pmatrix} 2 & 1 & -2 \\ 1 & 0 & 0 \\ -1 & 2 & 2 \\ 2 & -1 & 1 \end{pmatrix}$

   (d) $\begin{pmatrix} 1 \\ -1 \\ 3 \end{pmatrix} (1 \quad 3 \quad -4)$

   (e) $\begin{pmatrix} 2 & 2 \\ 3 & -2 \\ 1 & -1 \end{pmatrix} \begin{pmatrix} 2 & 1 & 4 & -2 & 1 \\ 0 & -3 & -2 & 3 & 0 \end{pmatrix}$

$$(f) \quad \begin{pmatrix} -3 & 1 & 1 \\ 2 & 0 & 3 \\ 5 & -2 & 0 \end{pmatrix} \begin{pmatrix} 1 & -2 & 1 \\ 1 & 1 & -2 \\ 4 & -3 & 0 \end{pmatrix}$$

3. With reference to the television-inventory matrix **R** of Example 7.3, suppose that the profits which the merchant makes on the five kinds of sets (regardless of brand) are given by the corresponding elements of the column vector

$$\begin{pmatrix} \$132 \\ \$75 \\ \$91 \\ \$83 \\ \$28 \end{pmatrix}$$

Multiply the inventory matrix **R** by this column vector, and explain what its elements represent.

4. The elements of the following row vector are the prices which a supermarket charges for a pound of butter, a dozen eggs, a loaf of bread, a pound of coffee, and a half gallon of milk.

$$\mathbf{P} = (\$1.30 \quad \$0.95 \quad \$1.19 \quad \$4.00 \quad \$1.15)$$

If the corresponding quantities of butter, eggs, bread, coffee, and milk which a housewife buys are given by the column vector

$$\mathbf{Q} = \begin{pmatrix} 1 \\ 2 \\ 1 \\ 1 \\ 3 \end{pmatrix}$$

calculate $\mathbf{P} \cdot \mathbf{Q}$ and explain its significance. What product should we have asked for instead of $\mathbf{P} \cdot \mathbf{Q}$ if $\mathbf{Q}$ had been given as row vector instead of a column vector?

5. An automobile dealer is offering a one-day special on tune-ups, oil changes, and brake repairs. The profits which the dealer makes on the three services are given by corresponding elements of the column vector

$$\mathbf{P} = \begin{pmatrix} \$25 \\ \$4 \\ \$50 \end{pmatrix}$$

If the number of tune-ups, oil changes, and brake repairs actually made are given by the column vector

$$Q = \begin{pmatrix} 3 \\ 8 \\ 2 \end{pmatrix}$$

write an expression for total daily profit in matrix terms and compute the value of the total daily profit.

7.4 THE INVERSE OF A MATRIX

The remainder of this chapter will be devoted for the most part to the solution of systems of linear equations. To begin with, let us demonstrate how systems of linear equations can be written in matrix form, using as an example a system of two linear equations in two variables. Following the notation introduced in Section 6.2, we write these equations as

$$a_{11}x_1 + a_{12}x_2 = b_1$$

$$a_{21}x_1 + a_{22}x_2 = b_2$$

where x_1 and x_2 are the two variables, b_1 and b_2 are the constant terms, and the subscripts of the coefficients a_{11}, a_{12}, a_{21}, and a_{22} tell us to which equation and to which variable each coefficient belongs—the first subscript is 1 or 2 depending on the equation, and the second subscript is the same as that of the corresponding variable. An obvious advantage of this notation is that it can easily be extended to n linear equations in n variables.

To write the above system of linear equations in matrix form, let us introduce the following three matrices, representing, in turn, the variables, the coefficients, and the constant terms.

$$X = \begin{pmatrix} x_1 \\ x_2 \end{pmatrix}, \qquad A = \begin{pmatrix} a_{11} & a_{12} \\ a_{21} & a_{22} \end{pmatrix}, \qquad B = \begin{pmatrix} b_1 \\ b_2 \end{pmatrix}$$

Calculating the product $A \cdot X$, we obtain

$$A \cdot X = \begin{pmatrix} a_{11} & a_{12} \\ a_{21} & a_{22} \end{pmatrix} \begin{pmatrix} x_1 \\ x_2 \end{pmatrix} = \begin{pmatrix} a_{11}x_1 + a_{12}x_2 \\ a_{21}x_1 + a_{22}x_2 \end{pmatrix}$$

and we see that the elements of the resulting column vector are precisely the left-hand members of the original equations. Thus we can substitute for them b_1 and b_2, getting

$$\mathbf{A} \cdot \mathbf{X} = \begin{pmatrix} a_{11}x_1 + a_{12}x_2 \\ a_{21}x_1 + a_{22}x_2 \end{pmatrix} = \begin{pmatrix} b_1 \\ b_2 \end{pmatrix} = \mathbf{B}$$

or simply

$$\boxed{\mathbf{A} \cdot \mathbf{X} = \mathbf{B}}$$

Although $\mathbf{A} \cdot \mathbf{X} = \mathbf{B}$ is one matrix equation, it is simply another way of writing the original pair of equations; had we begun with three equations in three variables, $\mathbf{A} \cdot \mathbf{X} = \mathbf{B}$ would have represented the *three* equations

$$a_{11}x_1 + a_{12}x_2 + a_{13}x_3 = b_1$$

$$a_{21}x_1 + a_{22}x_2 + a_{23}x_3 = b_2$$

$$a_{31}x_1 + a_{32}x_2 + a_{33}x_3 = b_3$$

In ordinary algebra, the equation $ax = b$ can be solved by dividing the expressions on both sides of the equation by a, getting $x = b/a$ provided that $a \neq 0$. The same could have been accomplished by *multiplying* the expressions on both sides of the equation by the *reciprocal* of a, or $1/a$, which is also written as a^{-1}. Thus we would have obtained

$$a^{-1} \cdot ax = a^{-1} \cdot b$$

$$(a^{-1} \cdot a)x = a^{-1} \cdot b$$

and hence,

$$x = a^{-1} \cdot b$$

since $a^{-1} \cdot a$ is equal to 1. To extend the concept of a *reciprocal* to matrix multiplication, let us now make the following definition.

*If $\mathbf{A}$ is a square matrix and there exists a square matrix $\mathbf{C}$ such that $\mathbf{C} \cdot \mathbf{A} = \mathbf{I}$, where $\mathbf{I}$ is the identity matrix of the same order as $\mathbf{A}$, then $\mathbf{C}$ is called the **inverse** of $\mathbf{A}$; it is denoted by $\mathbf{A}^{-1}$.*

EXAMPLE 7.10   The inverse of the matrix

$$\mathbf{A} = \begin{pmatrix} 2 & 3 \\ -5 & -2 \end{pmatrix}$$

is the matrix*

---

*The procedure for finding the inverse of a matrix will be taken up in Section 7.5.

$$\mathbf{A}^{-1} = \begin{pmatrix} -\dfrac{2}{11} & -\dfrac{3}{11} \\[2ex] \dfrac{5}{11} & \dfrac{2}{11} \end{pmatrix}$$

and to verify this we have only to show that $\mathbf{A}^{-1} \cdot \mathbf{A}$ equals the identity matrix of order 2×2. When we actually perform this multiplication, we get

$$
\mathbf{A}^{-1} \cdot \mathbf{A} = \begin{pmatrix} -\dfrac{2}{11} & -\dfrac{3}{11} \\[2ex] \dfrac{5}{11} & \dfrac{2}{11} \end{pmatrix} \begin{pmatrix} 2 & 3 \\ -5 & -2 \end{pmatrix}
$$

$$
= \begin{pmatrix} -\dfrac{2}{11} \cdot 2 + \left(-\dfrac{3}{11}\right)(-5) & -\dfrac{2}{11} \cdot 3 + \left(-\dfrac{3}{11}\right)(-2) \\[3ex] \dfrac{5}{11} \cdot 2 + \dfrac{2}{11}(-5) & \dfrac{5}{11} \cdot 3 + \dfrac{2}{11}(-2) \end{pmatrix}
$$

$$
= \begin{pmatrix} 1 & 0 \\ 0 & 1 \end{pmatrix}
$$

You can verify that we could obtain the same result for $\mathbf{A} \cdot \mathbf{A}^{-1}$.

It follows from our definition that the inverse of a square matrix $\mathbf{A}$ must be of the same order as $\mathbf{A}$, and it can also be shown that if $\mathbf{C}$ is the inverse of $\mathbf{A}$, then $\mathbf{A}$ is the inverse of $\mathbf{C}$, namely, that $\mathbf{A}^{-1} \cdot \mathbf{A} = \mathbf{A} \cdot \mathbf{A}^{-1}$ whenever $\mathbf{A}^{-1}$ exists. Our definition does not tell us, however, how we can check whether any given square matrix has an inverse, and it does not tell us how to find the inverse of a matrix when it does exist. The first of these two problems will be taken up in Section 7.6, where we shall study what is called the *determinant* of a matrix; the other problem will be treated in Section 7.5.

Let us now return to the problem of solving systems of linear equations. As we have shown we can write a system of linear equations in matrix form as $\mathbf{A} \cdot \mathbf{X} = \mathbf{B}$. Suppose that the coefficient matrix $\mathbf{A}$ has the inverse $\mathbf{A}^{-1}$. We can then multiply the expressions on both sides of this matrix equation by $\mathbf{A}^{-1}$ and get

$$\mathbf{A}^{-1} \cdot (\mathbf{A} \cdot \mathbf{X}) = \mathbf{A}^{-1} \cdot \mathbf{B}$$

We can write this result as*

---

*It can be shown that matrix multiplication is associative. That is, for matrices $\mathbf{A}$, $\mathbf{B}$, and $\mathbf{C}$, $\mathbf{A} \cdot (\mathbf{B} \cdot \mathbf{C}) = (\mathbf{A} \cdot \mathbf{B}) \cdot \mathbf{C}$. Thus $\mathbf{A}^{-1} \cdot (\mathbf{A} \cdot \mathbf{X}) = (\mathbf{A}^{-1}\mathbf{A}) \cdot \mathbf{X}$.

$$(\mathbf{A}^{-1} \cdot \mathbf{A}) \cdot \mathbf{X} = \mathbf{A}^{-1} \cdot \mathbf{B}$$

and since $\mathbf{A}^{-1} \mathbf{A} = \mathbf{I}$ and $\mathbf{IX} = \mathbf{X}$, we get

$$\boxed{\mathbf{X} = \mathbf{A}^{-1} \cdot \mathbf{B}}$$

This tells us that the solution for the x's are given by the elements of the matrix $\mathbf{A}^{-1} \cdot \mathbf{B}$.

EXAMPLE 7.11   To illustrate this technique, let us use it to solve the following system of two linear equations in two variables.

$$2x_1 + 3x_2 = 5$$
$$-5x_1 - 2x_2 = 4$$

This is going to be easy, since we already know the inverse of the coefficient matrix $\mathbf{A}$ from Example 7.10—that is

$$\begin{pmatrix} -\dfrac{2}{11} & -\dfrac{3}{11} \\ \dfrac{5}{11} & \dfrac{2}{11} \end{pmatrix}$$

Thus

$$\mathbf{A}^{-1} \cdot \mathbf{B} = \begin{pmatrix} -\dfrac{2}{11} & -\dfrac{3}{11} \\ \dfrac{5}{11} & \dfrac{2}{11} \end{pmatrix} \begin{pmatrix} 5 \\ 4 \end{pmatrix} = \begin{pmatrix} -\dfrac{2}{11} \cdot 5 + \left(-\dfrac{3}{11}\right)4 \\ \dfrac{5}{11} \cdot 5 + \dfrac{2}{11} \cdot 4 \end{pmatrix}$$

$$= \begin{pmatrix} -2 \\ 3 \end{pmatrix}$$

and this tells us that the solutions for x_1 and x_2 are $x_1 = -2$ and $x_2 = 3$.

We now have a systematic approach to the solution of systems of linear equations; all we have to do is multiply the inverse of the coefficient matrix $\mathbf{A}$ by the column vector $\mathbf{B}$ of constant terms and read the elements of the resulting column vector. This applies not only to two linear equations in two variables, but in general to n linear equations in n variables; in each case, the solutions for the x's are given by the respective elements of the product matrix $\mathbf{A}^{-1} \cdot \mathbf{B}$. Of course, there remains the question of *how* to obtain the inverse of a matrix, and (as we shall see later) this is just about as difficult as the original problem of solving a system of linear equations. Nevertheless, the method we introduced in this section provides us with a *systematic* way of solving systems of linear equations, and this is very important in this age of electronic computers. In the next section we study another matrix approach to the solution of a system of linear equations, which, at the same time, will serve to find the inverse of the coefficient matrix.

7.5 ELEMENTARY ROW OPERATIONS

In this section we demonstrate how the *method of elimination* of Section 6.2 can be simplified and unified by working only with the coefficients and constant terms in matrix form.

EXAMPLE 7.12 To illustrate this technique, let us return to Example 6.2, where we used the method of elimination to solve the system of equations

$$2x + 3y = 5$$
$$-5x - 2y = 4$$

Following the notation introduced in Section 6.2, we can rewrite this system of equations as

$$2x_1 + 3x_2 = 5$$
$$-5x_1 - 2x_2 = 4$$

The coefficient matrix and the column vector of constant terms are

$$\mathbf{A} = \begin{pmatrix} 2 & 3 \\ -5 & -2 \end{pmatrix} \quad \text{and} \quad \mathbf{B} = \begin{pmatrix} 5 \\ 4 \end{pmatrix}$$

respectively, and to simplify our notation we shall combine these two matrices into the one matrix

$$(\mathbf{A} \mid \mathbf{B}) = \begin{pmatrix} 2 & 3 & \mid & 5 \\ -5 & -2 & \mid & 4 \end{pmatrix}$$

where the vertical line serves to separate the elements of the coefficient matrix from the constant terms. This matrix is called the **augmented coefficient matrix**.

In the work which follows, we shall again solve the system

$$2x_1 + 3x_2 = 5$$

$$-5x_1 - 2x_2 = 4$$

by the method of elimination, but this time we shall indicate on the *left-hand side* of the page what each step does to the system of equations, and on the *right-hand side* what it does to the matrix $(\mathbf{A} \mid \mathbf{B})$. Proceeding as we did in Example 6.2, we eliminate x_2 from the first equation by multiplying the expressions on both sides of the first equation by 2, multiplying the expressions on both sides of the second equation by 3, and then adding the expressions on both sides of the second equation to those of the first. Symbolically, we thus get

$$
\begin{array}{cc}
\begin{array}{l}
4x_1 + 6x_2 = 10 \\
-15x_1 - 6x_2 = 12
\end{array}
&
\left(\begin{array}{cc|c}
4 & 6 & 10 \\
-15 & -6 & 12
\end{array} \right)
\end{array}
$$

and

$$
\begin{array}{cc}
\begin{array}{l}
-11x_1 \quad\quad = 22 \\
-15x_1 - 6x_2 = 12
\end{array}
&
\left(\begin{array}{cc|c}
-11 & 0 & 22 \\
-15 & -6 & 12
\end{array} \right)
\end{array}
$$

If we then divide the expressions on both sides of the first equation by -11, we get

$$
\begin{array}{cc}
\begin{array}{l}
x_1 \quad\quad = -2 \\
-15x_1 - 6x_2 = 12
\end{array}
&
\left(\begin{array}{cc|c}
1 & 0 & -2 \\
-15 & -6 & 12
\end{array} \right)
\end{array}
$$

and we can stop since we have found that $x_1 = -2$ (and can determine the value of x_2 by substituting $x_1 = -2$ into the second equation, as we did in Example 6.2).

To save time and labor in problems of this kind, we can omit the work on the original system of equations altogether; instead, we simply work with the augmented coefficient matrix $(\mathbf{A} \mid \mathbf{B})$, manipulating the elements in its rows by the following **elementary row operations**.

1. *Multiplying each element of a row by the same number, not zero.*
2. *Adding (subtracting) each element of a row to (from) the corresponding element of another row.*
3. *Interchanging two rows.*

We did not use the third operation in our example, but it is sometimes needed to put an augmented coefficient matrix $(\mathbf{A} \mid \mathbf{B})$ into a desired form.

When we solve a system of linear equations by this method, namely, by applying elementary row operations to the augmented coefficient matrix $(\mathbf{A} \mid \mathbf{B})$, we generally continue the process until the matrix is reduced to the form

$$\begin{pmatrix} 1 & 0 & ? \\ 0 & 1 & ? \end{pmatrix}, \quad \begin{pmatrix} 1 & 0 & 0 & ? \\ 0 & 1 & 0 & ? \\ 0 & 0 & 1 & ? \end{pmatrix}, \quad \begin{pmatrix} 1 & 0 & 0 & 0 & ? \\ 0 & 1 & 0 & 0 & ? \\ 0 & 0 & 1 & 0 & ? \\ 0 & 0 & 0 & 1 & ? \end{pmatrix}$$

and so on, because the solutions for the x's are then given by the numbers taking the place of the question marks. In other words, *we continue the process until the coefficient matrix to the left of the vertical line has been converted into an identity matrix, and the solutions for the x's are then given by the elements of the column vector to the right of the vertical line.*

In actual practice, it is often possible to reduce the required detail by combining several of the elementary row operations into a single step. This is illustrated in Example 7.13.

EXAMPLE 7.13   To solve the system of equations

$$x_1 - 2x_2 + x_3 = 8$$
$$3x_1 + 5x_2 + 7x_3 = 6$$
$$2x_1 - 3x_2 - 5x_3 = 7$$

we start with the matrix

$$\begin{pmatrix} 1 & -2 & 1 & 8 \\ 3 & 5 & 7 & 6 \\ 2 & -3 & -5 & 7 \end{pmatrix}$$

Then, to eliminate the 3 and the 2 in the *first column*, we subtract *three times* the elements of the first row from the corresponding elements of the second row and *twice* the elements of the first row from the corresponding elements of the third row and get

$$\begin{pmatrix} 1 & -2 & 1 & 8 \\ 0 & 11 & 4 & -18 \\ 2 & -3 & -5 & 7 \end{pmatrix} \quad \text{and} \quad \begin{pmatrix} 1 & -2 & 1 & 8 \\ 0 & 11 & 4 & -18 \\ 0 & 1 & -7 & -9 \end{pmatrix}$$

and, after dividing each element of the second row by 11,

$$\begin{pmatrix} 1 & -2 & 1 & 8 \\ 0 & 1 & \dfrac{4}{11} & -\dfrac{18}{11} \\ 0 & 1 & -7 & -9 \end{pmatrix}$$

To eliminate the -2 and the lower 1 from the *second column*, we then add *twice* the elements of the second row to the corresponding elements of the first row and subtract the elements of the second row from the corresponding elements of the third row. We thus obtain

$$\left(\begin{array}{ccc|c} 1 & 0 & \dfrac{19}{11} & \dfrac{52}{11} \\[2ex] 0 & 1 & \dfrac{4}{11} & -\dfrac{18}{11} \\[2ex] 0 & 1 & -7 & -9 \end{array}\right) \quad\text{and}\quad \left(\begin{array}{ccc|c} 1 & 0 & \dfrac{19}{11} & \dfrac{52}{11} \\[2ex] 0 & 1 & \dfrac{4}{11} & -\dfrac{18}{11} \\[2ex] 0 & 0 & -\dfrac{81}{11} & -\dfrac{81}{11} \end{array}\right)$$

and, after dividing each element of the third row by $-81/11$,

$$\left(\begin{array}{ccc|c} 1 & 0 & \dfrac{19}{11} & \dfrac{52}{11} \\[2ex] 0 & 1 & \dfrac{4}{11} & -\dfrac{18}{11} \\[2ex] 0 & 0 & 1 & 1 \end{array}\right)$$

Finally, to eliminate the $19/11$ and $4/11$ in the *third column*, we subtract $19/11$ times the elements of the third row from the corresponding elements of the first row and $4/11$ times the elements of the third row from the corresponding elements of the second row. This gives

$$\left(\begin{array}{ccc|c} 1 & 0 & 0 & 3 \\ 0 & 1 & 0 & -2 \\ 0 & 0 & 1 & 1 \end{array}\right)$$

and we can read the solutions as $x_1 = 3$, $x_2 = -2$, and $x_3 = 1$.

In case you feel that what we have done here is like shooting a duck with a cannon, let us hasten to add that the method is seldom, if ever, used to solve systems of linear equations in two or three variables. Its advantages would become apparent, though, if we had to work with systems of linear equations in many variables; furthermore, we shall see next that this method can also be used to find the inverse of a matrix.

If we perform elementary row operations on a square matrix $\mathbf{A}$ until it is changed into the identity matrix $\mathbf{I}$ of the same order, the total effect is the same as if we had multiplied $\mathbf{A}$ by its inverse $\mathbf{A}^{-1}$. Thus when we apply elementary row operations to the matrix $(\mathbf{A} \mid \mathbf{B})$ until $\mathbf{A}$ is changed to $\mathbf{I}$, the effect is the same as if we had multiplied by $\mathbf{A}^{-1}$, and we can write

$$\mathbf{A}^{-1}(\mathbf{A} \mid \mathbf{B}) = (\mathbf{A}^{-1}\cdot \mathbf{A} \mid \mathbf{A}^{-1}\cdot \mathbf{B}) = (\mathbf{I} \mid \mathbf{A}^{-1}\cdot \mathbf{B})$$

It is of interest to note that this agrees with the result obtained in Section 7.4—the solutions given by the elements of the column vector to the right of the vertical line are, in fact, the elements of $\mathbf{A}^{-1} \cdot \mathbf{B}$.

This analysis also suggests a way of calculating the inverse of a square matrix $\mathbf{A}$. Suppose that instead of $(\mathbf{A} \mid \mathbf{B})$ we start with the matrix $(\mathbf{A} \mid \mathbf{I})$, where $\mathbf{I}$ is the identity matrix of the same order as $\mathbf{A}$. For instance, when $\mathbf{A}$ is of order 2×2 or 3×3, we would start with

$$(\mathbf{A} \mid \mathbf{I}) = \begin{pmatrix} a_{11} & a_{12} & 1 & 0 \\ a_{21} & a_{22} & 0 & 1 \end{pmatrix}$$

or

$$(\mathbf{A} \mid \mathbf{I}) = \begin{pmatrix} a_{11} & a_{12} & a_{13} & 1 & 0 & 0 \\ a_{21} & a_{22} & a_{23} & 0 & 1 & 0 \\ a_{31} & a_{32} & a_{33} & 0 & 0 & 1 \end{pmatrix}$$

Then, if we perform elementary row operations until $\mathbf{A}$ is changed into $\mathbf{I}$, the total effect is the same as if we had multiplied by $\mathbf{A}^{-1}$, and we can write

$$\mathbf{A}^{-1}(\mathbf{A} \mid \mathbf{I}) = (\mathbf{A}^{-1} \cdot \mathbf{A} \mid \mathbf{A}^{-1} \cdot \mathbf{I}) = (\mathbf{I} \mid \mathbf{A}^{-1})$$

It follows that if we perform elementary row operations on $(\mathbf{A} \mid \mathbf{I})$ until $\mathbf{A}$ is changed to $\mathbf{I}$, then the matrix which consists of the elements to the right of the vertical line is converted into the inverse matrix $\mathbf{A}^{-1}$.

EXAMPLE 7.14 To illustrate this technique, let us find the inverse of the coefficient matrix of the system of equations in Example 7.12, namely, the inverse of the matrix

$$\mathbf{A} = \begin{pmatrix} 2 & 3 \\ -5 & -2 \end{pmatrix}$$

Using elementary row operations to change

$$\begin{pmatrix} 2 & 3 & 1 & 0 \\ -5 & -2 & 0 & 1 \end{pmatrix} \quad \text{into} \quad \begin{pmatrix} 1 & 0 & ? & ? \\ 0 & 1 & ? & ? \end{pmatrix}$$

let us first eliminate the 3 by adding $\frac{3}{2}$ of each element of the second row to the corresponding element of the first row. This gives

$$\begin{pmatrix} -\dfrac{11}{2} & 0 & 1 & \dfrac{3}{2} \\ -5 & -2 & 0 & 1 \end{pmatrix}$$

and, subtracting $\frac{10}{11}$ of each element of the first row from the corresponding element of the second row to eliminate the -5, we get

$$\left(\begin{array}{cc|cc} -\dfrac{11}{2} & 0 & 1 & \dfrac{3}{2} \\ 0 & -2 & -\dfrac{10}{11} & -\dfrac{4}{11} \end{array}\right)$$

Finally, if we divide each element of the first row by $-\frac{11}{2}$ and each element of the second row by -2, we obtain

$$\left(\begin{array}{cc|cc} 1 & 0 & -\dfrac{2}{11} & -\dfrac{3}{11} \\ 0 & 1 & \dfrac{5}{11} & \dfrac{2}{11} \end{array}\right)$$

and this verifies the result which we gave in Example 7.10, that the inverse of the given matrix **A** is

$$\mathbf{A}^{-1} = \left(\begin{array}{cc} -\dfrac{2}{11} & -\dfrac{3}{11} \\ \dfrac{5}{11} & \dfrac{2}{11} \end{array}\right)$$

When we use this method to find the inverse of the coefficient matrix of a system of linear equations (or, for that matter, the inverse of any square matrix), it can happen that we arrive at a row with nothing but zeros to the left of the vertical line. If this is the case, *the matrix does not have an inverse* (and *the system of equations does not have a unique solution*). The reason for this, as well as a more direct criterion for deciding whether or not any given square matrix has an inverse, will be discussed in Section 7.6.

EXERCISES

1. With reference to the two matrices **A** and **A**$^{-1}$ given in Example 7.10, verify that the product **A** · **A**$^{-1}$ is also equal to **I**.

2. Verify that the inverse of

$$\mathbf{A} = \begin{pmatrix} 1 & -2 \\ 2 & -3 \end{pmatrix} \quad \text{is} \quad \mathbf{A}^{-1} = \begin{pmatrix} -3 & 2 \\ -2 & 1 \end{pmatrix}$$

namely, that **A**$^{-1}$ · **A** = **I**, and use this result to solve each system of linear equations by evaluating the corresponding products **A**$^{-1}$ · **B**.

(a) $x_1 - 2x_2 = 2$ (b) $x_1 - 2x_2 = -7$ (c) $x_1 - 2x_2 = 5$
     $2x_1 - 3x_2 = 5$ $2x_1 - 3x_2 = -9$ $2x_1 - 3x_2 = 7$

Check each answer by substituting the values obtained for the x's into the original equations.

3. Evaluate the product $\mathbf{A}^{-1} \cdot \mathbf{A}$ to verify that the inverse of

$$\mathbf{A} = \begin{pmatrix} 1 & 2 \\ -2 & 1 \end{pmatrix} \quad \text{is} \quad \mathbf{A}^{-1} = \begin{pmatrix} \dfrac{1}{5} & -\dfrac{2}{5} \\ \dfrac{2}{5} & \dfrac{1}{5} \end{pmatrix}$$

and use this result to solve each system of linear equations by calculating the corresponding products $\mathbf{A}^{-1} \cdot \mathbf{B}$.

(a) $x_1 + 2x_2 = 7$ (b) $x_1 + 2x_2 = 6$ (c) $x_1 + 2x_2 = -8$
    $-2x_1 + x_2 = 1$ $-2x_1 + x_2 = 8$ $-2x_1 + x_2 = -9$

Check each answer by substituting the values obtained for the x's into the original equations.

4. Evaluate the product $\mathbf{A}^{-1} \cdot \mathbf{A}$ to verify that the inverse of

$$\mathbf{A} = \begin{pmatrix} 2 & 1 & -1 \\ 3 & 2 & 5 \\ 1 & 1 & 5 \end{pmatrix} \quad \text{is} \quad \mathbf{A}^{-1} = \begin{pmatrix} -5 & 6 & -7 \\ 10 & -11 & 13 \\ -1 & 1 & -1 \end{pmatrix}$$

and use this result to solve each system of linear equations by calculating the corresponding products $\mathbf{A}^{-1} \cdot \mathbf{B}$.

(a) $2x_1 + x_2 - x_3 = 6$ (b) $2x_1 + x_2 - x_3 = 7$
    $3x_1 + 2x_2 + 5x_3 = 3$ $3x_1 + 2x_2 + 5x_3 = -3$
     $x_1 + x_2 + 5x_3 = -2$ $x_1 + x_2 + 5x_3 = -8$

Check each answer by substituting the values obtained for the x's into the original equations.

5. Find the inverse of the matrix

$$\mathbf{A} = \begin{pmatrix} 1 & 4 \\ 2 & 9 \end{pmatrix}$$

and use it to solve the system of linear equations

$$x_1 + 4x_2 = 1$$

$$2x_1 + 9x_2 = -3$$

6. Find the inverse of the matrix

$$\mathbf{A} = \begin{pmatrix} 1 & 1 & -1 \\ 2 & 1 & 3 \\ 3 & 3 & 1 \end{pmatrix}$$

and use it to solve the system of linear equations

$$x_1 + x_2 - x_3 = -3$$
$$2x_1 + x_2 + 3x_3 = 7$$
$$3x_1 + 3x_2 + x_3 = -1$$

7. Solve the following system of linear equations by the method illustrated in Example 7.12; that is, by performing elementary row operations on the augmented coefficient matrix $(A \mid B)$.

$$2x_1 - x_2 = 5$$
$$5x_1 - 3x_2 = 11$$

8. Solve the following system of linear equations by the method illustrated in Example 7.12; that is, by performing elementary row operations on the augmented coefficient matrix $(A \mid B)$.

$$x_2 + 3x_3 = -4$$
$$x_1 + 2x_2 + x_3 = 7$$
$$x_1 - 2x_2 = 1$$

(*Hint:* The solution of this problem can be simplified by first changing the order of these equations, thus making use of the fact that some of the coefficients are already zero.)

7.6 THE DETERMINANT OF A MATRIX

As we saw in Section 7.5, the problem of solving a system of linear equations is closely related to that of finding the inverse of a matrix. Indeed, it can be shown that the condition for

$$a_{11}x_1 + a_{12}x_2 = b_1$$
$$a_{21}x_1 + a_{22}x_2 = b_2$$

to have a *unique solution* and the condition for

$$A = \begin{pmatrix} a_{11} & a_{12} \\ a_{21} & a_{22} \end{pmatrix}$$

to have an *inverse* are the same; *in either case, the quantity* $a_{11}a_{22} - a_{21}a_{12}$ *must not equal zero.* If $a_{11}a_{22} - a_{21}a_{12} = 0$—namely, if the matrix A does not have an inverse—we say that it is **singular**.

Since the quantity $a_{11}a_{22} - a_{21}a_{12}$ plays such an important role in problems involving 2×2 matrices, we denote it with a special symbol and give it a special name; we write it as

$$\begin{vmatrix} a_{11} & a_{12} \\ a_{21} & a_{22} \end{vmatrix} = a_{11}a_{22} - a_{21}a_{12}$$

and refer to it as the **determinant** of the 2×2 matrix **A**.

EXAMPLE 7.15   The determinants of the two matrices

$$\begin{pmatrix} 3 & -7 \\ -9 & 5 \end{pmatrix} \quad \text{and} \quad \begin{pmatrix} 2 & -6 \\ -4 & 12 \end{pmatrix}$$

are

$$\begin{vmatrix} 3 & -7 \\ -9 & 5 \end{vmatrix} = 3 \cdot 5 - (-9)(-7) = -48$$

and

$$\begin{vmatrix} 2 & -6 \\ -4 & 12 \end{vmatrix} = 2 \cdot 12 - (-4)(-6) = 0$$

respectively, and we can conclude that *the first matrix has an inverse, whereas the second is singular.*

The problem of solving a system of three linear equations in three variables is a direct extension of the two-equation problem. That is, it can be shown that the condition for

$$a_{11}x_1 + a_{12}x_2 + a_{13}x_3 = b_1$$
$$a_{21}x_1 + a_{22}x_2 + a_{23}x_3 = b_2$$
$$a_{31}x_1 + a_{32}x_2 + a_{33}x_3 = b_3$$

to have a unique solution and the condition for

$$\mathbf{A} = \begin{pmatrix} a_{11} & a_{12} & a_{13} \\ a_{21} & a_{22} & a_{23} \\ a_{31} & a_{32} & a_{33} \end{pmatrix}$$

to have an inverse are the same. Extending the notation and the terminology introduced above to 3×3 matrices, we write the quantity which must not equal zero for the inverse of **A** to exist as

$$\begin{vmatrix} a_{11} & a_{12} & a_{13} \\ a_{21} & a_{22} & a_{23} \\ a_{31} & a_{32} & a_{33} \end{vmatrix} = \begin{aligned} & a_{11}a_{22}a_{33} + a_{12}a_{23}a_{31} + a_{13}a_{21}a_{32} \\ & - a_{31}a_{22}a_{13} - a_{32}a_{23}a_{11} - a_{33}a_{21}a_{12} \end{aligned}$$

and we refer to it as the *determinant* of the 3 × 3 matrix **A**.

Since the expression which defines the determinant of a 3 × 3 matrix is fairly complicated (or, at least, difficult to remember), it is helpful to use the following scheme: *We begin by repeating the first two columns of the determinants as in the array*

$$\begin{vmatrix} a_{11} & a_{12} & a_{13} \\ a_{21} & a_{22} & a_{23} \\ a_{31} & a_{32} & a_{33} \end{vmatrix} \begin{matrix} a_{11} & a_{12} \\ a_{21} & a_{22} \\ a_{31} & a_{32} \end{matrix}$$

and then we multiply the three elements which lie on each of the diagonal lines. If the diagonal slopes downward (going from left to right) we add the corresponding product, and if the diagonal slopes upward, we subtract it.

EXAMPLE 7.16 Using this method to evaluate the determinant of the coefficient matrix of the system of linear equations of Example 7.13, we get

$$\begin{vmatrix} 1 & -2 & 1 \\ 3 & 5 & 7 \\ 2 & -3 & -5 \end{vmatrix} \begin{matrix} 1 & -2 \\ 3 & 5 \\ 2 & -3 \end{matrix} = \begin{aligned} & 1 \cdot 5(-5) + (-2)7 \cdot 2 + 1 \cdot 3(-3) \\ & -2 \cdot 5 \cdot 1 - (-3)7 \cdot 1 - (-5)3(-2) \end{aligned}$$

$$= -81$$

Since this result is not zero, we conclude that the given matrix has an inverse and that the system of equations has a unique solution (as we already know from Example 7.13).

It is of interest to note that there is a similar scheme for the evaluation of the determinant of a 2 × 2 matrix. Without even having to repeat any of the columns, we write

$$\begin{vmatrix} a_{11} & a_{12} \\ a_{21} & a_{22} \end{vmatrix} = a_{11}a_{22} - a_{21}a_{12}$$

and it can be seen that we have only to multiply the elements on the respective diagonals and subtract or add depending on whether the arrow points up or down.

Although determinants serve many purposes in various branches of mathematics, we have introduced them here for one reason only—to be able to decide whether any given matrix has an inverse. All we have to know, therefore, is whether a given determinant is zero, and as we shall see, this can often be resolved without actually having to evaluate the determinant. Instead, we make use of the fact that

if a row (or column) of a matrix contains nothing but zeros, then the determinant is equal to zero.

EXAMPLE 7.17   For instance

$$\begin{vmatrix} 0 & 0 \\ 3 & 4 \end{vmatrix} = 0 \cdot 4 + 0 \cdot 3 = 0$$

and

$$\begin{vmatrix} 1 & 0 & 2 \\ 3 & 0 & 4 \\ 5 & 0 & 7 \end{vmatrix} = 1 \cdot 0 \cdot 7 + 0 \cdot 4 \cdot 5 + 2 \cdot 3 \cdot 0 - 5 \cdot 0 \cdot 2 - 0 \cdot 4 \cdot 1 - 7 \cdot 3 \cdot 0$$

$$= 0$$

More generally, we have only to observe that each of the products (which we add or subtract in the formulas for 2×2 and 3×3 determinants) has among its factors *one element from each row and one element from each column.* (For instance, for a 3×3 determinant, $a_{12}a_{23}a_{31}$ has the factor a_{12}, which is in the *first* row and the *second* column; a_{23}, which is in the *second* row and the *third* column; and a_{31}, which is in the *third* row and the *first* column. Similarly, $a_{31}a_{22}a_{13}$ has the factor a_{31}, which is in the *third* row and the *first* column; a_{22}, which is in the *second* row and the *second* column; and a_{13}, which is in the *first* row and the *third* column.) Thus, if the elements of one row (or column) are all zeros, each product has at least one factor zero, and their sum (the value of the determinant) is equal to zero.*

In actual practice, we can hardly expect to find many determinants in which a row (or column) contains nothing but zeros, but there are certain rules according to which the elements of determinants can be manipulated, and *if a determinant equals zero, these manipulations (suitably applied) will lead to a determinant which has a row (or column) containing only zeros.* These manipulations are very similar to the elementary row operations of Section 7.5—corresponding to those operations, we now have the following rules:

---

*This also justifies the criterion on page 197, where we stated that the coefficient matrix does not have an inverse if we get a row containing nothing but zeros to the left of the vertical line.

1. *If each element of a row (or column) is multiplied by the same number, the value of the determinant is multiplied by that number.*

2. *If each element of a row (or column) is added to (or subtracted from) the corresponding element of another row (or column), the value of the determinant remains unchanged.*

3. *If two rows (or columns) are interchanged, the value of the determinant is multiplied by -1.*

Note that the first of these rules enables us to factor out, so to speak, a number from a row or a column of a determinant.

EXAMPLE 7.18 To illustrate, if we multiply each element of the second row of the determinant

$$\begin{vmatrix} 2 & -6 \\ -4 & 12 \end{vmatrix}$$

by $\frac{1}{2}$, the value of the determinant is multiplied by $\frac{1}{2}$, and we can compensate for this by multiplying the determinant by 2, namely, by writing

$$\begin{vmatrix} 2 & -6 \\ -4 & 12 \end{vmatrix} = 2\begin{vmatrix} 2 & -6 \\ -2 & 6 \end{vmatrix}$$

If we then apply the second rule and add each element of the second row to the corresponding element of the first row, we get

$$2\begin{vmatrix} 2 & -6 \\ -2 & 6 \end{vmatrix} = 2\begin{vmatrix} 0 & 0 \\ -2 & 6 \end{vmatrix}$$

Since the first row contains nothing but zeros, we conclude that the value of the original determinant is zero.

EXAMPLE 7.19 To give another example in which the above rules can be used to advantage, let us check whether the system of linear equations

$$x_1 - 2x_2 + 3x_3 = 5$$

$$2x_1 + 5x_2 + 2x_3 = 4$$

$$4x_1 + x_2 + 8x_3 = 12$$

has a unique solution; that is, let us check whether the determinant of the coefficient matrix

$$|\mathbf{A}| = \begin{vmatrix} 1 & -2 & 3 \\ 2 & 5 & 2 \\ 4 & 1 & 8 \end{vmatrix}$$

is equal to zero. There is really no set rule which tells us how to go about something like this, but suppose, for the sake of argument, that we begin by subtracting the elements of the second row from the corresponding elements of the third row.

$$|\mathbf{A}| = \begin{vmatrix} 1 & -2 & 3 \\ 2 & 5 & 2 \\ 2 & -4 & 6 \end{vmatrix}$$

Then if we divide each element of the third row by 2 (and compensate for it by multiplying the determinant by 2), we obtain

$$|\mathbf{A}| = 2\begin{vmatrix} 1 & -2 & 3 \\ 2 & 5 & 2 \\ 1 & -2 & 3 \end{vmatrix}$$

and it can be seen that if the elements of the first row are subtracted from the corresponding elements of the third row, we finally get

$$|\mathbf{A}| = 2\begin{vmatrix} 1 & -2 & 3 \\ 2 & 5 & 2 \\ 0 & 0 & 0 \end{vmatrix}$$

Thus $|\mathbf{A}| = 0$ and we have found that the given system of equations does not have a unique solution; in fact, further investigation will show that the system is inconsistent (and there are no solutions).

As should be apparent from Examples 7.18 and 7.19 we can also state that

a determinant is zero also if two rows (or columns) are equal or if the corresponding elements of two rows (or columns) are proportional.

Thus it can be seen that each of the determinants

$$\begin{vmatrix} 3 & -2 & 3 \\ 5 & 1 & 5 \\ 4 & -2 & 4 \end{vmatrix}, \qquad \begin{vmatrix} 2 & -6 \\ 10 & -30 \end{vmatrix}, \quad \text{and} \quad \begin{vmatrix} 2 & 0 & -3 \\ 8 & 16 & -4 \\ 2 & 4 & -1 \end{vmatrix}$$

and is equal to zero. In the first determinant the first and third columns are the same, in the second determinant each element of the second row is *five* times the corresponding element of the first row (and each element of the second column is *minus three* times the corresponding element of the first column), and in the third determinant each element of the second row is *four times* the corresponding element of the third row.

So far as determinants of $4 \times 4, 5 \times 5, \ldots$ matrices are concerned, let us merely point out that they obey the same general rules as 2×2 and 3×3 determinants, and they correspond to matrices having an inverse if and only if they are not equal to zero. In this book we shall not study determinants with more than 3 rows and 3 columns, but detailed treatments may be found in most college algebra texts. Let us point out, though, that *the special schemes with the upward and downward diagonals work only for determinants of 2×2 and 3×3 matrices.*

EXERCISES

1. Evaluate each determinant.

   (a) $\begin{vmatrix} 7 & 5 \\ 3 & 2 \end{vmatrix}$

   (c) $\begin{vmatrix} 4 & 0 & -2 \\ -1 & 5 & 1 \\ 0 & 6 & 3 \end{vmatrix}$

   (b) $\begin{vmatrix} -3 & -2 & 3 \\ 2 & 1 & 4 \\ 2 & -3 & 4 \end{vmatrix}$

   (d) $\begin{vmatrix} -3 & 8 \\ 9 & 6 \end{vmatrix}$

2. To verify the three rules of Section 7.6, evaluate the determinant

   $$\begin{vmatrix} 2 & 5 & 1 \\ 3 & 2 & -1 \\ 1 & 4 & -2 \end{vmatrix}$$

   and then *recalculate* its value after you have
   (a) multiplied each element of the second row by 3;
   (b) multiplied each element of the second column by 4;
   (c) added each element of the first row to the corresponding element of the second row;
   (d) subtracted each element of the third column from the corresponding element of the first column;
   (e) interchanged the first two rows;
   (f) interchanged the first and third columns.

3. Without using the formulas to evaluate the corresponding determinants, show that each matrix is singular.

   (a) $\begin{pmatrix} 12 & 6 \\ -6 & -3 \end{pmatrix}$

   (c) $\begin{pmatrix} -8 & -3 \\ 32 & 12 \end{pmatrix}$

   (b) $\begin{pmatrix} 5 & -2 & 7 \\ 3 & 11 & 14 \\ -2 & 13 & 7 \end{pmatrix}$

   (d) $\begin{pmatrix} 8 & 1 & 1 \\ 8 & 2 & -4 \\ 4 & 0 & 3 \end{pmatrix}$

Our goal in this chapter was twofold: (1) to provide you with the ability to describe a problem situation in *matrix notation*; and (2) to show how matrices can be used to solve a system of linear equations. To accomplish these objectives we first presented an introduction to matrix operations involving addition, subtraction, and multiplication. We then showed how a system of linear equations can be written in the matrix form $\mathbf{AX} = \mathbf{B}$, and how the solution to the system of equations depends upon obtaining the inverse of the matrix $\mathbf{A}$; that is, $\mathbf{X} = \mathbf{A}^{-1}\mathbf{B}$.

The remaining sections of the chapter focused on how *elementary row operations* can be used to develop the inverse of a matrix and how the method of elimination of Section 6.2 can be simplified and unified by working only with the coefficients ($\mathbf{A}$) and constant terms ($\mathbf{B}$) in matrix form. The chapter concluded with a brief introduction to the concept of the determinant of a matrix.

1. **Matrix**   A rectangular (or square) array of numbers arranged in rows and columns.
2. **Elements**   The individual entries of a matrix.
3. **Row Vector**   A matrix with one row.
4. **Column Vector**   A matrix with one column.
5. **Order, or Dimension**   The number of rows and columns of a matrix. Thus, if a matrix has m rows and n columns, we say that its order is $m \times n$, or its dimensions are $m \times n$.
6. **Matrix Algebra**   Rules according to which matrices are combined.
7. **Matrix Addition**   If $\mathbf{A}$ and $\mathbf{B}$ are $m \times n$ matrices with elements a_{ij} and b_{ij}, then $\mathbf{A} + \mathbf{B}$ is the $m \times n$ matrix which has the elements $a_{ij} + b_{ij}$. Thus we simply add corresponding elements to compute $\mathbf{A} + \mathbf{B}$.
8. **Matrix Subtraction**   If $\mathbf{A}$ and $\mathbf{B}$ are $m \times n$ matrices with the elements a_{ij} and b_{ij}, then $\mathbf{A} - \mathbf{B}$ is the $m \times n$ matrix which has the elements $a_{ij} - b_{ij}$. Thus we simply subtract corresponding elements to compute $\mathbf{A} - \mathbf{B}$.
9. **Transpose of a Matrix**   If $\mathbf{A}$ is an $m \times n$ matrix with elements a_{ij}, then $\mathbf{A}'$, the *transpose* of $\mathbf{A}$, is an $n \times m$ matrix with the elements $a'_{ij} = a_{ji}$. Thus the first row of $\mathbf{A}'$ is the same as the first column of $\mathbf{A}$, the second row of $\mathbf{A}'$ is the same as the second column of $\mathbf{A}$, and so on.
10. **Scalar Multiplication**   If $\mathbf{A}$ is an $m \times n$ matrix with elements a_{ij} and c is any constant, or *scalar*, then $c\mathbf{A}$ is an $m \times n$ matrix which has the elements ca_{ij}. In other words, every element of $\mathbf{A}$ is multiplied by c.
11. **Matrix Multiplication**   If $\mathbf{A}$ is an $m \times n$ matrix and $\mathbf{B}$ is an $n \times r$

matrix, then their product $C = A \cdot B$ is the $m \times r$ matrix whose elements are

$$c_{ij} = a_{i1}b_{1j} + a_{i2}b_{2j} + \cdots + a_{in}b_{nj}$$

In words, the element c_{ij} in the ith row and the jth column of the product matrix C is obtained by multiplying the ith row of A (looked upon as a row vector) by the jth column of B (looked upon as a column vector).

12. **Identity Matrix**   A square matrix for which the elements on the diagonal from upper left to lower right are 1s and all other elements are 0s.

13. **Inverse of a Matrix**   If A is a square matrix and there exists a square matrix C such that $C \cdot A = I$, where I is the identity matrix of the same order as A, then C is called the inverse of A and it is denoted by A^{-1}.

14. **Augmented Coefficient Matrix**   For a system of linear equations we denote the coefficient matrix by A and the column vector of constant terms by B. The augmented coefficient matrix is formed by combining these two matricies into the one matrix, $(A \mid B)$, where the vertical line serves to separate the elements of the coefficient matrix from the constant terms.

15. **Elementary Row Operations**   Operations used to manipulate the elements in the rows of the augmented coefficient matrix $(A \mid B)$:

   1. *Multiplying each element of a row by the same number, not zero.*

   2. *Adding (subtracting) each element of a row to (from) the corresponding element of another row.*

   3. *Interchanging two rows.*

16. **Determinant of a Matrix**   For a 2×2 matrix A, we refer to the determinant of A as

$$\begin{vmatrix} a_{11} & a_{12} \\ a_{21} & a_{22} \end{vmatrix} = a_{11}a_{22} - a_{21}a_{12}$$

(The determinant of a 3×3 matrix is presented in Section 7.6).

SUPPLEMENTARY EXERCISES

In **Exercises 1–8,** matrices A and B are as shown.

$$A = \begin{pmatrix} -2 & 5 \\ 7 & 6 \end{pmatrix} \qquad B = \begin{pmatrix} 4 & 3 \\ 10 & -6 \end{pmatrix}$$

1. Find $\mathbf{A} + \mathbf{B}$.
2. Find $\mathbf{A} - \mathbf{B}$.
3. Evaluate $\mathbf{A} \cdot \mathbf{B}$.
4. Evaluate $\mathbf{B} \cdot \mathbf{A}$.
5. Find $\mathbf{A}'$.
6. Find $\mathbf{B}'$.
7. Find $2 \cdot \mathbf{A}$.
8. Find $10 \cdot \mathbf{B}$.

In **Exercises 9–13**, matrices $\mathbf{A}$ and $\mathbf{B}$ are as shown.

$$\mathbf{A} = \begin{pmatrix} 2 & 5 & -1 \\ 7 & 3 & 2 \end{pmatrix} \quad \mathbf{B} = \begin{pmatrix} 10 & 4 & -3 \\ 6 & 5 & 1 \end{pmatrix}$$

9. Find $\mathbf{A} + \mathbf{B}$.
10. Find $\mathbf{A} - \mathbf{B}$.
11. Find $\mathbf{B}'$.
12. Evaluate $\mathbf{A} \cdot \mathbf{B}'$.
13. Evaluate $\mathbf{B}' \cdot \mathbf{A}$

In **Exercises 14–17**, vectors $\mathbf{A}$ and $\mathbf{B}$ are as shown.

$$\mathbf{A} = \begin{pmatrix} 5 \\ 10 \\ 15 \end{pmatrix} \quad \mathbf{B} = (1 \quad 2 \quad 3)$$

14. Find $\mathbf{A} \cdot \mathbf{B}$.
15. Compute $\mathbf{A} + \mathbf{B}'$.
16. Evaluate $\mathbf{A}' \cdot \mathbf{A}$.
17. Evaluate $\mathbf{A} \cdot \mathbf{A}'$.
18. A small business has five part-time employees. Vector $\mathbf{H}$ defines the number of hours each employee worked during the previous week, and vector $\mathbf{P}$ contains the pay rate in dollars per hour for each employee. Assume for a particular week that $\mathbf{H}$ and $\mathbf{P}$ are

$$\mathbf{H} = \begin{pmatrix} 20 \\ 25 \\ 10 \\ 15 \\ 30 \end{pmatrix} \quad \mathbf{P} = \begin{pmatrix} 4.50 \\ 5.00 \\ 3.75 \\ 4.00 \\ 4.00 \end{pmatrix}$$

Compute $\mathbf{W} = \mathbf{H}' \cdot \mathbf{P}$. In words, what is $\mathbf{W}$?

19. A hardware store sells three different types of lawnmowers. If vector **A** denotes the number of each type sold, vector **B** denotes the selling price, and vector **C** denotes the cost per unit, answer each question assuming

$$\mathbf{A} = \begin{pmatrix} 6 \\ 10 \\ 5 \end{pmatrix} \qquad \mathbf{B} = \begin{pmatrix} 350 \\ 200 \\ 425 \end{pmatrix} \qquad \mathbf{C} = \begin{pmatrix} 200 \\ 150 \\ 300 \end{pmatrix}$$

(a) Use matrix multiplication to compute the total revenue.
(b) Use matrix multiplication to compute the total cost.
(c) Use matrix subtraction to compute the profit, where profit equals total revenue minus total cost.

20. With reference to Exercise 1, find $\mathbf{A}^{-1}$.

21. With reference to Exercise 1, find $\mathbf{B}^{-1}$.

22. If $\mathbf{A} = \begin{pmatrix} 4 & 5 \\ 2 & 1 \end{pmatrix}$, find $\mathbf{A}^{-1}$.

23. Use the results of Exercise 22, to solve the following system of linear equations.

$$4x_1 + 5x_2 = 19$$
$$2x_1 + x_2 = 5$$

24. Use the results of Exercise 20 to solve the following system of linear equations.

$$-2x_1 + 5x_2 = 14$$
$$7x_1 + 6x_2 = 3$$

25. Use the results of Exercise 21 to solve the following system of linear equations.

$$4x_1 + 3x_2 = 15$$
$$10x_1 - 6x_2 = 42$$

26. Evaluate each determinant.

(a) $\begin{vmatrix} 1 & -2 \\ 2 & -3 \end{vmatrix}$ (d) $\begin{vmatrix} 4 & 3 \\ 10 & -6 \end{vmatrix}$

(b) $\begin{vmatrix} 1 & 4 \\ 2 & 9 \end{vmatrix}$ (e) $\begin{vmatrix} 2 & 1 & -1 \\ 3 & 2 & 5 \\ 1 & 1 & 5 \end{vmatrix}$

(c) $\begin{vmatrix} -2 & 5 \\ 7 & 6 \end{vmatrix}$ (f) $\begin{vmatrix} 1 & 1 & -1 \\ 2 & 1 & 3 \\ 3 & 3 & 1 \end{vmatrix}$

INEQUALITIES
AND SYSTEMS
OF LINEAR
INEQUALITIES

In this chapter we study situations which arise when the equal sign of a linear equation is replaced with $<$, $>$, $\leq$, or $\geq$, called **inequality signs**, and standing for *less than, greater than, less than or equal to,* and *greater than or equal to*, respectively. As you will see from the applications discussed, linear inequalities arise in a great many practical situations. Moreover, the concepts introduced in Section 8.3, where we discuss **systems of linear inequalities**, provide the necessary background for the study of linear programming applications in Chapter 9.

8.1 INEQUALITIES

For any two real numbers a and b, one (and only one) of the following conditions must be true.

1. a equals b, which we write as $a = b$.
2. a is greater than b, which we write as $a > b$.
3. a is less than b, which we write as $a < b$.

Many of the rules which apply to *equalities* apply also to *inequalities,* that is, to expressions involving inequality signs. For example, where $a = b$ and $b = c$ implies that $a = c$ for any real numbers a, b, and c, we now have

Rule 1

$$\text{If } a > b \text{ and } b > c, \text{ then } a > c$$
$$\text{If } a < b \text{ and } b < c, \text{ then } a < c.$$

Also, where $a = b$ implies that $a + c = b + c$ for any real numbers a, b, and c, we now have

Rule 2

> If a > b, then a + c > b + c
> If a < b, then a + c < b + c.

And where $a = b$ and $c = d$ implies that $a + c = b + d$ for any real numbers a, b, c, and d, we now have

Rule 3

> If a > b and c > d, then a + c > b + d
> If a < b and c < d, then a + c < b + d.

EXAMPLE 8.1   Rule 1 is illustrated by the fact that if Mr. Jones makes more money than Ms. Brown and Ms. Brown makes more money than Mr. Smith, then Mr. Jones makes more money than Mr. Smith. Rule 2 is illustrated by the fact that if one car is more expensive than another but the license fee is the same for both cars, then the total amount spent for the first car exceeds that spent for the second. Rule 3 is illustrated by the fact that if Mr. White is older than Mrs. White and Mr. Rogers is older than Mrs. Rogers, then the sum of the ages of the two men exceeds the sum of the ages of the two women.

Although we phrased Rule 2 so that it applies to the addition of equals to unequals, it applies also to the subtraction of equals from unequals. To understand why this is true, note that subtracting 3 is the same as adding -3, subtracting -5 is the same as adding $+5$, and so on. Note, however, that for Rule 3 this kind of argument does not apply— when we subtract unequals from unequals, anything can happen. For example, if $a = 5$, $b = 2$, $c = 12$, and $d = 7$, then $a - c = -7$ and $b - d = -5$. Clearly, -7 is not greater than -5, and thus we see that Rule 3 can not be generally applied for subtraction.

In multiplication by equals, we must be careful when it comes to inequalities. To multiply unequals by equals, we use Rule 4.

Rule 4

> If a > b, then ac > bc when c is positive and
> ac < bc when c is negative.

Observe that when c is positive the direction of the inequality remains the same, but when c is negative the direction of the inequality is reversed. For example, if $a = 5$, $b = 2$, and $c = -1$, we see that $a > b$.

Note, however, that $ac = -5$, and $bc = -2$, so $ac < bc$. Thus we see that multiplying by a negative number reverses the direction of the inequality.

We can also multiply unequals by unequals, provided the numbers are all positive and the inequalities have the same sense (go in the same direction); in that case we have Rule 5.

<table>
<tr><td>Rule 5</td><td>If a, b, c, and d are all positive and a > b and c > d, then ac > bd.</td></tr>
</table>

It should also be observed that Rules 4 and 5 also hold when we substitute $<$ for $>$ and vice versa.

EXAMPLE 8.2   Rule 4 is illustrated by the fact that if a share of IBM costs more than a share of GE, then 50 shares of IBM will cost more than 50 shares of GE; on the other hand, buying 50 shares of IBM will leave one with less money in the bank than buying 50 shares of GE. To illustrate Rule 5, note that if a pound of butter costs more than a pound of margarine, then 5 pounds of butter cost more than 3 pounds of margarine.

Although we phrased Rule 4 so that it applies to the multiplication of unequals by equals, it applies also to the division of unequals by equals. To demonstrate this we have only to point out that dividing by 4 is the same as multiplying by $\frac{1}{4}$, dividing by -7 is the same as multiplying by $-\frac{1}{7}$, and so on. Note however, that this kind of argument does not apply when we divide unequals by unequals, in which case anything can happen. For example, if $a = 10$, $b = 5$, $c = 100$, and $d = 20$, so that $a > b$ and $c > d$, then $\frac{a}{b} = \frac{10}{100} = 0.1$ and $\frac{b}{d} = \frac{5}{20} = 0.25$.

Clearly, $\frac{a}{c} = 0.1$ is not greater than $\frac{b}{d} = 0.25$.

It is customary to refer to $a > b$ and $a < b$ as **strict** (or **strong**) inequalities and to $a \geq b$ (which is read "a is greater than or equal to b") and $a \leq b$ (which is read "a is less than or equal to b") as the corresponding **weak** inequalities. This notation makes it possible to simplify (abbreviate) certain statements involving inequalities. For instance, the statement "the bank pays at least 4 percent interest" can be written as $i \geq 4\%$ (where i is the interest rate) instead of $i > 4\%$ or $i = 4\%$. Similarly, if a job is open to anyone who is at most 45 years old, we can express this by writing $y \leq 45$ (where y is the person's age) instead of $y < 45$ or $y = 45$. It can easily be shown that all the rules which apply to $>$ and $<$ also apply to $\geq$ and $\leq$.

In the study of equations we sometimes distinguish between those that hold for all values of the variable, such as $(x + 1)^2 = x^2 + 2x + 1$, and those that hold only for *some* values of the variable, such as $x + 3 = 5$ (which holds only for $x = 2$). Making a similar distinction in connection with inequalities, we refer to inequalities such as $3 > 2, 5 < 7$, and $x + 2 > x$ as **absolute inequalities**; the first two simply express true relationships between numbers, and the other one holds regardless of what value we might substitute for x. In contrast, $x > 3, 2x - 5 < 7$, and $x^2 > 4$ are called **conditional inequalities**; they hold for *some*, but not all, values of x. Among infinitely many other possibilities, $x > 3$ holds for $x = 5$ and $x = 12$, but not for $x = 0$ or $x = -3$; $2x - 5 < 7$ holds for $x = 1$ and $x = 2$, but not for $x = 6$ or $x = 9$; and $x^2 > 4$ holds for $x = -6$ and $x = 7$, but not for $x = \frac{1}{2}$ or $x = -1$.

EXAMPLE 8.3   Suppose that a used-car dealer budgets $750 for television advertising, and that a local television station charges $80 for a 30-second commercial during the late late show. How many of these commercials can the dealer afford? If x is the number of commercials, their cost is 80x, and we obtain the inequality

$$80x \leq 750$$

which simply expresses the fact that the cost of the commercials must not exceed $750. If we now multiply the expressions on both sides of this inequality by 1/80 (or divide by 80), we get

$$x \leq \frac{750}{80} \quad \text{or} \quad x \leq 9\frac{3}{8}$$

and we find that the used-car dealer can afford at most 9 of these commercials.

EXAMPLE 8.4   Suppose that Mrs. Lewis, who has $5312 in her savings account, wants to use some of her money to buy a certain kind of stock which sells for $74 a share, but she does not want the balance of her savings account to go below $2000. How many shares can she buy? If she buys x shares, she will have to take 74x dollars out of her savings account, which leaves her a balance of $5312 - 74x$ dollars. Since this balance is not supposed to go below $2000, we can write

$$5312 - 74x \geq 2000$$

and the problem is to solve this inequality for x. If we subtract 5312 from the expressions on both sides of the equation (or add −5312 in accordance with Rule 2), we get

$$-74x \geq 3312$$

If we multiply the expressions on the left- and right-hand sides of the inequality by −1, we reverse the direction of the inequality, obtaining

$$74x \leq 3312$$

If we then divide the expressions on both sides of the inequality by 74, we get

$$x \leq \frac{3312}{74} \quad \text{or} \quad x \leq 44\frac{56}{74}$$

Thus, since it is impossible to buy a fraction of a share, Mrs. Lewis can buy at most 44 shares.

To simplify our notation, we sometimes write two inequalities as one and call it a **double inequality**. For instance, if x, the asking price for a piece of property, exceeds $22,000 but is not more than $27,000, we can express this by writing

$$\$22,000 < x \leq \$27,000$$

instead of $x > \$22,000$ *and* $x \leq \$27,000$. This is simply a shorthand notation, and we can still apply the various rules so long as we keep in mind that we are actually dealing with two inequalities.

8.3 ABSOLUTE VALUES

Inequalities can also be simplified by using **absolute values**. The absolute value of any real number x is denoted $|x|$, and by definition

$$|x| = \begin{cases} x & \text{if } x > 0 \\ 0 & \text{if } x = 0 \\ -x & \text{if } x < 0 \end{cases}$$

For example, if $x = 7$, then $|x| = 7$; if $x = -7$, then $|x| = -(-7) = 7$. We use absolute value whenever we are interested in the magnitude of a quantity and not in its sign.

FIGURE 8.1
Diagrams
for Example 8.5

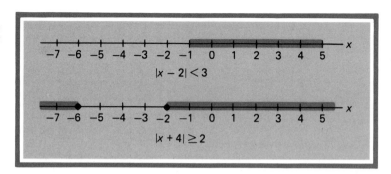

In general, if a is a positive real number, then $|x| < a$ means that x is *numerically less* than a, namely, that x falls *inside* the interval from $-a$ to a; symbolically, $|x| < a$ is thus equivalent to $-a < x < a$. By the same token, $|x| > a$ means that x is *numerically greater* than a, namely, that x falls *outside* the interval from $-a$ to a; symbolically, $|x| > a$ is equivalent to $x < -a$ or $x > a$.

EXAMPLE 8.5 For instance, $|x - 2| < 3$ is equivalent to $-3 < x - 2 < 3$ and, hence, to

$$-1 < x < 5$$

and $|x + 4| \geq 2$ is equivalent to $x + 4 \leq -2$ or $x + 4 \geq 2$ and, hence, to

$$x \leq -6 \quad \text{or} \quad x \geq -2$$

Geometrically, the values of x for which $|x - 2| < 3$ and $|x + 4| \geq 2$ are represented by the intervals shaded in the two diagrams of Figure 8.1. In the second diagram the shaded intervals should actually extend indefinitely in both directions. In addition, the ● at $x = -6$ and $x = -2$ indicates that the point is included in the interval.

EXERCISES

1. State whether each inequality is true or false.

   (a) $15 > -10$ (d) $4 \leq 4$ (g) $\dfrac{2}{5} < \dfrac{3}{6}$

   (b) $12 < 8$ (e) $-4 > -8$ (h) $-2 \geq -1$

   (c) $\dfrac{6}{5} > \dfrac{5}{4}$ (f) $-8 > -6$ (i) $-3 \geq 0$

2. Perform each operation.
   (a) Add 11 to the expressions on both sides of the inequality $x - 11 > 5$.
   (b) Multiply the expressions on both sides of the inequality $\frac{1}{3}x < 5$ by 3.
   (c) Divide the expressions on both sides of the inequality $-2x \le 6$ by -2.
   (d) Subtract 4 from the expressions on both sides of the inequality $3x + 4 > 13$, and then divide the expressions on both sides by 3.
   (e) Add 2 to the expressions on both sides of the inequality $-\frac{1}{5}x - 2 \ge 3$, and then multiply the expressions on both sides by -5.

3. When a variable must satisfy two inequalities, it can happen that the inequalities are *inconsistent* (that is, no value of x can satisfy both) or that one of them is *redundant* (that is, one of the inequalities automatically takes care of the other). Check whether either of these situations arises in each example.
   (a) $x > 5$ and $x > 4$ (d) $x < -1$ and $x > 1$
   (b) $x \ge 3$ and $x \le 4$ (e) $x \le -2$ and $x \ge -3$
   (c) $x < 4$ and $x \ge 7$ (f) $x > -20$ and $x \le 12$

4. Solve each inequality and indicate the result geometrically as in Figure 8.1.
   (a) $4x - 3 > 9$ (d) $7 - 2x > 3$
   (b) $3x + 5 \le 14$ (e) $2 + \frac{x}{2} \ge 3$
   (c) $\frac{1}{7}x - 2 > \frac{3}{7}$ (f) $\frac{3}{x} > \frac{1}{2}$

5. Mr. Knapp has a monthly budget of $5000 to run his office. If his overhead is $1450 and each secretary gets a monthly salary of $680, set up an inequality which must be satisfied by x, the number of secretaries he can employ. At most how many secretaries can he employ?

6. An automatic freight elevator designed to carry a maximum load of 5000 pounds is being used to lift pianos weighing 380 pounds each. Set up an inequality that must be satisfied by x, the number of pianos which the elevator can lift at one time. What is the greatest number of pianos the elevator can lift?

7. A certain health ordinance requires that there be at least 150 cubic feet of "breathing space" per customer in the banquet room of a hotel. Set up an inequality that must be satisfied by x, the number

of customers allowed in a banquet room which is 60 feet long, 40 feet wide, and 12 feet high. What is the greatest number of customers allowed in this banquet room?

8. A broker feels that by 1985 a mutual fund's shares should be worth about $35; in fact, she claims that this figure will not be off either way by more than $2. Set up an inequality for x, the 1985 value of such a mutual fund share, (a) using absolute values; (b) without using absolute values.

9. The professor of a large class in economics claims that 98 percent of the students will get final examination grades within 12 points of the expected norm of 68. If x is a student's final examination grade in this class, set up an inequality which should be satisfied by the grades of 98 percent of the students (a) using absolute values; (b) without using absolute values.

10. Rewrite each inequality without absolute values, and indicate the results graphically as in Figure 8.1.
    (a) $|x| < 5$ (c) $|3x - 7| \geq 8$
    (b) $|x - 3| \leq 1$ (d) $|2x + 3| > 5$

11. If $a > b$ and $c > d$, what relationship ($>$, $<$, or $=$) exists between $a - c$ and $b - d$ in each case?
    (a) $a = 6$, $b = 3$, $c = 2$, and $d = 1$
    (b) $a = 7$, $b = 4$, $c = 5$, and $d = 1$
    (c) $a = 8$, $b = 6$, $c = 4$, and $d = 2$
    What does this demonstrate?

12. If $a > b$ and $c > d$, what relationship ($>$, $<$, or $=$) exists between $\dfrac{a}{c}$ and $\dfrac{b}{d}$ in each case?
    (a) $a = 6$, $b = 2$, $c = 4$, and $d = 1$
    (b) $a = 9$, $b = 2$, $c = 3$, and $d = 2$
    (c) $a = 8$, $b = 6$, $c = 4$, and $d = 3$
    What does this demonstrate?

8.4 SYSTEMS OF LINEAR INEQUALITIES

If the equality sign of a linear equation is replaced by $<$, $>$, $\leq$, or $\geq$, we refer to the resulting inequality as **linear inequality**. For two variables, the *graph* of a linear inequality consists of one of the two regions into which the line representing the corresponding equation divides the plane, and whether or not the line, itself, is included depends on whether the inequality is *strong* or *weak*.

To plot the graph of a linear inequality in two variables, we first draw the line which represents the corresponding equality, and then we pick the correct region by making use of the fact that *the graph of an inequality is the set of all points whose coordinates satisfy (are solutions of) the inequality*. We take an arbitrary point that is *easy to plot* (the origin, for example, provided it does not lie on the line), and simply check whether or not its coordinates satisfy the inequality. If they do, the region containing the particular point is the graph of the given inequality; if they do not, the other region is the graph of the given inequality. Of course, we judge from the inequality, itself, whether the line is to be included.

EXAMPLE 8.6   To illustrate, let us plot the graphs of $2x + 3y < 12$ and $x - y \geq 3$. For the first inequality we begin by drawing the line $2x + 3y = 12$ as in the first diagram of Figure 8.2, and all that remains to be done is to check whether the origin (or some other point not on the line) satisfies the inequality. Since $2 \cdot 0 + 3 \cdot 0$ *is less than* 12, we conclude that the origin belongs to the graph, which thus consists of the region shaded in the first diagram of Figure 8.2. It does not contain the line itself, since $2x + 3y$ must be less than 12 and hence cannot equal 12. For the second inequality we begin by drawing the line $x - y = 3$, as in the second diagram of Figure 8.2. Then, since $x = 0$ and $y = 0$ do *not* satisfy the inequality $x - y \geq 3$, we find that the origin is *not* part of its graph, which thus consists of the region shaded in the second diagram of Figure 8.2. In this case, the line itself *is* included in the graph, and we have indicated this by drawing the line heavier than the other lines of the diagram.

FIGURE 8.2
Graphs of Linear
Inequalities

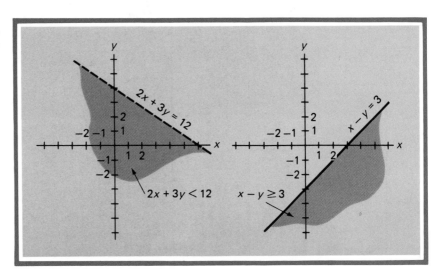

In business and economics, there are many applied problems in which several conditions expressed as linear inequalities must be satisfied at the same time. These conditions may be due to the scarcity of raw materials, restrictions on the time that is available for the manufacture of a product, limited capitalization, shortages in the labor force that can perform a given task, and so on. In general, when we ask for the *solution set* (or the *common solution*) of a system of linear inequalities, we are asking for the set of points whose coordinates satisfy (are solutions of) *all* the inequalities. In practice, this means that we must find the *intersection* of the solution sets of the individual inequalities, namely, *the region which their graphs have in common.*

EXAMPLE 8.6
(Continued)
If we combine the two inequalities of this example, we find that the solution set of the system of linear inequalities

$$2x + 3y < 12$$

$$x - y \geq 3$$

is given by the region common to the shaded regions of the two diagrams of Figure 8.3. Thus the solution of this system of inequalities is given by the shaded region of Figure 8.3, where the heavy line serves to indicate that the lower portion of the line $x - y = 3$ is included.

FIGURE 8.3
Solution of a System of Linear Inequalities

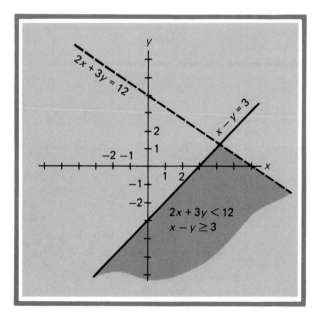

To study a practical application, we shall consider an example of a typical *mixing problem*, which requires that given resources be combined or "mixed" so that they can best be utilized.

EXAMPLE 8.7   A company makes two kinds of dietary food, referred to as food A and food B. These products contain, (among other ingredients) two important food supplements. Specifically, it takes 2 pounds of the first supplement and 1 pound of the second supplement to make a case (1 dozen cans) of food A and 4 pounds of the first supplement and 5 pounds of the second supplement to make a case of food B. Assume that on a given day, 80 pounds of the first supplement and 70 pounds of the second supplement are on hand (but need not be all used up), and the production manager of the company has to decide how many cases of each kind of food should be scheduled for that day.

So far as the work of this chapter is concerned, we shall merely investigate what kind of scheduling is feasible. Obviously, 50 cases of food A would not be feasible since this would require too much of the first supplement; similarly, 12 cases of each kind of food would not be feasible since this would require too much of the second supplement. On the other hand, 10 cases of each kind of food would be feasible, as would be 5 cases of the first kind and 12 cases of the other; observe, however, that in neither situation would all the food supplements be used up. In Chapter 9 we shall also consider the profit which the company makes on each of these two kinds of food; by combining this information with the results obtained here, we shall be able to decide which kind of scheduling is actually the most profitable.

If we let x and y denote the number of cases of foods A and B which the production manager schedules for the given day, the restrictions imposed on x and y by the conditions of the problem are given by the four inequalities

$$x \geq 0$$

$$y \geq 0$$

$$2x + 4y \leq 80$$

$$x + 5y \leq 70$$

The first two inequalities simply state that the quantities of food produced cannot be negative; the third inequality expresses the fact that only 80 pounds of the first supplement are available, while the fourth inequality expresses the fact that only 70 pounds of the second food supplement are available. Clearly, $2x + 4y$ pounds of the first food supplement and $x + 5y$ pounds of the second food supplement are needed to make x cases of food A and y cases of food B.

We thus have a system of *four* linear inequalities in two variables, and to solve it we must find the region which their respective graphs have in common. The first two inequalities tell us that we are limited to points to the right of (or on) the y-axis, and above (or on) the x-axis; in other words, we are restricted to the *first quadrant*. So far as the other two inequalities are concerned, we simply plot the lines $2x + 4y = 80$ and $x + 5y = 70$ as in Figure 8.4, and since $x = 0$ and $y = 0$ (the coordinates of the origin) satisfy both inequalities, we conclude that their respective graphs are the regions which lie below (or on) these two lines. Thus the solution of the whole system of linear inequalities is given by the shaded region of Figure 8.4 and it includes the boundary, as is indicated by the heavy lines.

As can be seen from the diagram of Figure 8.4, the points (10, 10) and (5, 12) are among those falling *inside* the shaded region, and this means that the production manager could schedule the production of 10 cases of each kind of food, or 5 cases of food A and 12 cases of food B. It can also be seen from this diagram that the manager cannot schedule the production of 50 cases of food A or 12 cases of each kind, for both points (50, 0) and (12, 12) lie outside the shaded region of Figure 8.4. This is as far as we shall go for now; to single out a particular point within the shaded region of feasible solutions requires further considerations, such as about the company's profit or the demand for the two products.

FIGURE 8.4
Set of Feasible
Solutions
for Example 8.7

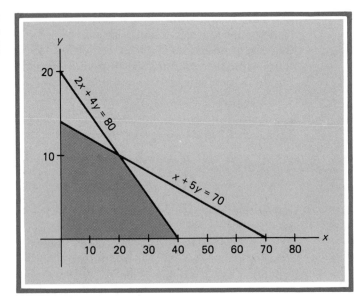

1. Draw a graph of the region which represents each inequality.
   (a) $x + 5y > 10$ (c) $5x + 2y \geq 20$;
   (b) $4x - 7y \leq 14$ (d) $4x + 3y < -24$.

2. Draw a graph of the solution set of each system of linear in-equalities.
   (a) $x + y > 3$ (d) $4x - 3y + 6 > 0$
   $\quad\ x - y > 0$ $\quad\ 3x + 5y + 15 \geq 0$
   (b) $4x - y \leq -11$ (e) $x + y < 4, x + y \geq 1$, and
   $\quad\ x + 2y > 4$ $\quad\ x \leq 3$
   (c) $y - x > 2, y - 3x < 2,$ (f) $3x + 2y < 18, x \geq 0, y \geq 0,$
   $\quad$ and $x \leq 4$ $\quad\ x \leq 5$, and $y \leq 7$

3. Draw a graph of the region which represents the solutions of each system of linear inequalities.
   (a) $x \geq 0, y \geq 0, z \geq 0, x \leq 5, y \leq 3$, and $2x + 3y + z \leq 24$
   (*Hint:* Draw the plane $2x + 3y + z = 24$ by joining the points at which it cuts the coordinate axes.)
   (b) $x \geq 0, y \geq 0, z \geq 0, x + y + 2z \leq 6$, and $x + z \leq 3$
   (*Hint:* Draw the plane $x + y + 2z = 6$ by joining the points at which it cuts the coordinate axes, and draw the plane $x + z = 3$ by joining the points at which it cuts the x- and z-axes, and then drawing lines through these points which are parallel to the y-axis.)

4. In a 60-minute "late movie" shown on television, anywhere from 2 to 5 minutes are devoted to public service announcements, and at least 10 minutes are devoted to commercials.
   (a) If x is the number of minutes devoted to commercials and y is the number of minutes actually taken up by the movie, give the four inequalities which completely determine what values can be assumed by x and y.
   (b) Sketch the region of feasible solutions and check whether it contains the points (12, 44), (11, 42), (15, 40), (8, 49), (18, 40), and (12, 57).

5. A manufacturer makes prefabricated desks and bookcases. The desks cost $25 to produce and require 3 cubic feet of storage space, while the bookcases cost $12 to produce and require 2 cubic feet of storage space.
   (a) If the manufacturer schedules the production of x desks and y bookcases, what inequalities must be satisfied by x and y if the total production cost must not exceed $52,000 and the total storage space available is 6800 cubic feet?

(b) Check whether the region of feasible solutions contains the points (2,000, 500), (1,500, 1,000), (1,800, 600), and (1,000, 4,000).

6. A baker wants to make two kinds of cookies, which both require pecans and walnuts as ingredients. A dozen of the first kind requires 3 ounces of pecans and 4 ounces of walnuts, and a dozen of the second kind requires 2 ounces of pecans and 5 ounces of walnuts.

   (a) If the baker plans to bake x dozen of the first kind and y dozen of the second kind, what inequalities must be satisfied by x and y if there are only 3 pounds of pecans and 5 pounds, 12 ounces of walnuts?

   (b) Sketch the region of feasible solutions and check whether it contains the points (10, 10), (9, 10), and (6, 15).

7. Mr. Jones is told by his doctor that he should supplement his daily diet with *at least* 50 milligrams of calcium and 8 milligrams of iron. He cannot buy these minerals separately, but 5 milligrams of calcium and 2 milligrams of iron are contained in each vitamin pill Q, while 10 milligrams of calcium and 1 milligram of iron are contained in each vitamin pill R.

   (a) If Mr. Jones takes x vitamin pills Q and y vitamin pills R per day, what linear inequalities must be satisfied by x and y in addition to $x \geq 0$ and $y \geq 0$ so that he will get enough of these mineral supplements?

   (b) Sketch the region of feasible solutions, and check whether it contains the points (9, 1), (1, 5), (5, 2), and (6, 3).

8. A contractor wants to complete three projects that require, respectively, 2000, 3000, and 2000 hours of labor. For the time period in which she wants to complete these projects, her work force can provide her with 5000 hours of regular time and 2000 hours of overtime.

   (a) If x hours of regular time are used to finish the first project and y hours of regular time are used to finish the second project, express in terms of x and y the amount of overtime that will be needed to complete the first project, the amount of overtime that will be needed to complete the second project, and the amounts of regular time and overtime that will be needed to complete the third project.

   (b) Determine the six inequalities that must be satisfied by x and y, sketch the region of feasible solutions, and check whether it contains the points (1500, 1800), (800, 2000), (1500, 2500), and (600, 3200).

9. Among the three secretaries working for the president of a com-

pany, Rose takes 2 minutes to answer a certain kind of form letter, Betty takes 3 minutes, and Robert takes 4 minutes.

(a) If only one typewriter is in working condition and 8 of these letters have to be answered within a maximum time of 20 minutes, what inequalities must be satisfied by x, y, and $8 - x - y$, the number of letters answered, respectively, by Rose, Betty, and Robert?

(b) Sketch the region of feasible solutions. Also, since x and y must be positive integers or zero, give the coordinates of all feasible points and indicate in each case how many letters are answered by Rose, by Betty, and by Robert.

10. A caterer, who can provide food for at most 600 persons on any one evening, is asked to provide the food for three parties given the same night. She is told that at the first party there will be at most 150 persons and at the second party there will be at most 250 persons.

(a) If x, y, and z denote the number of persons attending these three parties, what inequalities will have to be satisfied by x, y, and z so that the caterer will not run short on food?

(b) Sketch the region of feasible solutions. (*Hint:* Draw the plane $x + y + z = 600$ by joining the points at which the plane cuts the coordinate axes; also find the point on this plane for which $x = 150$ and $y = 250$.)

11. The manager of a supermarket has a maximum of 3800 cubic feet of storage space available for three kinds of merchandise, for which he can spend at most $19,000. The first kind of merchandise comes in 5-cubic-foot cartons costing $20 apiece, the second kind comes in 3-cubic-foot cartons costing $50 apiece, and the third kind comes in 4-cubic-foot cartons costing $20 apiece.

(a) If the manager of the supermarket orders x cartons of the first kind of merchandise, y cartons of the second kind, and z cartons of the third kind, what inequalities must be satisfied by x, y, and z?

(b) Sketch the region of feasible solutions. (*Hint:* Draw each plane by joining the points at which it cuts the coordinate axes.)

(c) Check whether the following points are in the region of feasible solutions: (600, 120, 50), (500, 200, 20), (550, 150, 40), and (608, 0, 190).

12. The personnel manager of a large department store can hire at most 7 of 15 applicants for sales positions, of which 5 have had no experience, 4 have had limited experience, and 6 have had extensive experience.

(a) If the personnel manager hires, respectively, x, y, and z applicants from these three groups, what inequalities will have to be satisfied by these variables?

(b) Sketch the region of feasible solutions and check whether it contains the points (1, 5, 1), (0, 3, 2), (3, 2, 3), (0, 0, 6), (2, 0, 4), and (1, 2, 5).

SUMMARY

Throughout the first seven chapters of this text we studied several types of problem situations which can be described by linear equations. In this chapter we introduced a different type of situation which arises when the equal sign of a linear equation is replaced with $<$, $>$, $\leq$, or $\geq$, creating an inequality which we call a *linear inequality*. A major objective of the chapter was to demonstrate how systems of linear inequalities can by used to describe problems in which several conditions expressed as linear inequalities must be satisfied at the same time.

GLOSSARY

1. **Linear Inequality**   An expression which arises when the equal sign of a linear equation is replaced with $<$ (less than), $>$ (greater than), $\leq$ (less than or equal to), or $\geq$ (greater than or equal to).

2. **Absolute Value**   The absolute value of any real number x is denoted by $|x|$, and by definition

$$|x| = \begin{cases} x & \text{if } x > 0 \\ 0 & \text{if } x = 0 \\ -x & \text{if } x < 0 \end{cases}$$

SUPPLEMENTARY EXERCISES

1. Which inequalities are true and which are false?
   - (a) $-2 > 4$
   - (b) $4 < -3$
   - (c) $\dfrac{3}{5} > \dfrac{6}{7}$
   - (d) $-5 > -6$
   - (e) $-9 > -4$

2. Which inequalities are true and which are false?
   - (a) $12 > -9$
   - (b) $13 < 10$
   - (c) $\dfrac{5}{4} > \dfrac{4}{3}$
   - (d) $3 \geq 3$
   - (e) $-6 > -8$
   - (f) $-5 > -3$
   - (g) $\dfrac{2}{5} < \dfrac{3}{6}$
   - (h) $-1 \geq -1$
   - (i) $-2 \geq 0$

3. Perform each operation.
   (a) Add 12 to the expressions on both sides of the inequality $x - 12 > 3$.
   (b) Multiply the expressions on both sides of the inequality $\frac{1}{2}x < 4$ by 2.
   (c) Multiply the expressions on both sides of the inequality $-3x \leq 6$ by $-\frac{1}{3}$.
   (d) Subtract 4 from the expressions on both sides of the inequality $2x + 4 > 7$.
   (e) Divide the expressions on both sides of the inequality $-5x < 15$ by -5.

4. Solve each inequality and indicate the result geometrically, as in Figure 8.1.
   (a) $5x + 5 \leq 45$ (c) $\frac{2}{3}x - \frac{4}{3} > 8$
   (b) $3x - 4 \geq 11$

5. Solve the following inequalities and indicate the result graphically, as in Figure 8.1.
   (a) $2x - 3 > 5$ (c) $\frac{1}{2}x - 2 > \frac{3}{2}$ (e) $3 + \frac{x}{3} \geq 1$
   (b) $3x + 2 \leq 14$ (d) $5 - 2x > 3$ (f) $\frac{2}{x} > \frac{3}{4}$

   (*Hint:* Note that x cannot be negative or zero in part (f).)

6. The sales manager of a department store predicts that next year's sales, x, will be within $200,000 of $3,000,000. Set up inequalities for x.

7. A grape-growers association has estimated that the selling price (p) for this year's grapes will be between $380 and $420 per ton. Write an inequality that expresses the association's price estimate.

8. The service manager at an automobile dealership believes that the total cost for repairing a customer's car will be between $250 and $400. Write an inequality that expresses the service manager's estimate.

9. A stockbroker claims that during the next 6 months the price of a certain stock will stay within $2.50 of its current price of $58.25. Express the broker's claim in terms of inequalities for x, the price of the stock, (a) using absolute values; (b) without using absolute values.

10. Rewrite each inequality without absolute values and indicate the result graphically, as in Figure 8.1.
    (a) $|2x - 5| \leq 9$ (b) $|x + 4| \geq 6$ (c) $|x| > 4$

11. Rewrite each inequality without absolute values and indicate the result graphically, as in Figure 8.1.

    (a) $|2x - 5| \leq 3$ (b) $|3x + 1| > 4$ (c) $|x + 5| \geq 1$

12. Draw the graph of the solution set of each system of inequalities.

    (a) $x + y \geq 9$ (b) $3x - y \leq 2$ (c) $2x - 5y > 15$
        $x - y \leq 1$ $x + 3y > 5$ $3x + y \leq 3$

13. Draw a graph of the region which represents each inequality.

    (a) $x + 2y > 6$ (c) $2x + 5y \geq 20$
    (b) $3x - 4y \leq 12$ (d) $3x + 4y < -12$

14. Draw a graph of the solutions set of each system of linear inequalities.

    (a) $x - y > 0$ (d) $4x - 3y + 11 > 0$
        $x + y > 4$ $3x + 5y + 1 \geq 0$
    (b) $4x - y \leq -2$ (e) $x + y < 5, x + y \geq 2,$
        $x + 2y > 1$ $x \leq 4,$ and $y < 2$
    (c) $y - x > 1$ (f) $x \geq 0, y \geq 0$
        $2y - 3x < 2$ $x \leq 5, y \leq 8$
           $x \leq 2$ $3x + 2y < 19$

15. A manufacturer makes two kinds of glass trays. The more solid ones cost $5.00 to produce and $0.20 to ship, while the more flimsy ones cost $2.00 to produce and $0.40 to ship.

    (a) If the manufacturer schedules the production of x of the more solid trays and y of the more flimsy trays, what inequalities must be satisfied by x and y if the total production cost must not exceed $3000 and the total shipping cost must not exceed $160?

    (b) Sketch the region of feasible solutions, and check whether it contains the points (500, 150), (580, 110), and (400, 210).

16. A jeweler buys gold from three different suppliers, among which the first can sell her at most 30 ounces, the second can sell her at most 50 ounces, and the third can sell her all she wants.

    (a) If x, y, and z denote the number of ounces the jeweler orders from each of these suppliers, what inequalities must be satisfied by x, y, and z if the jeweler's order does not exceed 120 ounces?

    (b) Sketch the region of feasible solutions. (*Hint:* Draw the plane $x + y + z = 120$ by joining the points at which the plane cuts the coordinate axes; also find the point on this plane for which $x = 30$ and $y = 50$.)

AN INTRODUCTION TO LINEAR PROGRAMMING

In recent years, a great deal of progress has been made in solving problems involving the allocation of limited resources to meet desired goals. The primary objective of these problems is to plan (or program) activities so that a required job can be done most efficiently with a given labor force, goods can be manufactured most economically with given ingredients, merchandise can be distributed at a minimum cost with existing facilities, and so on. The programming models we shall discuss in this chapter are all **linear models**; that is, we shall be interested in maximizing (or minimizing) linear expressions of the form

$$c_1 x_1 + c_2 x_2 + \cdots + c_k x_k$$

where the x's are variables and the c's are known constants, and where the x's are subject to **restrictions** (**limitations**, or **constraints**) expressed in terms of linear equations or linear inequalities. Hence we refer to these methods as **linear programming**. The linear expressions we maximize or minimize are referred to as **objective functions**, since they pertain to the objectives we are trying to achieve.

9.1 GRAPHICAL SOLUTIONS

A large class of linear programming problems consist of "mixing" problems, in which given resources must be combined, or "mixed," to produce specific outputs in the most efficient way.

EXAMPLE 9.1 Recall the problem introduced in Example 8.7, where two kinds of food supplements had to be mixed in the preparation of two dietary foods, A and B. Under the conditions of that problem, 80 pounds of the first supplement and 70 pounds of the second supplement are available; 2 pounds of the first supplement and 1 pound of the second supplement are needed to produce a case of food A; and 4 pounds of the first supplement and 5 pounds of the second supplement are needed to

FIGURE 9.1
Feasible Region
for Example 9.1

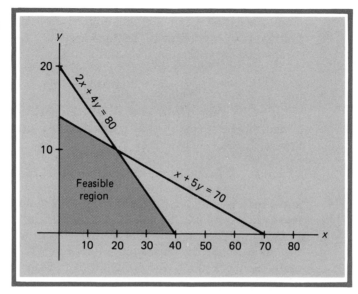

produce a case of food B. Using x and y to denote the number of cases of foods A and B that are to be scheduled for production, we expressed the restrictions or constraints imposed on these variables as

$$x \geq 0, \quad y \geq 0, \quad 2x + 4y \leq 80, \quad \text{and} \quad x + 5y \leq 70$$

and we showed that the solution set of this system of linear inequalities is given by the shaded region of Figure 8.4, which we have reproduced as Figure 9.1. From now on, we shall refer to such a solution set as the **region of feasible solutions,** or simply the **feasible region.**

If we now add the information that the company makes a profit of $3.00 per case of food A and a profit of $10.00 per case of food B, we can ask for the values of x and y that will maximize the company's profit; that is, the values of x and y for which

$$3x + 10y$$

is a maximum.

At a first glance it may seem that the production manager should forget about food A and concentrate on producing only food B, and this would be correct if there were an unlimited supply of all the necessary ingredients. Note, however, that if production is limited to food B, the maximum amount of B that can be produced is 14 cases. This would use up all of the second food supplement and yield a profit of $140, but $80 - 14(4) = 24$ pounds of the first supplement would be left over.

Since food A uses more of the first supplement (per case) than food B, it may be more profitable, perhaps, to produce a few cases of food A and fewer than 14 cases of food B. Indeed, before we start looking for the most profitable way of scheduling the production of these two dietary foods, let us see whether it might be possible to arrange things so that the company's profit will be increased to, for instance, $150. This means that we must choose x and y so that

$$3x + 10y = 150$$

while at the same time $x \geq 0$, $y \geq 0$, $2x + 4y \leq 80$, and $x + 5y \leq 70$. Geometrically speaking, this means that we must look for a point which lies on the line

$$3x + 10y = 150$$

and which is also in the shaded region of Figure 9.1. If we combine the two as in Figure 9.2, it can be seen that the line cuts the shaded region; in fact, any point on the line segment PQ satisfies *all* the conditions. Among them are the points (20, 9) and (10, 12), for example, and it can easily be checked that the production of 20 cases of food A and 9 cases of food B or 10 cases of food A and 12 cases of food B satisfy all the constraints. As you will be asked to verify in Exercise 6 at the end of this section, however, some of the first supplement will be left over in each case, and some of the second supplement will also be left over in the first case.

Instead of asking for a production schedule which will yield a profit of $150, we could have asked for a production schedule which will yield a profit of $50, a profit of $100, a profit of $200, and so on. This means that we would have had to look for points on the lines $3x + 10y = 50$, $3x + 10y = 100$, $3x + 10y = 200$, . . . , which are all

FIGURE 9.2
Feasible Region
for Example 9.1

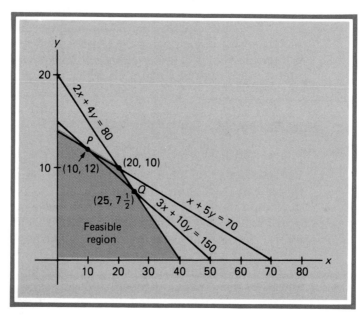

FIGURE 9.3
Feasible Region
for Example 9.1
and Lines
Representing Various
Profits

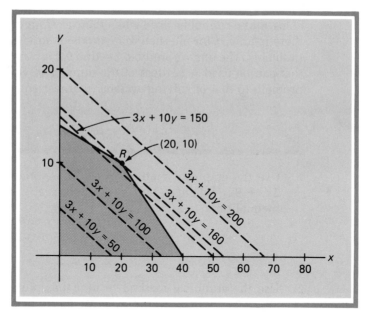

shown in Figure 9.3, together with the line $3x + 10y = 150$. An important feature of these lines is that they are *all parallel*; in fact, we will get a line parallel to $3x + 10y = 150$ no matter what profit we substitute for \$150, since the x- and y-coefficients (which determine the slope) are always the same. It can also be seen from Figure 9.3 that when the profit is decreased the line will move closer to the origin and when the profit is increased the line will move farther away. This suggests that we look for the line which is parallel to the line $3x + 10y = 150$, which is as far away from the origin as possible, and which has at least one point in common with the feasible region. Clearly, any point which is on this line and also in the feasible region will yield a maximum profit.

As can be seen from Figure 9.3, the line with all these properties is the one we have drawn parallel to $3x + 10y = 150$ through the point $(20, 10)$, namely, through the point R in which the two lines $2x + 4y = 80$ and $x + 5y = 70$ intersect. We have thus solved the problem of scheduling the company's production—its profit will be a maximum (in fact, it will equal $3 \cdot 20 + 10 \cdot 10 = \$160$) corresponding to the production of 20 cases of food A and 10 cases of food B. Observe that the point $(20, 10)$ lies on the boundary of the feasible region and that all the available amounts of the two food supplements $(20 \cdot 1 + 10 \cdot 5 = 70$ pounds of the second supplement) will be used up.

The geometrical, or graphical, method of solving linear programming problems works nicely for two variables, but it may involve configurations that are difficult to picture when there are three variables, and it cannot be used when there are four or more variables. Thus there is a need for alternative methods of solving linear programming problems. The one we study in Section 9.2 is a simple algebraic method that can be used regardless of the number of variables; it reduces the problem to that of solving systems of linear equations.

EXERCISES

1. Use the graphical method to find the solution which maximizes $2x_1 + 9x_2$, where x_1 and x_2 are nonnegative and must satisfy the inequalities

$$2x_1 + 3x_2 \leq 6$$

$$x_1 - x_2 \leq 1$$

2. Use the graphical method to find the solution which maximizes $3x_1 + 2x_2$, where x_1 and x_2 must be nonnegative and satisfy the inequalities

$$4x_1 + x_2 \leq 200$$

$$x_1 + x_2 \leq 80$$

$$\frac{1}{3}x_1 + x_2 \leq 60$$

3. Refer to Exercise 5 at the end of Section 8.4. How should the manufacturer schedule the production of the prefabricated furniture, if the manufacturer makes a profit of $12 on each desk, a profit of $7 on each bookcase, and the objective is to maximize total profit? What is this maximum profit?

4. Refer to Exercise 6 at the end of Section 8.4. How should the baker schedule the production of the two kinds of cookies in each case?
   (a) The baker makes a profit of 40¢ on each dozen of the first kind and a profit of 44¢ on each dozen of the second kind.
   (b) The baker makes a profit of 68¢ on each dozen of the first kind and a profit of 44¢ on each dozen of the second kind?

5. With reference to Example 9.1, suppose that the company which makes the dietary food decides to add a third food supplement, of which 1.4 pounds are required for a case of food A, 4 pounds are required for a case of food B, and 65 pounds are available on that day. Assuming that the profit figures remain unchanged, how many cases of each kind of food should the production manager schedule for that day to maximize the company's profit? What is the maximum profit?

6. With reference to Example 9.1, determine the amount of each food

supplement that is left over when they produce 20 cases of food A and 9 cases of food B, and when they produce 10 cases of food A and 12 cases of food B.

7. A company has the capacity to manufacture a maximum of 240 radios per day. The three kinds it makes require, respectively, 9 ounces, 6 ounces, and 2 ounces of copper wire, of which 900 ounces are available on a given day. How many radios of each kind should they produce that day to maximize their profit in each case?
   (a) The profits on the three kinds of radios are $6, $2, and $2 per radio, respectively.
   (b) The profits on the three kinds of radios are $4, $4, and $2 per radio, respectively.

8. Refer to Exercise 10 at the end of Section 8.4. What attendance at the three parties would maximize the caterer's total receipts in each case?
   (a) The caterer gets $3.25 per person at the first party, $3.50 per person at the second party, and $3.00 per person at the third party.
   (b) The caterer gets $2.50 per person at the first party, $3.25 per person at the second party, and $3.50 per person at the third party.
   Also find the corresponding total receipts.

9. Refer to Exercise 11 at the end of Section 8.4. How many cartons of each kind of merchandise should the supermarket manager order to maximize total profit in each case.
   (a) The profits on a carton of each of the three kinds of merchandise are $20, $10, and $15, respectively.
   (b) The profits on a carton of each of the three kinds of merchandise are $10, $20, and $8 respectively.
   Also find the corresponding total profits.

9.2 EXTREME POINTS AND THE OPTIMAL SOLUTION

Note that in Example 9.1 the optimal solution is given by a point on the boundary (the outside edge, or surface) of the feasible region. In linear programming terminology, such vertices or corners of the feasible region are referred to as **extreme points**. In general, it can be shown that for linear programming problems involving any number of variables, *the optimal solution to a linear system can be found at an extreme point of the feasible region.* It can also be shown that if the solution is not unique, at least two solutions must correspond to extreme points of the feasible region, and every point on the line segment joining them is also a solution.

Using these results (which are treated more formally in some of the books to which we refer to at the end of the chapter), we can now solve any linear programming problem by listing all the extreme points of the feasible region, calculating the corresponding values of the objective function (that is, the corresponding values of the linear expression which is to be maximized or minimized), and then choosing the extreme point(s) at which it is a maximum or minimum.

EXAMPLE 9.1
(Continued)

In Figure 9.4 we show the feasible region for the dietary food problem of Example 9.1. The four extreme points are identified as ①, ②, ③, and ④. Specifically, extreme point ① is the origin, extreme point ② occurs where the line $x + 5y = 70$ intersects, or cuts, and y-axis, extreme point ③ is the point of intersection of the lines $x + 5y = 70$ and $2x + 4y = 80$, and extreme point ④ is the point at which the line $2x + 4y = 80$ intersects the x-axis. The expression we want to maximize in this example, the company's profit, is given by $3x + 10y$, and if we calculate its value for each extreme point we obtain these values.

Extreme Point	Coordinates of Extreme Point (x, y)	Value of $3x + 10y$
①	(0, 0)	0
②	(0, 14)	140
③	(20, 10)	160
④	(40, 0)	120

As can be seen from this table, the company's profit is maximum at the point (20, 10).

The method of this section requires that we locate all the vertices, or extreme points, of the feasible region. In the two-variable case, the boundary of the feasible region consists of lines, which are obtained by substituting equal signs for the inequality signs in the restrictions (linear inequalities) imposed on the two variables. Furthermore, each extreme point of the feasible region is a point of intersection of two of these lines, and its coordinates are obtained by solving the corresponding system of two linear equations in the two variables. In a three-variable case, the boundary of the feasible region consists of planes, which are obtained by substituting equal signs for the inequality signs in the restrictions (linear inequalities) imposed on the three variables. Furthermore, each extreme point of the feasible region is a point of

FIGURE 9.4
Extreme Points
and the Optimal
Solution

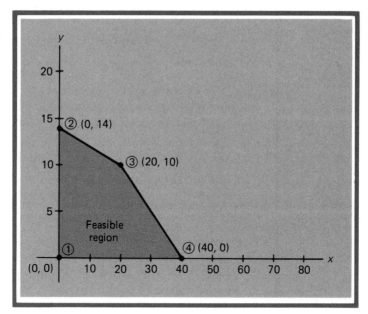

intersection of three of these planes, and its coordinates are obtained by solving a corresponding system of three linear equations in the three variables.

For problems that involve four or more variables, we not only cannot picture the region of feasible solutions, but the amount of algebraic detail involved in identifying all the extreme points becomes too cumbersome. Fortunately, a good deal of this work can be avoided by using an algebraic method called the **Simplex method.** This method, which was invented by G. B. Dantzig in 1947, is a highly efficient trial-and-error technique in which we begin with a feasible solution and check to see whether it maximizes (or minimizes) the *objective function.* If not, which is usually the case, the Simplex method indicates the direction we must take in searching for a maximum (or minimum) solution. A very important feature of the Simplex method is that it utilizes to great advantage some of the matrix techniques of Chapter 7.

EXERCISES

1. Rework Exercise 1 at the end of Section 9.1 by computing the value of $2x_1 + 9x_2$ for each extreme point.

2. Rework Exercise 2 at the end of Section 9.1 by computing the value of $3x_1 + 2x_2$ for each extreme point.

3. Rework Exercise 3 at the end of Section 9.1 by computing the value of total profit for each extreme point.

4. Rework both parts of Exercise 4 at the end of Section 9.1 by calculating the baker's profit for each extreme point.

5. Rework part (a) of Exercise 7 at the end of Section 9.1 by listing the vertices of the region of feasible solutions, calculating the company's total profit on the radios for each vertex, and thus determine how the profit can be maximized.

6. Use the method of this section to find the maximum value of $3.5x + 2.0y$, where x and y must be nonnegative and satisfy the inequalities $x + y \leq 6$, $5x + 3y \leq 20$, and $x - y \leq 1$.

7. With reference to Example 9.1, suppose that the company wants to expand its line by including two other dietary foods, C and D. A case of food C requires 3 pounds of each food supplement, while a case of food D requires 5 pounds of the first food supplement and 2 pounds of the second. If all other figures are the same as before, and a case of foods C and D yield profits of $8.00 and $9.00, respectively, how should one schedule the production of the four dietary foods to maximize the company's profit?

9.3 THE SIMPLEX METHOD

In the dietary-food problem of Example 9.1, we used the letters x and y to denote the amounts of foods A and B scheduled for production. As we consider linear programming problems with more and more variables, the practice of selecting a different letter to identify each variable becomes impractical, so the usual practice is to use the letter x with a subscript to identify each problem variable. In the dietary-food problem, if we let x_1 and x_2 (instead of x and y) denote the amounts of foods A and B scheduled for production, we can restate the problem as

$$\text{max} \quad 3x_1 + 10x_2$$

s.t.

$$2x_1 + 4x_2 \leq 80$$

$$x_1 + 5x_2 \leq 70$$

$$x_1, x_2 \geq 0$$

In the abbreviated form shown above *max* stands for *maximize*, *s.t.* stands for *subject to*, and $x_1, x_2 \geq 0$ simply denotes the fact that both x_1 and x_2 must be nonnegative variables. We refer to this mathematical statement, or formulation, as the *mathematical model* for the dietary-food problem.

To illustrate some of the main features of the Simplex method we shall initially restrict our discussion to mathematical models such as the one in the dietary-food problem. That is, we shall consider maximization linear programming problems involving less-than-or-equal-to constraints.

The first step of the Simplex method is the conversion of linear inequalities into linear equations. For less-than-or-equal-to constraints, this is done by adding a nonnegative **slack variable** to the expression on the left-hand side of the inequality. To illustrate this approach, recall the first constraint of the dietary food problem,

$$2x_1 + 4x_2 \leq 80$$

In order to make this constraint an equality we must add something on the left-hand side to make up for any difference between $2x_1 + 4x_2$ and 80. For example, the production of 8 cases of food A ($x_1 = 8$) and 10 cases of food B ($x_2 = 10$) results in the use of $2(8) + 4(10) = 16 + 40 = 56$ pounds of the first food supplement. Since 80 pounds are available, this production combination results in $80 - 56 = 24$ pounds of the first supplement left over. In linear programming terminology, this 24 pounds is called *slack*.

Note that the amount of slack depends upon the value of x_1 and x_2. Thus the amount we add to the left-hand side of the constraint must be variable. If we let s_1 denote the variable that is to be added to the first constraint in order to provide the necessary slack, we can rewrite the first constraint as

$$2x_1 + 4x_2 + s_1 = 80$$

Since s_1 can be interpreted as the amount of slack associated with the first constraint, s_1 is referred to as a *slack variable*. Similarly, if we add the slack variable s_2 to the left-hand side of the second constraint

$$x_1 + 5x_2 \leq 70$$

we can rewrite this constraint as

$$x_1 + 5x_2 + s_2 = 70$$

Using the slack variables s_1 and s_2, we can restate the dietary-food problem as

$$\max \quad 3x_1 + 10x_2$$

s.t.

$$2x_1 + 4x_2 + s_1 \qquad = 80$$
$$x_1 + 5x_2 \qquad + s_2 = 70$$
$$x_1, x_2, s_1, s_2 \geq 0$$

Note that since the slack variables do not contribute to profit, the profit coefficient associated with each slack variable is zero, and hence the objective function can be written as $3x_1 + 10x_2 + 0x_3 + 0x_4$, or simply $3x_1 + 10x_2$.

The form shown above, in which the constraints of the linear programming problem are written as linear equations, is referred to as the **standard form** of the problem. Thus the first step of the Simplex method is to write the linear programming problem in standard form. It is important to realize that the optimal solution to the standard form of the problem is the same as the optimal solution to the original problem. Thus using standard form does not change the basic problem, but only the way in which we write the constraints.

basic feasible *solutions*   What we have just done does not look like much of a simplification. In Example 9.1 we now have four variables instead of two. This does make it seem as if the problem has become more complicated, but there are compensations. For instance, we can now use a theorem which tells us that many of the variables must be zero—specifically,

> *if we have to maximize a linear expression in k nonnegative vari-*
> *ables which must satisfy m linear inequalities, and we introduce m*
> *nonnegative slack variables to convert the inequalities into equa-*
> *tions (as in the dietary-food example), then at least k of the k + m*
> *variables must be zero in the final solution.*

For example, for the dietary-food problem involving the variables x_1, x_2, s_1, and s_2, this theorem states that at least two of the four variables must be zero in the final solution. Note that although the connection may not be immediately apparent, this is simply another way of saying that the solution of a linear programming problem must correspond to an extreme point of the feasible region.

Thus *the key to the solution of any linear programming problem is to find the k variables which equal zero in the final solution;* once this has been accomplished, the only thing that remains to be done is to solve a system of m linear equations in the other m variables. For instance, if we knew which two variables are zero in the final solution of the dietary-food example, we could substitute zero for them in

$$2x_1 + 4x_2 + s_1 \qquad = 80$$
$$x_1 + 5x_2 \qquad + s_2 = 70$$

and this would leave us with the simple problem of having to solve the resulting system of two linear equations in the other two variables.

In the Simplex method, we look for these k variables beginning with a **basic feasible solution**, an extreme point of the feasible region which corresponds to a given set of k variables equaling zero. We then check whether it solves the problem, and if not, we go on to another extreme point by a method which we shall discuss in the next part of this section. Note that it is a simple matter to find a basic feasible solution when the constant terms of the linear equations are *all positive*—we simply let the *original k variables equal zero, so that the slack variables will be equal to the constant terms.*

EXAMPLE 9.1
(Continued)

As we already indicated in the dietary-food example, we have the two equations

$$2x_1 + 4x_2 + s_1 = 80$$
$$x_1 + 5x_2 + s_2 = 70$$

and it can be seen by inspection that if we let $x_1 = 0$ and $x_2 = 0$, the solutions for the other two variables are $s_1 = 80$ and $s_2 = 70$. Thus $x_1 = 0$, $x_2 = 0$, $s_1 = 80$, and $s_2 = 70$ is a *basic feasible solution;* whether it is the optimal solution is another matter, about which we shall not worry at this time.

---

transformation of feasible solutions

Based upon the graphical solution of the dietary-food problem, we know that the basic feasible solution $x_1 = 0$, $x_2 = 0$, $s_1 = 0$, and $s_2 = 70$ does not provide the optimal solution to the problem. In fact, the company's profit corresponding to this basic feasible solution is

$$3x_1 + 10x_2 = 3(0) + 10(0) = 0$$

Thus we shall have to look for other basic feasible solutions, namely, for other extreme points of the feasible region. In the Simplex method we proceed step by step from the initial basic feasible solution to other basic feasible solutions; in each step we change one of the zero variables to a nonzero variable (or, at least, to a variable which need not be zero), and vice versa, until the problem is solved.

EXAMPLE 9.1
(Continued)

To illustrate this technique, let us refer again to the dietary-food problem, where we had the system of equations

$$2x_1 + 4x_2 + s_1 = 80$$
$$x_1 + 5x_2 + s_2 = 70$$

and the initial basic feasible solution $x_1 = 0$, $x_2 = 0$, $s_1 = 80$, and $s_2 = 70$. Suppose, for the sake of argument, that we want to move from this extreme point at which $x_1 = 0$ and $x_2 = 0$ to the one which corresponds to $x_1 = 0$ and $s_2 = 0$. (Of course, we could substitute $x_1 = 0$ and $s_2 = 0$ in the above equations and solve for x_2 and s_1, but this is precisely the kind of work we want to avoid in problems where we have to work with a great number of variables.)

In the Simplex method we go from the case where $x_1 = 0$ and $x_2 = 0$ to the case where $x_1 = 0$ and $s_2 = 0$ by performing *elementary row operations* (see Section 7.5) on the augmented matrix $(\mathbf{A} \mid \mathbf{B})$ of coefficients and constant terms. For our example we have

$$\left(\begin{array}{cccc|c} 2 & 4 & 1 & 0 & 80 \\ 1 & 5 & 0 & 1 & 70 \end{array} \right)$$

and it should be observed that the third and fourth columns are like those of a 2×2 *identity matrix*; in fact, this is what made it possible to read the solutions for s_1 and s_2 when x_1 and x_2 are equal to zero. To change this so that we can *read* the solutions for x_2 and s_1 when x_1 and s_2 are equal to zero, we shall have to move the $\begin{smallmatrix}0\\1\end{smallmatrix}$ column from the fourth column of the matrix to the second; in other words, we shall have to convert the augmented matrix to the form

$$\left(\begin{array}{cccc|c} ? & 0 & 1 & ? & ? \\ ? & 1 & 0 & ? & ? \end{array} \right)$$

where the question marks will have to be replaced with numbers by operating on the rows of the matrix $(\mathbf{A} \mid \mathbf{B})$. Observe that this will make the second and third columns of the matrix like those of a 2×2 identity matrix; their order is reversed, but this does not matter.

To change the second element of the first row to 0, we simply subtract $\frac{4}{5}$ of each element of the second row from the corresponding element of the first row, getting $2 - \frac{4}{5}(1) = \frac{6}{5}$, $4 - \frac{4}{5}(5) = 0$, $1 - \frac{4}{5}(0) = 1$, $0 - \frac{4}{5}(1) = -\frac{4}{5}$, and $80 - \frac{4}{5}(70) = 24$, and, hence,

$$\left(\begin{array}{cccc|c} \dfrac{6}{5} & 0 & 1 & -\dfrac{4}{5} & 24 \\ 1 & 5 & 0 & 1 & 70 \end{array} \right)$$

To change the second element of the second row to 1, we have only to divide each element of this row by 5, getting

$$\left(\begin{array}{cccc|c} \dfrac{6}{5} & 0 & 1 & -\dfrac{4}{5} & 24 \\ \dfrac{1}{5} & 1 & 0 & \dfrac{1}{5} & 14 \end{array} \right)$$

which corresponds to the system of equations

$$\frac{6}{5}x_1 \qquad + s_1 - \frac{4}{5}s_2 = 24$$

$$\frac{1}{5}x_1 + x_2 \qquad + \frac{1}{5}s_2 = 14$$

Substituting $x_1 = 0$ and $s_2 = 0$ into these two equations, we can read the solutions for the other two variables as $s_1 = 24$ and $x_2 = 14$, which are simply the new *constant terms*.

So far we have discussed three important aspects of the Simplex method: (1) *the introduction of slack variables to convert linear inequalities into linear equations;* (2) *the theorem according to which at least k of the k + m original and slack variables must be zero in the final solution;* and (3) *the matrix technique, which enables us to transform basic feasible solutions, namely, the method which enabled us to go from one set of k zero solutions to another.* On the other hand, we have not yet learned how to decide whether a given basic feasible solution actually maximizes (or minimizes) the objective function; and if not, how to determine which variable should be deleted from the set of zero solutions, and how to choose the variable which must take its place.

tableau form   To simplify the computations involved in the Simplex method, we begin by setting up the initial **Simplex tableau.** For the dietary-food example, we have the following Simplex tableau.

c's		x_1	x_2	s_1	s_2		Quotients
0	s_1	2	4	1	0	80	$\dfrac{80}{4} = 20$
0	s_2	1	5	0	1	70	$\dfrac{70}{5} = 14$
Solution:		0	0	80	70		
c's:		3	10	0	0		
Indicators:		3	10	0	0		

Entering Departing
variable variable

On top of each column of the coefficient matrix, we indicate the variable to which it belongs, and to the left of each row we indicate which variable can be read from the corresponding equation; that is, the variable that equals the corresponding constant term in the given basic feasible solution. Further to the left we show the coefficients of these variables in the formula for the objective function.

The first line below the augmented matrix contains the basic feasible solution to which the tableau pertains, and the second line contains the corresponding coefficients of the variables in the formula for the objective function. Finally, the third line below the augmented matrix contains the **indicators**, *which are obtained by subtracting from the c (in the second line below the augmented matrix) the sum of the products obtained by multiplying each element of the corresponding column of the augmented matrix by the corresponding c on the extreme left.* Thus for the dietary-food example the indicators were calculated as shown below.

$$\text{Indicator } 1 = \quad 3 - (2 \cdot 0 + 1 \cdot 0) = \quad 3$$

$$\text{Indicator } 2 = 10 - (4 \cdot 0 + 5 \cdot 0) = 10$$

$$\text{Indicator } 3 = \quad 0 - (1 \cdot 0 + 0 \cdot 0) = \quad 0$$

$$\text{Indicator } 4 = \quad 0 - (0 \cdot 0 + 1 \cdot 0) = \quad 0$$

The practical significance of these indicators is provided by the following statement.

> *A given basic solution is not optimal (that is, the value of the objective function can be increased) if at least one of the indicators is positive. Otherwise, the solution maximizes the objective function, although it may not be unique when one or more of the indicators is zero for one of the variables not in solution.*

Thus, since two of the indicators in our initial Simplex tableau are positive, we conclude that the given basic feasible solution is not optimal—that is, it does not maximize the objective function.

The indicators also tell us which variable should be deleted from the set of zero solutions. Since this variable enters the set of variables whose solution need not be zero, it is officially called the **entering variable**. The rule which we follow in selecting the entering variable is:

> *The entering variable corresponds to the column whose indicator is largest.*

Although this will not guarantee that the corresponding improvement of the objective function is a maximum, *we are assured, at least, that we are going in the right direction.* Note that in our example, 10 is the largest indicator and hence x_2 is the entering variable. It is convenient to indicate the entering variable by means of an arrow pointing upward, as in the tableau shown above.

After we have determined the entering variable, the next step is to choose the **departing variable**, the variable which must take the place of the entering variable among the zero solutions. The purpose of the column labeled **quotients** is to determine the departing variable. The elements in this column are obtained by dividing the constant terms, the b's, by the corresponding coefficients of the entering variable. Thus for the dietary-food example, these quotients were obtained by dividing the constant terms, 80 and 70, by the respective elements of the second column of the matrix, 4 and 5. Hence we obtained $80/4 = 20$ and $70/5 = 14$. The significance of these quotients is provided by the following rule.

The departing variable corresponds to the row for which the quotient in the right-hand column is as small as possible, yet nonnegative. *

Since 14 is positive and the smaller of the two quotients on the right-hand side of the tableau, the departing variable is s_2.

To complete the picture, we draw an arrow pointing downward below the column corresponding to the departing variable (s_2), as we did in the tableau shown above. Based upon the above analyses, use of the Simplex method has determined that we must go from the basic feasible solution in which $x_1 = 0$ and $x_2 = 0$ to the basic feasible solution in which $x_1 = 0$ and $s_2 = 0$, a job which was done previously in the preceding subsection. As we showed, the corresponding solutions for x_2 and s_1 are $x_2 = 14$ and $s_1 = 24$. Copying the resulting augmented matrix, we obtain the following *second Simplex tableau*:

c's		x_1	x_2	s_1	s_2		Quotients
0	s_1	$\frac{6}{5}$	0	1	$-\frac{4}{5}$	24	$24 \div \frac{6}{5} = 20$
10	x_2	$\frac{1}{5}$	1	0	$\frac{1}{5}$	14	$14 \div \frac{1}{5} = 70$
Solution:		0	14	24	0		
c's:		3	10	0	0		
Indicators:		1	0	0	-2		

Entering variable (↑) — under x_1 Departing variable (↓) — under s_2

---

*Special problems arise when the smallest of these non-negative quotients is zero or not unique; such situations are referred to as *degeneracies*, and they are discussed in more advanced texts on linear programming.

where the indicators are

$$\text{Indicator 1} = 3 - \left(\frac{6}{5} \cdot 0 + \frac{1}{5} \cdot 10\right) = 1$$

$$\text{Indicator 2} = 10 - (0 \cdot 0 + 1 \cdot 10) = 0$$

$$\text{Indicator 3} = 0 - (1 \cdot 0 + 0 \cdot 10) = 0$$

$$\text{Indicator 4} = 0 - \left(-\frac{4}{5} \cdot 0 + \frac{1}{5} \cdot 10\right) = -2$$

Since indicator 1 is positive, we conclude that the solution is not optimal. Moreover, since indicator 1 is the only positive indicator, x_1 will have to be the *entering variable* for the next step. The quotients that are required for the determination of the departing variable are again shown on the right, and since 20 is the smaller of the two, we find that the departing variable must be s_1. This means that we shall now have to go from the basic feasible solution in which the zero variables are x_1 and s_2 to the basic feasible solution in which the zero variables are s_1 and s_2.

Proceeding as in the subsection "Transformation of Feasible Solutions," we shall thus have to change the augmented matrix

$$\begin{pmatrix} \frac{6}{5} & 0 & 1 & -\frac{4}{5} & 24 \\ \frac{1}{5} & 1 & 0 & \frac{1}{5} & 14 \end{pmatrix}$$

to the form

$$\begin{pmatrix} 1 & 0 & ? & ? & ? \\ 0 & 1 & ? & ? & ? \end{pmatrix}$$

where the question marks will have to be replaced with numbers by performing suitable operations on the rows. This will make the first two columns of the augmented matrix like those of a 2×2 identity matrix, and we will be able to read off the solutions for x_1 and x_2 when s_1 and s_2 are equal to zero.

To change the first element of the second row to 0, we subtract $\frac{1}{6}$ of each element of the first row from the corresponding element of the second row, getting $\frac{1}{5} - \frac{1}{6}\left(\frac{6}{5}\right) = 0$, $1 - \frac{1}{6}(0) = 1$, $0 - \frac{1}{6}(1) = -\frac{1}{6}$, $\frac{1}{5} - \frac{1}{6}\left(-\frac{4}{5}\right) = \frac{1}{3}$, and $14 - \frac{1}{6}(24) = 10$. Then, to change the first element of the first row to 1, we multiply each element of this row by $\frac{5}{6}$, so that the new augmented matrix becomes

$$\begin{pmatrix} 1 & 0 & \dfrac{5}{6} & -\dfrac{2}{3} & \Big| & 20 \\[2mm] 0 & 1 & -\dfrac{1}{6} & \dfrac{1}{3} & \Big| & 10 \end{pmatrix}$$

As can be seen by inspection, the corresponding basic feasible solution is $x_1 = 20$, $x_2 = 10$, $s_1 = 0$, and $s_2 = 0$, and the *third Simplex tableau* becomes

$c's$		x_1	x_2	s_1	s_2	
3	x_1	1	0	$\dfrac{5}{6}$	$-\dfrac{2}{3}$	20
10	x_2	0	1	$-\dfrac{1}{6}$	$\dfrac{1}{3}$	10
Solution:		20	10	0	0	
$c's$:		3	10	0	0	
Indicators:		0	0	$-\dfrac{5}{6}$	$-\dfrac{4}{3}$	

where the indicators are

$$\text{Indicator 1} = 3 - (1 \cdot 3 + 0 \cdot 10) = 0$$

$$\text{Indicator 2} = 10 - (0 \cdot 3 + 1 \cdot 10) = 0$$

$$\text{Indicator 3} = 0 - \left(\frac{5}{6} \cdot 3 - \frac{1}{6} \cdot 10\right) = -\frac{5}{6}$$

$$\text{Indicator 4} = 0 - \left(-\frac{2}{3} \cdot 3 + \frac{1}{3} \cdot 10\right) = -\frac{4}{3}$$

Since none of these indicators is positive, we conclude that the solution is optimal: the company's profit will be a maximum if they produce (and sell) $x_1 = 20$ cases of food A and $x_2 = 10$ cases of food B.

EXERCISES

In **Exercises 1–5**, restate the linear programming problem in standard form and find the basic feasible solution in which the original problem variables are zero.

1. Restate the problem of Exercise 1 at the end of Section 9.1.
2. Restate the problem of Exercise 2 at the end of Section 9.1.

3. Restate the problem of Exercise 3 at the end of Section 9.1.

4. Restate the problem of Exercise 4(a) at the end of Section 9.1.

5. Restate the problem of Exercise 7 at the end of Section 9.1.

6. The following is the *first Simplex tableau* for Exercise 1 at the end of Section 9.1.

c's		X_1	X_2	S_1	S_2		Quotients
0	S_1	2	3	1	0	6	
0	S_2	1	-1	0	1	1	
Solutions:		0	0	6	1		
c's:		2	9	0	0		
Indicators:							

Complete this tableau by calculating the indicators, determining the entering variable, calculating the corresponding quotients, and determining the departing variable.

7. Use the results of Exercise 6 to complete the Simplex solution.

8. The following is the *second Simplex tableau* for Exercise 2 at the end of Section 9.1.

c's		X_1	X_2	S_1	S_2	S_3		Quotients
3	X_1	1	$\frac{1}{4}$	$\frac{1}{4}$	0	0	50	
0	S_2	0	$\frac{3}{4}$	$-\frac{1}{4}$	1	0	30	
0	S_3	0	$\frac{11}{12}$	$-\frac{1}{12}$	0	1	$43\frac{1}{3}$	
Solution:		50	0	0	30	$43\frac{1}{3}$		
c's:		3	2	0	0	0		
Indicators:								

Complete this tableau by calculating the indicators, determining the entering variable, calculating the corresponding quotients, and determining the departing variable.

9. Use the results of Exercise 8 to complete the Simplex solution.

10. Solve Exercise 3 at the end of Section 9.1 using the Simplex method.

11. Solve Exercise 4(a) at the end of Section 9.1 using the Simplex method.

12. Solve Exercise 7 at the end of Section 9.1 using the Simplex method.

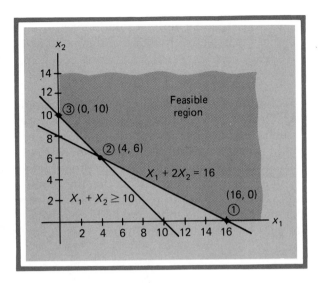

FIGURE 9.5
Graph
of the Feasible Region
for Example 9.2

9.4 ADDITIONAL CONSIDERATIONS

In this section we discuss how to solve linear programming problems for which the objective is to minimize a linear function of the problem variables. In addition, we show how the Simplex method can be used to solve problems involving greater-than-or-equal-to constraints as well as equality constraints. Example 9.2 introduces these concepts.

EXAMPLE 9.2 Consider a linear programming problem involving the variables x_1 and x_2. The objective is to minimize $3x_1 + 5x_2$, where x_1 and x_2 must be nonnegative variables and solutions of the system of linear inequalities $x_1 + 2x_2 \geq 16$ and $x_1 + x_2 \geq 10$. The graph of the feasible region for this problem is shown in Figure 9.5. Since the optimal solution to a linear programming problem occurs at an extreme point, we can determine the optimal solution to this problem by finding which extreme point minimizes $3x_1 + 5x_2$. The following table provides the necessary computations.

Extreme Point	Coordinates (x_1, x_2)	Value of $3x_1 + 5x_2$
①	(16, 0)	$3(16) + 5(0) = 48$
②	(4, 6)	$3(4) + 5(6) = 42$
③	(0, 10)	$3(0) + 5(10) = 50$

Thus we see that the optimal solution is $x_1 = 4$ and $x_2 = 6$ and that the value of the objective function at this point is 42.

---

solving minimization problems using the Simplex method

To solve minimization problems using the Simplex method, we replace each term of the objective function with its negative and then treat the problem as a maximization problem. For example, in Example 9.2 we would solve a maximization problem with an objective function of $-3x_1 - 5x_2$. To understand why this procedure works, first note that the feasible region does not change for the modified problem. Thus the optimal solution to the revised problem must be one of the original extreme points. The following table compares the value of $3x_1 + 5x_2$ and the modified objective function $-3x_1 - 5x_2$ for each extreme point.

Extreme Point	Coordinates (x_1, x_2)	Value of $3x_1 + 5x_2$	Value of $-3x_1 - 5x_2$
①	(16, 0)	48	−48
②	(4, 6)	42	−42
③	(0, 10)	50	−50

Thus we see that the extreme point which minimizes $3x_1 + 5x_2$ is also the solution which maximizes $-3x_1 - 5x_2$. Consequently, in order to solve a minimization problem we can follow the procedure illustrated for the maximization case. The only change required is that we multiply each coefficient of the objective function by -1 before starting the solution procedure.

surplus variables

In order to apply the Simplex method to problems with greater-than-or-equal-to constraints, we must first convert each constraint into a linear equation. To illustrate the approach used, consider the first constraint of Example 9.2.

$$x_1 + 2x_2 \geq 16$$

Since the left-hand side of this constraint is always greater than or equal to the right-hand side, we must subtract something on the left-hand side in order to make up for any difference between $x_1 + 2x_2$ and 16. For example, if $x_1 = 6$ and $x_2 = 9$, then $x_1 + 2x_2 = 6 + 2(9) = 24$, so for this case the left-hand side has a **surplus** of $24 - 16 = 8$ when compared to the right-hand side of the constraint. Thus we must subtract 8 on the left-hand side to make the constraint an equality.

In general, since the surplus depends upon the value of x_1 and x_2, the amount we subtract on the left-hand side of a greater-than-or-equal-to constraint must be variable. If we let s_1 denote the variable that must be subtracted on the left-hand side of $x_1 + 2x_2 \geq 16$ to account for any surplus, we can rewrite this inequality as $x_1 + 2x_2 - s_1 = 16$. Since s_1 can be interpreted as the amount of surplus associated with the constraint, s_1 is called a **surplus variable**. Similarly, if we let s_2 denote the surplus variable that must be subtracted on the left-hand side of the second constraint of Example 9.2, $x_1 + x_2 \geq 10$, we can rewrite this constraint as $x_1 + x_2 - s_2 = 10$. Note that once both constraints are written as linear equations, we have the standard form of the problem.

At first it may appear that some confusion may result by using the same letter to refer to both slack and surplus variables. However, note that slack variables are added on the left-hand side of a constraint, while surplus variables are subtracted. Thus surplus variables always have a negative sign associated with them in the standard form of the problem; the letter s can therefore be used in both cases without confusion.

After multiplying the objective function of Example 9.2 by -1 and then subtracting surplus variables s_1 and s_2 from constraints 1 and 2, respectively, we obtain the following equivalent maximization problem.

$$\max \quad -3x_1 - 5x_2$$

s.t.

$$x_1 + 2x_2 - s_1 \qquad = 16$$

$$x_1 + x_2 \qquad - s_2 = 10$$

$$x_1, x_2, s_1, s_2 \geq 0$$

Note that the surplus variables are similar to slack variables in that they do not contribute to profit; hence the profit coefficient associated with each surplus variable is zero. Thus the objective function can be written as $-3x_1 - 5x_2 + 0s_1 + 0s_2$, or simply $-3x_1 - 5x_2$.

artificial variables   For linear programming problems with greater-than-or-equal-to constraints, we can not obtain an initial basic feasible solution by simply setting the problem variables equal to zero. For example, in Example 9.2 if we set x_1 and x_2 equal to zero in the standard form of the problem, the constraints become

$$-s_1 \quad = 16$$

$$-s_2 = 10$$

and thus we obtain the solution $s_1 = -16$ and $s_2 = -10$. However, this is not a feasible solution since s_1 and s_2 are negative. What we do in situations like this is relatively simple—we add one new variable to each equation that led to the negative solution. For example, if we let a_1 denote the variable added to the first constraint of Example 9.2 and a_2 the variable added to the second constraint, we can rewrite the two constraints as

$$x_1 + 2x_2 - s_1 \qquad + a_1 \qquad = 16$$
$$x_1 + x_2 \qquad - s_2 \qquad + a_2 = 10$$

Now, if we set x_1, x_2, s_1, and s_2 equal to 0, we get the basic feasible solution $a_1 = 16$ and $a_2 = 10$. Although this solution does not make sense in the physical problem, it is a basic feasible solution as far as the application of the Simplex method is concerned.

The extra variables (a_1 and a_2) used in the preceding example are referred to as **artificial variables**; unlike slack and surplus variables, artificial variables do not have any "real" significance and are introduced for the sole purpose of getting the Simplex method started. Thus we can guarantee that they will be removed before the optimal solution is reached by assigning a very low profit coefficient to each of these variables. The actual value selected is unimportant as long as it is low enough to force the total profit to be substantially reduced if any artificial variable is in the solution. For example, if we assign a profit coefficient of -100 to each artificial variable, the objective function becomes

$$\max \quad -3x_1 - 5x_2 + 0s_1 + 0s_2 - 100a_1 - 100a_2$$

The corresponding initial Simplex tableau is shown below.

c's		x_1	x_2	s_1	s_2	a_1	a_2		Quotients
-100	a_1	1	2	-1	0	1	0	16	$\dfrac{16}{2} = 8$
-100	a_2	1	1	0	-1	0	1	10	$\dfrac{10}{1} = 10$
Solution:		0	0	0	0	16	10		
c's:		-3	-5	0	0	-100	-100		
Indicators:		197	295	-100	-100	0	0		

Entering variable (↑ under x_2)

Departing variable (↓ under s_2)

After two iterations we reach the optimal solution of $x_1 = 4$ and $x_2 = 6$. The Simplex tableaux used to obtain this solution are shown below.

c's		x_1	x_2	s_1	s_2	a_1	a_2			Quotients
-5	x_2	$\dfrac{1}{2}$	1	$-\dfrac{1}{2}$	0	$\dfrac{1}{2}$	0		8	$8 \div \dfrac{1}{2} = 16$
-100	a_2	$\dfrac{1}{2}$	0	$\dfrac{1}{2}$	-1	$-\dfrac{1}{2}$	1		2	$2 \div \dfrac{1}{2} = 4$
Solution:		0	8	0	0	0	2			
c's:		-3	-5	0	0	-100	-100			
Indicators:		$\dfrac{99}{2}$	0	$\dfrac{95}{2}$	-100	$\dfrac{-295}{2}$	0			

$\uparrow$ $\downarrow$

Entering   Departing
variable   variable

c's		x_1	x_2	s_1	s_2	a_1	a_2		
-5	x_2	0	1	-1	1	1	-1		6
-3	x_1	1	0	1	-2	-1	2		4
Solution:		4	6	0	0	0	0		
c's:		-3	-5	0	0	-100	-100		
Indicators:		0	0	-2	-1	-98	-99		

equality constraints   In order to use the Simplex method to solve linear programming problems with equality constraints, we must add an artificial variable to each equality constraint to obtain an initial basic feasible solution. For example, consider an equality constraint such as

$$2x_1 + 5x_2 + 4x_3 = 20$$

where x_1, x_2, and x_3 are the original problem variables. If we add the artificial variable a_1 to this constraint, we obtain

$$2x_1 + 5x_2 + 4x_3 + a_1 = 20$$

Once we add an artificial variable to each equality constraint, the Simplex method proceeds *exactly* as for the greater-than-or-equal-to constraint case.

To obtain an initial basic feasible solution, the Simplex method requires that the constant terms of the linear equations all be nonnegative. When the right-hand side of the original constraint is negative, however, this will not be the case. Thus if a constant term *is* negative, we simply multiply the expressions on both sides of the original by -1. For instance, if a linear programming problem involves the inequality

$$3x_1 - 7x_2 \geq -4$$

we simply rewrite it as

$$-3x_1 + 7x_2 \leq 4$$

remembering that when we multiply by a negative number, the inequality must be reversed. After doing so, we have the usual situation for less-than-or-equal-to constraints.

For a less-than-or-equal-to constraint with a negative value on the right-hand side, the procedure is similar; that is, we multiply on both sides by -1 in order to obtain a greater-than-or-equal-to constraint with a nonnegative right-hand side value. Note that for an equality constraint with a negative value on the right-hand side, the above procedure simply results in an equivalent equality constraint with a positive constant term.

solving larger
problems

Although we have discussed the solution of linear programming problems primarily from the viewpoint of maximization problems with less-than-or-equal-to constraints and minimization problems with greater-than-or-equal-to constraints, most real-world linear programming problems consist of a combination of less-than-or-equal-to constraints, greater-than-or-equal-to constraints, and equality constraints. Because of the computational effort involved in solving larger problems that involve a mixture of constraint types, a computer program that performs the steps of the Simplex method is necessary to solve most practical problems. If you have access to such a program, we suggest that you use the program to re-solve some of the problems you have worked in this chapter.

EXERCISES

1. Assume in Exercise 7 at the end of Section 8.4 that Mr. Jones wants to minimize the cost of adding the necessary minerals to his diet.

Write the standard form of this problem if each vitamin pill Q costs 3¢ and each vitamin pill R costs 4¢.

2. Use the graphical method to solve Exercise 1.

3. Re-solve Exercise 1 by computing the value of the objective function at each extreme point.

4. Use the Simplex method to solve Exercise 1.

5. With reference to Exercise 8 at the end of Section 8.4, use the graphical method to determine how the contractor can minimize the cost of completing the three projects, in each case.

   (a) On the first project the contractor has to pay $8 per hour for regular time and $12 per hour for overtime, on the second project the contractor has to pay $6 per hour for regular time and $11 for overtime, and on the third project the contractor has to pay $9 per hour for regular time and $12.40 per hour for overtime.

   (b) On the second project the contractor has to pay $10 per hour for overtime, on the third project the contractor has to pay $13 for overtime, but otherwise the figures are the same as in part (a).

6. A wholesale distributor of art reproductions manufactures two kinds of wooden frames, which she gives away free with the paintings. It takes 20, 10, and 10 minutes to *cut, assemble,* and *finish* the first kind of frame, which cost her $1.20 apiece, and 10, 20, and 60 minutes to *cut, assemble,* and *finish* the other kind of frame, which cost her $3.60 apiece. A certain production run calls for at least 8 hours of cutting, at least 10 hours of assembling, and at least 18 hours of finishing. The distributor wants to determine how many frames of each kind she should schedule to minimize cost. Write the standard form of this problem.

7. Use the graphical method to solve Exercise 6.

8. Solve the linear programming problem of Exercise 6 by computing the value of the objective function at each extreme point.

9. Write the following linear programming problem in standard form and find the basic feasible solution in which the original problem variables are zero: Minimize $-4x_1 + 5x_2$, where x_1 and x_2 must be nonnegative and satisfy the inequalities

$$x_1 + 4x_2 \leq 12$$

$$3x_1 + 2x_2 \leq 12$$

$$x_1 - x_2 \geq -2$$

10. The following is the first Simplex tableau for Exercise 9.

c's		x_1	x_2	s_1	s_2	s_3	Quotients
0	s_1	1	4	1	0	0	12
0	s_2	3	2	0	1	0	12
0	s_3	-1	1	0	0	1	2
Solution:		0	0	12	12	2	
	c's:	4	-5	0	0	0	
Indicators:							

Complete this tableau by calculating the indicators, determining the entering variable, calculating the corresponding quotients, and determining the departing variable.

11. Use the results of Exercise 10 to complete the solution of the linear programming problem of Exercise 9.

12. Write the following linear programming problem in standard form: Minimize $5x_1 - 10x_2$, where x_1 and x_2 must be nonnegative and satisfy the inequalities

$$x_1 + 3x_2 \leq 30$$
$$2x_1 - x_2 \leq 20$$
$$x_1 - 10x_2 \leq -10$$

13. Solve Exercise 12 using the Simplex method.

14. Write the following problem in standard form: Minimize $2x_1 + 1.5x_2$, where x_1 and x_2 must be nonnegative and satisfy the inequalities

$$x_1 + x_2 \geq 1$$
$$x_1 + 3x_2 \leq 3$$

15. Solve Exercise 14 using the Simplex method.

In Chapter 8 we introduced *systems of linear inequalities* and their use in describing problems in which several conditions expressed as linear inequalities must be satisfied at the same time. We continued that introduction by discussing problems in which the objective is to maximize or minimize some linear function of the problem variables, while at the same time satisfying a system of linear inequalities. Such problems are called *linear programming problems.*

We first discussed a graphical procedure for solving linear programming problems involving two (or at most three) variables. Then we showed how a simple algebraic method, which involved determining the value of the objective function at each extreme point, could be used to determine the optimal solution.

In order to reduce the amount of algebraic detail involved in solving linear programming problems by identifying the value of the objective function at each extreme point, the *Simplex method* was introduced. This method is a technique in which we begin with a feasible solution and check to see whether it maximizes (or minimizes) the objective function. If the solution does neither, the Simplex method indicates the direction we must take in searching for an optimal solution and, if such a solution exists, identifying when it is reached.

A complete discussion of the Simplex method with all its facets and ramifications would require considerably more space than we can devote in this book. Special problems that arise in connection with the Simplex method and alternative techniques that are easier to use in special kinds of problems are treated in the books to which we refer at the end of the chapter.

1. **Linear Program** A mathematical model with a linear objective function, a set of linear constraints, and nonnegative variables.
2. **Objective Function** The linear expression to be maximized or minimized.
3. **Constraint** An equation or inequality which restricts the values of the variables.
4. **Feasible Region** The set of solutions satisfing all the constraints.
5. **Extreme Points** The vertices, or corners, of the feasible region.
6. **Simplex Method** An efficient algebraic trial-and-error technique for solving linear programming problems.
7. **Slack Variable** A nonnegative variable used to convert a less-than-or-equal-to constraint into a linear equation.
8. **Basic Feasible Solution** A solution corresponding to an extreme point of the feasible region.
9. **Standard Form** A linear programming problem for which the constant terms of the linear equations (replacing the inequalities) are all nonnegative.
10. **Surplus Variable** A nonnegative variable used to convert a greater-than-or-equal-to constraint into a linear equation.
11. **Artificial Variable** A variable introduced with greater-than-or-equal-to constraints or equality constraints which enables us to obtain an initial basic feasible solution when using the Simplex method.
12. **Simplex Tableau** A table used to keep track of the calculations made when using the Simplex method.

1. Consider a company which makes two kinds of wine racks, a standard model and a deluxe model. It processes these racks on three different machines, I, II, and III; specifically, it takes 2.0, 1.2, and 2.4 hours on machines I, II, and III to make a standard rack, and 2.0, 2.4 and 0.8 hours on machines I, II, and III to make a deluxe rack. The profit which the company makes on these racks is $2.40 for each standard model and $4.80 for each deluxe model. Use the graphical approach to determine how many racks of each kind should be scheduled to maximize the total profit from a production run during which 48 hours are available on each machine.

2. Solve Exercise 1 by determining the profit corresponding to each extreme point.

3. Restate the linear programming problem of Exercise 1 in standard form and find the basic feasible solution in which the original variables are zero.

4. Solve the linear programming problem of Exercise 1 using the Simplex method.

5. Restate the following linear programming problem in standard form and find the basic feasible solution in which the original variables are zero: Maximize $3x_1 - 2x_2 + 5x_3$, where x_1, x_2, and x_3 must be nonnegative and satisfy the inequalities

$$6x_1 + 2x_2 + 3x_3 \leq 6$$
$$- 2x_2 + x_3 \leq 3$$
$$5x_1 - x_3 \geq -4$$

6. Solve the linear programming problem of Exercise 5 using the Simplex method.

7. Restate the following linear programming problem in standard form and determine the basic feasible solution in which the original problem variables are equal to zero.

$$\max \quad 28x_1 + 21x_2 + 10x_3$$

s.t.

$$3x_1 + 2x_2 + 4x_3 \leq 12$$
$$x_1 + 2x_2 + 4x_3 \leq 8$$
$$x_1 + 3x_2 + 2x_3 \leq 6$$

8. Suppose, for instance, that the manager of an oil refinery has to schedule the blending of four kinds of gasoline, A, B, C, and D. The refinery's facilities permit the blending of *at most* 10 million gallons

during the period under consideration, and there is the further restriction that only 2000 pounds of a secret anti-knock ingredient are available. It takes 200 pounds of this ingredient to blend a million gallons of gasoline A, 100 pounds for a million gallons of gasoline B, 400 pounds for a million gallons of gasoline C, and 100 pounds for a million gallons of gasoline D. If the refinery makes a profit of 2.4¢ per gallon on gasoline A, 3.0¢ per gallon on gasoline B, 4.8¢ per gallon on gasoline C, and 3.6¢ per gallon on gasoline D, *how should the manager schedule the production of the four gasolines to maximize the refinery's profit?* Show the linear programming model that can be used to solve this problem.

9. Solve Exercise 8 using the Simplex method.

REFERENCES

Anderson, D. R., D. J. Sweeney, and T. A. Williams, *An Introduction to Management Science: Quantitative Approaches to Decision Making* (3rd ed.). St. Paul, MN: West Publishing Co., 1982.

Dantzig, G. B., *Linear Programming and Extensions*. Princeton, N.J.: Princeton University Press, 1963.

Gass, S., *Linear Programming* (4th ed.). New York: McGraw-Hill Book Co., 1975.

DIFFERENTIAL CALCULUS

The purpose of this chapter is to provide an introduction to the basic ideas of differential calculus. First, we introduce a concept needed for the study of differential calculus—the limit of a function. Then we show how the fundamental ideas of differential calculus are based upon a special kind of limit called a derivative. The process of finding such a limit is referred to as differentiation. This chapter is primarily devoted to the basic ideas of differential calculus and the mechanics of differentiation, while Chapter 11 is devoted to its applications. In Chapter 12 we discuss the theory and applications of another branch of calculus called integral calculus.

10.1 THE LIMIT OF A FUNCTION

Example 10.1, which involves the quadratic function $y = 3x^2 + 1$, illustrates the concept of the limit of a function.

EXAMPLE 10.1 Let us investigate what happens to the values of $y = 3x^2 + 1$ when x takes on values that are close to but not equal to 2, as shown in the following table.

x	$y = 3x^2 + 1$
1.990	12.88
1.995	12.94
1.999	12.99
2.001	13.01
2.005	13.06
2.010	13.12

We see that as x approaches 2, the value of y approaches 13. In mathematical terms we say that the given function has the *limit* 13 when x approaches 2. Symbolically, we write this as $\lim\limits_{x \to 2} (3x^2 + 1) = 13$ or as $\lim\limits_{x \to 2} y = 13$, where $\lim\limits_{x \to 2} y$ is read "the limit of y when x approaches 2."

To generalize the above concept let us now consider a more formal definition of the limit of a function. In essence, what we mean by "the function y = f(x) has the limit L when x approaches a" is that we can make f(x) differ from L by as little as we please by confining x to a sufficiently small interval about a, excluding x = a. Consequently, in our example involving the function $y = 3x^2 + 1$, we were able to conclude that the limit is 13 as x approaches 2 since we can make $3x^2 + 1$ differ from 13 by as little as we please by confining x to a sufficiently small interval about 2. For example, based upon the analysis in Example 10.1, we know that when x is greater than 1.99 but less than 2.01, the value of y is between 12.88 and 13.12; similarly, when x is greater than 1.995 but less than 2.005, the value of y is between 12.94 and 13.06; and so on. Thus we see that we can make f(x) differ from 13 by smaller and smaller amounts as we choose values of x closer and closer to 2; hence the limit of $3x^2 + 1$ at x = 2 is 13.

There is an easy way to find the limit of the given function in Example 10.1. To find the limit of $3x^2 + 1$ at x = 2, all we really need to do is to substitute the value of x = 2 into $3x^2 + 1$; doing so, we obtain $3(2)^2 + 1 = 13$. However, it is important to understand that the concept of the limit of a function does not depend upon the value of f(x) at the point in question, or even upon whether f(x) is defined at that point. The following examples will help in clarifying these concepts. We first illustrate a situation in which the limit of a function does not exist.

EXAMPLE 10.2 Consider, for example, what happens to the values of the function given by

$$y = \frac{1}{x^2}$$

when x takes on values very close to 0. For example, if x takes on the values

0.1,   0.01,   0.001,   0.0001

the corresponding values of y are

100;   10,000;   1,000,000;   100,000,000

and it can be observed that these values of y increase beyond any bound as x takes on values closer and closer to 0. In other words, $\lim_{x \to 0} y$ does not exist in this case. This is illustrated in Figure 10.1, which shows the graph of $y = 1/x^2$.

Example 10.3 shows what happens to the limit of a function at a point where the value of the function is not defined.

EXAMPLE 10.3   Let us consider the function given by $y = (x^2 - 4)/(x - 2)$ for all real values of x except $x = 2$, and let us see what happens to the values of y when x takes on values close to 2. Rather than pick values of x and calculate the corresponding values of y, let us simplify the equation of the function by writing

$$y = \frac{x^2 - 4}{x - 2} = \frac{(x - 2)(x + 2)}{x - 2} = x + 2$$

which can be done since we excluded $x = 2$. Thus the graph of this function is like that of the line $y = x + 2$ (see Figure 10.2) without the point $(2, 4)$, and we can see that y will be close to 4 when x is close to (but not equal to) 2. Indeed, $\lim_{x \to 2} y = 4$ even though the value of the function is *not defined* for $x = 2$.

FIGURE 10.1
Graph of $y = 1/(x^2)$

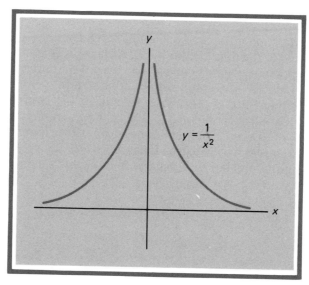

$$y = \frac{1}{x^2}$$

FIGURE 10.2
Diagram
for Example 10.3

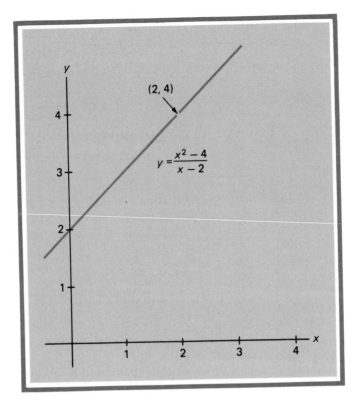

$$y = \frac{x^2 - 4}{x - 2}$$

(2, 4)

10.2 CONTINUITY

The difficulties we encountered in Examples 10.2 and 10.3 are closely tied to the idea of **continuity**. As far as Example 10.2 is concerned, it is apparent from Figure 10.1 that the function is **discontinuous**— evidently, the graph cannot be drawn in a continuous stroke, that is, without lifting the pen or pencil off the paper. In Example 10.3 the function is not defined for $x = 2$ and its graph is discontinuous because there is a gap, a point missing, at $x = 2$ (see Figure 10.2). In each of these examples we have used the terms *continuous* and *discontinuous* rather intuitively, but they suggest the following definition.

> A function with the values $f(x)$ is continuous at $x = a$ if and only if (1) $\lim_{x \to a} f(x)$ exists, (2) $f(a)$ is defined, and (3) $\lim_{x \to a} f(x) = f(a)$.

Furthermore, we say that a function is **continuous in an interval** if it is continuous at each point of the interval. Thus the function of Example 10.2, $y = 1/x^2$, is continuous in the interval from 1 to 2 or in the

FIGURE 10.3
Example where the
Limit of a Function
does not Equal the
Value of the Function

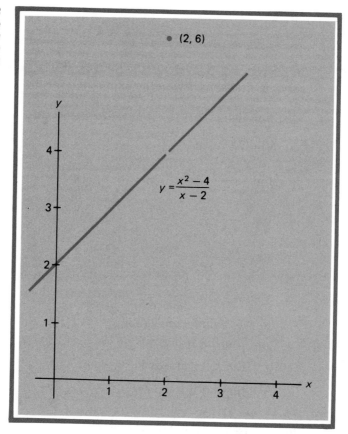

interval from 4 to 10, but not in the interval from -1 to 5 or in the interval from -3 to 2, for the latter two intervals both contain $x = 0$.

As far as the respective discontinuities are concerned, note that in Example 10.2 we violated condition 1 of the above definition, and that in Example 10.3 we violated condition 2. The next example shows how we violate condition 3.

EXAMPLE 10.3
(Continued)

Suppose that we modify the function of Example 10.3 so that it is given by $y = (x^2 - 4)/(x - 2)$ for all real values of x except $x = 2$, and that for $x = 2$ the value of the function is defined as $y = 6$. Now we get the graph shown in Figure 10.3, which differs from that of Figure 10.2 only in that we added the point $(2, 6)$. Note that $\lim_{x \to 2} y$ is still equal to 4, but that for $x = 2$ the value of the function is 6. Thus the function is discontinuous at this point.

In **Exercises 1–5,** evaluate the limit by direct substitution or, if necessary, by first simplifying the expression for $f(x)$.

1. $\lim\limits_{x \to 3} 18$

2. $\lim\limits_{x \to 4} (2x + 2)$

3. $\lim\limits_{x \to 3} \dfrac{x - 3}{x^2 - 9}$

4. $\lim\limits_{x \to 2} \dfrac{x^2 - 3x}{x - 3}$

5. $\lim\limits_{x \to 8} \dfrac{x + 4}{x^2 - 16}$

6. Given $f(x) = \dfrac{3(x^2 - 9)}{2x(x + 3)}$ for all real values of x except $x = 0$ and

    $x = -3$, find each value.

    (a) $\lim\limits_{x \to -3} f(x)$ if it exists.

    (b) $\lim\limits_{x \to 3} f(x)$ if it exists.

    (c) $\lim\limits_{x \to 0} f(x)$ if it exists.

In **Exercises 7–11,** determine whether or not the function is continuous
at the point(s) specified. If not, which of the conditions for continuity
are violated?

7. $f(x) = 4x + 16$ at $x = 2$

8. $y = 2x^2 - 4x$ at $x = 1$

9. $f(x) = \dfrac{1}{x}$ at $x = 0$ and at $x = 2$

10. $y = \dfrac{1}{x^2 - 4}$ at $x = 2$ and at $x = -2$

11. $f(x) = \dfrac{x - 3}{x^2 + 9}$ at $x = 3$

10.3   RATES OF CHANGE

Few things are more important in business and economics than the
study of *changes*: changes in a company's sales, changes in the value of
the dollar, changes in the gross national product, changes in the values

of stocks, changes in hourly wages, changes in interest rates, and so on. Equally important, though, are the **rates** at which these changes are taking place. After all, if we were told that a company's sales increased by $2,000,000, the significance of this information would depend largely on whether this change took place over 1 year, 2 years, or perhaps even 10 years. Similarly, if we are told that the Consumer Price Index has gone down by 0.3 point, this does not mean very much until we find out whether this change took place over a week, a month, or a year.

So far, we have limited our study of *rates of change* to phenomena represented by linear functions, and we have done this for the very simple reason that they are the only functions whose values change at a *constant rate*. As we saw in Section 3.1, this constant rate of change is given by the slope, m, of the line $y = mx + b$; in fact, m represents the change in y which corresponds to an *increase of one unit* in x. When it comes to other kinds of functions, we run into difficulties trying to measure both the rate of change and the related concept of the slope (direction, or steepness).

EXAMPLE 10.4 To illustrate these problems, let us suppose that the supply for a certain small bearing is given by the equation

$$f(x) = 2000x + 5000x^2$$

where x is the price per bearing in cents. If we look at the graph of this function in Figure 10.4, we find that (going from left to right) the values of the function increase, and that they do so at a *faster and faster rate*; at least, the curve gets steeper and steeper, and this suggests an increasing rate of change.

To investigate this more closely, let us see what happens when the price of the bearings in increased from 2¢ to 6¢ apiece. When we make the necessary substitutions, we find that for $x = 2$ the supply is given by

$$f(2) = 2000(2) + 5000(2)^2 = 24,000$$

and that for $x = 6$ it is given by

$$f(6) = 2000(6) + 5000(6)^2 = 192,000$$

Hence, the supply increases by $192,000 - 24,000 = 168,000$ bearings when x changes from 2¢ to 6¢ and we could say that *on the average* the supply of the bearings increased by $168,000/4 = 42,000$ bearings for each 1¢ increase in x. In other words, the average rate of change for this interval is 42,000 and, geometrically speaking,

$$\frac{192,000 - 24,000}{6 - 2} = 42,000$$

FIGURE 10.4
Graph of Supply
Function

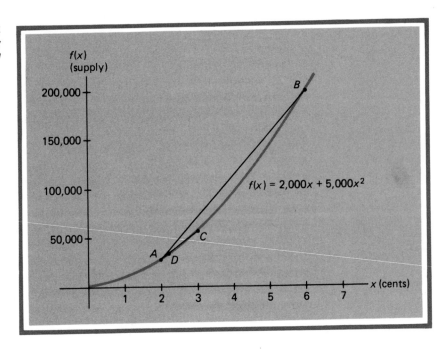

is the *slope* of the line segment joining points *A* and *B* of Figure 10.4.

As is evident from this diagram, the slope of the line segment *AB* does not really reflect what we might refer to as the slope, direction, or steepness of the curve at point *A* or at point *B*, and it does not tell us that the curve is actually *steeper* (and the rate of change is *greater*) at *B* than it is at *A*. If, for the sake of argument, we are interested primarily in what happens in the vicinity of point *A*, it might be better to see what happens when x changes by a smaller amount, such as when it changes from 2 to 3. Since we already know that $f(2) = 24,000$, we have only to calculate $f(3)$, for which we get

$$f(3) = 2000(3) + 5000(3)^2 = 51,000$$

Thus the *average rate of change* for the interval from x = 2 to x = 3 is

$$\frac{f(3) - f(2)}{3 - 2} = \frac{51,000 - 24,000}{3 - 2} = 27,000$$

and, geometrically speaking, this is the *slope* of the line segment *AC* of Figure 10.4. This is less than the average rate which we obtained for the interval from x = 2 to x = 6, but it is apparent that the line segment *AC* is still "steeper" than the curve appears to be at point *A*.

To get even closer, let us find the slope of the line segment *AD* of Figure 10.4, namely, the *average rate* at which the values of the function change on the very small interval from x = 2 to x = 2.1. Since

$$f(2.1) = 2000(2.1) + 5000(2.1)^2 = 26{,}250$$

and $f(2) = 24{,}000$, we get

$$\frac{f(2.1) - f(2)}{2.1 - 2} = \frac{26{,}250 - 24{,}000}{0.1} = 22{,}500$$

and this pretty well tells the story of what happens in the vicinity of point A. The slope of line segment AD is 22,500, which is just about indicative of the direction, steepness, or slope of the curve at point A. Also, 22,500 is pretty nearly the *average rate* at which the values of the function increase in the vicinity of point A, namely, in the vicinity of $x = 2$. Of course, we could approximate this situation even more closely by considering the interval from $x = 2$ to $x = 2.01$, or the interval from $x = 2$ to $x = 2.001$, but we shall leave it to you to show in Exercise 1 at the end of the next section that the corresponding average rates of change are, respectively, 22,050 and 22,005.

10.4 INSTANTANEOUS RATES OF CHANGE

The purpose of Example 10.4 was to illustrate some of the difficulties in measuring rates of change. However, it suggests the "ultimate" step of letting the second point on the curve approach the first *in the sense of a limit*. For instance, the values we computed for the slopes of the different line segments, 27,000, 22,500, 22,050, and 22,005, seem to come closer and closer to 22,000. We shall show next that this is, indeed, the *limit*, or *limiting value*, approached by these slopes.

In Figure 10.5 we show the curve $y = f(x)$ and two points identified as $P(x_1, y_1)$ and $Q(x_2, y_2)$. The slope of the line segment joining P and Q is

$$m_{PQ} = \frac{y_2 - y_1}{x_2 - x_1}$$

This equation also defines the average rate of change in y over the interval from x_1 to x_2. Suppose we hold point P fixed and move point Q along the curve toward P. What we shall observe for most curves encountered in practice is that as we do so, the slope of the line segment joining P and Q will vary by smaller and smaller amounts as Q gets closer and closer to P; in fact, the value of the slope approaches a limiting value, which we call the **slope of the tangent line** to the curve at the point P, or simply the **slope of the curve** at the point P. Moreover,

FIGURE 10.5
Diagram for Definition
of the Slope of Line
Segment PQ

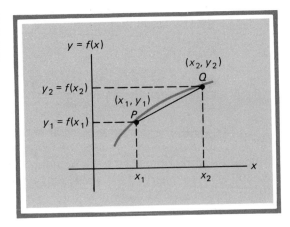

since the value of the slope of the line segment joining points P and Q and the average rate of change in y over the corresponding interval of x are the same, we refer to the slope of the curve at P as the **instantaneous rate** at which the values of this function change at $x = x_1$.

To emphasize the fact that point Q is moving closer and closer to point P, we shall rewrite the x-coordinate of Q as $x_1 + \Delta x$, where Δx (delta x) is some very small quantity. Using this notation, the slope of the line segment joining P and Q is written as

$$m_{PQ} = \frac{y_2 - y_1}{(x_1 + \Delta x) - x_1}$$

$$= \frac{y_2 - y_1}{\Delta x}$$

Another way to look at this result is to recognize that Δx simply represents the difference in the x-coordinates between points P and Q.

When the value of the x-coordinate is x_1, the value of y is $f(x_1)$; similarly, when the value of the x-coordinate is $x_1 + \Delta x$, the value of y is $f(x_1 + \Delta x)$. Thus we can write the slope of the line segment PQ as

$$m_{PQ} = \frac{f(x_1 + \Delta x) - f(x_1)}{\Delta x}$$

Figure 10.6 shows the curve $y = f(x)$ with this revised notation, including the tangent line to the curve at point P.

To determine the slope of the curve at point P—that of the tangent line touching the curve at point P—we must find the limiting value of the slope of the line segment joining points P and Q, as Q approaches P. As Q approaches P, however, the value of Δx gets smaller and smaller, and thus we define the slope of the curve at point P as

FIGURE 10.6
Revised Diagram
for the Definition
of the Slope
of the Curve
at Point P

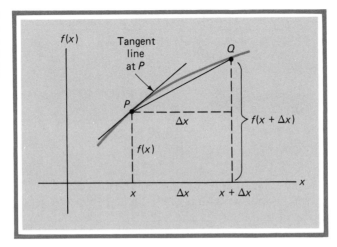

$$\text{Slope at point } P = \lim_{\Delta x \to 0} \frac{f(x + \Delta x) - f(x)}{\Delta x}$$

In this expression, *lim* stands for *limit*, $\Delta x \to 0$ stands for Δx *approaches zero*, and we refer to $\lim_{\Delta x \to 0}$ as *the limit as Δx approaches zero*. Since we previously indicated that this limiting value also defines what we mean by the instantaneous rate of change of the function, we write

$$\text{Instantaneous rate of change at } x = \lim_{\Delta x \to 0} \frac{f(x + \Delta x) - f(x)}{\Delta x}$$

EXAMPLE 10.4
(Continued)

If we let the x-coordinate of the second point on the curve be $2 + \Delta x$, where Δx is presumably very small, then the slope of the line segment which joins point A and this nearby point is given by

$$\frac{f(2 + \Delta x) - f(2)}{(2 + \Delta x) - 2} = \frac{f(2 + \Delta x) - f(2)}{\Delta x}$$

and we can evaluate this quantity by making use of the fact that the equation of the given function is $f(x) = 2000x + 5000x^2$. When we substitute $2 + \Delta x$ for x, we get

$$f(2 + \Delta x) = 2000(2 + \Delta x) + 5000(2 + \Delta x)^2$$

$$= 4000 + 2000(\Delta x) + 5000[4 + 4(\Delta x) + (\Delta x)^2]$$

$$= 24,000 + 22,000(\Delta x) + 5000(\Delta x)^2$$

Since we already know that $f(2) = 24,000$ we get

$$\frac{f(2 + \Delta x) - f(2)}{\Delta x} = \frac{24,000 + 22,000(\Delta x) + 5,000(\Delta x)^2 - 24,000}{\Delta x}$$

$$= 22,000 + 5000(\Delta x)$$

Finally, letting $\Delta x \rightarrow 0$ (that is, letting the second point on the curve approach point A), we find that

$$\lim_{\Delta x \to 0} \frac{f(2 + \Delta x) - f(2)}{\Delta x} = 22,000$$

and this value is the slope of the curve at $x = 2$, as well as the instantaneous rate at which the values of this function change when $x = 2$.

EXERCISES

1. Verify that for Example 10.4 the average rate of change is **(a)** 22,050 for the interval from $x = 2$ to $x = 2.01$; **(b)** 22,005 for the interval from $x = 2$ to $x = 2.001$.

2. Consider the function $y = 10x^2$. Find the average rate of change for each interval.
   (a) $x = 4$ to $x = 5$ **(c)** $x = 4$ to $x = 4.01$
   (b) $x = 4$ to $x = 4.1$ **(d)** $x = 4$ to $x = 4.001$

3. Find the slope of the graph of $y = 10x^2$ at $x = 4$. What is the relationship between the slope at $x = 4$ and the average rate of change over the intervals listed in Exercise 2.

4. What is the slope of the curve corresponding to $y = 3x^2$ at $x = 1$?

5. Compute the slope of the graph of $y = 3x^2$ at $x = 2$.

6. Find the rate at which values of $y = x^2 + 3x$ change when $x = 4$.

7. Compute the slope of the graph of $y = x^2 - 2x + 1$ at $x = 1$.

8. Compute the slope of the graph of $y = x^2 - 2x + 1$ at $x = 2$.

9. Determine the slope of the graph of $x + 3$ at $x = 1$. Is the slope different at $x = 2$? Explain.

10. Suppose that the demand for a portable television set is given by the equation

$$d = 600p - p^2$$

where p is the price in dollars and d is the number of units sold. At a price of $200, find the rate at which the values of this function change.

The special kind of limit which we discussed in section 10.4 is called a **derivative**, and the process of finding it is called **differentiation**. Thus, by definition, the derivative of the function f with respect to the variable x is

$$\text{Derivative of the function } f \text{ with respect to } x = \lim_{\Delta x \to 0} \frac{f(x + \Delta x) - f(x)}{\Delta x}$$

Because they are used in many different areas, derivatives are denoted by many different symbols. If the values of a function are given by $y = f(x)$, the corresponding values of the derivative can be written as

$$f'(x), \quad \frac{dy}{dx}, \quad f', \quad y', \quad D_x y, \quad D_x f(x), \quad \frac{d}{dx} f(x)$$

and, although this is mainly a matter of personal taste, we shall mostly use the first two. The notation $f'(x)$ has the advantage that it makes it clear that *the derivative of a function is, itself, a function*; furthermore, it makes it easy to write the value of the derivative at $x = a$ as $f'(a)$. The notation $\frac{dy}{dx}$ has the advantage that it states explicitly that we are dealing with the *derivative of y with respect to x*. In other words, this derivative measures the rate of change of y when there is a change in x. The symbol $\frac{dy}{dx}$ has the *serious disadvantage* of looking like a fraction, which it is *not*; the whole expression stands for the special limit called a derivative.

Since many beginners seem to have some purely technical difficulties with the basic mechanics of differentiation, it will help to approach the problem systematically in *four* steps, where the first three steps consist of setting up the *slope* (or difference quotient)

$$\frac{f(x + \Delta x) - f(x)}{\Delta x}$$

and the fourth step consists of taking the limit of this quantity as $\Delta x \to 0$.

1. *Find $f(x + \Delta x)$ by substituting $x + \Delta x$ into the expression, or formula, for the values of the function and simplify if possible.*
2. *Subtract $f(x)$ from $f(x + \Delta x)$ and simplify, if possible.*
3. *Divide the difference obtained in the second step by Δx.*

4. Find the limit of the expression (slope, or difference quotient) obtained in the third step as $\Delta x \to 0$; very often this can be done by simply substituting 0 for Δx.

EXAMPLE 10.5 To illustrate these four steps (which are sometimes referred to as the **delta process**), let us differentiate the function

$$f(x) = 4x^2 + 2$$

We proceed as indicated above.

Step 1
$$f(x + \Delta x) = 4(x + \Delta x)^2 + 2$$
$$= 4[x^2 + 2x(\Delta x) + (\Delta x)^2] + 2$$
$$= 4x^2 + 8x(\Delta x) + 4(\Delta x)^2 + 2$$

Step 2
$$f(x + \Delta x) - f(x) = [4x^2 + 8x(\Delta x) + 4(\Delta x)^2 + 2] - [4x^2 + 2]$$
$$= 8x(\Delta x) + 4(\Delta x)^2$$

Step 3
$$\frac{f(x + \Delta x) - f(x)}{\Delta x} = \frac{8x(\Delta x) + 4(\Delta x)^2}{\Delta x} = 8x + 4(\Delta x)$$

Step 4
$$\frac{dy}{dx} = f'(x) = \lim_{\Delta x \to 0} \frac{f(x + \Delta x) - f(x)}{\Delta x}$$
$$= \lim_{\Delta x \to 0}[8x + 4(\Delta x)]$$
$$= 8x$$

Thus the derivative of the function $4x^2 + 2$ is $8x$; hence at $x = 1$ the derivative is $8(1) = 8$, at $x = 2$ the derivative is $8(2) = 16$, and so on.

EXAMPLE 10.4
(Continued) As another example of the delta process for finding the derivative of a function, let us differentiate the function of Example 10.4

$$f(x) = 2000x + 5000x^2$$

Step 1
$$f(x + \Delta x) = 2000(x + \Delta x) + 5000(x + \Delta x)^2$$
$$= 2000x + 2000(\Delta x) + 5000[x^2 + 2x(\Delta x) + (\Delta x)^2]$$
$$= 2000x + 2000(\Delta x) + 5000x^2 + 10,000x(\Delta x)$$
$$+ 5000(\Delta x)^2$$

Step 2 $f(x + \Delta x) - f(x) = [2000x + 2000(\Delta x) + 5000x^2 + 10000x(\Delta x)$

$$+ 5000(\Delta x)^2] - [2000x + 5000x^2]$$

$$= 2000(\Delta x) + 10000x(\Delta x) + 5000(\Delta x)^2$$

Step 3 $\dfrac{f(x + \Delta x) - f(x)}{\Delta x} = 2000 + 10000x + 5000(\Delta x)$

Step 4 $\dfrac{dy}{dx} = f'(x) = \lim\limits_{\Delta x \to 0} \dfrac{f(x + \Delta x) - f(x)}{\Delta x} = 2000 + 10000x$

This enables us to calculate the *instantaneous* (or *marginal*) *rate* at which $f(x)$, the supply of the bearings, is increasing for any price x. For x = 1, for example, the values of the function are increasing at an instantaneous rate of 2000 + 10000(1) = 12,000 (bearings); for x = 2 the instantaneous rate is 22,000; for x = 5 the instantaneous rate is 52,000; and for x = 10 it is 102,000. Of course, the value we got here for x = 2 agrees with the result previously obtained. Note that we could write the above results as $f'(1) = 12,000$, $f'(2) = 22,000$, $f'(5) = 52,000$, and $f'(10) = 102,000$.

EXAMPLE 10.6   To differentiate the function $f(x) = 4x + 2$ using the four-step process, we proceed as follows.

Step 1 $$f(x + \Delta x) = 4(x + \Delta x) + 2$$

$$= 4x + 4(\Delta x) + 2$$

Step 2 $$f(x + \Delta x) - f(x) = [4x + 4(\Delta x) + 2] - (4x + 2)$$

$$= 4(\Delta x)$$

Step 3 $$\dfrac{f(x + \Delta x) - f(x)}{\Delta x} = \dfrac{4(\Delta x)}{\Delta x} = 4$$

Step 4 $$\dfrac{dy}{dx} = f'(x) = \lim\limits_{\Delta x \to 0} \dfrac{f(x + \Delta x) - f(x)}{\Delta x}$$

$$= \lim\limits_{\Delta x \to 0} (4)$$

$$= 4$$

Thus for the function $4x + 2$, the derivative is 4 at every value of x. Clearly this makes sense, because $4x + 2$ is a linear function with a constant rate of change, or slope, of 4.

FIGURE 10.7
Diagram
for Example 10.7

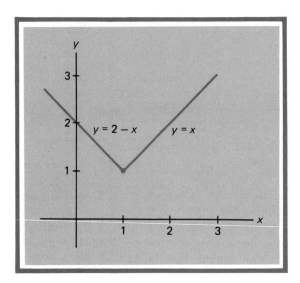

To conclude this introduction to the concept of a derivative, let us add that there *are* functions whose derivatives *do not exist;* or at least, their derivatives may not exist for all values of x within their domain. For one thing, a function has to be *continuous* before it can be differentiated, but even if it is continuous it may not have a derivative at some point (or points) as is illustrated by Example 10.7.

EXAMPLE 10.7 Consider the function given by $y = x$ for $x \geq 1$ and by $y = 2 - x$ for $x < 1$. As can be seen from the graph of this function in Figure 10.7, the function is continuous at $x = 1$, but if we take a sequence of x's which approach 1 but alternate between values less than and greater than 1, the slopes of the line segments joining the corresponding points on the graph to the point (1,1) will alternate between -1 and 1 and hence will *not* approach a limit. In other words, the derivative does not exist at $x = 1$.

EXERCISES

In **Exercises 1–5,** use the four-step delta process to find the derivative of the given function.

1. $f(x) = 6$
2. $y = 5 - 4x$

3. $f(t) = 2t + 5$

4. $f(x) = -x^2$

5. $f(x) = 5x^2 - 1$

6. Assume that the weekly demand for a frozen dessert (in thousands) is given by the equation

$$D = 1260 - 98p + 2p^2$$

where p is its price in cents. What is the instantaneous (or *marginal*) rate of change of the demand for the dessert when it is priced at 16 cents?

7. Assume that the supply for a certain small ceramic insulator is given by the equation

$$S = 2p + 4p^2$$

where p is the price per insulator in cents and the supply is in units of 100 insulators. What is the instantaneous (or marginal) rate at which the supply for the insulators is changing when the price is 5¢? What is the *average* rate of change when the price is increased from 5¢ to 5.5¢, and why are the two answers different? Draw a graph, if necessary.

8. Draw the graph of the function given by $y = x^2$ for $x \leq 0$ and $y = 0$ for $x > 0$, and judge whether the function is (a) continuous at $x = 0$; (b) differentiable at $x = 0$.

9. Draw the graph of the function given by $y = x$ for $x \leq 1$ and $y = 2 - x$ for $x > 1$, and judge whether the function is (a) continuous at $x = 1$; (b) differentiable at $x = 1$.

10.6 RULES OF DIFFERENTIATION

The four-step process for finding the derivative of a function is used only when absolutely necessary, which is fairly seldom; in actual practice, the derivatives of most functions can be written directly by following a few relatively simple rules. Some of these rules will be given below, while others will be discussed in later sections of this chapter. To simplify our work, it will be assumed throughout that $f(x)$, $g(x)$, and $h(x)$ are the values of **differentiable functions**, namely, functions whose derivatives exist.

The first rule we shall consider asserts that if the values of a function are *all equal*, the derivative of the function is 0 for all values of x. Formally,

if f(x) = k, where k is a constant, then f'(x) = 0

and it would hardly seem necessary to require a proof that the derivative of a constant is zero. After all, $y = k$ is the equation of a *horizontal line*, whose slope (and hence the derivative for all values of x) is zero.

The next rule pertains to functions given by equations of the form $f(x) = x^n$, where n is a *positive integer*. Later, we shall extend the rule to the case where n can also be a negative integer or even a fraction, but for the time being let us merely state that

if f(x) = x^n, where n is a positive integer, then f'(x) = $n \cdot x^{n-1}$.

In words, to differentiate x^n we reduce the exponent by 1 and multiply by n. *

EXAMPLE 10.8 If we want to differentiate $f(x) = x^8$, for example, or $g(x) = x^{11}$, we can immediately write $f'(x) = 8x^7$ and $g'(x) = 11x^{10}$.

The third rule which we shall consider in this section asserts that if the values of a function are all multiplied by a constant, then the values of the derivative are multiplied by the same constant. Formally,

if f(x) = $k \cdot g(x)$, where k is a constant, then f'(x) = $k \cdot g'(x)$.

EXAMPLE 10.9 To differentiate $y = 12x^4$, for example, all we have to do is multiply 12 by the derivative of x^4, $4x^3$, and we get

$$\frac{dy}{dx} = 12 \cdot 4x^3 = 48x^3$$

Similarly, if $g(x) = \frac{1}{2}x^6$, then $g'(x) = \frac{1}{2} \cdot 6x^5, = 3x^5$, and if $h(x) = 13x$, then $h'(x) = 13(1 \cdot x^{1-1}) = 13 \cdot x^0 = 13 \cdot 1 = 13$.

The fourth rule pertains to functions whose values are sums or differences of several terms. We shall state it for *sums of two terms*, but we shall then demonstrate how it can easily be generalized to sums and

---

*A proof of this rule may be found in most college textbooks on calculus.

differences involving more than two terms. Formally,

$$if\ f(x) = g(x) + h(x),\ then\ f'(x) = g'(x) + h'(x)$$

which means, in fact, that we can differentiate term by term.

EXAMPLE 10.10 Applying this rule, we can immediately write the derivative of $f(x) = 4x^3 + 5x^2$ as

$$f'(x) = 4 \cdot 3x^2 + 5 \cdot 2x = 12x^2 + 10x$$

Also, to differentiate $y = 2x^5 - 3x^7$ we could first write this equation as $y = 2x^5 + (-3)x^7$, so we get

$$\frac{dy}{dx} = 2 \cdot 5x^4 + (-3) \cdot 7x^6 = 10x^4 - 21x^6$$

but we could just as well have differentiated term by term, writing directly

$$\frac{dy}{dx} = 2 \cdot 5x^4 - 3 \cdot 7x^6 = 10x^4 - 21x^6$$

When there are *more than two* terms, as in $f(x) = 3x^2 + 5x^3 + 3x^4$, we could first write this equation as $f(x) = (3x^2 + 5x^3) + 3x^4$ and apply the rule *twice*, but this would not differ from differentiating term by term and we might just as well write directly

$$\frac{dy}{dx} = 3 \cdot 2x + 5 \cdot 3x^2 + 3 \cdot 4x^3 = 6x + 15x^2 + 12x^3$$

There are two more rules of differentiation that we shall take up in this section—the **product rule** and the **quotient rule**. The first of these applies to functions whose values are products of two factors involving x, and formally it states that

$$if\ f(x) = g(x) \cdot h(x),\ then\ f'(x) = g(x) \cdot h'(x) + h(x) \cdot g'(x).$$

This tells us that the derivative of $g(x) \cdot h(x)$ is given by g(x) *times the derivative of h(x) plus h(x) times the derivative of g(x)*.

EXAMPLE 10.11 To illustrate this rule, let us differentiate $y = (x^2 - 1)(3x + 4)$ without first multiplying out the product term by term and then check the answer by doing so. Since the derivative of $x^2 - 1$ is $2x$ and the derivative of $3x + 4$ is 3, we get

$$\frac{dy}{dx} = (x^2 - 1) \cdot 3 + (3x + 4) \cdot 2x$$

$$= 3x^2 - 3 + 6x^2 + 8x$$

$$= 9x^2 + 8x - 3$$

If we first multiply out term by term, we get

$$y = (x^2 - 1)(3x + 4)$$

$$= 3x^3 + 4x^2 - 3x - 4$$

so

$$\frac{dy}{dx} = 9x^2 + 8x - 3$$

The sixth, and final, rule of this section is the quotient rule, which applies to functions whose values are the ratios of two expressions involving x. Formally,

$$\text{if } f(x) = \frac{g(x)}{h(x)}, \text{ then } f'(x) = \frac{h(x) \cdot g'(x) - g(x) \cdot h'(x)}{h(x)^2}$$

which tells us to multiply the denominator by the derivative of the numerator, subtract the product of the numerator and the derivative of the denominator, and then divide by the square of the denominator.

An important application of the quotient rule is its use in demonstrating that the formula for differentiating x^n holds also for *negative integral exponents*, such as when $f(x) = x^{-3}$ or $f(x) = x^{-1}$. Thus we shall want to show that

if $f(x) = x^{-n}$, *where n is a positive integer, then* $f'(x) = -n \cdot x^{-n-1}$.

To this end, let us write the equation of the function as

$$f(x) = \frac{1}{x^n}$$

where the numerator is $g(x) = 1$, the denominator is $h(x) = x^n$, and n is a positive integer. Then $g'(x) = 0$ according to the first rule of this section, $h'(x) = n \cdot x^{n-1}$ according to the second rule, and substitution into the formula for the quotient rule yields

$$f'(x) = \frac{x^n \cdot 0 - 1(n \cdot x^{n-1})}{(x^n)^2} = \frac{-n \cdot x^{n-1}}{x^{2n}}$$

$$= -n \cdot x^{(n-1)-2n}$$

$$= -n \cdot x^{-n-1}$$

EXAMPLE 10.12   To illustrate this rule, let us differentiate $f(x) = x^{-3}$, $u(x) = 4x^{-5}$, and $c(x) = 1/x$. For the first two functions we get directly

$$f'(x) = -3 \cdot x^{-4} \quad \text{and} \quad u'(x) = 4(-5 \cdot x^{-6}) = -20x^{-6}$$

and after writing the equation of the third function as $c(x) = x^{-1}$, we also get

$$c'(x) = -1 \cdot x^{-2} = \frac{-1}{x^2}$$

You may have observed that we took certain linguistic liberties in the examples of this section. Instead of saying that we differentiate $y = (x^2 - 1)(3x + 4)$, we should really have said that we *differentiate the function* given by this particular equation, and instead of referring to $f'(x) = -3x^{-4}$ as the derivative of $f(x) = x^{-3}$, we should really have referred to $f'(x)$ as the *value of the derivative* of the given function at x. However, it is customary to take these liberties in order to simplify our language, and there is no danger in doing this, as long as we always remember that there is a difference between the values of a function and the function itself. Keep this in mind as we continue to refer to $f'(x) = 60x^4$ as the derivative of $f(x) = 12x^5$, continue to say that the derivative of $4x^{-5}$ is $-20x^{-6}$, and continue to say that if we differentiate $f(x) = 3x^2 + 5x^4$, we get $f'(x) = 6x + 20x^3$.

EXERCISES

In **Exercises 1–6**, differentiate each function using the rules of Section 10.4 and find their derivatives at x = 1 and x = 3.

1. $f(x) = 14$
2. $f(x) = -1.5x$
3. $f(x) = 3x^7$

4. $f(x) = 2x - 9$

5. $f(x) = x + 8x^2 - x^3$

6. $f(x) = 2 - 18x + 3x^5$

In **Exercises 7–12,** differentiate each function using the rules of Section 10.4 and find the values of their derivatives at $x = 4$ (if they exist).

7. $f(x) = (1 - x^3)(1 + 2x)$

8. $f(x) = \dfrac{x^2 - x + 3}{x}$

9. $f(x) = x^4(1 + x^2)$

10. $f(x) = x^{-3} + 2x^{-4}$

11. $f(x) = \dfrac{x + 4}{x - 4}$

12. $f(x) = 6 + \dfrac{12}{x^6}$

In **Exercises 13–18,** differentiate each function using the rules of Section 10.3 and find the values of their derivatives at $x = 0$ (if they exist).

13. $f(x) = \dfrac{2}{x} - \dfrac{3}{x^2}$

14. $f(x) = (x - 3)(x^2 + 1)(2x - 6)$

15. $f(x) = \dfrac{(x^3 + 1)(7x^2 - x)}{x + 3}$

16. $f(x) = x^4(x^2 + 1)(x - 3)$

17. $f(x) = \dfrac{x + 5}{(x^2 + 1)(x - 4)}$

18. $f(x) = 2x + 3x^{-1} - 6x^{-2}$

19. Assume that a company's total receipts for manufacturing and selling x television sets is given by the equation

$$R = 120x - 0.012x^2$$

Find the instantaneous (marginal) rate at which these total receipts are changing when (**a**) $x = 200$ and (**b**) $x = 400$.

20. A company's total sales revenue is given by the equation $y = x + 2x^2$, where x is the number of years the company has been in business and y is in millions of dollars.

(a) At what rate is the company's total sales revenue growing after 4 years, that is, for x = 4?

(b) Find the equation of the tangent line at x = 4 and use it to predict the company's total sales revenue for the sixth year assuming that the growth rate remains constant after the fourth year. How does this compare with the corresponding value obtained by substituting x = 6 into the original equation?

10.7 SPECIAL METHODS OF DIFFERENTIATION

In this section we present two special methods of differentiation which often provide great simplifications when the rules of the preceding section cannot easily be applied.

the chain rule To introduce the first of these techniques, suppose we are asked to differentiate

$$y = (1 + 7x^3)^{25}$$

To differentiate this function, we begin by denoting the expression in parentheses with the letter u. Thus we have

$$y = u^{25} \quad \text{where} \quad u = 1 + 7x^3$$

and the rules of Section 10.6 yield

$$\frac{dy}{du} = 25u^{24} \quad \text{and} \quad \frac{du}{dx} = 21x^2$$

This does not give us $\dfrac{dy}{dx}$, but we can obtain this derivative in one more step by applying the **chain rule of differentiation.***

$$\boxed{\frac{dy}{dx} = \frac{dy}{du} \cdot \frac{du}{dx}}$$

Before we apply this rule, let us make it very clear that the formula does *not* pertain to fractions and that we are *not canceling* the quantity

---

*A proof of this rule may be found in most college textbooks on calculus.

du; each of the symbols $\dfrac{dy}{dx}$, $\dfrac{dy}{du}$, and $\dfrac{du}{dx}$ represents a separate derivative, and the chain rule simply states that *the first is given by the product of the other two*. Returning now to our illustration, we get

$$\frac{dy}{dx} = (25u^{24})(21x^2)$$

$$= 25(1 + 7x^3)^{24} \cdot 21x^2$$

$$= 525x^2(1 + 7x^3)^{24}$$

EXAMPLE 10.13   For instance, when we use this kind of *mental substitution*, we can immediately write the derivative of

$$f(x) = 24(2 + 5x + 3x^2)^7$$

as

$$f'(x) = 24 \cdot 7(2 + 5x + 3x^2)^6(5 + 6x)$$

where $5 + 6x$ is the derivative of $2 + 5 + 3x^2$. Hence the result is

$$f'(x) = 168(5 + 6x)(2 + 5x + 3x^2)^6$$

Also, if we apply the chain rule separately to each term, we can immediately write the derivative of

$$y = 2(1 + 5x)^3 + 12(2 - 7x^2)^5$$

$$\frac{dy}{dx} = 2 \cdot 3(1 + 5x)^2 \cdot 5 + 12 \cdot 5(2 - 7x^2)^4(-14x)$$

where 5 is the derivative of $1 + 5x$ and $-14x$ is the derivative of $2 - 7x^2$. Hence the result is

$$\frac{dy}{dx} = 30(1 + 5x)^2 - 840x(2 - 7x^2)^4$$

In some of its applications, the chain rule consists of several "links," as is illustrated by Example 10.14.

EXAMPLE 10.14   To differentiate

$$y = 4[1 + (5 + x^4)^3]^6$$

for example, we could substitute u for $1 + (5 + x^4)^3$ and r for $(5 + x^4)$, so that we can write

$$y = 4u^6, \quad u = 1 + r^3, \quad \text{and} \quad r = 5 + x^4$$

and hence

$$\frac{dy}{du} = 24u^5, \quad \frac{du}{dr} = 3r^2, \quad \text{and} \quad \frac{dr}{dx} = 4x^3$$

Using the chain rule *twice*, we can write

$$\frac{dy}{dx} = \frac{dy}{du} \cdot \frac{du}{dx}, \quad \frac{du}{dx} = \frac{du}{dr} \cdot \frac{dr}{dx}, \quad \text{and, hence,} \quad \frac{dy}{dx} = \frac{dy}{du} \cdot \frac{du}{dr} \cdot \frac{dr}{dx}$$

It follows that the answer to our problem is given by

$$\frac{dy}{dx} = 24u^5 \cdot 3r^2 \cdot 4x^3$$

$$= 24[1 + (5 + x^4)^3]^5 \cdot 3(5 + x^4)^2 \cdot 4x^3$$

$$= 288x^3(5 + x^4)^2[1 + (5 + x^4)^3]^5$$

With some practice, problems like this can also be done mentally, that is, without actually introducing the letters u and r.

---

implicit differentiation The second special method of differentiation that we present in this section applies to functions that are solved for neither y nor x. Such functions are called *implicit* and are given by an equation such as

$$x^2 + y^3 = 5x + 4y \quad \text{or} \quad 5xy = x^3 - y^2$$

namely, by an equation *not* of the form $y = f(x)$ or $x = g(y)$. To differentiate functions like these (with respect to x or with respect to y) it is sometimes possible to solve first for y in terms of x or x in terms of y, but it is generally much easier to use what is called **implicit differentiation**.

Actually, all this amounts to is *differentiating term by term and using the chain rule where necessary*. To illustrate this technique, it will be convenient to use the symbol $\frac{d}{dx} f(x)$ instead of $f'(x)$. Using the chain rule, we shall write the derivative of the function $h(y)$ with respect to x as

$$\frac{d}{dx} h(y) = \frac{d}{dy} h(y) \cdot \frac{dy}{dx} = h'(y) \cdot \frac{dy}{dx}$$

where it must be understood, of course, that the *prime in h′(y) denotes differentiation with respect to y. This is the key to the whole situation.*

EXAMPLE 10.15   To illustrate this kind of differentiation, let us refer to the first of the above equations, namely,

$$x^2 + y^3 = 5x + 4y$$

and find $\dfrac{dy}{dx}$. Showing more detail than is really necessary, we differentiate each term with respect to x, getting

$$\frac{d}{dx}(x^2) + \frac{d}{dx}(y^3) = \frac{d}{dx}(5x) + \frac{d}{dx}(4y)$$

$$2x + \frac{d}{dy}(y^3)\cdot\frac{dy}{dx} = 5 + \frac{d}{dy}(4y)\cdot\frac{dy}{dx}$$

$$2x + 3y^2\cdot\frac{dy}{dx} = 5 + 4\cdot\frac{dy}{dx}$$

and all that remains to be done is to solve this equation for $\dfrac{dy}{dx}$. Collecting all terms involving $\dfrac{dy}{dx}$ on the left-hand side of the equation and all the other terms on the right-hand side, we get

$$3y^2\cdot\frac{dy}{dx} - 4\cdot\frac{dy}{dx} = 5 - 2x$$

$$(3y^2 - 4)\frac{dy}{dx} = 5 - 2x$$

and, finally,

$$\frac{dy}{dx} = \frac{5 - 2x}{3y^2 - 4}$$

It is typical of this kind of differentiation that the answer will be in terms of both x and y, but this seldom poses any difficulties so far as further work or applications are concerned.

EXAMPLE 10.16   To give another example of implicit differentiation, let us refer to the second of the equations given above,

$$5xy = x^3 - y^2$$

We *could* solve this equation for y by means of the *quadratic formula* of Section 3.3, but this would involve a considerable amount of work. To differentiate implicitly, we use the *product rule* on the left-hand side, getting

$$\frac{d}{dx}(5xy) = \frac{d}{dx}(x^3) - \frac{d}{dx}(y^2)$$

$$5x \cdot \frac{d}{dx}(y) + y \cdot \frac{d}{dx}(5x) = \frac{d}{dx}(x^3) - \frac{d}{dy}(y^2) \cdot \frac{dy}{dx}$$

$$5x \cdot \frac{dy}{dx} + 5y = 3x^2 - 2y \cdot \frac{dy}{dx}$$

Collecting terms, we then get

$$5x \cdot \frac{dy}{dx} + 2y \cdot \frac{dy}{dx} = 3x^2 - 5y$$

$$(5x + 2y) \cdot \frac{dy}{dx} = 3x^2 - 5y$$

and, finally,

$$\frac{dy}{dx} = \frac{3x^2 - 5y}{5x + 2y}$$

Next, let us use implicit differentiation to demonstrate that the rule for differentiating x^n also holds when n is a positive fraction. Thus we shall show that

If $y = x^{r/s}$ where r and s are positive integers and $x > 0$, then

$$\boxed{\frac{dy}{dx} = \frac{r}{s} \cdot x^{(r/s)-1}}$$

If we raise the expressions on both sides of the equation $y = x^{r/s}$ to the power s, we get

$$y^s = (x^{r/s})^s = x^r$$

and implicit differentiation yields

$$s \cdot y^{s-1} \cdot \frac{dy}{dx} = r \cdot x^{r-1}$$

or

$$\frac{dy}{dx} = \frac{r \cdot x^{r-1}}{s \cdot y^{s-1}}$$

Now, if we substitute $x^{r/s}$ for y in the denominator, we get

$$\frac{dy}{dx} = \frac{r \cdot x^{r-1}}{s(x^{r/s})^{s-1}} = \frac{r \cdot x^{r-1}}{s \cdot x^{r(s-1)/s}} = \frac{r \cdot x^{r-1}}{s \cdot x^{r-(r/s)}} = \frac{r}{s} \cdot x^{(r/s)-1}$$

and this completes the proof.

EXAMPLE 10.17

If $f(x) = x^{4/3}$, then $f'(x) = (4/3)x^{1/3}$; and if $y = x^{2/5}$, then $\dfrac{dy}{dx} = (2/5)x^{-3/5}$; in each case *we multiply f(x) by the exponent and reduce the exponent by 1.*

In Exercise 12 at the end of this section you will be asked to show that the rule for differentiating x^n holds also when n is a *negative fraction.*

EXERCISES

In **Exercises 1–6,** differentiate each function.

1. $y = (1 + 3x^2)^7$
2. $f(x) = (3 - x + 4x^2)^5$
3. $g(x) = 4\left(x - \dfrac{1}{x}\right)^3$
4. $f(x) = (1 + 3x - 2x^2)^{-4}$
5. $F(x) = x^3(2x^2 - 3)^6$
6. $y = 2\left(\dfrac{x - 2}{x + 2}\right)^3$
7. Given $x = 2 - 3y + 2y^2$, find each.
   (a) $\dfrac{dy}{dx}$
   (b) The value of this derivative at the point $(1, 1)$.
8. The relationship between the price for a product (in cents) and the demand (in thousands of units) is given by

$$p = \sqrt{29 - 3D - D^2}$$

Find $\dfrac{dD}{dp}$ at $p = 5$, namely, the marginal rate at which the demand is changing when the price of the product is 5¢.

9. Given $3x^3y^2 = 3x + 5y - 2$, find dy/dx.

10. Given $y^2 = x^3 + 4x + 9$, find each.

   (a) $\dfrac{dy}{dx}$

   (b) The values of this derivative at the points on the curve where $x = 2$.

   (c) The equations of the tangents to the curve at the points where $x = 2$.

11. Differentiate $y = \sqrt[3]{x}$ by first writing this equation as $y^3 = x$ and then finding $\dfrac{dx}{dy}$ and, hence, $\dfrac{dy}{dx}$. Verify that the result agrees with the rule for differentiating x^n when n is a positive fraction.

12. Use the rule for differentiating x^n when n is a positive fraction and the quotient rule to show that the rule holds also when n is a negative fraction, that is, when $n = -r/s$, where r and s are positive integers.

13. Use the rule for differentiating x^n when n is a positive fraction and the result of the preceding exercise to differentiate each.

   (a) $y = 3x^{3/2}$

   (b) $f(x) = (1 + x^2)^{-1/4}$

   (c) $g(x) = x(1 + 3x - x^2)^{2/3}$

   (d) $y = \dfrac{3}{\sqrt{x}}$

   (e) $y = \dfrac{x}{(2 + x)^{5/2}}$

   (f) $f(x) = 25x(1 + 3x^2)^{3/5}$

14. The demand for a product (in hundreds of cartons) is related to its price (in dollars per carton) by means of the equation

$$d = \frac{4,000}{\sqrt{p}}$$

Use the result of Exercise 12 to find the instantaneous (marginal) rate at which the demand is increasing when the price is $16 per carton.

15. The profit of a business venture (in thousands of dollars) is related to the promotional expenses (in thousands of dollars) by means of the equation

$$P = 20 + 8\sqrt{E}$$

   (a) Find the marginal rate at which the profits of this business venture are increasing when the promotional expenses are $4000.

(b) Find the amount by which the profits are actually increased when the promotional expenses are increased from $4000 to $5000.

10.8 THE DERIVATIVES OF SPECIAL FUNCTIONS

In this section we study the differentiation of several types of exponential and logarithmic functions.*

exponential functions The derivative of the exponential function given by $f(x) = e^x$ is the function itself;

if $f(x) = e^x$, then $f'(x) = e^x$.

The rule for differentiating e^x can easily be generalized with the use of the chain rule so that it applies also to the differentiation of e^{ax}, where a is a constant. In fact

if $f(x) = e^{ax}$, then $f'(x) = ae^{ax}$.

EXAMPLE 10.18 Recall Example 4.1 (page 112), where the demand curve for a new product is given by the equation

$$D = 1280e^{-0.0726p}$$

where D is the demand (in thousands) for the new product and p is the price in cents. Thus to differentiate the demand function, we can write

$$\frac{dD}{dp} = 1280(-0.0726)e^{-0.0726p} = -92.8e^{-0.0726p}$$

and for $p = 20$, for example, we find that the demand changes at a marginal rate of $-92.8e^{-0.0726(20)} = -22$ (approximately). The fact that the rate is negative implies that the demand *decreases*, which is apparent also from Figure 4.3. Thus when the new product sells for 20¢, there is a marginal *decrease of demand* of 22 thousand units corresponding to a 1¢ increase in price.

The rule for differentiating e^x can also be generalized to the differentiation of b^x, where b is a positive constant.

---

*Proofs for the results in this section may be found in most college textbooks on calculus.

$$\text{If } y = b^x, \text{ then } \frac{dy}{dx} = b^x(\ln b).$$

EXAMPLE 10.19 For instance, if $y = 2^x$ we can immediately write $\dfrac{dy}{dx} = 2^x(\ln 2)$, and if we refer to the first form of the demand function of Example 4.1 (page 97) which was

$$D = 1280(0.93)^p$$

we get

$$\frac{dD}{dp} = 1280(0.93)^p(\ln 0.93) = -92.9(0.93)^p$$

where we made use of the value of $\ln 0.93$ obtained on page 113.

Most of the *growth curves* studied in business and economics involve variations of the exponential function. We already met the *modified exponential function* in Section 4.1, where a function of this kind was used to describe how the demand for a new meat tenderizer changes with time.

Another important growth curve which has roughly the shape of an elongated letter **S** (see Figure 10.8) is the logistic curve

$$y = \frac{k}{c + ae^{bx}}$$

where k, a, b, and c are appropriate constants.

EXAMPLE 10.20 To give an example, let us consider the relationship given by

$$y = \frac{20,000}{1 + 50e^{-0.5x}}$$

where y is the expected (or predicted) enrollment at a relatively new university and x is the number of years that have elapsed since the enrollment of the first freshman class. Note that if we substitute $x = 0$, we find that the original enrollment was slightly below 400; it is also apparent from the equation that the enrollment will eventually *approach* (but never exceed) 20,000 students. Suppose now that we would like to know the *annual rate* at which the school can be expected to

FIGURE 10.8
A Logistic Curve

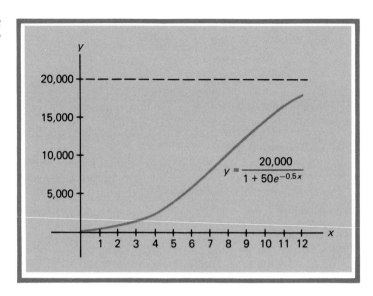

grow 3 years after the enrollment of the first freshman class. To find $\dfrac{dy}{dx}$ at x = 3, which is the quantity we are trying to determine, let us first write the equation as

$$y = 20{,}000(1 + 50e^{-0.5x})^{-1}$$

Then, repeatedly applying the chain rule, we get

$$\frac{dy}{dx} = 20{,}000(-1)(1 + 50e^{-0.5x})^{-2} \cdot \frac{d}{dx}(1 + 50e^{-0.5x})$$

$$= -20{,}000(1 + 50e^{-0.5x})^{-2} \cdot 50e^{-0.5x} \cdot \frac{d}{dx}(-0.5x)$$

$$= -20{,}000(1 + 50e^{-0.5x})^{-2} \cdot 50e^{-0.5x}(-0.5)$$

$$= \frac{500{,}000e^{-0.5x}}{(1 + 50e^{-0.5x})^2}$$

If we substitute x = 3, this becomes

$$\frac{dy}{dx} = \frac{500{,}000e^{-1.5}}{(1 + 50e^{-1.5})^2}$$

$$= \frac{500{,}000(0.223)}{[1 + 50(0.223)]^2}$$

$$= 755$$

where $e^{-1.5} = 0.223$ was obtained from Table III in the appendix. Thus after 3 years the university's enrollment is growing at an annual rate of 755 students.

---

logarithmic functions   To differentiate logarithmic functions of the form $y = \ln x$, we can use the following result.

$$\text{If } y = \ln x, \text{ then } \frac{dy}{dx} = \frac{1}{x}.$$

The above rule can be generalized with the use of the chain rule so that it applies to the differentiation of $\ln u$, where u is a function of x. Specifically,

$$\text{If } y = \ln u, \text{ then } \frac{dy}{dx} = \frac{1}{u}\frac{du}{dx}$$

EXAMPLE 10.21   The supply of one brand of automobile tires (in thousands) is given by

$$S = 320 \cdot \ln (1 + p)$$

where p is the price per tire (in dollars). To find the marginal rate at which the supply increases when $p = \$49.95$, we differentiate the given function, getting

$$\frac{dS}{dp} = 320 \cdot \frac{1}{1 + p} \cdot 1 = \frac{320}{1 + p}$$

Then, substituting $p = 49.95$, we find that

$$\frac{dS}{dp} = \frac{320}{50.95} = 6.28$$

which means that the marginal rate at which the supply increases is 6280 tires corresponding to a $1 increase in price.

The rule for differentiating logarithmic functions can also be generalized so that it applies when the base is not e (which it is when we work with natural logarithms). In such cases it can be shown that

$$\boxed{\text{if } y = \log_b x, \text{ then } \frac{dy}{dx} = \frac{1}{x(\ln b)}.}$$

EXAMPLE 10.22 For instance, if $y = \log_{10} x$, then $\dfrac{dy}{dx} = \dfrac{1}{x(\ln 10)}$, where $\ln 10$ is approximately equal to 2.30.

EXERCISES

1. Differentiate.
   (a) $f(x) = e^{5x}$
   (b) $f(x) = e^{-15x}$
   (c) $g(x) = 5^{2x}$
   (d) $y = 6e^{5x^3}$
   (e) $f(x) = x^2 \cdot e^x$
   (f) $y = (1 + 2e^x)^3$
   (g) $y = \dfrac{3 - 2e^x}{1 + 3e^x}$
   (h) $f(x) = (1 + 3x^4)e^{-x}$
   (i) $F(x) = x^3 \cdot 2^{4x}$
   (j) $g(x) = \dfrac{1 + 4^x}{1 - 4^x}$

2. In Example 4.2 (Section 4.1) we expressed the annual demand for a new meat tenderizer (in thousands of packages) by means of the equation

   $$y = 100 - 94e^{-x}$$

   where x is the number of years the product has been on the market. At what *annual rate* is the demand growing after 3 years? Compare this with the actual change in the demand between $x = 3$ and $x = 4$, and explain why there is a difference between the two results.

3. In Exercise 7 at the end of Section 4.1 we used the equation

   $$y = 100e^{-0.000025x}$$

   to determine y, the proportion of radial tires (made by one manufacturer) that are still usable after having been driven for x miles. Find the values of $\dfrac{dy}{dx}$ at $x = 20{,}000$ and $x = 40{,}000$, and explain the significance of these results.

4. If D is the demand for a product (in thousands of units), the total sales revenue in thousands of dollars is given by

   $$R = 500D \cdot e^{-0.2D}$$

Find the derivative of R with respect to D at $D = 2$ and $D = 5$, and explain the significance of these results.

5. With reference to Exercise 4, calculate the quantity $\dfrac{\frac{dR}{dD}}{R} \cdot 100$ for $D = 2$. What does this result *mean*?

6. Differentiate.

(a) $f(x) = \ln 3x$
(b) $y = \ln x^3$
(c) $f(x) = 3x^2 - 2(\ln x)^2$
(d) $g(x) = x^3(\log_5 x)$

(e) $g(x) = \dfrac{1}{x} \cdot \ln x$
(f) $y = (\ln x)^6$
(g) $f(x) = (2 + x)(\log_{10} x)$
(h) $y = \dfrac{3x^2}{\log_{10} x}$

7. The relationship between the weekly demand for new television sets in a certain market area and their price (in dollars) is given by

$$D = 1500 - 200 \cdot \ln p$$

for $300 \leq p \leq 500$. Find $\dfrac{dD}{dp}$ at $p = 400$ and explain its significance.

10.9 HIGHER DERIVATIVES

Since the derivative of a function is also a function, there is no reason why we cannot *differentiate a derivative*. It is customary to refer to the function thus obtained as the **second derivative**, and if the values of the original function and its derivative are denoted by $f(x)$ and $f'(x)$, those of the second derivative are denoted by $f''(x)$. In the $\dfrac{dy}{dx}$ notation, it is customary to write the second derivative as $\dfrac{d^2y}{dx^2}$.

EXAMPLE 10.23 If $f(x) = x^4$, then $f'(x) = 4x^3$ and $f''(x) = 4 \cdot 3x^2 = 12x^2$. Also, if $y = e^{3x^2}$ we get

$$\frac{dy}{dx} = e^{3x^2} \cdot 6x = 6xe^{3x^2}$$

for the first derivative and

$$\frac{d^2y}{dx^2} = 6x(e^{3x^2} \cdot 6x) + e^{3x^2} \cdot 6$$

$$= (36x^2 + 6)e^{3x^2}$$

If we continue this process and differentiate again—if we differentiate the second derivative—we obtain the **third derivative**, which we denote by $f'''(x)$ or $\dfrac{d^3y}{dx^3}$. Continuing in this way, we can also define a **fourth derivative**, a **fifth derivative**, a **sixth derivative**, and so forth.*

EXAMPLE 10.23
(Continued) Referring again to $f(x) = x^4$, for which we already showed that $f'(x) = 4x^3$ and $f''(x) = 12x^2$, we can now add that $f'''(x) = 24x$, $f^{(iv)}(x) = 24$, and that from then on all higher derivatives are zero for all values of x.

EXERCISES

1. Find the first four derivatives of the function given by

$$f(x) = x^3 + 4x^2 - 5x + 7$$

In **Exercises 2–7,** find the first two derivatives.

2. $f(x) = x^4 - 3x^2 + 7$
3. $g(x) = 3x^5 - 4x^3$
4. $y = x^5 - 8x^3 + 1$
5. $f(x) = xe^{-x}$
6. $y = x^2 \cdot \ln x$
7. $f(x) = (1 + x)^3 e^{2x}$

SUMMARY

In this chapter we provided an introduction to the basic ideas of differential calculus. To begin with, we showed how the concept of the *limit of a function* can be used to measure the slope of a curve at a point, a

---

*When using the $f'(x), f''(x), \ldots$ notation, small Roman numerals in parentheses are used instead of the primes for any derivative higher than the third.

process which is equivalent to measuring the instantaneous rate of change of a function.

In Section 10.2 we indicated that the special type of limit defined in Section 10.1 is a *derivative*, and that the process of finding the derivative is called *differentiation*. A four-step process, known as the *delta process*, was introduced to perform the actual mechanics of differentiation. Then, in Section 10.3, we introduced several rules to simplify the four-step process for finding the derivative.

Subsequent sections discussed special methods of differentiation that often provide great simplifications when the rules we introduced cannot be easily applied. Specifically, we discussed the use of the *chain rule* and *implicit differentiation*, followed by a discussion of methods for differentiating several types of exponential and logarithmic functions. The chapter concluded with a brief introduction to *higher derivatives*.

1. Consider the function $y = 4x^2 + 2x + 8$. Find the average rate of change for the interval from:
   (a) $x = 2$ to $x = 3$
   (b) $x = 2$ to $x = 2.1$
   (c) $x = 2$ to $x = 2.01$

2. Use the four-step delta process to differentiate the function of Exercise 1.

3. Use the rules of differentiation presented in Section 10.4 to differentiate the function given in Exercise 1.

In **Exercises 4–7**, evaluate the limits by direct substitution, or, if necessary, by first simplifying the expression for $f(x)$.

4. $\lim\limits_{x \to 2}(3x^2 + 2)$

5. $\lim\limits_{x \to 1}\dfrac{x^2 + x - 2}{x - 1}$

6. $\lim\limits_{x \to 1}\dfrac{x^2 + x - 2}{x + 1}$

7. $\lim\limits_{x \to 5}\dfrac{4x^2 - 100}{2x(x - 5)}$

In **Exercises 8–10**, determine whether or not the function is continuous at the point specified. If not, which of the conditions for continuity is violated?

8. $f(x) = \dfrac{x + 2}{x - 2}$ at $x = 2$

9. $f(x) = \dfrac{x^2 + 3x}{x + 3}$ at $x = 3$

10. $f(x) = 8x^2 + 4x$ at $x = 4$

In **Exercises 11–13**, use the four-step delta process to differentiate each function.

11. $y = 2x^2$

12. $y = x + 5$

13. $y = x^2 + 6x + 9$

In **Exercises 14–22,** use the rules of differentiation given in Section 10.6 to differentiate each function.

14. $f(x) = -2x^2$

15. $y = (x + 3)(x + 3)$

16. $y = 5x^2 + 2x^{-4}$

17. $f(x) = 3x^2 + 4x + 5$

18. $y = \dfrac{x^2 + 2x}{x + 2}$

19. $y = 15x$

20. $y = -2x + 4$

21. $y = \dfrac{2x^3 - x^2 + 4}{x}$

22. $y = \dfrac{1}{x^3}$

In **Exercises 23–29,** use the methods of differentiation presented in Sections 10.4 and 10.5 to differentiate each function.

23. $y = (x + 3)^2$

24. $y = (2x^2 + 6x)^3$

25. $f(x) = 10(3x^2 + 5x)^2$

26. $y = x^{1/2}$

27. $f(x) = (x^2 + 8x)^{1/2}$

28. Given $2xy = 4x + 2y - 6$, find $\dfrac{dy}{dx}$.

29. Given $x^3 - 2y^2 + xy = 0$, find $\dfrac{dy}{dx}$.

In **Exercises 30–35,** use the methods of differentiation given in Sections 10.6 and 10.7 to differentiate each function.

30. $f(x) = e^{-5x}$

31. $y = (4e^x)^2$

32. $f(x) = (\ln x)^2$

33. $y = \ln 5x$

34. $y = \ln x^{-2}$

35. Find the second derivative of each function.
    (a) $y = x^2 + 6x + 9$
    (b) $f(x) = -4x^3$
    (c) $y = x^4 - 2x^2 + 3$

36. A department store's profit is given by $P = 250{,}000 + 3600x - 40x^2$, where x is the daily expenditure on advertising. Without actually calculating any values of this function or plotting its graph, judge whether it would be profitable for them to increase their advertising budget if the current advertising expenditures are (a) $40 per day, and (b) $60 per day.

37. The relationship between the weekly demand for a radio in a certain market area and its price (in dollars) is given by

$$D = \ln (p + 100)$$

Find the derivative of D with respect to p at $p = 20$ and $p = 50$. What is the significance of these two derivatives?

38. A company's total sales revenue is given by the equation $f(x) = 2x + x^2$, where x is the number of years the company has been in business and $f(x)$ is in millions of dollars.
    (a) At what rate is the company's total sales revenue growing after 3 years?
    (b) Find the equation of the tangent line at $x = 3$ and use it to predict the company's total sales revenue for the fifth year *if the growth rate were to remain constant after the third year.* How does this compare with the corresponding value obtained by substituting $x = 5$ into the original formula?

39. The demand for a product (in hundreds of units) is related to its price (in cents) by means of the equation

$$D = \frac{500}{\sqrt{p}}$$

Find the instantaneous (marginal) rate at which the demand is decreasing when the price is 25¢ per unit.

40. A new company's gross earnings are given by

$$y = 24{,}000e^{0.2t}$$

where y is in dollars and t is the number of years the company has been in business. At what rate will the company's gross earnings be growing after it has been in business for 8 years?

DIFFERENTIAL CALCULUS APPLICATIONS

Most applications of differential calculus to business and economics arise in optimization problems, namely, in problems in which we want to find the best way of performing a certain operation. The theory of Chapter 10 is thus used to find the conditions which will maximize a company's profit, which will minimize the cost of production, which will maximize the efficiency of a process, which will hold losses to a minimum, which will maximize the yield of investments, and so on.

11.1 MAXIMA AND MINIMA

In each of the problems which we shall study in this section there will be one *independent variable* (whose values can presumably be controlled) and one *dependent variable* (whose values we hope to maximize or minimize). To make this possible, it will always be assumed that the two variables are related by means of a known function, so our problem reduces to that of *maximizing or minimizing* the values of this function. (Situations in which there are several independent variables will be treated separately in Section 11.2.)

When we look at problems of this kind geometrically, we say that a point on the graph of $y = f(x)$ is a relative maximum if it is higher than any nearby point and that it is a relative minimum if it is lower than any nearby point. Thus in Figure 11.1, there is a relative maximum at point P, a relative minimum at point Q, and another relative maximum at point R. It is apparent from this graph that a relative maximum need not be the *highest* point on a curve and that a relative minimum need not be the *lowest*; although there is a relative maximum at point P of Figure 11.1 (which is higher than any *nearby* point), the function assumes greater values further to the right, and although there is a relative minimum at point Q, the function assumes smaller values further to the left. It should also be noted that as we have drawn the graph of Figure 11.1, the curve has a *horizontal slope* (so the function has a

FIGURE 11.1
Relative Maxima
and Minima

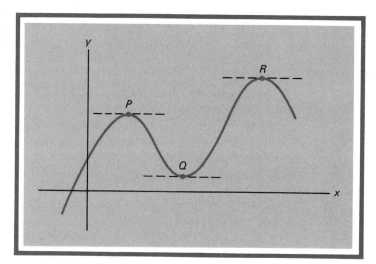

zero *derivative*) at points P, Q, and R. Although it is very often true that a zero derivative implies that there is a relative maximum or a relative minimum, and vice versa, there are exceptions.

EXAMPLE 11.1   In the graph of Figure 10.7, there is a relative minimum at $x = 1$ but the derivative does not exist. Another exception of this kind may be found in the graph of Figure 11.2, where at $x = 2$ the function has a zero

FIGURE 11.2
Graph of Curve
without Relative
Maximum or Minimum

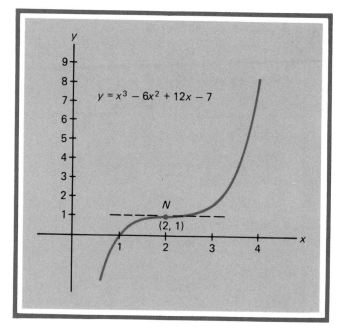

$$y = x^3 - 6x^2 + 12x - 7$$

N

(2, 1)

derivative (and its graph a horizontal slope) without there being a relative maximum or a relative minimum.

If a function is differentiable, however, *a relative maximum or minimum can exist only when the slope of its graph is horizontal*, and we therefore begin all optimization problems (to which calculus applies) by looking for the values of the independent variable at which the derivative of the function is zero. Then we must check whether there is a relative maximum or a relative minimum for each of these values, or whether we are faced with a situation like that shown in Figure 11.2. This could be done geometrically by plotting a few nearby points (the points corresponding to x = 1 and x = 3, for instance, in Figure 11.2), but there exists a systematic way which is generally much easier. To explain how it works, let us inspect the two diagrams of Figure 11.3. In the first diagram there is a relative maximum, and if we move *from left to right* it can be seen that the slope (and, hence, the derivative of the function) is at first positive, but it decreases, becoming zero and then negative. This means that the derivative is *decreasing*, namely, that its rate of change—the *second derivative*—must be *negative*. Similarly, in the second diagram, there is a relative minimum, and if we move *from left to right* it can be seen that the slope (and, hence, the derivative of the function) is at first negative, but it increases, becoming zero and then positive. This means that now the derivative is *increasing*, namely, that its rate of change—the *second derivative*—must be *positive*. We thus have the following criterion.

If the first derivative is zero at a given point and the second derivative is negative, there must be a relative maximum; if the first derivative is zero at a given point and the second derivative is positive, there must be a relative minimum.

FIGURE 11.3
Relative Maximum
and Relative Minimum

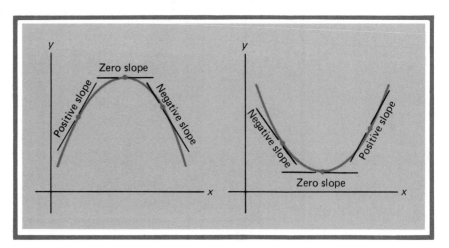

If the first and second derivatives are *both* zero at a given point, we simply resort to the method suggested first, plotting a few nearby points.

If the second derivative is *zero* at $x = a$ and has opposite signs for values of x slightly less than and slightly greater than a, the point is referred to as an **inflection point**. More intuitively, it is a point at which the tangent to the curve *changes from rotating in one direction to rotating in the opposite direction*. For example, the point N in Figure 11.2 is an inflection point.

EXAMPLE 11.2   To illustrate this theory, let us refer to the function given by $y = x^3 - 9x^2 + 24x$, whose graph we plotted in Figure 2.6. When we differentiate twice with respect to x, we get

$$\frac{dy}{dx} = 3x^2 - 18x + 24$$

and

$$\frac{d^2y}{dx^2} = 6x - 18$$

To find the values of x at which the first derivative is zero, we shall have to solve the quadratic equation $3x^2 - 18x + 24 = 0$, which simplifies to

$$x^2 - 6x + 8 = 0$$

Using the quadratic formula or any of the other techniques of Section 3.3, we get $x = 2$ and $x = 4$, and, substituting these values into the formula obtained for the second derivative, we get $6(2) - 18 = -6$ and $6(4) - 18 = 6$. Thus, there is a *relative maximum* at $x = 2$ (where the second derivative is negative) and a *relative minimum* at $x = 4$ (where the second derivative is positive). These results are shown in Figure 11.4, and they answer the question asked in Example 2.6, namely, whether the graph of the function might not oscillate wildly between the five points through which we drew its graph in Figure 2.6. *Our analysis has shown that the curve cannot have any "turning points" (that is, relative maxima or minima) other than those at $x = 2$ and $x = 4$.*

EXAMPLE 11.3   To give another illustration of this technique, let us analyze the function of Figure 11.2, whose equation was $y = x^3 - 6x^2 + 12x - 7$. Differentiating twice with respect to x, we get

$$\frac{dy}{dx} = 3x^2 - 12x + 12$$

FIGURE 11.4
*Diagram
for Example 11.2*

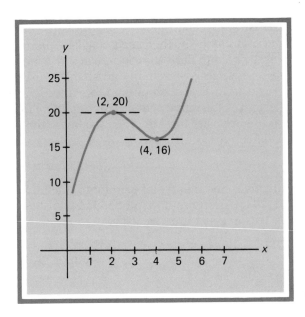

and

$$\frac{d^2y}{dx^2} = 6x - 12$$

To find the values at which the first derivative is zero, we have to solve the quadratic equation $3x^2 - 12x + 12 = 0$, which simplifies to

$$x^2 - 4x + 4 = 0$$

The only solution of this equation is $x = 2$, and if we substitute this value of x into $6x - 12$, the expression we obtained for the second derivative, we get $6(2) - 12 = 0$. Since the second derivative is thus also zero at $x = 2$, we continue by investigating the values of the function at two nearby points, such as at $x = 1.9$ and $x = 2.1$, for which we get

$$f(1.9) = (1.9)^3 - 6(1.9)^2 + 12(1.9) - 7 = 0.999$$

and

$$f(2.1) = (2.1)^3 - 6(2.1)^2 + 12(2.1) - 7 = 1.001$$

Since one of these values is less than $f(2) = 1$ while the other is greater than 1, we conclude that there is *neither a relative maximum nor a relative minimum* at $x = 2$ (as is apparent, of course, from Figure 11.2). Actually, a function *could* have a relative maximum or minimum at a point where its first two derivatives are both zero; this is illustrated in the two parts of Exercise 6 at the end of this section.

Next, let us study some situations in which the theory of relative maxima and minima, which we have studied, can be applied.

EXAMPLE 11.4   Consider a retailer's problem of pricing an alarm clock which costs the retailer $4.00. Assume that if the price is x dollars per clock, the retailer will be able to sell 480 − 40x clocks. The problem is to determine how much to charge per clock to maximize total profit. Since total profit is given by the product of the number of clocks sold and the profit per clock, namely, the product of 480 − 40x and x − 4, the quantity the retailer wants to maximize is given by

$$\text{Total profit} = (480 - 40x)(x - 4)$$

Differentiating twice, first by the product rule, we get

$$\frac{dy}{dx} = (480 - 40x) \cdot 1 + (x - 4) \cdot (-40) = 640 - 80x$$

and

$$\frac{d^2y}{dx^2} = -80$$

so that there is the possibility for a relative maximum or minimum when

$$640 - 80x = 0$$

namely, at x = 8. Since the second derivative is *negative* for that value of x (or, for that matter, for any value of x), we conclude that the function has a relative maximum at x = 8; in other words, profit will be maximized if the retailer charges $8.00 for each of the clocks. In fact, this maximum profit will be $640, as can easily be verified by substituting x = 8 into the original equation.

EXAMPLE 11.5   To consider one more example, suppose that the relationship between the demand for a product (say, a new kind of battery) and its price (in cents) is given by the equation

$$D = 25,000e^{-0.05p}$$

and that we want to find the value of p for which the *total sales revenue* will be a maximum. Since the total sales revenue is given by the product of p (price) and D (demand), the function whose values we shall want to maximize is given by

$$f(p) = 25{,}000p \cdot e^{-0.05p}$$

When we differentiate with respect to p, we get

$$f'(p) = 25{,}000p\,(-0.05)e^{-0.05p} + 25{,}000e^{-0.05p}$$
$$= 25{,}000e^{-0.05p}(-0.05p + 1)$$

which can equal zero only when

$$-0.05p + 1 = 0$$

namely, when $0.05p = 1$, or $p = 20$. It will be left to you to verify that the second derivative is *negative* at $p = 20$, so that the total sales revenue will, indeed, be a *maximum* when the price per battery is 20¢.

Before we turn to other applications of differential calculus, let us caution you against the indiscriminate application of the method which we have just discussed. As we already pointed out, there are situations where the derivative at a maximum or minimum point of a curve does not exist. Also, we must always be careful to check *whether the answers we get fall within the domain for which the function is defined, or for which it has meaningful applications.*

EXAMPLE 11.6   In Section 3.3 we introduced the concept of quadratic functions with an illustration that involved the relationship between the weekly demand for a new frozen dessert and the price at which it is sold. Specifically, a market research study showed that 240,000 of the desserts were sold when they were priced at 15¢, 100,000 were sold when they were priced at 20¢, and 60,000 were sold when they were priced at 24¢. It can be shown that the demand curve corresponding to these observations is

$$y = 1260 - 98x + 2x^2$$

where x is the price in cents and y is the demand in thousands. Differentiating twice with respect to x, we get

$$\frac{dy}{dx} = -98 + 4x \quad \text{and} \quad \frac{d^2y}{dx^2} = 4$$

and we might be tempted to conclude that the demand is a minimum when $-98 + 4x = 0$, namely, when the frozen dessert sells at *two for 49¢*. This is quite unreasonable, however, because the given funcion provides a suitable model only for a limited set of values of x. For example, suppose the processor of the desserts wants to use this parabolic model to see how many desserts can be sold if they charge either 10¢ or 30¢. When we substitute x = 10, we find that in the first case

$$y = 1260 - 98(10) + 2(10)^2 = 480$$

or, that there would be a demand for 480,000 of the frozen desserts. In the second case, substitution of x = 30 yields

$$y = 1260 - 98(30) + 2(30)^2 = 120$$

which represents a demand for 120,000 of the frozen desserts per week. The first of these results seems rather high and it may well raise some doubts about the appropriateness of the equation with which it was obtained. So far as the second result is concerned, something must definitely be wrong—according to the original data, 60,000 of the desserts were sold when they were priced at 24¢, and it simply does not make sense that the demand should go up when the price is increased to 30¢. What we are observing is an example of the problems that arise when we attempt to extrapolate beyond the price range to which the quadratic function was meant to apply. Thus, if we limit the domain of the function, for example, to the interval from x = 15 to x = 24, it is apparent from Figure 11.5 that the demand is a minimum at x = 24 cents.

Since situations like this are by no means rare, we must always be on the alert for the possibility that the desired maximum or minimum may occur at the endpoint (or endpoints) of the interval (or intervals) to which the independent variable is restricted.

To summarize the method of this section, let us list the following steps for determining the relative maxima and minima of functions whose first and second derivatives exist.

1. *Find the first and second derivatives $f'(x)$ and $f''(x)$.*
2. *Solve the equation $f'(x) = 0$ for x, but eliminate those solutions which do not fall within the domain of x dictated by the nature of the problem.*
3. *Find the value of $f''(x)$ for each x obtained in Step 2; then*
    (a) *if $f''(x)$ is negative, there is a relative maximum;*
    (b) *if $f''(x)$ is positive, there is a relative minimum;*
    (c) *if $f''(x)$ is zero, check the values of the original function at nearby points.*

FIGURE 11.5
Diagram
for Example 11.6

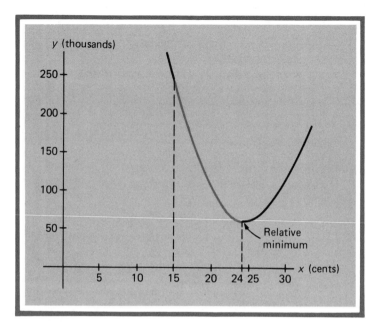

1. Find the value of x for which $y = 5 - 8x + 2x^2$ is a relative minimum.

2. Find the value of x for which $y = 6x - x^2$ is a relative maximum. If the domain of x is the set of all real numbers, is the corresponding value of y actually the maximum value of this function?

3. Find the relative maxima and minima of

$$y = x^3 - 9x^2 + 15x + 2$$

   and plot the graph of this function.

4. Find the relative maxima and minima of

$$y = 3x^4 - 16x^3 + 6x^2 + 72x$$

   and plot the graph of this function (*Hint*: Solve the resulting equation by factoring.)

5. Investigate the relative maxima and minima of each function and plot its graph.
   (a) $y = x^3 - 9x^2 + 27x - 20$
   (b) $y = 3x^5 - 5x^3$

6. Investigate the relative maxima and minima of each function and plot its graph.

(a) $y = -x^4$

(b) $y = 3(x - 2)^4 + 2$

7. A company which leases fleets of cars to large corporations discounts the total bill by 2 percent for each car in excess of 20 (up to a maximum discount of 50 percent).

(a) If they charge K dollars per car without the discount, find an expression for their total receipts for x + 20 cars.

(b) For how many cars would their total receipts be a maximum?

8. The management of a company making optical equipment has found that the demand for one kind of lens is given by

$$D = 112e^{-0.02p}$$

where p is the price per lens in dollars. How many of these lenses should they make to maximize their total sales revenue?

9. The manufacturer of a new alloy knows that at p dollars a ton, $240 - p$ tons can be sold at a cost of $8,000/(240 - p) + 30$ dollars per ton. How much should be charged and how many tons should be manufactured to maximize his total profit?

10. A manufacturer of cardboard boxes wants to make open boxes out of pieces of cardboard 30 inches long and 30 inches wide by cutting squares out of the corners (see Figure 11.6) and folding up the sides.

(a) Show that if x is the side of these squares, then the volume of the boxes is given by

$$V = 4x^3 - 120x^2 + 900x$$

FIGURE 11.6
Diagram
for Exercise 10

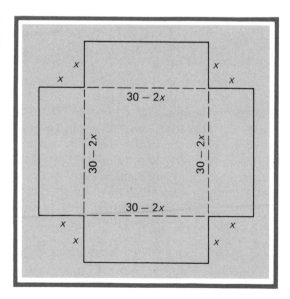

(b) Squares of what size should be cut out of the corners of the pieces of cardboard so as to maximize the volume of these open boxes?

11. Importers claim that if the government charges a tax of t cents on an ounce of a certain kind of perfume imported from an Asian country, they will be able to sell $48,000 - 200t$ ounces of the perfume. Assuming that this claim is correct, what tax should the government charge so as to maximize its total tax revenue on this perfume?

12. The operator of a boat dock figures that with y sailboats the weekly profit from their rental will be $120\sqrt{y} - 15y$ dollars. How many sailboats should the operator keep so as to maximize profit?

13. A certain study showed that a person with x years of formal education (grade school, high school, college) can expect lifetime earnings of $750,000 - 360,000e^{-x/6}$ dollars, and that a year of formal education costs on the average \$3000. How many years of formal education will thus maximize a person's net lifetime earnings (namely, earnings minus the expense of formal education)?

11.2 PARTIAL DIFFERENTIATION

In Section 2.3 we touched only very briefly upon functions of *several independent variables*, but it is important to appreciate the fact that in most practical applications, situations involving several independent variables are more common than those in which there is only one. Retail prices, for example, depend on salaries paid to salespeople, store rental, advertising, wholesale prices, and so on; dividends paid by corporations depend on factors such as their earnings per share, their overall financial condition, their policy concerning research and development, and taxes; and interest rates, to mention one more example, depend on the demand for mortgage money, the availability of cash, government regulations, and numerous other factors.

When we deal with more than one independent variable, everything becomes (mathematically speaking) much more complicated, and this applies particularly to rates of change. When several independent variables are all changing at the same time, it can be very difficult to determine how these changes *interact* (that is, how they affect each other), and it can be very difficult, indeed, to determine how the rate of change of a dependent variable is related to those of all the independent variables.

In this section, we shall study **partial derivatives**, namely, *derivatives with respect to one of the independent variables when all the* other *independent variables are treated as constants.* Given $z = f(x, y)$, for instance, we are said to be differentiating **partially** with respect to x, if we treat y as a constant and otherwise proceed as in ordinary differentiation. This partial derivative of z with respect to x is written as $\frac{\partial z}{\partial x}$ (where the symbol ∂ is used instead of the letter d to distinguish partial derivatives from "ordinary" derivatives), and we similarly write $\frac{\partial z}{\partial y}$ for the partial derivative of z with respect to y, which is obtained by differentiating with respect to y while treating x as a constant. More generally, if $u = f(x, y, z)$, the partial derivative of u with respect to x, $\frac{\partial u}{\partial x}$, is obtained by differentiating with respect to x while treating y and z as constants, and $\frac{\partial u}{\partial y}$ and $\frac{\partial u}{\partial z}$ are defined in the same way.

EXAMPLE 11.7 If

$$z = 2x^2 + 4xy - y^2 + 5x - 3y$$

then

$$\frac{\partial z}{\partial x} = 4x + 4y + 5 \quad \text{and} \quad \frac{\partial z}{\partial y} = 4x - 2y - 3$$

and if

$$z = u^2 + uvw + uw^2$$

then

$$\frac{\partial z}{\partial u} = 2u + vw + w^2, \quad \frac{\partial z}{\partial v} = uw, \quad \frac{\partial z}{\partial w} = uv + 2uw$$

EXAMPLE 11.8 In Example 2.7 we expressed the relationship among z (the cost of a certain product in dollars), x (the cost of raw materials in dollars per pound), and y (the cost of labor in dollars per hour) by means of the equation

$$z = 130 + 12x + 27y$$

If we now differentiate partially with respect to x and y, we get

$$\frac{\partial z}{\partial x} = 12 \quad \text{and} \quad \frac{\partial z}{\partial y} = 27$$

and this means that *when the cost of labor is held fixed, an increase of $1 per pound in the cost of raw materials brings about an increase of $12 in the cost of the product, and that when the cost of raw materials is held fixed, an increase of $1 in the hourly cost of labor brings about an increase of $27 in the cost of the product.*

If we differentiate $\dfrac{\partial z}{\partial x}$ partially with respect to x (that is, if we differentiate $\dfrac{\partial z}{\partial x}$ with respect to x while treating y as a constant), we get the **second partial derivative** $\dfrac{\partial^2 z}{\partial x^2}$, and if we differentiate $\dfrac{\partial z}{\partial x}$ partially with respect to y (that is, if we differentiate $\dfrac{\partial z}{\partial x}$ with respect to y while treating x as a constant), we get the *second partial derivative* $\dfrac{\partial^2 z}{(\partial y\,\partial x)}$. The other two *second partial derivatives*, $\dfrac{\partial^2 z}{\partial y^2}$ and $\dfrac{\partial^2 z}{(\partial x\,\partial y)}$, are defined in the same way, and it should be noted that $\dfrac{\partial^2 z}{(\partial x\,\partial y)}$ is equal to $\dfrac{\partial^2 z}{(\partial y\,\partial x)}$.*

EXAMPLE 11.7
(Continued)

Referring again to the function of Example 11.7, for which we obtained

$$\frac{\partial z}{\partial x} = 4x + 4y + 5 \quad \text{and} \quad \frac{\partial z}{\partial y} = 4x - 2y - 3$$

we now get

$$\frac{\partial^2 z}{\partial x^2} = 4, \qquad \frac{\partial^2 z}{\partial y^2} = -2, \qquad \frac{\partial^2 z}{\partial y\,\partial x} = 4, \qquad \frac{\partial^2 z}{\partial x\,\partial y} = 4$$

We have introduced these *higher* partial derivatives primarily because they are needed to decide whether $z = f(x, y)$ has a relative maximum, a relative minimum, or neither for given values of x and y.

For a relative maximum or a relative minimum, it is necessary that

---

*In certain rare cases, $\dfrac{\partial^2 z}{(\partial x\,\partial y)}$ and $\dfrac{\partial^2 z}{(\partial y\,\partial x)}$ are not equal. In this text we are not interested in such cases, so we shall assume that these two second partials are always equal.

$$\frac{\partial z}{\partial x} = 0 \quad \text{and} \quad \frac{\partial z}{\partial y} = 0$$

There is a relative maximum if

$$\frac{\partial^2 z}{\partial x^2} < 0 \quad \text{and} \quad \frac{\partial^2 z}{\partial x^2} \cdot \frac{\partial^2 z}{\partial y^2} - \left(\frac{\partial^2 z}{\partial x\,\partial y}\right)^2 > 0$$

and a relative minimum if

$$\frac{\partial^2 z}{\partial x^2} > 0 \quad \text{and} \quad \frac{\partial^2 z}{\partial x^2} \cdot \frac{\partial^2 z}{\partial y^2} - \left(\frac{\partial^2 z}{\partial x\,\partial y}\right)^2 > 0$$

If $\left(\frac{\partial^2 z}{\partial x^2}\right)\left(\frac{\partial^2 z}{\partial y^2}\right) - \left(\frac{\partial^2 z}{\partial x\,\partial y}\right)^2 < 0$, then there is a saddle point, which is neither a relative maximum nor a relative minimum. A complete discussion of saddle points is beyond the scope of this text.

EXAMPLE 11.9 To illustrate this theory, which is proved in most advanced calculus texts, let us investigate the function given by

$$z = x^2 + y^2 - 6x - 4y + 18$$

When we perform the necessary partial differentiations, we get

$$\frac{\partial z}{\partial x} = 2x - 6 \quad \frac{\partial z}{\partial y} = 2y - 4, \quad \frac{\partial^2 z}{\partial x^2} = 2, \quad \frac{\partial^2 z}{\partial y^2} = 2, \quad \frac{\partial^2 z}{\partial x\,\partial y} = 0$$

and it follows that $\frac{\partial z}{\partial x}$ and $\frac{\partial z}{\partial y}$ are zero when $2x - 6 = 0$ and $2y - 4 = 0$ namely, when $x = 3$ and $y = 2$. Since $\frac{\partial^2 z}{\partial x^2}$ is *positive* (regardless of the values of x and y), there is the possibility of a relative minimum, and since

$$\frac{\partial^2 z}{\partial x^2} \cdot \frac{\partial^2 z}{\partial y^2} - \left(\frac{\partial^2 z}{\partial x\,\partial y}\right)^2 = 2 \cdot 2 - 0^2 = 4 > 0$$

we conclude that the function *has* a relative minimum at $x = 3$ and

$y = 2$. In fact, this minimum value of the function is

$$z = 3^2 + 2^2 - 6(3) - 4(2) + 18 = 5$$

As a check, you may wish to calculate z for some values of x and y close to $x = 3$ and $y = 2$, respectively.

EXAMPLE 11.10 To consider a practical application, suppose that a manufacturer who makes shirts out of two kinds of material knows from past experience that if the firm makes x dozen shirts out of the first kind of material and y dozen shirts out of the second kind of material, they will sell for $80 - 3x$ and $60 - 2y$ dollars per dozen, respectively. How many dozens of each kind should the firm schedule for production *to maximize profit*, knowing that the cost of manufacturing x dozen shirts out of the first kind of material and y dozen shirts out of the second kind of material is $12x + 8y + 4xy$ dollars?

Since total sales revenue is given by $x(80 - 3x) + y(60 - 2y)$, where $x(80 - x)$ is the amount of money received for the shirts made out of the first kind of material and $y(60 - 2y)$ is the amount of money received for the shirts made out of the second kind of material, the profit is

$$z = x(80 - 3x) + y(60 - 2y) - (12x + 8y + 4xy)$$
$$= 80x - 3x^2 + 60y - 2y^2 - 12x - 8y - 4xy$$

If we differentiate partially with respect to x and y, we get

$$\frac{\partial z}{\partial x} = 80 - 6x - 12 - 4y$$

and

$$\frac{\partial z}{\partial y} = 60 - 4y - 8 - 4x$$

and the values of these two partial derivatives are zero when $80 - 6x - 12 - 4y = 0$ and $60 - 4y - 8 - 4x = 0$, namely, when

$$6x + 4y = 68$$
$$4x + 4y = 52$$

Subtracting, we get $2x = 16$; hence $x = 8$, and if we then substitute this value of x into the second equation, we get $4(8) + 4y = 52$, $4y = 20$, and $y = 5$.

To check whether $x = 8$ and $y = 5$ will actually maximize the manufacturer's profit, we shall have to investigate the second partial derivatives, which are

$$\frac{\partial^2 z}{\partial x^2} = -6, \qquad \frac{\partial^2 z}{\partial y^2} = -4, \qquad \frac{\partial^2 z}{\partial x \, \partial y} = -4$$

Since the first is *negative* and

$$\frac{\partial^2 z}{\partial x^2} \cdot \frac{\partial^2 z}{\partial y^2} - \left(\frac{\partial^2 z}{\partial x \, \partial y}\right)^2 = (-6)(-4) - (-4)^2 = 8 > 0$$

it follows that the manufacturer's profit will indeed be a *maximum* for production of 8 dozen shirts made out of the first kind of material and 5 dozen shirts made out of the second kind of material. In fact, this maximum profit will be

$$z = 80(8) - 3(8)^2 + 60(5) - 2(5)^2 - 12(8) - 8(5) - 4(8)(5)$$

$$= \$402$$

In **Exercises 1–6**, calculate $\dfrac{\partial z}{\partial x}, \dfrac{\partial z}{\partial y}, \dfrac{\partial^2 z}{\partial x^2}$, and $\dfrac{\partial^2 z}{\partial y^2}$ for each.

1. $z = x^2 + 4xy - y^2$
2. $z = x^3 + x^2 y^2 = 6y^3$
3. $z = 2x + y^2 - \dfrac{x}{y}$
4. $z = 3x^3 + 2y - x \cdot e^y$
5. $z = \ln x + 3x^2 y^2$
6. $z = x(\ln y) + y(\ln x)$

7. Verify for Exercises 1–6 that $\dfrac{\partial^2 z}{\partial y \, \partial x} = \dfrac{\partial^2 z}{\partial x \, \partial y}$.

8. In a certain city, the daily demand for beef (in pounds) is given by

$$z = 32{,}400 - 260x + 310y$$

where x is the average retail price of beef (in cents per pound) and y is the average retail price of pork (in cents per pound). Calculate the two partial derivatives $\dfrac{\partial z}{\partial x}$ and $\dfrac{\partial z}{\partial y}$ and explain what they mean.

9. A banker figures the size of a 25-year mortgage she is willing to give on a one-family house by means of the formula

$$z = 3x_1 + 0.025(x_2)^2$$

where x_1 is the size of the down payment (in dollars) and x_2 is the applicant's monthly salary (also in dollars). Calculate the two partial derivatives $\dfrac{\partial z}{\partial x_1}$ and $\dfrac{\partial z}{\partial x_2}$ and explain what they mean.

In **Exercises 10–12**, check for the possible existence of a relative maximum or a relative minimum.

10. $z = 2x^2 - 2xy + y^2 - 16x + 10y + 12$

11. $z = x^2 - 3xy - 2y^2 - 5x + y$

12. $z = e^{-(x^2+y^2)}$

13. A construction company pays untrained workers $5.00 an hour and trained workers $9.00 an hour. Knowing that the cost of a certain job (in dollars) will be

$$z = 2000 + 27x^3 - 72xy + 8y^2$$

if they use x untrained workers and y trained workers, how many workers of each kind should they use to *minimize their cost?*

14. A pharmaceutical firm can make $20 - \dfrac{50}{x} - \dfrac{24}{y}$ pounds of an antibiotic out of x pounds of ingredient A and y pounds of ingredient B, where ingredient A cost $3 a pound, ingredient B costs $4 a pound, and the antibiotic sells for $24 a pound.
 (a) Subtract the cost of the ingredients, $3x + 4y$, from the total sales revenue to express the pharmaceutical firm's profit, z, in terms of x and y.
 (b) Use the result of part (a) to determine how many pounds of each ingredient the firm should use to *maximize profit.* What is this maximum profit?

15. A company makes two kinds of detergents which are competitive, so that if D_1 and D_2 are the respective demands (in thousands of boxes) when they are priced at p_1 and p_2 cents per box, then

$$D_1 = 250 - 4p_1 + p_2 \quad \text{and} \quad D_2 = 760 + 3p_1 - 6p_2$$

Express the company's total sales revenue on the two kinds of detergents in terms of p_1 and p_2, and find the values of p_1 and p_2 for which it will be a maximum.

In this section we discuss how to solve an optimization problem involving two independent variables and one equality constraint.

EXAMPLE 11.11   Suppose that the *percentage reliability* of an opinion poll in which 400 persons are interviewed is given by

$$R = 100 - \frac{x^2 + 9y^2}{20,000}$$

where x is the number of persons who have lived in the city where the poll is conducted for at least 2 years, and y is the number of persons who have moved there more recently. Clearly, the "independent" variables are subject to the restriction $x + y = 400$, and one way to handle this kind of problem is to use the restriction to *eliminate* one of the independent variables. For example, we could substitute $y = 400 - x$ into the above formula for R and then use the method of Section 11.1 to find the value of x (and, hence, the value of y) which maximizes the percentage reliability. In Exercise 1 at the end of this section, you will be asked to use this procedure to show that $x = 360$ and $y = 40$ maximizes the percentage reliability.

Example 11.11 illustrates a typical optimization problem in which a function of two variables is subject to an equality constraint. In general this type of problem can be written as follows

$$\text{max or min } f(x, y)$$

s.t.

$$g(x, y) = b$$

An approach to such problems that often simplifies matters is to introduce a new variable, called a *Lagrange multiplier*; this variable is used to form a new function that combines the objective function and the equality constraint. The resulting function that we obtain is called a **Lagrangian function**; it is written

$$L(x, y, \lambda) = f(x, y) + \lambda[g(x, y) - b]$$

where λ (lambda) is the **Lagrange multiplier**. For this function to have a relative maximum or minimum at a point, the partial derivatives with respect to x, y, and λ must all equal zero at that point. Thus we must differentiate $L(x, y, \lambda)$ partially with respect to x, y, and λ, equate these partial derivatives to 0, and solve the resulting system of equations for x, y, and λ.

EXAMPLE 11.11
(Continued)

To solve the problem of Example 11.11 using the Lagrange multiplier approach, we form the Lagrangian function

$$L(x, y, \lambda) = \left(100 - \frac{x^2 + 9y^2}{200}\right) + \lambda(x + y - 400)$$

Taking the partial derivatives with respect to x, y, and λ and setting them equal to zero, we obtain

$$\frac{\partial L}{\partial x} = -\frac{x}{100} + \lambda = 0$$

$$\frac{\partial L}{\partial y} = -\frac{9y}{100} + \lambda = 0$$

$$\frac{\partial L}{\partial \lambda} = x + y - 400 = 0$$

Thus we now have a system of three equations involving three variables. Solving this system of equations, we obtain the solution x = 360, y = 40, and $\lambda = 3.6$.

To check if the solution truly yields a relative maximum for the problem, we first substitute the value of λ obtained above back into the original Lagrangian function. We obtain

$$L(x, y, \lambda = 3.6) = \left(100 - \frac{x^2 + 9y^2}{200}\right) + 3.6(x + y - 400)$$

Since this results in a function of two variables, the rules of Section 11.2 can be used to determine if the solution x = 360 and y = 40 is a relative maximum. In Exercise 2 at the end of this section, you will be asked to verify that this solution does result in a relative maximum.

The Lagrange multiplier approach can be generalized to problems involving more than two independent variables and several equality constraints. In addition, calculus-based techniques also exist for other types of nonlinear optimization problems that involve inequality constraints, as well as a mixture of inequality and equality constraints. The details of such procedures are beyond the scope of this text.

1. With reference to Example 11.11, substitute the value of $y = 400 - x$ into the formula for R and then use the method of Section 11.1 to find the value of x (and, hence, the value of y) which maximizes the percentage reliability.

2. With reference to Example 11.11, where we used the Lagrange multiplier approach to obtain the solution $x = 360$ and $y = 40$, use the rules of Section 11.2 to verify that this solution is a relative maximum.

3. Consider the problem

$$\min \quad 2x^2 - 10x + y^2 - 4y + 100$$
$$\text{s.t.}$$
$$x + 2y = 8$$

Find the minimum solution to this problem by substituting $x = 8 - 2y$ into the objective function and then applying the procedure of Section 11.1.

4. Use the Lagrange multiplier approach to solve Exercise 3.

5. A department store's average daily budget for placing ads is $100, which is spent partly on newspaper ads and partly on television commercials. If, on the average, x dollars per day are spent on newspaper ads and y dollars on television commercials, the store's total annual cost of running its advertising department is given by

$$C = 20,000 + 20x^2 + xy + 12y^2 - 440x - 300y$$

By first eliminating y, find the value of x which will minimize the store's total annual cost of running its advertising department.

6. Use the Lagrange multiplier approach to solve Exercise 5.

Many problems in business and economics are concerned with finding the best way to perform a certain operation. For example, a company wants to determine what price it should charge for a new product in order to maximize total sales revenue, a truck rental firm wants to determine how often it should perform engine tune ups in order to minimize operating costs, and so on. In this chapter we showed how differential calculus can be used to solve optimization problems such as these.

We first considered situations involving two variables that are related by means of a known function whose first and second derivatives exist. In such cases, we can determine the relative maximum and minimum by performing the following steps.

1. Find $f'(x)$ and $f''(x)$.

2. Solve the equation $f'(x) = 0$ for x, but eliminate those solutions which do not fall with the domain of x dictated by the nature of the problem.

3. Find the values of $f''(x)$ for each x obtained in Step 2; then
   (a) if $f''(x)$ is negative, there is a relative maximum;
   (b) if $f''(x)$ is positive, there is a relative minimum;
   (c) if $f''(x)$ is zero, check the values of the original function at nearby points.

In Section 11.2 we introduced the concept of a *partial derivative*, namely, derivatives with respect to one of the independent variables when all the other independent variables are treated as constants. Using the concept of the partial derivative and the *second partial derivative*, we presented a set of rules for deciding whether $z = f(x, y)$ has a relative maximum, a relative minimum, or neither. The chapter concluded with a brief introduction to the use of Lagrange multipliers in solving optimization problems involving two independent variables and one equality constraint.

GLOSSARY

1. **Optimization Problem**   A problem in which we want to find the best way of performing a certain operation.

2. **Independent Variable**   A variable whose values can presumably be controlled.

3. **Dependent Variable**   A variable whose values we hope to maximize or minimize.

4. **Relative Maximum**   A point on the graph of $y = f(x)$ is a relative maximum if it is higher than any nearby point.

5. **Relative Minimum**   A point on the graph of $y = f(x)$ is a relative minimum if it is lower than any nearby point.

6. **Partial Derivatives**   Derivatives with respect to one of the independent variables when all the other independent variables are treated as constants.

7. **Lagrange Multiplier**   A new variable added to an optimization problem involving an equality constraint.

8. **Lagrangian Function**   A function formed using a Lagrange multiplier to combine the original objective function and the equality constraint.

1. Find the value of x for which $y = 4x^2 - 16x + 4$ is a relative minimum.

2. Find the value of x for which $y = -3x^2 + 24x - 8$ is a relative maximum.

3. Find the relative maximum and minimum of $y = 2x^3 - 15x^2 + 36$.

4. Find the relative maximum and minimum of $y = 2x^3 - 3x^2 - 12x$.

5. Find the values of x for which $y = 10x - 5x^2 - 20$ is a relative maximum.

6. Find the relative minimum of the function $f(x) = 4x^3 - 12x^2 + 60$.

7. A real estate investor feels that in n years he will be able to sell an apartment house for 350,000 + 40,000n dollars. If the interest rate paid by banks is 7 percent compounded annually, the *present value* of the sales price of the apartment house n years hence is

$$P = (350,000 + 40,000n)(1.07)^{-n}$$

(where we simply discounted the sales price for n years at 7 percent). For how many years should the investor hold on to the apartment house to maximize its present value, and, hence, his profit on the transaction? (Use ln 1.07 = 0.06766.)

8. A television executive claims that if a soap manufacturer will spend an extra x thousand dollars on television commercials, her total profit will be increased by $32x^2e^{-0.5x}$ thousand dollars. By how much should the soap manufacturer increase her advertising budget to maximize her profit, and what will be the corresponding increase in profit?

9. A rectangular warehouse with a floor space of 6000 square feet is to be built in a county where zoning regulations require a 20-foot utility easement in the front and in the back and a 12-foot utility easement on each side. What are the dimensions of the smallest rectangular piece of land on which this warehouse can be built? (*Hint*: Let the two sides of the warehouse be x and 6000/x.)

10. The management of a company has found that the demand for a product is given by

$$D = 85e^{-0.01p}$$

where p is the price per unit in dollars. How many units should they make to maximize their total sales revenue?

11. In a certain city, the daily demand for beef (in pounds) is given by the equation

$$z = 3800 - 27x + 33y$$

where x is the average retail price of beef (in cents per pound) and y is the average retail price of pork (in cents per pound). Calculate the two partial derivatives $\frac{\partial z}{\partial x}$ and $\frac{\partial z}{\partial y}$ and explain precisely what they mean.

12. A banker figures the size of a 20-year mortgage he is willing to give on a one-family house by means of the formula

$$z = 2x_1 + 0.02(x_2)^2$$

where x_1 is the size of the downpayment, x_2 is the applicant's monthly salary, and all figures are in dollars. Calculate the two partial derivatives $\frac{\partial z}{\partial x_1}$ and $\frac{\partial z}{\partial x_2}$ and explain precisely what they mean.

13. If $z = 3x^2 - 6xy + y^2 + 24x + 8y + 50$, find the values of x and y for which z is a relative maximum or minimum.

14. If $z = 80 - x^2 - 2y^2 - 6x + 12y$, find the values of x and y for which z is a maximum, and also calculate this maximum value of z.

15. The total profit of a restaurant was found to depend mostly on the amount of money spent on advertising and the quality of the preparation of the food (measured in terms of the salaries paid to the chefs). In fact, the manager of the restaurant found that if she pays her chefs x dollars per hour and spends y dollars a week on advertising, the restaurant's weekly profit (in dollars) will be

$$z = 516x + 1008y - x^2 - y^2 - xy$$

What hourly wages should the manager pay her chefs and how much should she spend on advertising to maximize the restaurant's profit?

16. The gross sales of a product is believed to be related to the amount spent on radio advertising and newspaper advertising by the function

$$z = -2x^2 + 4xy - 6y^2 + 20x + 36y - 100$$

where

z = gross sales in thousands of units

x = thousands of dollars spent on radio advertising

y = thousands of dollars spent on newspaper advertising

Find the values of x and y which will maximize gross sales.

17. Refer to Exercise 16. Because of a recent budget cut, the firm is limited to a budget of $15,000 for radio and newspaper advertising. By first eliminating y, find the value of x which will maximize gross sales.

18. Refer to Exercise 16. Use the Lagrange multiplier approach to find the values of x and y which will maximize gross sales if the total budget for radio and newspaper advertising is $10,000.

INTEGRAL
CALCULUS

In the introduction to Chapter 10 we stated that calculus deals with two special kinds of limits called *derivatives* and *integrals*. Then we proceeded to introduce the derivative as a *limit of a function* which represents the slope, steepness, or direction, of a curve at a point. In contrast, an integral is a *limit of a sequence*, and it also has an important geometrical interpretation—as we shall see in Section 12.2, *integrals represent areas under curves*.

Integrals do not have as many *direct* applications as derivatives to problems of business and economics. *Indirectly*, though, they play a very important role in the definition of *probability*, and, hence, they are of basic importance in statistics and in the many areas of management science which involve elements of uncertainty.

12.1 THE AREA UNDER A CURVE

When we deal with *continuously changing quantities*, it is easy to misinterpret what they actually represent. This is illustrated in Example 12.1.

EXAMPLE 12.1

Suppose that the demand for a new kind of high-intensity reading lamp is given by the equation

$$f(x) = 120 + 144x^2$$

where x is the number of years that have lapsed since the lamp was first put on the market. If we substitute x = 1 into this equation, we get

$$f(1) = 120 + 144(1)^2 = 264$$

and we might say that there is a demand for 264 lamps one year after they have been introduced. This would be correct, but only if the demand is interpreted as an *annual rate*. They will not sell 264 of these lamps in a fraction of a second or even on the day that the product has been on the market for exactly one year—*but they would sell 264 of the lamps during the second year provided the demand remained constant at the level at which it was at the end of the first year.*

Of course, this is not going to happen. According to the given equation the demand will *not* remain constant: After a year and a half it will have become

$$f(1.5) = 120 + 144(1.5)^2 = 444$$

and after two years it will have become

$$f(2) = 120 + 144(2)^2 = 696$$

This raises a very interesting question—*how many of the lamps will they actually sell during the second year that the product is on the market?*

If we were satisfied with a rough estimate of their second-year sales, we could say that since the demand is increasing from an annual rate of 264 at $x = 1$ to an annual rate of 696 at $x = 2$, they will sell anywhere from 264 to 696 of the lamps. If we wanted to narrow this down a bit, we could say that they will sell *at least* $\frac{1}{2}(264) = 132$ lamps during the first half of the second year, *at least* $\frac{1}{2}(444) = 222$ lamps during the second half, and hence, *at least* $132 + 222 = 354$ lamps during the second year. This situation is pictured in Figure 12.1,

FIGURE 12.1
First Approximation
of Second-year
Demand

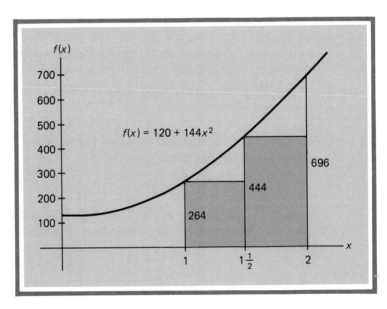

where we have drawn the graph of $f(x) = 120 + 144x^2$ and also the two rectangles whose *areas* represent the respective half-year sales (assuming that the demand remains at the constant annual rate of $f(1) = 264$ during the first half of the year and at the constant annual rate of $f(1.5) = 444$ during the second half of the year). Note that the first rectangle has a height of $f(1) = 264$, a base of $\frac{1}{2}$, and, hence, an area of $\frac{1}{2}(264) = 132$, while the second rectangle has a height of $f(1.5) = 444$, a base of $\frac{1}{2}$, and, hence, an area of $\frac{1}{2}(444) = 222$.

To get a better approximation of the second-year sales, let us suppose that the demand remains constant throughout each month *at the level at which it is at the beginning of the month,* and (as a matter of convenience) let us suppose, furthermore, that each month is $\frac{1}{12}$ of a year. In the *first month* of the second year they would thus sell $\frac{1}{12} \cdot f(1) = \frac{1}{12}(264) = 22$ lamps, in the *second month* they would sell $\frac{1}{12} \cdot f(1\frac{1}{12}) = \frac{1}{12}(289) = 24\frac{1}{12}$ lamps, in the *third month* they would sell $\frac{1}{12} \cdot f(1\frac{2}{12}) = \frac{1}{12}(316) = 26\frac{4}{12}$ lamps,..., and in the *twelfth month* they would sell $\frac{1}{12} \cdot f(1\frac{11}{12}) = \frac{1}{12}(649) = 54\frac{1}{12}$ lamps. We leave it to you to find the corresponding figures for the other eight months; we find that their second-year sales will total

$$22 + 24\tfrac{1}{12} + 26\tfrac{4}{12} + \cdots + 54\tfrac{1}{12} = 438\tfrac{2}{12}$$

If we picture this approximation of the second-year sales as in Figure 12.2, we find that the total of $438\frac{2}{12}$ is actually *the sum of the areas of the twelve shaded rectangles.* The height of the first rectangle is $f(1) = 264$ and its base is $\frac{1}{12}$, so its *area* is $\frac{1}{12}(264) = 22$; the height of the second rectangle is $f(1\frac{1}{12}) = 289$, and its base is $\frac{1}{12}$, so its *area* is

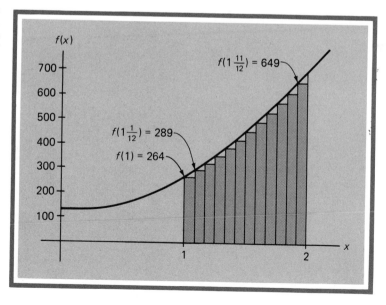

FIGURE 12.2
Second Approximation
of Second-year
Demand

$\frac{1}{12}(289) = 24\frac{1}{12}, \dots$; the height of the twelfth rectangle is $f(1\frac{11}{12}) = 649$, and its base is $\frac{1}{12}$, so its *area* is $\frac{1}{12}(649) = 54\frac{1}{12}$.

There is no reason why this kind of approximation cannot be improved, for instance, by holding the demand constant for several days—as in Figure 12.3—or for each day, when the result would be given by the sum of the areas of 365 rectangles, which is approximately 455.41. This value may be perfectly adequate to predict the total second-year sales, but more important by far is the idea which our method suggests—*if we choose smaller and smaller intervals over which the demand is assumed to be constant, then the total second-year sales will approach the corresponding area under the curve, namely, the shaded area of Figure 12.4.*

This last argument of Example 12.1 sounds very reasonable, but let us point out that as far as elementary geometry is concerned, such an area is *not even defined;* all we talk about in elementary geometry are the areas of regions made up of rectangles, triangles, circles, or parts of circles. However, if we follow the suggestion made above, we can now *define* an area like that of Figure 12.4 as *the limit approached by the sum of the areas of appropriate rectangles* (like those of Figures 12.1, 12.2, and 12.3) *when the number of rectangles increases beyond any bound, and, at the same time, the base of each rectangle gets smaller and smaller, namely, when the base of each rectangle approaches zero as a limit.*

FIGURE 12.3
Third Approximation of Second-year Demand

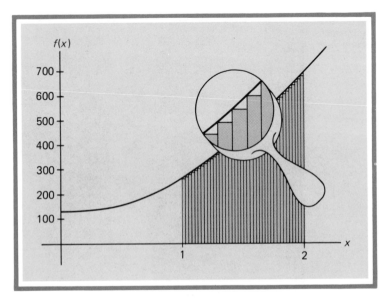

EXAMPLE 12.1
(Continued)
To evaluate this limit for our numerical example, let us divide the interval from $x = 1$ to $x = 2$ into n equal parts, where n is an arbitrary positive integer. The base of each rectangle will then be $1/n$, as is indicated in Figure 12.5, and the heights of the n rectangles are, respectively,

$$f(1) = 120 + 144\,(1)^2$$

$$f\left(1 + \frac{1}{n}\right) = 120 + 144\left(1 + \frac{1}{n}\right)^2$$

$$f\left(1 + \frac{2}{n}\right) = 120 + 144\left(1 + \frac{2}{n}\right)^2$$

$$\vdots \qquad\qquad \vdots$$

$$f\left(1 + \frac{n-1}{n}\right) = 120 + 144\left(1 + \frac{n-1}{n}\right)^2$$

The sum of the areas of the n rectangles of Figure 12.5, which we shall denote S_n, is thus given by

$$S_n = \frac{1}{n}[120 + 144(1)^2] + \frac{1}{n}\left[120 + 144\left(1 + \frac{1}{n}\right)^2\right]$$

$$+ \frac{1}{n}\left[120 + 144\left(1 + \frac{2}{n}\right)^2\right] + \cdots + \frac{1}{n}\left[120 + 144\left(1 + \frac{n-1}{n}\right)^2\right]$$

FIGURE 12.4
Second-year Demand
Represented by Area
under Curve

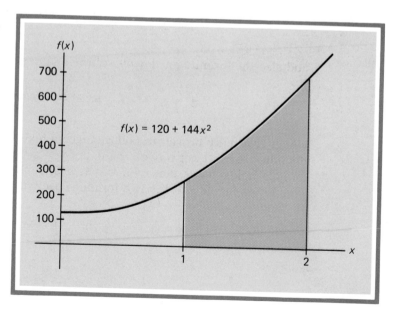

$f(x)$

$f(x) = 120 + 144x^2$

FIGURE 12.5
Diagram
for Continuation
of Example 12.1

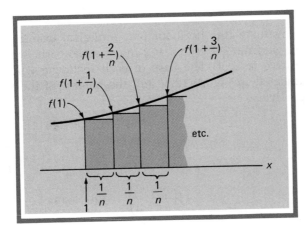

and (after collecting terms and performing other simplifications which we shall omit) it can be written as

$$S_n = 264 + \frac{288}{n^2}[1 + 2 + \cdots + (n - 1)]$$

$$+ \frac{144}{n^3}[1^2 + 2^2 + \cdots + (n - 1)^2]$$

To simplify this further, we shall have to use the formula for the sum of the first k positive integers, namely,

$$1 + 2 + 3 + \cdots + k = \frac{k(k + 1)}{2}$$

and also the formula for the sum of their squares.

$$1^2 + 2^2 + 3^2 + \cdots + k^2 = \frac{k(k + 1)(2k + 1)}{6}$$

which is usually proved in college algebra texts by *mathematical induction*; we shall not prove it here, but you can easily check that the formula holds, for instance, for k = 1, 2, 3, 4, and 5.

When k = n − 1, the two formulas become

$$1 + 2 + 3 + \cdots + (n - 1) = \frac{(n - 1)n}{2}$$

and

$$1^2 + 2^2 + 3^2 + \cdots + (n - 1)^2 = \frac{(n - 1)n(2n - 1)}{6}$$

so that the expression which we obtained for the sum of the n rectangles of Figure 12.5 can now be written as

$$S_n = 264 + \frac{288}{n^2}\left[\frac{(n-1)n}{2}\right] + \frac{144}{n^3}\left[\frac{(n-1)n(2n-1)}{6}\right]$$

Further simplifications lead to the final result, that

$$S_n = 456 - \frac{216}{n} + \frac{24}{n^2}$$

Had we treated this general case first, we could have saved ourselves a good deal of work. When we substitute $n = 12$ into the formula obtained for S_n, we get

$$456 - \frac{216}{12} + \frac{24}{12^2} = 456 - 18 + \frac{2}{12} = 438\frac{2}{12}$$

without having to go to the trouble of calculating the area of each rectangle. Incidentally, it was with the use of this formula that we obtained 455.41 (rounded to two decimals) for the case where $n = 365$, namely, for the case where the demand was held constant each day.

Finally, to complete the solution of our problem, we shall have to perform one more step—we shall have to find the *limit* of the sum of the areas of the n rectangles when their base, $1/n$, approaches zero. Note that when $1/n \to 0$, then n must increase beyond any bound, and we write $n \to \infty$. Since $216/n$ and $24/n^2$ both approach zero when $n \to \infty$, we get

$$\lim_{n \to \infty}\left(456 - \frac{216}{n} + \frac{24}{n^2}\right) = 456$$

and this figure represents the *actual second-year sales of the given kind of lamp*. Geometrically speaking, it *is* the area of the shaded region of Figure 12.4, namely, the area of the region bounded by the x-axis, the graph of $f(x) = 120 + 144x^2$, and the two vertical lines $x = 1$ and $x = 2$.

12.2 THE DEFINITE INTEGRAL

The argument which we used in the preceding section is not limited to the special example where the demand for a product increases continuously with time in accordance with the formula $f(x) = 120 + 144x^2$.

Areas under curves arise in many applications (relating to all sorts of situations), and it is for this reason that the kind of limit which we determined in the preceding section, namely, the limit of the sum of the areas of *more and more rectangles which become narrower and narrower*, has a special symbol and also a special name. It is denoted by

$$\int_a^b f(x)\, dx$$

and it is referred to as the **definite integral** (*of the given function*) *from a to b*. For any *continuous* function with the values $f(x)$, it *defines the area* of the region bounded by the x-axis, the graph of $y = f(x)$, and the two vertical lines $x = a$ and $x = b$, as in Figure 12.6. (Actually, definite integrals can also be defined for some functions which have discontinuities, but we shall not be concerned with this here.)

The symbol $\int$ is called the **integral sign**, and it is really an elongated **S**, standing for *sum*. The function whose values $f(x)$ are the heights of the rectangles (as in Figure 12.5) is called the **integrand**, and a and b are called the **limits of integration**; they tell us *from where to where along the x-axis* the area is determined. The dx serves to indicate that we divide the interval from a to b along the x-axis into n equal parts, which we might denote Δx in accordance with the notation of Section 10.1, and then take the limit as $\Delta x \to 0$. It must be understood, however, and it cannot be too strongly emphasized, that the symbol

$\int_b^a f(x)\, dx$ *as a whole* represents the limit which we refer to as a definite

integral; individually, $\int$ and dx do not really have any significance.

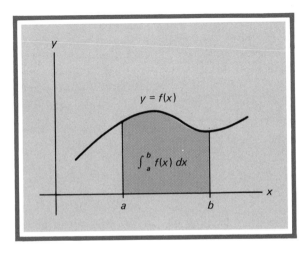

FIGURE 12.6
Area Represented
by Definite Integral

$y = f(x)$

$\int_a^b f(x)\, dx$

EXAMPLE 12.1
(Continued)

Using this notation, we can now write the second-year sales which we obtained in Example 12.1 as

$$\int_1^2 (120 + 144x^2)\, dx$$

As should be apparent from Section 12.1, the evaluation of a definite integral by the method we used can be quite involved. Even though $f(x) = 120 + 144x^2$ represents a relatively simple kind of function, a good deal of work was needed to find a general expression for the sum of the areas of the n rectangles, simplify this sum (that is, put it into a manageable form), and then take the limit as $n \to \infty$. Fortunately, there exists a theorem, to be introduced in Section 12.3, which makes it possible to avoid most of this work; until then, however, you will have to use the method of Section 12.1.

EXERCISES

1. Suppose that in Example 12.1 the growth of the demand for the lamps had been linear, so that $f(x) = 120 + 144x$, where the significance of x and $f(x)$ are the same as before.
   (a) Subdividing the interval from $x = 1$ to $x = 2$ into n equal intervals (as in Figure 12.7 for $n = 13$), show that the sum of the areas of the n rectangles (which approximates the second-year sales) can be written as

FIGURE 12.7
Diagram for Exercise 1

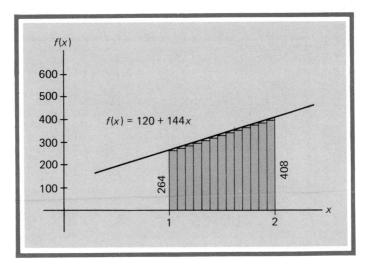

$$264 + \frac{144}{n^2}[1 + 2 + 3 + \cdots + (n-1)]$$

(b) Use the formula for the sum of the first k positive integers (Section 12.1) to show that the sum of the areas of the n rectangles can be written as

$$336 - \frac{72}{n}$$

(c) Find the actual second-year sales by taking the limit of the expression obtained in part (b) as $n \to \infty$.

(d) The result of part (c) gives the area of the region bounded by the x-axis, the line $f(x) = 120 + 144x$, and the two vertical lines $x = 1$ and $x = 2$. Since this is a *trapezoid*, verify the result of part (c) by making use of the formula according to which the area of a trapezoid is *half* the product of the *sum of the two parallel sides* and the *altitude*, namely, the perpendicular distance between the two parallel sides.

2. To find the area of the region bounded by the x-axis, the graph of $f(x) = x^2$, and the vertical line $x = 1$, we divide the interval from 0 to 1 into n equal parts and then form rectangles, as in either of the two diagrams of Figure 12.8.

(a) Show that if we form the rectangles as in the *first diagram*, the sum of the areas of the n rectangles is

$$\frac{1}{3} - \frac{1}{2n} + \frac{1}{6n^2}$$

and if we form the rectangles as in the *second diagram*, the sum of the areas of the n rectangles is

FIGURE 12.8
Diagram for Exercise 2

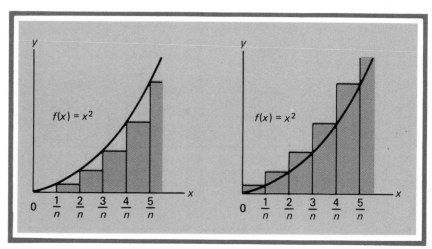

$$\frac{1}{3} + \frac{1}{2n} + \frac{1}{6n^2}$$

(*Hint:* Make use of the formula for the sum of the squares of the first k positive integers.)

(b) Explain why the *actual* area under this parabola from $x = 0$ to $x = 1$ must lie *between* the two expressions obtained in part (a), and why it must be equal to $1/3$.

3. Make use of the formula $1^3 + 2^3 + 3^3 + \cdots + k^3 = k^2(k + 1)^2/4$ to find the area bounded by the x-axis, the graph of $y = -x^3$, and the vertical line $x = 1$. Note that the heights of the rectangles, being given by the values of the function, will be *negative*, and, hence, the final answer will be *negative*. What general rule can we derive from this? (*Hint:* Form the rectangles as in the second diagram of Figure 12.8, so that the height of the first rectangle will be $-(1/n)^3$, that of the second rectangle will be $-(2/n)^3$, and so on.)

In **Exercises 4–9,** draw the regions whose areas are given by the definite integral shown in the exercise.

4. $\displaystyle\int_1^3 (1 + 2x)\,dx$

5. $\displaystyle\int_{-1}^1 (4 + x)\,dx$

6. $\displaystyle\int_1^2 (x^2 - 4x + 3)\,dx$

7. $\displaystyle\int_1^5 e^x\,dx$

8. $\displaystyle\int_0^3 (3x - x^2)\,dx$

9. $\displaystyle\int_2^3 (1 - e^{-x})\,dx$

10. Show in detail the simplifications we omitted in the last step of the derivation of the formula for S_n.

12.3 THE FUNDAMENTAL THEOREM

After we defined derivatives in the beginning of Chapter 10, we showed that there are many special formulas and special methods which enable us to differentiate *without having to go through the whole detailed* process of evaluating the necessary limits by means of the four-step delta process. Similar simplifications are possible in the evaluation of definite integrals; by use of a special theorem, called the **fundamental theorem of integral calculus,** we can find the values of many definite integrals *without having to go through the cumbersome process of determining the limit of the sum of the areas of rectangles (as we did in the preceding sections).* The proof of this theorem is difficult, but to express it *in words,* the value of the definite integral

$$\int_a^b f(x)\,dx$$

can be obtained by finding a function *whose derivative equals the integrand* $f(x)$, and then subtracting the value of this function at $x = a$ from its value at $x = b$. More formally,

if $f(x)$ *is the derivative of* $F(x)$, *and both of these functions are continuous on the interval from a to b, then*

$$\int_a^b f(x)\,dx = F(b) - F(a)$$

and we find that the whole problem of evaluating a definite integral reduces to that of finding a function (or functions) whose derivative is of a given form. This process is referred to as **antidifferentiation,** and it is amazing, to say the least, that the two basic concepts of calculus, derivatives and integrals, are related in this way. Note that we used the corresponding *capital letter* to denote the antiderivative of the given function. This is common practice, and we might similarly write the antiderivative of $g(x)$ as $G(x)$, the antiderivative of $q(x)$ as $Q(x)$, and so forth.

EXAMPLE 12.1
(Continued)
Since we have not yet learned how to antidifferentiate, it is difficult to illustrate the fundamental theorem; nevertheless, let us use it to reevaluate the second-year sales of the lamps, with which we were concerned in Example 12.1, making use of the fact that $f(x) = 120 + 144x^2$ is the derivative of $F(x) = 120x + 48x^3$. This is easily verified, since

$$F'(x) = 120 \cdot 1 + 48 \cdot 3x^2 = 120 + 144x^2$$

Thus we can write

$$\int_1^2 (120 + 144x^2)\,dx = F(2) - F(1)$$

where

$$F(2) = 120(2) + 48(2)^3 = 624$$

and

$$F(1) = 120(1) + 48(1)^3 = 168$$

It follows that

$$\int_1^2 (120 + 144x^2)\,dx = 624 - 168 = 456$$

This agrees with the result obtained in Section 12.1.

12.4 ANTIDIFFERENTIATION

Although the terms *antiderivative* and *antidifferentiation* are widely used, it is more common to refer to the antiderivative of a function as its **indefinite integral**, and to refer to the process of antidifferentiation simply as **integration**. Thus if $F'(x) = f(x)$, we refer to $F(x)$ as the *indefinite integral* of $f(x)$ and write it as

$$F(x) = \int f(x)\,dx$$

The symbols $\int$ and dx, individually, do not have any significance; the whole expression $\int f(x)\,dx$ represents the function (or, perhaps, functions) whose derivative is $f(x)$.

In the example of Section 12.3, we gave the antiderivative of $f(x) = 120 + 144x^2$ as $F(x) = 120x + 48x^3$, and it may have occurred to you that $F(x) = 120x + 48x^3$ is *not* the only function whose derivative is $f(x) = 120 + 144x^2$; other possibilities are $F(x) = 120x + 48x^3 + 3$, $F(x) = 120x + 48x^3 - 17$, and, in general, any function of the form $F(x) = 120x + 48x^3 + C$, where C is an arbitrary constant. This simply expresses the fact that *the derivative of a constant is zero*, and if we turn this argument around, we can now say that the *antiderivative of zero is a constant*.

In general, if $F(x)$ is an *antiderivative* of $f(x)$, then so is $F(x) + C$, and to allow for the existence of this constant we always write

$$\int f(x)\ dx = F(x) + C \quad \text{instead of} \quad \int f(x)\ dx = F(x)$$

where C is called the **constant of integration**. How the value of this constant is determined in any given example will be illustrated in Example 12.4.

To obtain some general rules of integration, let us refer to the first four rules of Section 10.6. In the first rule we asserted that if k is a constant and $f(x) = k$, then $f'(x) = 0$; thus, as we already said, *the antiderivative of 0 is a constant*, namely,

$$\int 0\ dx = C$$

This result is rather trivial, but more important is the one about integrating $f(x) = k$. Since the derivative of kx is k according to the second rule of Section 10.6 (the one for differentiating x^n) with $n = 1$, it follows immediately that

$$\int k\ dx = kx + C$$

More generally, the derivative of x^n is $n \cdot x^{n-1}$, where n can be any positive or negative integer or fraction. Thus the derivative of $\frac{1}{n + 1} \cdot x^{n+1}$ is $\frac{1}{n + 1} \cdot (n + 1)x^n = x^n$, the antiderivative of x^n is $\frac{1}{n + 1} \cdot x^{n+1}$, and we write

$$\int x^n\ dx = \frac{1}{n + 1} \cdot x^{n+1} + C$$

where n can be any positive or negative integer or fraction except -1; what happens when $n = -1$ will be explained shortly. This result is very easy to remember.

To integrate a power of x, we increase the exponent by 1 and divide by the new exponent.

EXAMPLE 12.2

$$\int x^5 \, dx = \frac{1}{6} \cdot x^6 + C$$

$$\int \frac{1}{x^3} \, dx = \int x^{-3} \, dx = \frac{1}{-2} \cdot x^{-2} + C = -\frac{1}{2x^2} + C$$

and

$$\int \sqrt{x} \, dx = \int x^{1/2} \, dx = \frac{1}{3/2} \cdot x^{3/2} + C = \frac{2}{3} \cdot x^{3/2} + C = \frac{2}{3} \cdot x\sqrt{x} + C$$

Note that the above formula for integrating x^n holds also for $n = 0$, and hence for all *rational numbers* n except $n = -1$; for $n = 0$ the formula yields

$$\int x^0 \, dx = \frac{1}{1} \cdot x^{0+1} + C = x + C$$

and this is correct since $x^0 = 1$ and the antiderivative of 1 is x. Usually, we write $\int 1 \, dx$ simply as $\int dx$.

Having discussed rules of integration analogous to the first two rules of Section 10.6, let us now give the rules

$$\int k \cdot f(x) \, dx = k \cdot \int f(x) \, dx$$

where k is a constant, and

$$\int [f(x) + g(x)] \, dx = \int f(x) \, dx + \int g(x) \, dx$$

which are analogous to the third and fourth rules of Section 10.6. Thus we can "factor a constant out of an integral," and integrate "term by term." Note that if we substitute $-g(x)$ for $g(x)$, the last rule leads to

$$\int [f(x) - g(x)] \, dx = \int f(x) \, dx - \int g(x) \, dx$$

EXAMPLE 12.3 To illustrate all these rules, let us integrate (antidifferentiate) $12x^5 - 5/x^2 + 3$. Leaving it to you to find the rule which justifies each step, we get

$$\int \left(12x^5 - \frac{5}{x^2} + 3 \right) dx = \int (12x^5 - 5x^{-2} + 3)\, dx$$

$$= \int 12x^5\, dx - \int 5x^{-2}\, dx + \int 3\, dx$$

$$= 12 \cdot \int x^5\, dx - 5 \cdot \int x^{-2}\, dx + \int 3\, dx$$

$$= 12 \cdot \frac{1}{6} \cdot x^6 - 5 \cdot \frac{1}{-1} \cdot x^{-1} + 3x + C$$

$$= 2x^6 + \frac{5}{x} + 3x + C$$

Before we give another example, we observe that there is also a method of integration analogous to the *product rule*, the fifth rule of Section 10.6; this method, called **integration by parts**, is discussed in more advanced texts.

EXAMPLE 12.4 To give an applied problem which is solved by antidifferentiation, suppose that the *marginal productivity* of an industrial operation (say, the production of electric furnaces) is given by

$$f(x) = \frac{60}{x^2} + 10$$

where x is the capitalization in millions of dollars. [Note that the term *marginal productivity* is the *rate* at which production increases (or decreases) when there is a unit increase in capitalization; in other words, it is the *derivative of production with respect to capitalization*.] Suppose, furthermore, that when the capitalization is $5,000,000 they can produce 62 of these furnaces per week, and they want to know *how many they will be able to produce if their capitalization is increased to $10,000,000*. To express production in terms of capitalization, we shall have to *antidifferentiate* the marginal productivity, namely, $60/x^2 + 10$; thus we get

$$F(x) = \int \left(\frac{60}{x^2} + 10 \right) dx = \int (60x^{-2} + 10)\, dx$$

$$= 60 \cdot \frac{1}{-1} \cdot x^{-1} + 10x + C$$

$$= -\frac{60}{x} + 10x + C$$

The next step is to evaluate the constant of integration C, and to this end we make use of the fact that for x = 5 (million dollars) the production is $F(5) = 62$. When we substitute these values into the equation $F(x) = -60/x + 10x + C$, we get

$$62 = -\frac{60}{5} + 10 \cdot 5 + C = -12 + 50 + C$$

and, solving for C, this becomes C = 62 + 12 − 50 = 24. Thus the equation which expresses production in terms of capitalization is

$$F(x) = -\frac{60}{x} + 10x + 24$$

and it follows that for x = 10 (namely, when their capitalization is $10,000,000) they will be able to produce

$$F(10) = -\frac{60}{10} + 10 \cdot 10 + 24 = 118$$

electric furnaces.

When it comes to the special functions whose derivatives we discussed in Section 10.8, we merely list the following integration formulas, which can all be verified by simply differentiating the results and observing that the derivatives we obtain equal the respective integrands.

$$\int e^x \, dx = e^x + C$$

$$\int b^x \, dx = \frac{b^x}{\ln b} + C$$

$$\int \frac{1}{x} \, dx = \ln x + C$$

Note that the third of these integration formulas demonstrates why we had to exclude n = −1 when we gave the general rule for integrating x^n.

EXAMPLE 12.5 The following integrations illustrate the use of the above formulas.

$$\int 7e^x\,dx = 7e^x + C$$

$$\int 10^x\,dx = \frac{10^x}{\ln 10} + C = 0.4343 \cdot 10^x + C$$

and

$$\int \frac{5}{x}\,dx = 5 \cdot \ln x + C$$

If we wanted to use the first of these results to evaluate the area of the shaded region of Figure 12.9, we would get

$$\int_2^4 7e^x\,dx = (7e^4 + C) - (7e^2 + C)$$

$$= 7e^4 - 7e^2$$

$$= 7(54.60) - 7(7.389)$$

$$= 330.48$$

where the values of e^4 and e^2 were obtained from Table III. Note that *when we evaluate a definite integral the constant of integration cancels, so that it may just as well be left out.*

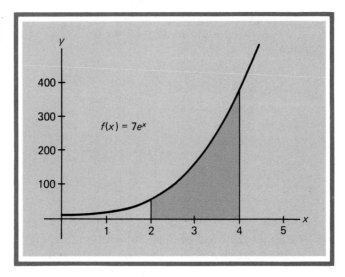

FIGURE 12.9
Diagram
for Example 12.5

$f(x) = 7e^x$

1. Evaluate each indefinite integral.

   (a) $\displaystyle\int x^4\, dx$ (b) $\displaystyle\int \frac{1}{x^4}\, dx$

   Also use the results of parts (a) and (b), respectively, to find each value.
   (c) The area of the region bounded by the x-axis, the graph of $f(x) = x^4$, and the line $x = 2$.
   (d) The area of the region bounded by the x-axis, the graph of $f(x) = 1/x^4$, the line $x = 1$, and the line $x = 2$.

2. Evaluate each indefinite integral.

   (a) $\displaystyle\int 15\, dx$ (b) $\displaystyle\int x^{2/3}\, dx$

3. Evaluate each indefinite integral.

   (a) $\displaystyle\int (3 - x)\, dx$ (b) $\displaystyle\int (2x + 6x^5)\, dx$

   Also use the results of parts (a) and (b), respectively, to find each.
   (c) The area of the region bounded by the x-axis, the y-axis, the graph of $y = 3 - x$, and the line $x = 2$.
   (d) The area of the region bounded by the x-axis, the graph of $y = 2x + 6x^5$, and the line $x = 1$.

4. Evaluate each indefinite integral.

   (a) $\displaystyle\int \left(\frac{1}{2}\sqrt{x} - \frac{1}{2\sqrt{x}}\right) dx$ (b) $\displaystyle\int (5 - 3x^2 + 5x^4)\, dx$

5. Evaluate the following indefinite integral and use the result to find the area of the region bounded by the x-axis, the y-axis, the graph of $f(x) = 2x + 4e^x$, and the line $x = 2$:

$$\int (2x + 4e^x)\, dx$$

6. Evaluate each indefinite integral.

   (a) $\displaystyle\int 6^x\, dx$ (b) $\displaystyle\int \left(x + 2 + \frac{2}{x}\right) dx$ (c) $\displaystyle\int 5 \cdot 3^x\, dx$

Note: In **Exercises 7** and **8** the following definitions apply.

- The *marginal cost* of an item is the *rate* at which the total production cost changes when there is a change in the quantity produced, namely, the derivative of the total cost with respect to the quantity produced.

- The *marginal revenue* of an item is the *rate* at which its total sales revenue changes when there is a change in demand, namely, the derivative of its total sales revenue with respect to demand.

7. The marginal cost of producing a certain kind of baby food is given by
$$c(x) = 40 \cdot x^{-2/3}$$
where x, the number of cans produced, is in thousands, and the cost is in dollars. Find a formula for $C(x)$, the total cost of producing x thousand cans of the baby food, given that 8000 cans can be produced at a cost of $700. How much will it cost to produce 125,000 cans?

8. For a certain kind of leather belt, the marginal revenue is given by
$$9 - \frac{4}{\sqrt{D}}$$
when there is a demand for D belts; the sales revenue, itself, is in dollars. Find a formula expressing the total sales revenue in terms of the demand, making use of the fact that for $D = 0$ the total sales revenue is also zero. What total sales revenue corresponds to a demand for 400 of these belts?

9. For the monthly operation of a large turkey farm, the *marginal productivity* (see Example 12.4) is given by
$$n(x) = 50 - \frac{1000}{x}$$
where x is the capitalization of the farm in thousands of dollars. Find a formula giving the number of turkeys they can produce per month in terms of x, if they can produce 10,000 turkeys per month when their capitalization is $300,000. What would be their monthly production if they increased the capitalization to $500,000? (Use $\ln 300 = 5.7$ and $\ln 500 = 6.2$.)

10. The rate at which a worker's efficiency (expressed as a percentage) changes with respect to time is given by
$$e(t) = \frac{40}{9} - \frac{20}{9}t$$
where t is the number of hours he or she has been at work. If the worker's efficiency is 100 after having been at work for 2 hours, what is his or her efficiency in each case?

(a) At $t = 0$, namely, when starting out in the morning.
(b) At $t = 8$, namely, when ready to quit in the afternoon.

11. The rate at which a newly built skyscraper is settling into the ground is $3e^{-3t}$ inches per year, where t is its age in years. Find a formula which expresses the number of inches the building has settled into the ground in terms of t, making use of the fact that the whole process begins when $t = 0$. How many inches will the building have settled **(a)** after 1 year, and **(b)** after 2 years?

12.5 SOME FURTHER APPLICATIONS

In this section we shall return to our original problem, namely, that of evaluating *definite integrals*. To this end, let us simplify our notation by writing

$$\int_a^b f(x)\ dx = F(b) - F(a) \quad \text{as} \quad \int_a^b f(x)\ dx = F(x)\Bigg]_a^b$$

EXAMPLE 12.1
(Continued)

In the continuation of Example 12.1, we could have written

$$\int_1^2 (120 + 144x^2)\ dx = (120x + 48x^3)\Bigg]_1^2$$

$$= (120 \cdot 2 + 48 \cdot 2^3) - (120 \cdot 1 + 48 \cdot 1^3)$$

$$= 456$$

This is no different from what we did previously, but it saves us the trouble of having to write down *separately* the values of $F(x)$, $F(1)$, and $F(2)$, and finally $F(2) - F(1)$; also, there is no need now for the constant of integration.

The next two examples pertain to applied problems in which the solution requires the evaluation of a definite integral.

EXAMPLE 12.6

In Example 6.6, the demand and the supply for one type of ceramic insulators (in hundreds) were related to their price (in cents) by means of the equations

$$D(p) = 231 - 18p \quad \text{and} \quad S(p) = 2p + 4p^2$$

When we solved these two equations simultaneously, we showed that

FIGURE 12.10
Diagram
for Example 12.6

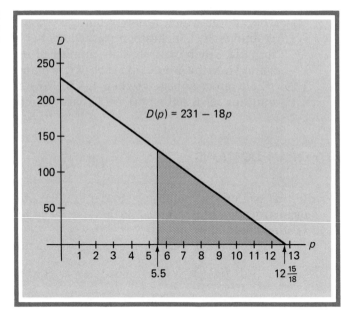

the market for the insulators would be in *equilibrium* (that is, supply would equal demand) when $p = 5.5$¢, in which case there is a demand for $D(5.5) = 231 - 18(5.5) = 132$ hundred of the ceramic insulators. It is clear from the equation

$$D(p) = 231 - 18p$$

that some persons would buy the insulators even if they cost more than 5.5¢; for $p = 8$¢ there would be a demand for $231 - 18(8) = 87$ hundred, for $p = 10$¢ there would be a demand for $231 - 18(10) = 51$ hundred, and only for $p = 231/18 = 12\frac{15}{18}$¢ would the demand be zero. Thus some consumers benefit from the fact that the market is in equilibrium when the price is 5.5¢ and their combined overall gain, called the *consumers' surplus*, is given by the area of the region under the demand curve shaded in Figure 12.10. This area is given by the definite integral

$$\int_{5.5}^{231/18} (231 - 18p)\, dp$$

which equals

$$(231p - 9p^2)\Big]_{5.5}^{231/18} = \left[231\left(\frac{231}{18}\right) - 9\left(\frac{231}{18}\right)^2 \right] - \left[231(5.5) - 9(5.5)^2 \right]$$

$$= 484$$

FIGURE 12.11
Diagram
for Example 12.7

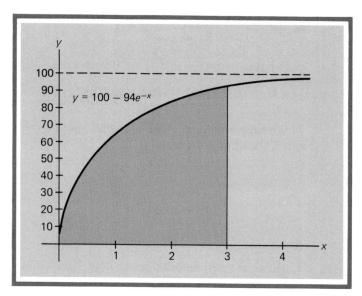

where the result is in *dollars*, since $D(p)$ was given in hundreds (of insulators) and p in cents. Since the shaded region of Figure 12.10 is a triangle, it would actually have been easier to get this result by making use of the fact that the area of a triangle is half the product of the base and the height; we would thus have gotten $1/2(231/18 - 5.5) \times [231 - 18(5.5)] = \frac{1}{2} \cdot \frac{22}{3} \cdot 132 = 484$. Incidentally, this $484 represents the consumers' combined savings that are due to the existence of a market in which everybody can buy the insulators at the price for which supply equals demand.

EXAMPLE 12.7 In Example 4.2, we illustrated *modified exponential functions* by giving the sales of a new meat tenderizer (in thousands of packages) as

$$y = 100 - 94e^{-x}$$

where x represents the number of years this product has been on the market. To determine its *total sales* during the first three years, we must find the area of the region shaded in Figure 12.11; that is, we must evaluate the definite integral

$$\int_0^3 (100 - 94e^{-x}) \, dx$$

Using the result that

$$\int e^{ax} \, dx = \frac{1}{a} e^{ax} + C$$

we get

$$\left(100x - 94 \cdot \frac{e^{-x}}{-1}\right)\Bigg]_0^3 = (100 \cdot 3 + 94e^{-3}) - (100 \cdot 0 + 94e^0)$$

$$= 210.7 \text{ thousand packages}$$

where the value of e^{-3} was obtained using a calculator with an e^x key, and e^0 is, of course, equal to 1.

EXERCISES

1. Evaluate the definite integral of Exercise 4 at the end of Section 12.2.

2. Evaluate the definite integral of Exercise 6 at the end of Section 12.2.

3. Evaluate the definite integral of Exercise 8 at the end of Section 12.2.

4. Evaluate the definite integral

$$\int_{-2}^2 (x^3 - 4x)\, dx$$

and *explain* the result by drawing the region whose area the definite integral is supposed to represent (see also Exercise 3 at the end of Section 12.2).

5. A company's total sales revenue is

$$y = x + 2x^2$$

where x is the number of years the company has been in business and y is in millions of dollars.

(a) Find the company's total sales revenue for the first 6 years.

(b) Find n, if the company's *average* annual sales revenue for the first n years is $7.5 million.

6. A new company's gross earnings are given by

$$y = 120{,}000e^{0.15t}$$

where y is in dollars and t is the number of years the company has been in business. Find the company's total gross earnings for the first 4 years it was in business.

7. A company which leases office equipment has found that the maintenance cost of an electric typewriter increases continuously with its age, and that it equals

$$22.4 + 0.1e^t$$

dollars when the typewriter is t years old. If 20 new typewriters are to be leased to a firm for 5 years and the *same* maintenance charge is to be included in the total fee for each year, what should this charge be?

SUMMARY

In this chapter we showed that the definite integral $\int_a^b f(x) \, d(x)$ defines the area of the region bounded by the x-axis, the graph of the continuous function $y = f(x)$, and the two vertical lines $x = a$ and $x = b$. According to the *fundamental theorem of integral calculus*, the value of the definite integral can be obtained by finding a function whose derivative equals the integrand $f(x)$ and then subtracting the value of this function at $x = a$ from its value at $x = b$. Thus the whole problem of evaluating a definite integral reduces to that of finding a function (or functions) whose derivative is of a given form, a process referred to as *antidifferentiation*. You should now understand why the two basic concepts of calculus, derivatives and integrals, are so closely related.

GLOSSARY

1. **Definite Integral** For any continuous function with the values $f(x)$, the definite integral (of the given function) from a to b defines the area of the region bounded by the x-axis, the graph of $y = f(x)$, and the two vertical lines $x = a$ and $x = b$. Symbolically, we refer to the definite integral as

$$\int_a^b f(x) \, dx$$

2. **Integral Sign** The symbol $\int$ denotes integration.
3. **Integrand** The function to which the definition of an integral refers.
4. **Limits of Integration** The values a and b to which the definition of the definite integral refers.
5. **Fundamental Theorem of Integral Calculus** A theorem which states that the value of the definite integral

$$\int_a^b f(x) \, dx$$

can be obtained by finding a function whose derivative equals the integrand $f(x)$ and then subtracting the value of this function at $x = a$ from its value at $x = b$.

6. **Antidifferentiation** The process of evaluating a definite integral by finding a function (or functions) whose derivative is of a given form.

7. **Indefinite Integral** We refer to the antiderivative of a function as its indefinite integral. Thus if $F'(x) = f(x)$, we call $F(x)$ the indefinite integral of $f(x)$ and write it as

$$F(x) = \int f(x)\ dx$$

8. **Integration** The process of antidifferentiation.

1. Draw the region whose area is given by each definite integral.

   (a) $\displaystyle\int_1^3 (1 + 3x)\ dx$ (b) $\displaystyle\int_{-1}^1 (4 - x)\ dx$ (c) $\displaystyle\int_2^5 (1 + x^2)\ dx$

2. Draw the region whose area is given by each definite integral.

   (a) $\displaystyle\int_2^4 (1 + x^2)\ dx$ (b) $\displaystyle\int_2^5 \frac{1}{x}\ dx$ (c) $\displaystyle\int_2^6 \frac{1}{x}\ dx$

3. Evaluate each indefinite integral.

   (a) $\displaystyle\int \frac{4}{x\sqrt{x}}\ dx$ (c) $\displaystyle\int (4 - x + 3x^2 - 3x^5)\ dx$

   (b) $\displaystyle\int x^{3/5}\ dx$ (d) $\displaystyle\int (5x + 5x^{3/2})\ dx$

4. Evaluate each indefinite integral.

   (a) $\displaystyle\int x^3\ dx$ (c) $\displaystyle\int 12\ dx$

   (b) $\displaystyle\int x^{3/4}\ dx$ (d) $\displaystyle\int \frac{1}{\sqrt{x}}\ dx$

5. Evaluate each integral.

   (a) $\displaystyle\int (1 + 3x)\ dx$ (d) $\displaystyle\int (2 - 4x + 5x^2 - 4x^3)\ dx$

   (b) $\displaystyle\int (2x + 5x^4)\ dx$ (e) $\displaystyle\int (7 - 3x^2 + 6x^5)\ dx$

   (c) $\displaystyle\int \frac{3\sqrt{x} - 2}{\sqrt{x}}\ dx$ (f) $\displaystyle\int (5x^{1/4} - 3x^{1/2})\ dx$

6. Evaluate each integral.

(a) $\int (3x - 5e^x)\, dx$

(d) $\int (1 - e^x)\, dx$

(b) $\int \left(x + 1 + \dfrac{1}{x} \right) dx$

(e) $\int 3 \cdot 2^x\, dx$

(c) $\int 5^x\, dx$

(f) $\int \dfrac{15}{x}\, dx$

7. The marginal cost of producing a certain kind of cake mix is given by

$$c(x) = 325 - 1200e^{-2x}$$

where x, the number of packages produced, is in dozens, and the cost is in cents. Find a formula for $C(x)$, the total cost of producing x dozen packages of the cake mix, given that 2 dozen can be produced at a cost of $8.00. How much will it cost to produce 3 dozen packages of the mix?

8. For a certain kind of watch, the marginal revenue is given by

$$3000 - \frac{2000}{(1 + D)^2}$$

where the demand is in hundreds of watches and the total sales revenue is in dollars. Find a formula which expresses the total sales revenue in terms of D, making use of the fact that for $D = 0$ the total sales revenue is also zero. What would be the total sales revenue when there is a demand for 300 of the watches?

9. Evaluate the definite integrals of Exercise 1.

10. Evaluate the definite integrals of Exercise 2.

11. The manager of a new donut shop expects daily sales to grow continuously so that sales of donuts after t days will be $100 + 4t$ donuts after t days. On which day should the manager expect to sell the 10,000th donut? (Hint: Set up the definite integral which represents the total sales during the first x days, put it equal to 10,000, and solve for x.)

12. The rate at which a secretary's efficiency (expressed as a percentage) changes with respect to time is given by

$$40 - 10t$$

where t is the number of hours the secretary has been at work. If the secretary's efficiency is 76 percent after the secretary has worked for 2 hours, find a formula which expresses efficiency in terms of t, and use it to determine the secretary's efficiency after working (a) for 4 hours, and (b) for 8 hours.

13. The rate at which a building is settling into the ground is $12e^{-4t}$ inches per year, where t is its age in years. Find a formula which expresses the number of inches the building has settled into the ground in terms of t, making use of the fact that the whole process begins when $t = 0$. How many inches will the building have settled (a) after 1 year, and (b) after 2 years?

PROBABILITY: PRELIMINARY CONCEPTS

The mathematical models which we have studied have all been **deterministic**; that is, the relationships between the variables were always expressed in terms of mathematical equations *which left nothing to chance*. Thus when we said in Example 6.1 that a manufacturer's cost of producing x television sets is

$$C = 12{,}000 + 80x$$

dollars, we were able to substitute x = 300 and arrive at the conclusion that the cost of producing 300 sets is $36,000, *not a penny more nor a penny less*. Similarly, when we claimed in Example 4.2 that the sales of a meat tenderizer are given by

$$y = 100 - 94e^{-x}$$

we were able to substitute x = 5 (among other values) and conclude that the product will sell at an annual rate of 99.4 million packages after it has been on the market for 5 years—not 99.8 million packages nor 98.7, but 99.4 million packages *on the nose*.

To a practical businessperson, results like these (or, at least, their interpretation) must surely seem very unreasonable. In the first example the person might be willing to say, though, that the *expected* production cost is $36,000 (without having to guarantee that it will not turn out to be $35,750 or $36,455), and in the second example the person might feel "pretty sure" that after 5 years the product will sell at an annual rate of anywhere from 99 to 100 million packages. All this serves to illustrate that many of the models which we have discussed apply only in the sense of approximations (not necessarily bad ones), or that they must be interpreted as *averages* or *expectations*. Thus we shall devote the remainder of this book to **probabilistic models**, also called **stochastic models**, which are mathematical models that allow for the uncertainty observable in most practical decision-making situations.

The key to these models is the concept of **probability**, which we shall study in Chapter 14. In this chapter we shall study some preliminaries, mainly, methods which enable us to determine *what is possible in a given situation*. After all, we cannot very well be expected to judge what is likely or unlikely, what is probable or improbable, or what is credible or incredible, unless we know at least what is possible.

13.1 COUNTING

In the study of "what is possible," there are essentially two kinds of problems: First there is the problem of *listing everything that can happen in a given situation*, and then there is the problem of *determining how many different things can happen (without actually constructing a complete list)*. The second kind of problem is especially important, because there are many problems in which we really do not need a complete list, and, hence, can save ourselves a great deal of unnecessary work.

Although the first kind of problem may seem straightforward and easy, this is not always the case, as is illustrated by the following examples.

EXAMPLE 13.1   Suppose that three persons need new cars, and that, among others, they are considering a compact Ford, a compact Chevrolet, and a Volkswagen. What we would like to determine is the number of ways in which they can make their choice, caring only *how many of them* (not which ones) will buy a compact Ford, *how many of them* will buy a compact Chevrolet, and *how many of them* will buy a Volkswagen. Clearly, there are many possibilities: All three of them might buy compact Fords; one might buy a compact Ford and another a Volkswagen, while the third buys neither of the three kinds of cars; one might buy a compact Ford while the other two buy compact Chevrolets; and to mention one more possibility, all three of them might buy other kinds of cars.

To handle problems like this systematically, it helps to refer to a diagram like that of Figure 13.1, which is called a **tree diagram**. This diagram shows that for the first kind of car there are four possibilities (four branches) corresponding to 0, 1, 2, or 3 of the persons buying a compact Ford; for the second kind of car there are four branches emanating from the top branch, three from the second branch, two from the third branch, and none from the bottom branch. This is indicative of the fact that there are still four possibilities (0, 1, 2, or 3) when none of them buys a compact Ford, but only three possibilities (0, 1, or 2) when one of them buys a compact Ford, two possibilities (0 or 1) when two of them buy compact Fords, and there is no need to go on when all three

FIGURE 13.1
Tree Diagram
for Example 13.1

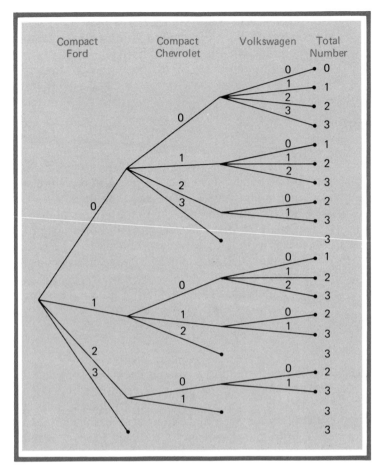

of them buy compact Fords. The same sort of reasoning applies also to the third kind of car, and we thus find that (going from left to right) there are altogether 20 different paths along the "branches" of the tree diagram of Figure 13.1; in other words, *the answer to our problem is that there are 20 different possibilities*. It can also be seen from the tree diagram that in 10 cases all three of the persons buy one of the three kinds of cars, in 6 cases only two of the persons buy one of the three kinds of cars, in 3 cases only one of the persons buys one of the three kinds of cars, and in 1 case none of them buys one of the three kinds of cars.

EXAMPLE 13.2   To consider another example in which a tree diagram can be of some aid (at least, until we shall have studied other techniques), suppose that a brokerage house asks its stock analyst to examine six stocks with regard to their potential long-term growth, and to come up with a first and a second choice. The question is, *in how many different ways can this be*

FIGURE 13.2
Tree Diagram
for Example 13.2

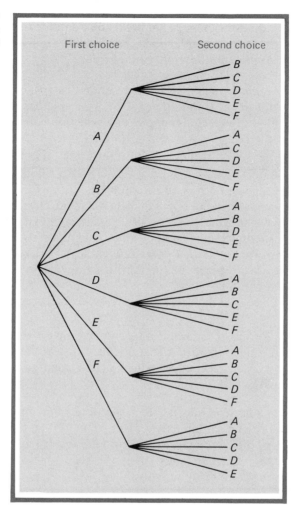

First choice   Second choice

done? Drawing a tree diagram like that of Figure 13.2, where the stocks are labeled A, B, C, D, E, and F, we find practically by inspection that there are 30 possibilities, corresponding to the 30 different paths along the branches of the tree. Starting at the top, the first path corresponds to the first choice being stock A and the second choice being stock B, the second path corresponds to the first choice being stock A and the second choice being stock C, . . . , and the 30th path (namely, the one along the bottom branches of the tree) corresponds to the first choice being stock F and the second choice being stock E.

Note that the answer we obtained in Example 13.2 is the *product* of 6 and 5, namely, the product of the number of ways in which the stock analyst can make her first choice and the number of ways in which she can subsequently make her second choice. In fact, our example illustrates the following general rule.

If a selection consists of two separate steps, of which the first can be made in m different ways and for each of these the second in n different ways, then the whole selection can be made in m · n different ways.

EXAMPLE 13.3 If a restaurant offers 12 different desserts, which it serves with coffee, Sanka, tea, milk, or hot chocolate, there are altogether $12 \cdot 5 = 60$ different ways in which one can order a dessert and a drink. Also, if someone wants to buy one of eight different toys as a birthday gift for a child, and have it sent by parcel post, by first class mail, or by express mail, then there are altogether $8 \cdot 3 = 24$ different ways in which the whole transaction can take place.

By use of appropriate tree diagrams, it is easy to generalize the above rule so that it will apply also to selections involving more than two steps. For k steps, where k is a positive integer, we obtain the following rule.

If a selection consists of k separate steps, of which the first can be made in n_1 different ways, for each of these the second can be made in n_2 different ways, . . . , and for each of these the kth can be made in n_k different ways, then the whole selection can be made in $n_1 \cdot n_2 \cdots n_k$ different ways.

Thus we simply multiply the number of ways in which each step can be made.

EXAMPLE 13.4 If the stock market analyst of Example 13.2 had been asked to include a third choice, the total number of possibilities would have been $6 \cdot 5 \cdot 4 = 120$; also if a new housing development advertises 2-, 3-, and 4-bedroom houses which can be had in 4 different exterior finishes, with or without a fireplace, and with or without a garage, there are altogether $3 \cdot 4 \cdot 2 \cdot 2 = 48$ different selections a homebuyer can make. Finally, if a true-false test consists of 10 questions, there are altogether $2^{10} = 1024$ different ways in which the answers can be checked; unfortunately, only one of them corresponds to the case in which all answers are correct.

1. Two insurance salespeople make a small bet each month as to who will be the first to sell two policies. (Thus, if we refer to the two insurance salespeople as *A* and *B*, the sequence *ABA* represents the case where *A* makes the first sale, then *B* makes a sale, and then *A* makes another sale and wins the bet; similarly, *BB* represents the case where the second insurance salesperson makes two sales and wins the bet before *A* makes one sale.)
   (a) Construct a tree diagram showing the 6 possible outcomes of this "game," and indicate in each case who wins the bet.
   (b) How many possible outcomes are left if we *know* that *A* makes the first sale, and in how many of them will *B* win the bet?

2. A bank classifies its delinquent installment-loan accounts according to whether or not they have ever been delinquent before, according to whether the amount owed is less than $100 or $100 or more, and according to whether payments are overdue by less than 2 months or by 2 months or more.
   (a) Construct a tree diagram showing the various ways in which the bank classifies its delinquent installment-loan accounts.
   (b) If there are 60 accounts in each of the categories of part (a) and a courteous reminder is sent to all those whose accounts are delinquent for the first time *or* who owe less than $100, how many of these courteous reminders will the bank have to mail out?
   (c) If a warning is sent to all those whose payments are overdue by 2 months or more, how many of these warnings will the bank have to mail out?
   (d) How many persons with delinquent installment-loan accounts at this bank will receive a courteous reminder as well as a warning?

3. The manager of a TV-stereo shop stocks two color television sets of the same kind, reordering at the end of each day (for delivery early the next morning) if and only if both sets have been sold. Construct a tree diagram which shows that if the manager starts on a Monday with two of the color television sets in stock, there are altogether eight different ways in which the manager can make sales on Monday and Tuesday of that week. (Note that if the manager sells one of the sets on Monday, there are only two possibilities, 0 and 1, for Tuesday.)

4. If a chain of drug stores has 4 warehouses and 14 retail outlets, in how many different ways can an item be shipped from one of the warehouses to one of the stores?

5. If the five finalists in the Miss California contest are Miss Santa Barbara, Miss Orange County, Miss San Diego, Miss Los Angeles, and Miss San Francisco, in how many ways can the judges choose the winner and the first runner-up?

6. In a primary election there are three candidates for mayor and four candidates for county attorney. In how many different ways can a voter mark a ballot in each case?
   (a) If he or she votes for one candidate for each office.
   (b) If he or she votes only for one candidate for one of the two offices?

7. Given that five airlines provide direct service between two Eastern cities, in how many different ways can a person fly from one city to the other and back in each case?
   (a) He or she must take the same airline both ways.
   (b) He or she can but need not take the same airline both ways.
   (c) He or she cannot take the same airline both ways.

8. A psychologist preparing four-letter nonsense words for use in a memory test chooses the first letter from among the consonants q, r, t, w, and z; the second letter from among the vowels a, e, i, o, and u; the third letter from among the consonants k, x, and v; and the fourth letter from among the vowels a, o, and u.
   (a) How many different nonsense words can be constructed?
   (b) How many of these nonsense words will begin either with the letter t or the letter w?
   (c) How many of these nonsense words will have the vowel a in both places?

9. With reference to Exercise 5, in how many ways can the judges choose the winner, the first runner-up, and the second runner-up from among the five finalists in the Miss California contest?

10. In a certain city, a child watching television on a Saturday morning has the choice between two different cartoon shows from 8 to 8:30, three different cartoon shows from 8:30 to 9, three different cartoon shows from 9 to 9:30, and two different cartoon shows from 9:30 to 10. In how many different ways can a child plan Saturday morning entertainment of watching cartoons continuously from 8 to 10?

11. A cafeteria offers 11 different soups or salads, 14 main dishes, and 9 desserts. In how many different ways can one choose a soup or salad, a main dish, and a dessert?

12. In a drive-in restaurant, a customer can order a hamburger rare, medium rare, medium, or well done, and also with or without mustard, with or without onions, and with or without relish. In how many different ways can a person order a hamburger in this restaurant?

The rules of Section 13.1 are often applied to problems in which repeated selections are made from *one and the same set,* and the order in which the selections are made *is* of significance. This was the case, for example, in Example 13.2 where the stock market analyst had to make a first choice and a second choice from among six stocks, and in Exercises 5 and 9 of the preceding set of exercises, where the judges had to make several selections from among the finalists of a beauty contest.

In general, *if* r *objects are selected from a set of* n *objects, any particular arrangement of these* r *objects is called a* **permutation.**The following are some examples.

EXAMPLE 13.5   Vermont, Maine, and Connecticut constitute a permutation (a particular ordered arrangement) of three of the six New England states; RCA, SCM, AT&T, MCA, and IBM constitute a permutation (a particular ordered arrangement) of five of the many corporations listed on the New York Stock Exchange; 45132 is one of many possible permutations of the first five positive integers, as are 32145 and 24531; and if we were asked to list *all possible* permutations of 2 of the 5 vowels *a, e, i, o,* and u, our answer would be

ae	ai	ao	au	ei	eo	eu	io	iu	ou
ea	ia	oa	ua	ie	oe	ue	oi	ui	uo

When it comes to the counting of all possible permutations, we can use the following result.

> *The number of permutations of* r *objects selected from a set of* n *objects is**

$$_nP_r = n(n-1)(n-2)\cdots(n-r+1)$$

To prove this formula, we have only to observe that the first selection is made from the whole set of n objects, the second selection is made from the n − 1 objects which remain after the first selection has been

---

*The following are some alternative symbols used to denote the number of permutations of r objects selected from a set of n objects; $P(n, r)$, P_r^n, $P_{n,r}$, and $(n)_r$.

made, the third selection is made from the $n - 2$ objects which remain after the first two selections have been made, and the rth and final selection is made from the $n - (r - 1) = n - r + 1$ objects which remain after the first $r - 1$ selections have been made.

EXAMPLE 13.6   The number of ways in which 4 sales territories can be assigned (one each) to 4 of a company's 9 salesmen is $9 \cdot 8 \cdot 7 \cdot 6 = 3024$, and the number of ways in which a graduate of an M.B.A. program can make a first, second, and third choice among 24 potential employers is $24 \cdot 23 \cdot 22 = 12,144$.

Note that it has been assumed in our discussion that the objects with which we are dealing are *distinguishable* in some way, for otherwise there are complications, which go beyond the scope of this text.

When *all* the elements of a set are selected in some order, namely, when $r = n$, we get the special rule

The number of permutations of n objects taken all together is

$$_nP_n = n(n - 1)(n - 2) \cdots 3 \cdot 2 \cdot 1$$

EXAMPLE 13.7   If the stock analyst of Example 13.2 ranks all six of the stocks, for instance, with regard to their potential long-term growth, this can be done in $6 \cdot 5 \cdot 4 \cdot 3 \cdot 2 \cdot 1 = 720$ different ways (barring ties); if 7 drivers had to be assigned to 7 delivery trucks, this could be done in $7 \cdot 6 \cdot 5 \cdot 4 \cdot 3 \cdot 2 \cdot 1 = 5040$ different ways.

Since products of consecutive integers arise in many problems involving permutations or other kinds of special arrangements, it generally simplifies matters if we use **factorial notation**.

In this notation, $1! = 1$, $2! = 2 \cdot 1 = 2$, $3! = 3 \cdot 2 \cdot 1 = 6$, $4! = 4 \cdot 3 \cdot 2 \cdot 1 = 24, \ldots$, and in general, $n!$, which is read "n factorial," denotes the product

$$n(n - 1)(n - 2) \cdots 3 \cdot 2 \cdot 1$$

for any positive integer n. It is also customary, to let $0! = 1$ (by definition) because this makes it easier to express certain formulas relating to permutations and other kinds of special arrangements. Incidentally, a table of *factorials*, from n = 0 to n = 15, may be found in Table VI in the Appendix.

We can now use the factorial notation to write the formula for the number of permutations of r objects selected from a set of n objects as

$$_nP_r = \frac{n!}{(n-r)!}$$

To prove this, we have only to take the preceding formula for $_nP_r$, and divide by (n − r)!, and make use of the fact that

$$n(n-1)(n-2)\cdots(n-r+1)\cdot(n-r)! = n!$$

EXAMPLE 13.8 The number of ways in which a chairman, a vice-chairman, a secretary, and a treasurer can be chosen from among the nine members of the executive council of a union is

$$_9P_4 = \frac{9!}{(9-4)!} = \frac{9!}{5!} = \frac{362,880}{120} = 3024$$

where the values of 9! and 5! were obtained from Table VII, and it should be noted that the result is the same as in the first part of Example 6. Also, the number of ways in which the defensive unit of a professional football team can be introduced before a game is

$$_{11}P_{11} = \frac{11!}{(11-11)!} = \frac{11!}{0!} = \frac{11!}{1} = 39,916,800$$

Of course, it follows that $_nP_n$ is simply n!.

13.3 COMBINATIONS

In contrast to problems concerning permutations, there are also many problems in which we select r objects from a set of n objects, but are *not* interested in the order in which they are selected.

EXAMPLE 13.9 Suppose, for example, that a person gathering data for a market research organization has to interview 3 of the 48 families living in an apartment building. As we shall show, these families can be selected in 17,296 different ways, but this is *not* the number of permutations of 3 objects selected from a set of 48 objects. If we did care about the order in which the person visits these families, the answer would be

$$_{48}P_3 = 48 \cdot 47 \cdot 46 = 103{,}776$$

but each set of 3 families would then be counted *six times*. For instance, if the letters *J, M,* and *S* stand for Jones, Morris, and Smith (namely, three of the families who live in the given apartment house), then

$$JMS, \quad JSM, \quad MJS, \quad MSJ, \quad SMJ, \quad SJM$$

constitute six *different permutations*, but they all represent the same three families, namely, the *same subset* of 3 of the 48 families. Since this argument holds for any three families who live in the given apartment house, the total number of ways in which 3 of the 48 families can be selected (without paying attention to the order in which they are selected) is given by

$$\frac{_{48}P_3}{6} = \frac{103{,}776}{6} = 17{,}296$$

The answer obtained in the last example is referred to as the number of **combinations** of 3 objects selected from a set of 48 objects. Thus, *combination* has the same meaning as *subset*, and when we ask for the *number of combinations of r objects selected from a set of n objects,* we are simply trying to find out *how many different subsets of r objects can be selected from a set of n objects.* To obtain a formula for this, we have only to observe that any r objects can be rearranged into r! different permutations; in other words, the r! permutations of the elements of any subset of r objects count only as *one combination.* Hence the $_nP_r$ permutations of r objects selected from a set of n objects contain each combination r! times, and $_nC_r$, the corresponding number of combinations, is given by $_nP_r$ divided by r!. Consequently,

the number of combinations of r objects selected from a set of n objects is

$$_nC_r = \frac{_nP_r}{r!} = \frac{n(n-1)\cdots(n-r+1)}{r!}$$

where we substituted $n(n-1)\cdots(n-r+1)$ for $_nP_r$. Some alternative symbols used to denote the number of combinations of r objects selected from a set of n objects are $C(n, r)$, C_r^n, $C_{n,r}$, and above all $\binom{n}{r}$, which is referred to as a **binomial coefficient**

EXAMPLE 13.10 To illustrate the use of the formula for $_nC_r$, let us see in how many ways a committee of 4 can be selected from among the 120 employees of a company and in how many ways a social scientist conducting a sample survey can select 5 of the 14 counties of Arizona. In the first case, we find that there are

$$_{120}C_4 = \frac{120 \cdot 119 \cdot 118 \cdot 117}{4!} = \frac{197,149,680}{24} = 8,214,570$$

ways of selecting the committee; and in the second case, we find that there are

$$_{14}C_5 = \frac{14 \cdot 13 \cdot 12 \cdot 11 \cdot 10}{5!} = \frac{240,240}{120} = 2002$$

ways of selecting the 5 counties. Of course, these are *combinations*, and the internal order of the committee and the order in which the social scientist might visit the 5 counties are not taken into consideration.

We can also write the formula for the number of combinations of r objects selected from a set of n objects as*

$$_nC_r = \frac{n!}{(n - r)! \cdot r!}$$

Had we used this formula in Example 13.10 to determine the number of ways in which the social scientist can select 5 of the 14 counties, we would have obtained $(14!)/(9! \cdot 5!)$, and we could then have continued by looking up the values of 14!, 9!, and 5! in Table VI. *This would have entailed a considerable amount of work, all of which can be avoided by looking up the answer, 2002, directly in Table VII.*

As we indicated above, the number of combinations of r objects selected from a set of n objects is often written as $\binom{n}{r}$ instead of $_nC_r$ and called a *binomial coefficient*; this is the notation and terminology used in Table VII, which contains the values of $\binom{n}{r}$ for $n = 0, 1, 2, \ldots$, and

---

*Note that this formula and the one for $_nP_r$ hold also when $n = 0$ and $r = 0$; in that case, trivially, $_0C_0 = 1$ and $_0P_0 = 1$.

20. When n is greater than 10 and r is large, the use of Table VII may require that we refer to the identity

$$_nC_{n-r} = {_nC_r} \quad \text{or, in the alternative notation,} \quad \binom{n}{n-r} = \binom{n}{r}$$

To prove this, we might argue that each time we select a subset of r objects we *leave* a subset of $n - r$ objects, so, there are as many ways of selecting r objects as there are ways of leaving (or selecting) $n - r$ objects. To prove the identity algebraically we have only to write

$$_nC_{n-r} = \frac{n!}{[n - (n - r)]!\,(n - r)!} = \frac{n!}{r!\,(n - r)!} = \frac{n!}{(n - r)!\,r!} = {_nC_r}$$

EXAMPLE 13.11 To determine the number of ways in which a police captain can choose 15 of 20 detectives for a special assignment, we look up $\binom{20}{5}$ in Table VII, getting

$$\binom{20}{15} = \binom{20}{5} = 15{,}504$$

Also, to determine the number of ways in which a child can choose 12 of the 16 most popular rides in Disneyland, we look up $\binom{16}{4}$ in Table VII, getting

$$\binom{16}{12} = \binom{16}{4} = 1820$$

EXERCISES

1. On each trip to Chicago, a salesperson visits 6 of 10 customers. In how many different ways can appointments be scheduled for a forthcoming trip to Chicago?

2. Find the number of ways in which 3 parties can be assigned to 3 of the 12 empty booths of a restaurant.

3. In how many ways can 5 government officials each choose a car from a car pool of 18 cars?

4. A company has 15 applicants for four different executive positions within its organization.
   (a) In how many ways can these positions be filled?
   (b) In how many ways can these positions be filled if 5 of the applicants are ruled out for various reasons?
   (c) In how many ways can the position be filled if there are 6 applicants for one of the positions and 9 applicants for the other three positions? (*Hint:* Multiply the number of ways in which the first position can be filled by the number of ways the other three positions can be filled.)

5. Four married couples have 8 seats in a row for a concert.
   (a) In how many ways can they be seated?
   (b) In how many ways can they be seated if none of the men are to sit together and none of the women are to sit together? (*Hint:* Add the number of possibilities where the first seat on the left is occupied by a man to the number of possibilities where the first seat on the left is occupied by a woman.)
   (c) In how many ways can they be seated if all the men are to sit together and all the women are to sit together?
   (d) In how many ways can they be seated if each couple is to sit together with the husband to the left of his wife?

6. In how many ways can a lumber company select 4 of 12 possible sites for the construction of new saw mills? Use one of the formulas for $_nC_r$ and check your answer in Table VII.

7. In how many ways can a 4-person committee be chosen from among the 24 doctors practicing in a certain city?

8. Find the number of ways in which an accountant working for the IRS can select 3 of 50 tax returns for a special audit in each case. (a) The order in which the chosen returns will be audited does not matter. (b) The order in which the chosen returns will be audited does matter.

9. If Mrs. Brown has 4 purses and 9 pairs of shoes, in how many ways can she choose 2 purses and 3 pairs of shoes to take along on a trip?

10. A shipment of 16 typewriters contains 1 that is defective. In how many ways can one choose 3 of these typewriters so that (a) the defective one is not included; (b) the defective one is included?

11. In hiring a staff, the manager of a new furniture store has to choose 6 salespeople from among 8 applicants, 2 buyers from among 4 applicants, 2 secretaries from among 12 applicants, and 3 stockroom clerks from among 6 applicants. Find the total number of ways in which the staff can be selected.

Borrowing from the language of statistics, we shall refer to the various things that can happen in a given situation (namely, the set of all possible outcomes) as the corresponding **sample space**. For instance, in Example 13.2 the sample space consists of the 30 different recommendations which the stock market analyst can make, in Example 13.6 the sample space consists of the 3024 ways in which the new sales territories can be assigned to the salespeople, and in Example 13.9 the sample space consists of the 17,296 ways in which the person gathering the data can choose 3 of the 48 families living in the given building.

In most work connected with sample spaces it is advantageous to identify the various possibilities with numbers or points—we can then talk about the things that can happen *mathematically,* without having to go through lengthy verbal details. Actually, this is what we do in sports when we refer to players by their numbers; it is what the Internal Revenue Service does when it refers to taxpayers by their social security numbers; and it is precisely what we do when we identify cities with points on a map.

The use of points rather than numbers has the added advantage that it makes it easier to visualize the various possibilities, and perhaps discover some of the features which various different outcomes have in common.

EXAMPLE 13.12 To illustrate this, consider an opinion poll, in which registered voters are asked whether they oppose a new bond issue for civic improvements, whether they are for it, or whether they are undecided. The possible responses of *one* voter can be pictured as in Figure 13.3, where we have identified the three answers with three points and also assigned to them the (code) numbers 1, 2, and 3. (Actually, these points could have been drawn in any pattern, and we could have assigned to the three possibilities any arbitrary set of numbers.)

Had we been interested in the responses of *two* voters, we could have represented the various possibilities by means of the nine points of Figure 13.4, where 1, 2, and 3 again stand for being opposed to the new bond issue, being for it, and being undecided. The advantage of the

FIGURE 13.3
Sample Space
for Responses
of One Voter

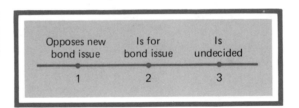

FIGURE 13.4
Sample Space
for Responses
of Two Voters

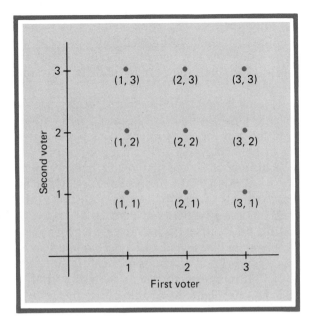

particular arrangement of Figure 13.4 is that we can use the coordinates of the points to identify the various possibilities. For instance, the point (1, 2) represents the case where the first voter opposes the new bond issue while the second voter is for it; similarly, (3, 1) represents the case where the first voter is undecided and the second voter is opposed to the new bond issue, and (2, 2) represents the case where both voters are for it. Note that the response of the first voter is always given by the first coordinate, while that of the second voter is given by the second coordinate.

If we were interested in the responses of n voters, there would be 3^n possibilities and as many points (in accordance with the rule on page 360). For n = 4, for example, there would be $3^4 = 81$ possibilities, that is, 81 points, among which (1, 3, 1, 2) represents the case where the first and third voters oppose the new bond issue, the second voter is undecided, and the fourth voter is against it. (Since each possibility is thus represented by four numbers, we cannot picture the corresponding points as readily as in Figures 13.3 and 13.4; in fact, this would require a diagram of *four* dimensions. Of course, we could identify the 81 possibilities with any arbitrary set of 81 points, but the chances are that this would not be of much help.)

Sample spaces are usually classified according to the number of points which they contain; especially, whether they are **finite** or **infinite**. All the sample spaces mentioned so far in this section have been *finite;* that is, they contained a finite, or fixed, number of points. In this text we shall limit our discussion to sample spaces containing only a finite number of points; in other words, we shall consider only situations in which the number of different things that can happen is finite.

Having defined sample space, let us now state what we mean by an **event**. This is important because probabilities (to which we shall devote most of the remainder of this book) always refer to the occurrence or nonoccurrence of events. For instance, we may want to assign a probability to the event that the price of anywhere from 24 to 30 public utility stocks will go down on a certain day, the event that there will be at least 6 heads in 10 flips of a coin, the event that a new tire will last at most 32,000 miles before it has to be recapped, and so forth. Generally speaking, *all events with which we are concerned in probability theory are represented by sets of outcomes, namely, by subsets of appropriate sample spaces,* and as you will recall from Chapter 1, a subset is any part of a set including the set as a whole and, trivially, the empty set $\emptyset$ which has no elements at all. Thus, *the term event corresponds to subset of a sample space in the language of mathematics.*

EXAMPLE 13.12
(Continued)

When we refer to Figure 13.4, for example, we find that the subset which consists of the point (2, 3) represents the *event* that the first voter is for the new bond issue while the second voter is undecided; the subset which consists of the points (1, 1), (2,2), and (3, 3) represents the *event* that both voters respond in the same way; and the subset which consists of the points (1, 2), (2, 1), (3,2), and (2,3) represents the *event* that one of the two voters is for the new bond issue while the other one either opposes it or is undecided.

EXAMPLE 13.13

Suppose that we are looking for a new house, and that we classify all houses advertised for sale according to whether they have 1, 2, 3, or 4 bedrooms, and also according to whether they have 1, 2, or 3 baths. *None of the houses has fewer bedrooms than baths.* To study the situation, we first draw a tree diagram like that of Figure 13.5, and we find that there are 9 possibilities altogether. Then, using coordinates to denote the number of bedrooms and the number of baths, we construct the sample space shown in Figure 13.6. Here (2, 1) represents the *event* that we choose a house with 2 bedrooms and 1 bath, while (4, 3) represents the *event* that we choose a house with 4 bedrooms and 3 baths. Also, the subset which consists of the points (3, 2) and (4, 1) represents the *event* that we choose a house in which the number of bedrooms and baths add up to 5; the set which consists of the points (2, 1), (3,1), (3,2), (4, 1), (4,2), and (4,3) represents the *event* that we choose a house with more bedrooms than baths; (1, 1), (2, 1) and (2, 2) represent the *event*

FIGURE 13.5
Tree Diagram
for Example 13.13

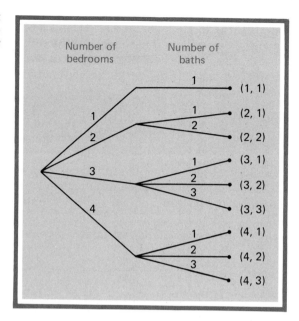

that we choose a house which has at most 2 bedrooms; and (3, 1), (3, 2) and (3, 3) represent the *event* that we choose a 3-bedroom house. Now, if we denote these four sets by D, E, F, and G (see Figure 13.6), we can form numerous other subsets (events) by applying the set operations we discussed in Section 1.1. For instance, it can be seen from Figure 13.6 that $E \cap F$ consists of the point (2, 1) and hence that it represents the *event* that we choose a 2-bedroom house with 1 bath; $D \cup G$ consists of

FIGURE 13.6
Sample Space
for Example 13.13

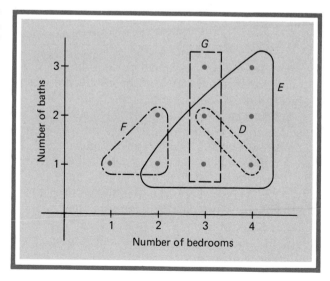

the points (3, 1), (3, 2), (3, 3), and (4, 1), and it represents the *event* that we choose a 3-bedroom house or a 4-bedroom house with only 1 bath; and that E', the complement of E, consists of the points (1, 1), (2, 2), and (3, 3), and it represents the *event* that we choose a house with as many bedrooms as baths.

Still referring to the sample space of Example 13.13 (that is, Figure 13.6), note that $F \cap D$ represents the *event* that we choose a 1- or 2-bedroom house for which the number of bedrooms and baths add up to 5. Clearly, this is impossible in the given situation; $F \cap D$ does not contain any of the nine points of the sample space and we write $F \cap D = \emptyset$. If two events such as F and D have no points in common, we refer to them as **mutually exclusive**

EXAMPLE 13.13
(Continued)

As can be seen from Figure 13.6, D and E' are mutually exclusive, as are F and G. On the other hand, D and G are *not* mutually exclusive—they both contain the point (3, 2)—and neither are F' and G. In fact, G is *contained* in F' and we can write $G \subset F'$. Obviously, 3-bedroom houses are included among those having 3 bedrooms or more.

As we indicated in the beginning of this chapter, counting possibilities often plays an important role in determining probabilities. Thus let us indicate briefly how *Venn diagrams* (see Chapter 1) can be used to count the elements of subsets, namely, to determine *how many individual outcomes comprise given events*.

EXAMPLE 13.14

Suppose, for instance, that a stock broker wants to call one of 234 clients. Assume that 157 of the clients are wealthy and 65 are retired. In addition, 43 of the retired clients are wealthy. *In how many different ways can the broker decide whom to call, if the broker wants the person called to be neither wealthy nor retired?* Drawing the circles which represent wealthy clients (set W) and retired clients (set R) as in the Venn diagrams of Figure 13.7, we begin by writing the 43 in the region common to the two circles, namely, the one which represents the set $W \cap R$. Then we observe that $157 - 43 = 114$ of the broker's clients must be in W but outside R, and that $65 - 43 = 22$ of the clients must be in R but outside W. This accounts for $114 + 43 + 22 = 179$ of the clients, and we conclude that the remaining $234 - 179 = 55$ clients are neither wealthy nor retired.

FIGURE 13.7
Venn Diagrams
for Example 13.14

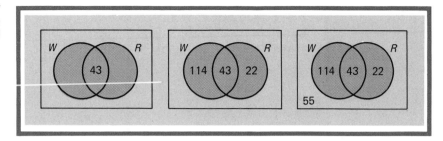

EXAMPLE 13.15 The following example is very similar, but we shall have to work with percentages rather than numbers and with three circles instead of two. It concerns a survey in which shoppers were interviewed in a supermarket and the following results were obtained: 68 percent shop there regularly, 53 percent are satisfied with the service, 82 percent collect trading stamps, 47 percent shop there regularly and are satisfied with the service, 50 percent are satisfied with the service and collect trading stamps, 64 percent shop there regularly and collect trading stamps, while 46 percent shop there regularly, are satisfied with the service, and collect trading stamps.

(a) What percentage of these shoppers shop there regularly but do not like the service and do not collect trading stamps?

(b) What percentage of these shoppers do not shop there regularly, do not like the service, and do not collect trading stamps?

(c) What fraction of the shoppers who shop there regularly do not collect trading stamps?

Drawing the circles which represent shoppers who shop there regularly (set A), shoppers who like the service (set B), and shoppers who collect trading stamps (set C) as in the Venn diagrams of Figure 13.8, we begin by writing 46 in the region common to A, B, and C. Then

FIGURE 13.8
Venn Diagrams
for Example 13.15

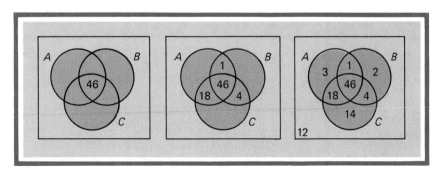

we observe that $47 - 46 = 1$ percent of the people shop there regularly and like the service but do *not* collect trading stamps, that $50 - 46 = 4$ percent of the shoppers belong to $B \cap C$ but *not* to A, and that $64 - 46 = 18$ percent of them belong to $A \cap C$ but *not* to B. Filling in these percentages as in the second Venn diagram of Figure 13.8, we then continue by arguing that

$$68 - (18 + 46 + 1) = 3\%$$

of the people shop there regularly but do *not* like the service and do *not* collect trading stamps, *which answers* (a). Similarly, we find that

$$53 - (1 + 46 + 4) = 2\%$$

of the shoppers must be in set B but outside A as well as C, while

$$82 - (18 + 46 + 4) = 14\%$$

of the shoppers must be in set C but outside A as well as B. When we add all the percentages shown in the third diagram of Figure 13.8, we get

$$3 + 1 + 46 + 18 + 2 + 4 + 14 = 88\%$$

and we conclude that the remaining 12 percent of the shoppers do *not* shop there regularly, do *not* like the service, and do *not* collect trading stamps; *this answers* (b).

To find the answer to (c), observe that among the 68 percent of the people who shop there regularly, $3 + 1 = 4$ percent are outside circle C and hence do *not* collect trading stamps. Four percent compared to 68 percent is $4/68$ or $1/17$, and this is the desired fraction of the shoppers who shop there regularly that do *not* collect trading stamps.

---

1. With reference to the sample space of Figure 13.4, describe in *words* the event represented by each set of points.
   (a) (1, 1)
   (b) (1, 2), (2, 2), and (3, 2)
   (c) (1, 1), (1, 2), (2, 1), and (2, 2)
   (d) (2, 1), (2, 2), (2, 3), (1, 2), and (3, 2)
2. With reference to the sample space of Figure 13.6, describe in *words* the event represented by each set of points.

(a) (3, 1)

(b) (3, 3) and (4, 3)

(c) (2, 1), (3, 2), and (4, 3)

(d) (1, 1), (2, 2), and (3, 3)

3. In a small restaurant, guests are served in two dining rooms, of which the smaller has three tables and the larger has four tables. Using two coordinates so that (1, 2), for example, represents the event that at a given moment one table in the smaller room and two tables in the larger room are being used, and (2, 0) represents the event that two tables in the smaller room and none in the larger room are being used, draw a diagram (similar to that of Figure 13.4) which shows the 20 points of the corresponding sample space. Also, if K is the event that at least five tables in the restaurant are being used, L is the event that the same number of tables is being used in both rooms, and M is the event that fewer tables are being used in the larger room than in the smaller room, list the points which comprise each event.

(a) K (b) L (c) M

Also indicate events K, L, and M on the diagram of the sample space by enclosing the points which they contain with a solid line, a dashed line, and a dotted line.

4. With reference to Exercise 3, express in words what event is represented by each set of points.

(a) (0, 3), (1, 2), (2, 1), and (3, 0)

(b) (3, 3), (2, 3), (1, 3), and (0, 3)

(c) (0, 2), (1, 1), and (2, 0)

(d) (0, 0), (0, 1), (0, 2), (0, 3), (0, 4), (1, 0), (2, 0), and (3, 0)

5. With reference to Exercise 3, which of the following pairs of events are mutually exclusive?

(a) K and L (c) L and M

(b) K and M (d) $K \cap L$ and M

6. Suppose that in Example 13.12 three voters had been interviewed, but that 1, 2, and 3 stand, as before, for being "opposed to the bond issue," "for it," and "undecided."

(a) Draw a tree diagram to show that there are altogether 27 different ways in which these voters can respond.

(b) Using three coordinates so that (2, 1, 3), for example, represents the event that the first voter is for the new bond issue, the second voter opposes it, and the third voter is undecided, list the points of the sample space which represent the following events.

(i) The first and third voters are undecided.

(ii) The first voter is opposed to the new bond issue, but the other two voters are not opposed to it.

(iii) Exactly two of the voters are for the new bond issue.

(c) Describe *in words* the event which is represented by each set of points.

P = {(1, 1, 1), (1, 1, 2), (1, 1, 3)}
Q = {(1, 1, 1), (2, 2, 2), (3, 3, 3)}
R = {(1, 2, 3), (1, 3, 2), (2, 1, 3), (2, 3, 1), (3, 1, 2), (3, 2, 1)}
S = {(2, 1, 1), (2, 1, 2), (2, 1, 3), (2, 2, 1), (2, 2, 2), (2, 2, 3), (2, 3, 1), (2, 3, 2), (2, 3, 3)}

7. With reference to part (c) of Exercise 6, list the points of the sample space which belong to each subset, and describe *in words* the event represented.
   (a) $P \cap Q$ (c) $P \cap R'$ (e) $P \cap S$
   (b) $Q \cup R$ (d) $Q \cap S$ (f) $R \cap S$

8. With reference to part (c) of Exercise 6, which pairs of subsets represent mutually exclusive events?
   (a) P and Q   (c) P and S   (e) Q and $R \cap S$
   (b) Q and S   (d) P and R   (f) Q and R'

9. If we let 1 and 0 represent *heads* and *tails*, the results obtained in three successive flips of a coin can be represented by means of points such as (1, 1, 0) and (0, 1, 0), where the first point represents *heads, heads, tails*, and the second point represents *tails, heads, tails*.
   (a) Copy the diagram of Figure 13.9 and complete it by filling in the coordinates of the other six points of the sample space.
   (b) If X represents the event that the first two tosses are *tails*, Y represents the event that at least one of the three tosses is *heads*, and Z represents the event that the tosses are either *all heads* or *all tails*, list the points of the sample space which belong to each of these subsets. Also describe *in words* the events represented by $X \cap Y$, $X \cup Z$, and $Y' \cap Z$.

10. Which of the following pairs of events are mutually exclusive? Explain your answers.
    (a) Being a woman and being president of a large corporation.
    (b) Being under 35 and being President of the United States.
    (c) Wearing a white shirt and having brown eyes.
    (d) Scoring a touchdown and hitting a home run in the same game.
    (e) Getting a ticket for speeding and getting a ticket for going through a red light.
    (f) Having rain and sunshine on the 4th of July, 1985.
    (g) Leaving Los Angeles by jet at 11 P.M. and arriving in Chicago on the same day.

11. A company has 380 employees, of which 274 got a raise, 86 got a promotion, and 55 got both. How many of the employees got neither a raise nor a promotion?

12. The manager of a baseball park knows from experience that 37

FIGURE 13.9
Diagram for Exercise 9

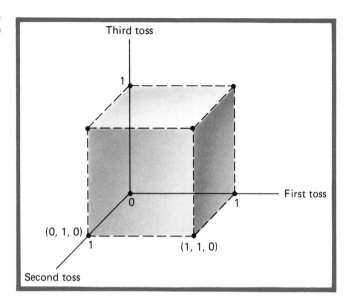

percent of all persons attending games buy a program, 54 percent buy peanuts, 67 percent buy a soft drink, 23 percent buy a program and peanuts, 34 percent buy peanuts and a soft drink, 28 percent buy a program and a soft drink, and 16 percent buy a program, peanuts, and a soft drink. What percentages of persons attending a baseball game at this park will do each of the following?

(a) Buy a program and a soft drink, but no peanuts.

(b) Buy peanuts, but neither a program nor a soft drink.

(c) Buy either peanuts or a soft drink.

(d) Buy a soft drink, but no peanuts.

(e) Buy neither a program, nor peanuts, nor a soft drink.

13. Among 60 new cars shipped to a dealer, there are 8 with air-conditioning, bucket seats, and automatic transmission; 5 with air-conditioning, automatic transmission, but no bucket seats; 3 with air-conditioning, bucket seats, but no automatic transmission; 8 with air-conditioning, but neither bucket seats nor automatic transmission; 24 with automatic transmission, but neither air-conditioning nor bucket seats; 2 with automatic transmission, bucket seats, but no air-conditioning; 3 with bucket seats, but neither air-conditioning nor automatic transmission; and 7 without any of these features.

(a) How many of these cars have bucket seats?

(b) How many of these cars have air-conditioning?

(c) How many of these cars have automatic transmissions as well as bucket seats?

(d) How many of these cars have neither air-conditioning nor bucket seats?

To provide the necessary background for an introduction to probability, this chapter introduced methods which enable you to determine what is possible in a given situation. First, we introduced *counting methods,* followed by a discussion of *permutations* and *combinations.* The chapter concluded with a discussion of the concept of a *sample space* and the importance of *events* in the study of probability.

1. **Deterministic Model** A mathematical model in which the relationships between the variables are always expressed in terms of mathematical equations that leave nothing to chance.
2. **Probabilistic, or Stochastic Model** A mathematical model which allows for the uncertaintly observable in most practical decision-making situations.
3. **Tree Diagram** A graphical method of listing all possibilities in a given situation.
4. **Permutation** Any particular arrangement of *r* objects selected from a set of *n* objects.
5. **Factorial Notation** A notation that enables us to show the product of consecutive integers from 1 to *n* as *n*!.
6. **Combination** The number of subsets of *r* objects that can be selected from a set of *n* objects.
7. **Sample Space** The set of possible outcomes in a given situation.
8. **Event** A subset of the sample space.
9. **Mutually Exclusive Events** Two events that have no sample points in common.

1. A vice-president of a publishing firm has to schedule the company's annual sales meetings for the next 3 years. If the locations are limited to Montreal, Philadelphia, and Atlanta and cannot be scheduled in the same city two years in a row, construct a tree diagram showing the 12 ways in which the job can be done.
2. Standard and Poor's regularly rates common stocks, assigning them the ratings A+, A, A−, B+, B, B−, and C.
   (a) In how many ways could they rate two different common stocks?
   (b) In how many ways could they have rated two different common stocks, if all we know is that their ratings are not the same?
   (c) In how many ways can they rate three different common stocks, if each of the stocks rates at least A−?

3. A new-car buyer finds that she must not only choose between 6 different models, but that each model can be had with 3 different engines, with or without air-conditioning, and in 9 different colors. Altogether, in how many different ways can her order be placed?

4. A multiple-choice test consists of 6 questions, each permitting a choice of 4 alternatives. In how many different ways can a student check off his answers to these questions?

5. A firm is considering building three new convenience food stores. If 8 possible locations are being evaluated, in how many ways can the firm select 3 of the 8 possible sites for the construction of the new stores?

6. In how many ways can 6 new accounts be distributed among 14 advertising executives, if none of them is to receive more than 1 of the new accounts?

7. In how many ways can a television director schedule a sponsor's 6 different commercials during the 6 time slots allocated to commercials during a 60-minute "special"?

8. An appliance salesman has four customers in El Paso, whom he may or may not visit on a 2-day trip to that city.
   (a) If we are interested only in how many of these customers he visits on each day, draw a tree diagram showing the 15 possibilities.
   (b) Using two coordinates so that (2, 1), for example, represents the event that he visits two of the customers on the first day and one on the second day and (3, 0) represents the event that he visits three of the customers on the first day and none on the second day, draw a diagram similar to that of Figure 13.4 which shows the 15 points of the corresponding sample space.
   (c) Describe in words the event which is represented by each of the following sets of points.
   $A = \{(0, 4), (1, 3), (2, 2), (3, 1), (4, 0)\}$;
   $B = \{(0, 2), (1, 2), (2,2)\}$;
   $C = \{(1, 0), (2, 1)\}$;
   $D = \{(0, 3), (1, 3), (0, 4)\}$;
   $E = \{(0, 0), (1, 0), (0, 1), (2, 0), (1, 1), (0, 2)\}$.

9. With reference to part (c) of Exercise 8, list the points of the sample space which belong to each subset, and describe in words the event each represents.
   (a) $A \cap B$ (c) E' (e) $C \cap D$
   (b) $A \cap D$ (d) $B \cup C$ (f) $A' \cap E$

10. With reference to part (c) of Exercise 8, which pairs of subsets represent mutually exclusive events?
   (a) A and B (c) B and D (e) C and E
   (b) C and D (d) B and E (f) A and D

11. In a group of 160 students, 92 are enrolled in a course in accounting, 63 are enrolled in a course in statistics, and 40 are enrolled in both. How many of these students are not enrolled in either course?

12. A market research organization claims that among 400 people interviewed in a large city, 312 regularly look at the food ads in the daily paper, 248 regularly look at the "Dear Abby" column, 173 regularly look at both, and 43 look at neither on a regular basis. Draw a Venn diagram and fill in the figures which correspond to the various regions to check whether the results of this survey should be questioned.

AN INTRODUCTION TO PROBABILITY AND DECISION MAKING

In Chapter 13 we studied what is possible in a given situation. In some instances we listed all possibilities, and in others we merely determined the number of different possibilities. Now we shall go one step further and judge also what is likely or probable, and what is unlikely or improbable. First, there is the question of what we *mean*, for example, when we say that the probability for rain is 0.80, when we say that the probability for the success of a new venture is 0.35, or when we say that the probability for a candidate's election is 0.63; then there is the question of how probabilities are actually determined; and finally there is the question of what mathematical rules probabilities have to obey. In order to illustrate the increasing role played by mathematics and probability in decision making, the chapter concludes with an introduction to **decision theory**, or **decision analysis**.

14.1 AN INTRODUCTION TO PROBABILITY

In everyday terms, **probability** can be thought of as a numerical measure of the "chance" that a particular event will occur. For example, consider the event, a successful advertising campaign. If an advertising agency indicates a near-zero probability for a successful advertising campaign, we interpret this statement to mean that it is very unlikely the advertising campaign will be a success. On the other hand, if the advertising agency indicates a 90 percent chance of success, which corresponds to a probability of 0.90, we would conclude that it is very likely the advertising campaign will be successful. A 0.50 probability (in other words, a 50 percent chance of success) indicates that a successful advertising campaign is just as likely to occur as not. Historically, the oldest way of measuring probabilities is the **classical concept of probability**. It was developed originally in connection with games of chance, and it lends itself most readily to bridging the gap between possibilities and probabilities. This concept applies only when all possible outcomes are equally likely, in which case we can say that

*if there are n equally likely possibilities, of which one must occur
and s are regarded as favorable, or as a success, then the probability
of a success is given by s/n.*

In the application of this rule, the terms *favorable* and *success* are used
rather loosely—what is a success from one point of view is a failure
from another. Thus *favorable* and *success* can be applied to any kind of
outcome, even if favorable means that a house gets struck by lightning,
or success means that a person catches pneumonia. This usage dates
back to the days when probabilities were quoted only in connection
with games of chance.

EXAMPLE 14.1   A shipment of 50 automobile batteries is known to contain 4 defective
batteries. If one of the batteries is randomly selected from the batch of
50, what is the probability of selecting a defective battery? Since there
are $s = 4$ defective units among the $n = 50$ batteries, we get

$$\frac{s}{n} = \frac{4}{50} = 0.08$$

A major shortcoming of the concept of classical probability is its
limited applicability, for there are many situations in which the various
possibilities cannot all be regarded as equally likely. This would be the
case, for instance, if we are concerned with the question of whether it
will rain on the next day. Surely, it would be nonsensical to say that
either it will rain or it will not rain, and hence the probability for rain
is $\frac{1}{2}$. Also, the various possibilities cannot be regarded as equaly likely
when we wonder whether a person will get a raise, when we want to
predict the outcome of an election or the score of a football game, or
when we want to judge whether food prices will go up or remain the
same.

Among the various probability concepts, the most widely held is
the **frequency interpretation**, according to which

*the probability of an event (happening or outcome) is the proportion
of the time that events of the same kind will occur in the long run.*

If we say that the probability is 0.88 that a jet from Denver to Seattle will
arrive on time, we mean that such flights arrive on time 88 percent of
the time. Also, if the weather service predicts that there is a 40 percent
chance for rain (namely, that the probability is 0.40 that it will rain), this
is meant to imply that under the same weather conditions it will rain 40
percent of the time. More generally, we say that an event has a probability of, say, 0.90, in the same sense in which we might say that in cold
weather our car will start 90 percent of the time. We cannot guarantee

what will happen on any particular occasion—the car may start and then it may not—but if we kept records over a long period of time, we should find that the proportion of successes is very close of 0.90.

In accordance with the frequency interpretation of probability, we estimate the probability of an event by observing what fraction of the time similar events have occurred in the past.

EXAMPLE 14.2 If data kept by a government agency show that (over a period of time) 528 of 600 jets from Denver to Seattle arrived on time, what is the probability that any one jet from Denver to Seattle will arrive on time?

Since in the past $\frac{528}{600} = 0.88$ of the flights arrived on time, we use this figure as an estimate of the desired probability; or we say that there is an 88 percent chance that such a flight will arrive on time.

EXAMPLE 14.3 If records show that 506 of 814 automatic dishwashers sold by a large retailer required repairs within the warranty year, what is the probability that an automatic dishwasher sold by this retailer will not require repairs within the warranty year?

Since $814 - 506 = 308$ of the dishwashers did not require repairs, we estimate the desired probability as $\frac{308}{814} = 0.38$ (rounded to two decimal places).

In the frequency interpretation, the probability of an event is defined in terms of what happens to similar events in the long run, so let us examine briefly whether it is at all meaningful to talk about the probability of an event which can occur only once. For instance, can we assign a probability to the event that Ms. Jones will be able to leave the hospital within 4 days after having an appendectomy, or to the event that a certain major-party candidate will win an upcoming gubernatorial election? If we put ourselves in the position of Ms. Jones' doctor, we might check medical records, discover that patients left the hospital within four days after an appendectomy in, say, 34 percent of hundreds of cases, and apply this figure to Ms. Jones. This may not be of much comfort to Ms. Jones, but it does to provide a meaning for a probability statement about her leaving the hospital within 4 days—the probability is 0.34.

This illustrates that when we make a probability statement about a specific (nonrepeatable) event, the frequency interpretation of probability leaves us no choice but to refer to a set of similar events. As can well be imagined, however, this can easily lead to complications, since the choice of "similar" events is generally neither obvious nor straightforward. With reference to Ms. Jones' appendectomy, we might consider as similar only cases in which the patients were of the same sex, only cases in which the patients were also of the same age as Ms. Jones, or only cases in which the patients were also of the same height and weight as Ms. Jones. Ultimately, the choice of similar events is a matter of personal judgment, and it is by no means contradictory that we can arrive at different probabilities, all valid, conerning the same event.

With regard to the question whether a certain major-party candidate will win an upcoming gubernatorial election, suppose that we ask the persons who have conducted a poll "how sure" they are that the candidate will win. If they say they are 95 percent sure (that is, if they assign a probability of 0.95 to the candidate's winning the election), this is not meant to imply that the candidate would win 95 percent of the time when running for office a great number of times. Rather, it means that the pollsters' prediction is based on a method which "works" 95 percent of the time. It is in this way that we must interpret many of the probabilities attached to statistical results.

Finally, let us mention an alternative concept of probability which is currently gaining in favor. According to this point of view, probabilities are interpreted as **personal** or **subjective evaluations**; they measure one's belief with regard to the uncertainties that are involved. Such probabilities apply especially when there is little or no direct evidence, so that there is really no choice but to consider collateral (indirect) information, educated guesses, and perhaps intuition and other subjective factors. Thus a manager may "feel" that the probability of success of a new venture, such as a new bookstore, is 0.60. In this way the manager would be expressing the strength of his or her belief regarding the uncertainties connected with the success of the store, and it may be based on business conditions in general, the opinion of an expert, or the manager's own subjective evaluation of the whole situation, including, perhaps, a small dose of optimism.

Regardless of which theory of probability is used, two basic rules* must be followed when assigning probabilities to the individual outcomes (points) of the sample space S.

Rule 1	*The probability associated with each individual outcome of the sample space must be on the interval from 0 to 1.*
Rule 2	*The sum of the probabilities of all the individual outcomes must be 1.*

EXAMPLE 14.4 Let us refer again to Example 13.12, the two-voter interview example. Suppose that the nine points of the sample space are assigned the probabilities shown in Figure 14.1. Clearly, Rule 1 is satisfied since

---

*These rules are appropriate for finite sample spaces; the modifications needed when S is infinite are discussed in texts on probability and statistics.

FIGURE 14.1
Sample Space
for Responses
of Two Voters

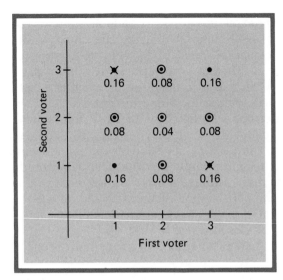

Note: 1 = Opposes new bond issue; 2 = Is for bond issue; 3 = Is undecided.

each of the nine points has a probability between 0 and 1. Moreover, since $0.16 + 0.08 + 0.16 + 0.08 + 0.04 + 0.08 + 0.16 + 0.08 + 0.16 = 1.00$, Rule 2 is also satisfied, and hence this set of probabilities represents a valid set of assignments.

To determine the probability of any event on the basis of the probabilities assigned to the individual outcomes we make use of the following definition.

The probability of any event A is given by the sum of the probabilities of the individual outcomes comprising A.

EXAMPLE 14.4
(Continued)

For instance, to find the probability that *at least one* of the two voters will be for the new bond issue, we have only to add the probabilities of the five points circled in Figure 14.1, and we get

$$0.08 + 0.08 + 0.04 + 0.08 + 0.08 = 0.36$$

Similarly, to find the probability that one of the voters will be opposed to the bond issue while the other is undecided, we have only to add the probabilities of the two points marked by an × in Figure 14.1, and we get

$$0.16 + 0.16 = 0.32$$

1. A study made by the management of a department store shows that 1643 of 2650 customers who came to the store during a special sale purchased at least one item that was not on sale. Estimate the probability that a customer who comes to this store during such a sale will buy at least one item that is not on sale.

2. A study made by a city's traffic engineer shows that among 2150 cars approaching a certain intersection from the north, 559 made a left turn. Estimate the probability that a car approaching this intersection from the north will make a left turn.

3. If 779 of 1025 people interviewed in a poll say that they favor certain environmental protection legislation, what is the probability that any one person (in the area surveyed) will favor this legislation?

4. Weather bureau statistics show that in a certain community it has rained 24 times in the last 60 years on the first Sunday in June, the day which a service club has chosen for its annual picnic. What is the probability that it will rain on the day which the service club has chosen for its picnic?

5. In a survey of the 88 lakes, ponds, and streams in a certain state, 56 were found to contain excessive amounts of pollutants. Estimate the probability that if a fisherman chooses any one of the lakes, ponds, or streams in this state, it will contain an excessive amount of pollutants.

6. In a sample of 116 cans of mixed nuts (taken from a very large shipment), 87 were found to contain mostly peanuts. Estimate the probability that one of these cans will contain mostly peanuts.

7. After an analysis of research done at their schools, three college presidents made the following claims: The first college president claims that the probabilities for more federal support, less federal support, or no change are, respectively, 0.07, 0.25, and 0.65; the second college president claims that these probabilities are, respectively, 0.14, 0.38, and 0.48; and the third college president claims that these probabilities are, respectively, 0.09, 0.38, and 0.56. Comment on these claims.

8. Explain why there must be a *mistake* in each statement.
    (a) The probability that a certain stock will go up in price is 0.43 and the probability that it will go down in price is 0.67.
    (b) The probability that a new restaurant will lose money during its first year of operation is 0.36 and the probability that it will either make a profit or break even is 0.54.

(c) The probability that the IRS will audit Mr. Smith's income tax return is 0.19, and the probability that it will audit either Mr. Smith's tax return or that of his brother is 0.05.

(d) The probability that there will be exactly one accident at a busy intersection on Labor Day is 0.23 and the probability that there will be at least one accident is 0.19.

(e) The probability that a professional football team will win its first game is 0.63, the probability that it will win its second game is 0.84, and the probability that it will win both games is 0.45.

(f) Mrs. Miller has two daughters. The probability that her older daughter will decide to go to college is 0.47, and the probability that both her daughters will decide to go to college is 0.62.

(g) The probability that an insurance salesperson will sell a life insurance policy to a friend is 0.48, the probability that he will sell him car insurance but no life insurance is 0.36, and the probability that he will sell him neither kind of insurance is 0.12.

9. Suppose that in Exercise 3 at the end of Section 13.4, the one dealing with the restaurant with two dining rooms, the points $(0, 0)$, $(0, 1)$, $(0, 2)$, $(0, 3)$, $(0, 4)$, $(1, 0)$, $(1, 1)$, $(1, 2)$, $(1, 3)$, $(1, 4)$, $(2, 0)$, $(2, 1)$, $(2, 2)$, $(2, 3)$, $(2, 4)$, $(3, 0)$, $(3, 1)$, $(3, 2)$, $(3, 3)$, and $(3, 4)$ of the sample space are assigned the respective probabilities 0.01, 0.01, 0.01, 0.03, 0.04, 0.01, 0.01, 0.01, 0.03, 0.04, 0.03, 0.03, 0.03, 0.09, 0.09, 0.05, 0.06, 0.07, 0.14, and 0.21.

(a) What are the probabilities that 0, 1, 2, or 3 of the tables in the smaller dining room are being used (at any given time)?

(b) What are the probabilities that 0, 1, 2, 3, or 4 of the tables in the larger dining room are being used (at any given time)?

(c) Find the probabilities associated with the events K, L, and M.

10. Sometimes the chef of a restaurant puts too much vinegar into the salad dressing, sometimes the chef puts in too little, sometimes the chef forgets to put any vinegar into the salad dressing, and sometimes the chef puts in exactly the right amount. If the corresponding probabilities are 0.21, 0.09, 0.14, and 0.56, respectively, find each probability.

(a) The chef will put too much or too little vinegar into the salad dressing.

(b) The chef will put too little vinegar, no vinegar at all, or exactly the right amount of vinegar into the salad dressing.

(c) The chef will put exactly the right amount or no vinegar at all into the salad dressing.

11. The probabilities that a student will get an A, B, C, D, or F in a

course of economics are 0.03, 0.25, 0.44, 0.21, and 0.07, respectively.

(a) What is the probability that the student will get at least a B?
(b) What is the probability that the student will get at most a C?
(c) What is the probability that the student will get a B or a C?
(d) What is the probability that the student will get neither an A nor an F?

14.2 MATHEMATICAL EXPECTATION

If we hear that in the United States a 45-year-old woman can expect to live 33 more years, this does not mean that anyone really expects a 45-year-old woman to live until her 78th birthday and then drop dead on the next day. Similarly, if we read that, based on 1982 data, a person living in the United States can expect to eat 113.6 pounds of beef and 321 eggs per year, or that a child can be expected to be absent from school because of illness 5.4 days per year, it must be apparent that the word *expect* is not being used in its colloquial sense. A child cannot very well be absent 5.4 days, and it would be surprising, indeed, if we found somebody who actually eats 113.6 pounds of beef and 321 eggs in a year. So far as the first statement is concerned, some 45-year-old women will live another 12 years, some will live another 35 years, some will live another 50 years, . . . , and the life expectancy of 33 more years will have to be interpreted as an average, namely, as a **mathematical expectation.**

Originally, the concept of a mathematical expectation arose in connection with games of chance, and in its simplest form it is *the product of the probability that a player will win and the amount the player stands to win.*

EXAMPLE 14.5 If we stand to receive $10 if a balanced coin comes up *tails*, and nothing if it comes up *heads*, our mathematical expectation is $10 \cdot 1/2 = \$5.00$. Similarly, if we consider buying one of 1000 raffle tickets issued for a prize worth $420, our mathematical expectation is $420 \cdot 1/1000 = \$0.42$; thus, it would be foolish to pay more than 42 cents for the ticket (unless the proceeds of the raffle went to a worthy cause, or the difference could be credited to whatever pleasure we might derive from placing a bet). Note that in this last example 999 of the tickets will not pay anything at all, one of the tickets will pay $420 (or the equivalent in merchandise), so that altogether the 1000 tickets pay $420, or on the average $0.42 per ticket.

So far, we have considered only examples in which there was a single payoff, namely, one prize or a single payment. To demonstrate how the concept of a mathematical expectation can be generalized, let us study the following modification of the raffle of Example 14.5.

EXAMPLE 14.5
(Continued) Suppose that the raffle is changed so that there is also a second prize (such as a portable television set) worth $180 and a third prize (such as a clock-radio) worth $60. Now we can argue that 997 of the tickets will not pay anything at all, one ticket will pay the equivalent of $420, another will pay the equivalent of $180, and a third will pay the equivalent of $60; altogether, the 1000 raffle tickets will thus pay $420 + $180 + 60 = $660, or on the average, $0.66 per ticket. Looking at the problem in a different way, we could argue that if the raffle were repeated many times, we would hold a losing ticket 99.7 percent of the time and win each of the three prizes 0.1 percent of the time. On the average we would thus win

$$0(0.997) + 420(0.001) + 180(0.001) + 60(0.001) = \$0.66$$

which is the sum of the products obtained by multiplying each amount by the corresponding proportion or probability.

Generalizing from this example, let us now make the following definition.

If the probabilities of obtaining the amounts a_1, a_2, a_3, . . . , or a_k are p_1, p_2, p_3, . . . , and p_k, respectively, then the mathematical expectation is

$$E = a_1 p_1 + a_2 p_2 + a_3 p_3 + \cdots + a_k p_k$$

Each amount is multiplied by the corresponding probability, and the mathematical expectation, E, is given by the sum of all these products. So far as the a's are concerned, it is important to remember that they are *positive* when they represent profits, winnings, or gains (namely, amounts which we receive), and that they are *negative* when they represent losses, penalties, or deficits (namely, amounts which we have to pay).

EXAMPLE 14.6 If we bet $2 on the flip of a coin (that is, we either win $2 or lose $2 depending on the outcome), the amounts a_1 and a_2 are $+2$ and -2, the probabilities are $p_1 = \frac{1}{2}$ and $p_2 = \frac{1}{2}$, and the mathematical expectation is

$$E = 2 \cdot \frac{1}{2} + (-2) \cdot \frac{1}{2} = 0$$

Indeed, that is what the mathematical expectation should be in an **equitable** or **fair game**, namely, in a game which does not favor either player. Although we referred to the quantities $a_1, a_2, a_3, \ldots,$ and a_k in the formula for a mathematical expectation as amount, they need not be *cash* winnings, losses, penalties, or rewards. When we said in the introduction to this section that a child can be expected to be absent from school 5.4 days, we referred to a result which was obtained by multiplying $0, 1, 2, 3, \ldots$ by the respective probabilities that a child is absent from school for that many days. Similarly, if we say that a person living in the United States can be expected to make 0.81 flights a year on commercial airlines, the a's refer to the number of flights, and 0.81 is the sum of the products obtained by multiplying $0, 1, 2, 3, \ldots$ by the respective probabilities that a person living in the United States makes that many flights.

EXAMPLE 14.7 Suppose that it is known from weather bureau records that in a certain county the probabilities for 0, 1, 2, 3, 4, 5, 6, or 7 hurricanes in any given year are 0.09, 0.22, 0.26, 0.21, 0.13, 0.06, 0.02, and 0.01, respectively. Thus we find that in this county they can expect

$$0(0.09) + 1(0.22) + 2(0.26) + 3(0.21) + 4(0.13) + 5(0.06)$$
$$+ 6(0.02) + 7(0.01) = 2.38$$

hurricanes per year.

EXERCISES

1. As part of a promotional scheme, a soap manufacturer offers a first prize of $80,000 and a second prize of $30,000 to persons willing to try a new product (distributed without charge) and send in their names on the label. The winners will be drawn at random in front of a large television audience.

(a) What would be each entrant's mathematical expectation if 1,500,000 persons were to send in their names?

(b) Would this make it worthwhile to spend the money it costs to mail in an entry?

2. A jeweler wants to "unload" 5 watches that cost $60.00 each and 45 watches that cost $15.00 each. If the jeweler wraps these watches in identically shaped unmarked boxes and lets each customer choose, find each of the following.

(a) Each customer's mathematical expectation.

(b) The jeweler's expected profit per customer if the jeweler charges $22.00 for the privilege of taking a pick.

3. The two finalists in a golf tournament play 18 holes, with the winner getting $20,000 and the runner-up getting $12,000. What are the two players' mathematical expectations if they are evenly matched?

4. If the two league champions are evenly matched, the probabilities that a best-of-seven basketball play-off will take 4, 5, 6, or 7 games are $\frac{1}{8}$, $\frac{1}{4}$, $\frac{5}{16}$, and $\frac{5}{16}$, respectively. Under these conditions, how many games can we expect such a play-off to last?

5. An importer is offered a shipment of bananas for $6000, and the probabilities that the importer will be able to sell them for $7000, $6500, $6000, or $5500 are 0.25, 0.46, 0.19, and 0.10, respectively. If the importer buys the shipment, what is the expected gross profit?

6. If it is extremely cold in the East, a guest ranch in Arizona will have 160 guests during the Christmas season; if it is cold (but not extremely cold) in the East they will have 104 guests, and if the weather is moderate in the East they will have only 78 guests. How many guests can they expect if the probabilities for extremely cold, cold, or moderate weather in the East are 0.34, 0.54, and 0.12, respectively?

7. The following table gives the probabilities that a customer who enters a certain shoe store will buy 0, 1, 2, 3, or 4 pairs of shoes.

Pairs of shoes	0	1	2	3	4
Probability	0.42	0.36	0.10	0.08	0.04

How many pairs of shoes can a customer entering this store be expected to buy?

8. The probabilities that the office of an airline at Sky Harbor Airport will get 0, 1, 2, 3, 4, 5, 6, 7, or 8 complaints per day about the handling of luggare are, respectively, 0.04, 0.15, 0.22, 0.24, 0.18, 0.11, 0.03, 0.02, and 0.01. How many complaints about the handling of luggage can they expect per day?

Decision analysis can be used to determine the "best" possible decision when a decision maker is faced with several possible decisions and an uncertain pattern of future events. For example, consider the following problem faced by the manager of a summer resort. The manager must decide whether to expand the facilities now or wait at least another year. The two possible decisions, denoted by d_1 and d_2, are

$$d_1 = \text{expand the facilities right away}$$

$$d_2 = \text{delay the expansion at least one year}$$

Determining the best decision will obviously depend upon what type of season the resort has. In this regard, the manager believes the resort will experience one of two possibilities: a good season or a bad season. In decision-analysis terminology, the possible future events that are not under control of the decision maker are referred to as the **states of nature**. Thus the states of nature for the resort problem, denoted by s_1 and s_2, are

$$s_1 = \text{the resort has a good season}$$

$$s_2 = \text{the resort has a bad season}$$

Given the two possible decisions and the two states of nature, which decision should the resort manager make? In order to answer this question, we need to determine the profit, or **payoff**, associated with each possible combination of a decision and a state of nature. For example, what profit would result if the manager decided to expand the facilities right away (d_1) and the resort has a good season (s_1)? What profit would result if the manager decided to delay the expansion at least one year (d_2) and the resort has a good season (s_1)?

Using the best information available, the manager of the resort has estimated the payoffs or profits for each of the decision and state of nature combinations. These estimates are presented in Table 14.1. In decision-analysis terminology, this table is referred to as a **payoff table**.

Table 14.1
Payoff Table for the Resort Problem

States of Nature	DECISION ALTERNATIVES	
	Expand Right Away d_1	Delay at Least 1 Year d_2
Good Season s_1	$246,000	$120,000
Bad Season s_2	−$60,000	$12,000

Payoff, or Profit

decision analysis without probabilities

Let us examine how decisions might be made when there is no information whatsoever about the probabilities associated with the various states of nature. Although there are quite a few criteria on which decisions can be based in the absence of any knowledge about the probabilities, in this text we shall only consider four possible criteria: the maximax criterion, the maximin criterion, the minimum criterion, and the mimimax criterion.

The **maximax decision criterion** is an optimistic approach to arriving at a decision. In this case the decision maker selects the decision that maximizes the maximum possible profit. Since the maximum profit for d_1 is $246,000 and the maximum profit for d_2 is $120,000, the manager would select d_1 using the maximax criterion. We might say that by doing so, the manager is maximizing the resort's maximum profit. When dealing with problems in which costs are to be minimized, an equivalent criterion referred to as the **minimin decision criterion** is used. In such problems the decision maker selects the decision that minimizes the minimum cost values.

The **maximin decision criterion** offers a pessimistic or conservative, approach to decision making. For this criterion, the decision maker selects the decision that maximizes the minimum possible profit. Since the minimum profit for d_1 is $-$60,000$ and the minimum profit for d_2 is $12,000, the manager selects d_2 using this criterion. In other terms, the manager chooses the alternative for which the minimum possible profit is maximized. For minimization problems the maximin decision criterion becomes the **minimax decision criterion**; in this case, the recommended decision then corresponds to the minimum of the maximum costs.

Note that the two decision criterion have each led to different recommendations. There is nothing wrong with this; it simply reflects the difference in philosophy between an optimistic and pessimistic approach to decision making.

decision analysis with probabilities

Let us assume that on the basis of general economic conditions, the resort manager has estimated that the probability of a good season is $\frac{1}{3}$ and the probability of a bad season is $\frac{2}{3}$. Consequently, the expected profit associated with expanding the facilities right away (d_1) is

$$246,000 \cdot \frac{1}{3} + (-60,000) \cdot \frac{2}{3} = \$42,000$$

and if the expansion of the facilities is delayed (d_2) the expected profit is

$$120,000 \cdot \frac{1}{3} + 12,000 \cdot \frac{2}{3} = \$48,000$$

Note that in determining the expected profits associated with each decision, we really just applied the concept of mathematical expectation introduced in Section 14.2.

Generally speaking, if we have to choose between several alternatives, it is considered "rational" to select the one with the most promising mathematical expectation: the one which maximizes expected profits, minimizes expected costs, maximizes expected tax advantages, minimizes expected losses, and so on. In decision analysis, this concept is the basis for the **expected monetary-value criterion**. Thus, following the expected monetary-value criterion, the expected payoff, or profit, of $48,000 is obviously preferable to an expected profit of $42,000. Hence the manager of the resort should decide to delay the expansion of the facilities.

Of course, the conclusion at which we arrived in our example is based on the assumption that the resort manager's appraisal of the chances for a good season is correct. As you will be asked to show in Exercise 1 at the end of this section, the manager should decide to expand the facilities right away if the probability of a good season is 0.40. The point we are trying to make is that *when decisions are based on mathematical expectations, we must be fairly sure that our estimates of the probabilities p are "correct" (or at least reasonably close).*

EXERCISES

1. With reference to the example discussed in Section 15.3, find the resort's expected profits with and without expanded facilities if the probability of a good season is 0.40.

2. The management of an oil company must decide whether to continue drilling at a certain location. If they continue to drill and there is oil, this will be worth $2,000,000 to their company; if they continue to drill and there is no oil, this will entail a loss of $1,200,000; if they stop drilling and there is oil (for their competitor to use), this will entail a loss of $800,000; and if they stop drilling and there is no oil, this will be worth $200,000 to their company (because funds allocated to the project will remain unspent).
   (a) Develop a payoff table for this problem.
   (b) What decision would maximize their company's expected gain if the probability of finding oil is 0.40?
   (c) Repeat part (b) when the probability of finding oil is 0.20.

3. Mr. Cooper is planning to attend a convention in Washington, D.C., and he must send in his room reservation immediately. The convention is so large that the activities are held partly in Hotel I and partly in Hotel II, and Mr. Cooper does not know whether the

particular session he wants to attend will be held at Hotel I or Hotel II. He is planning to stay only one day, which would cost him $25.20 at Hotel I and $21.60 at Hotel II, but it will cost him an extra $6.00 for cab fare if he stays at the wrong hotel.

(a) Develop a payoff table for the problem.

(b) Where should he make his reservation if he wants to minimize his expected expenses and believes that the probability is $\frac{2}{3}$ that the session he wants to attend will be held at Hotel I?

(c) Where should he make his reservation if he were a confirmed pessimist?

(d) Where should he make his reservation if he were a confirmed optimist?

4. Mrs. Green, who lives in a suburb, plans to spend an afternoon shopping in downtown Boston, and she has some difficulty deciding whether or not to take along her raincoat. If it rains, she will be inconvenienced if she does not bring it along, and if it does not rain, she will be inconvenienced if she does. On the other hand, it will be convenient to have the raincoat if it rains, and it would seem reasonable to say that she is neither convenienced nor inconvenienced if she does not bring her raincoat and it does not rain. To express all this numerically, suppose that the numbers in the following table are in *units of inconvenience*, so that the negative value reflects *convenience*.

	Takes raincoat	Does not take raincoat
It rains	−50	100
It does not rain	30	0

(a) What should Mrs. Green do to minimize her expected inconvenience if she feels the probability of rain is 0.10?

(b) What should Mrs. Green do to minimize her expected inconvenience if she feels that the probability of rain is $\frac{1}{5}$?

(c) What will Mrs. Green do if she is a confirmed optimist?

(d) What will Mrs. Green do if she is a confirmed pessimist?

5. A contractor has to choose between two jobs. The first job promises a profit of $120,000 with a probablity of $\frac{3}{4}$ or a loss of $30,000 (due to strikes and other delays) with a probability of $\frac{1}{4}$; the second job promises a profit of $180,000 with a probability of $\frac{1}{2}$ or a loss of $45,000 with a probability of $\frac{1}{2}$.

(a) Which job should the contractor choose to maximize expected profit?

(b) Which job would the contractor probably choose if the business is in fairly bad shape and the contractor will go broke unless there is a profit of at least $150,000 on the next job?

6. With reference to Exercise 2, what can the management of the oil company be expected to decide if their financial advisers tell them each of the following?

(a) The company will be bankrupt unless the drilling operation yields at least $1,000,000.

(b) The company will be bankrupt if the drilling operation shows a loss greater than $1,000,000.

SUMMARY

In this chapter we provided an introduction to the study of probability and its role in the decision-making process. We began with a discussion of the various approaches to probability; that is, the classical concept, the frequency interpretation, and the personal or subjective approach. Rules which must be followed when assigning probabilities to the individual outcomes of the sample space were provided, followed by a discussion of the use of probability in computing mathematical expectation. To illustrate an important application of probability, the chapter concluded with a brief introduction to decision analysis, and, in particular, to the expected monetary-value criterion of decision making.

GLOSSARY

1. **Probability**   A numerical measure (on a scale from 0 to 1) of the chance that a particular event will occur.
2. **Classical Concept of Probability**   This concept applies only when all possible outcomes are equally likely.
3. **Frequency Concept of Probability**   The probability of an event interpreted as the proportion of the time that such kind of event will occur in the long run.
4. **Subjective Concept of Probability**   The probability of an event expressed in terms of the strength of one's belief that the event will occur.
5. **Mathematical Expectation**   *If the probabilities of obtaining the values* a_1, a_2, a_3, . . . , *or* a_k *are* p_1, p_2, p_3, . . . , *and* p_k, *respectively, then the mathematical expectation is*

$$E = a_1 p_1 + a_2 p_2 + a_3 p_3 + \cdots + a_k p_k$$

6. **Decision Analysis**   A mathematical approach used to determine the "best" possible decision when a decision maker is faced with several possible decisions and an uncertain pattern of future events.

7. **Maximax Decision Criterion**   An optimistic approach to decision making. In this, the decision maker selects the decision that maximizes the maximum possible profit.

8. **Minimin Decision Criterion**   An approach to decision making in which the decision maker selects the decision that minimizes the minimum cost values.

9. **Maximin Decision Criterion**   A pessimistic or conservative approach to decision making. In this case the decision maker selects the decision that maximizes the minimum possible profit.

10. **Minimax Decision Criterion**   An approach to decision making in which the recommended decision corresponds to the minimum of the maximum costs.

11. **Expected Monetary-Value Criterion**   The decision maker selects the decision with the most promising mathematical expectation.

1. A county has narrowed its selection of the new county manager to six possible candidates. If each candidate has an equal chance of being selected and if two of the candidates have had previous experience as a county manager, what is the probability that the individual selected will not have had previous experience as a county manager?

2. In order to evaluate the quality of a new type of engine, the manufacturer carefully tested 25 engines selected at random from a recent production run. In that test 3 engines were found that needed some type of service. Estimate the probability that an engine purchased by a customer will need some type of repair.

3. A tire manufacturer requires that 4 of the 20 tires in each production lot must be inspected before they are shipped. If the tires are all satisfactory the whole lot is shipped, but if they are not all satisfactory the remaining 16 tires in the lot are also inspected. What is the probability that such a production lot will pass the inspection when actually 2 of the tires are defective?

4. A bus company's records show that over a period of time, 912 of 1200 buses from San Diego to Los Angeles arrived on time. Estimate the probability that the next bus from San Diego to Los Angeles will arrive on time.

5. Over a number of years 105 to 525 restaurants in a certain resort

city failed during their first 3 years of operation. Estimate the probability that any new restaurant in this city will fail during its first 3 years of operation.

6. Two well-known economists have estimated that the probabilities mortgage rates will be less than 10 percent, 10 percent to 14 percent, 15 percent to 19 percent, or 20 percent or more in 5 years are 0.05, 0.60, 0.25, and 0.10, respectively.
   (a) What is the probability that mortgage rates will be at least 15 percent in 5 years.
   (b) What is the probability that mortgage rates will be less than 20 percent in 5 years.

7. In order to construct an apartment building, a developer realizes that two sequential stages must be completed: stage I—design; stage II—construction. That is, stage II can not be started until stage I is completed. Based on previous experience the developer believes that stage I will either take 6 months, 9 months, or 12 months to complete. The estimate for stage II is 12 months, 15 months, or 18 months. The following table shows the sample space and a set of probabilities which were developed based upon an analysis of similar projects.

		6	9	12
			Design	
Construction	18	0.11	0.09	0.05
	15	0.10	0.30	0.03
	12	0.04	0.18	0.10

   (a) What is the probability that both stages will be completed in 18 months?
   (b) What is the probability that both stages will be completed in 21 months or less?
   (c) What is the probability that both stages will take longer than 2 years to complete?

8. An individual has $10,000 to invest in a speculative oil-drilling venture. The projected return at the end of one year is $0, $10,000, $20,000, $30,000, $40,000, or $50,000. If the probabilities of these returns are 0.50, 0.25, 0.10, 0.08, 0.05, and 0.02, respectively, what is the expected return for this investment?

9. An investment results in a gross profit of −$25,000, $0, $25,000, $50,000, or $75,000 with probabilities 0.10, 0.25, 0.45, 0.15, and

0.05, respectively. What is the expected gross profit for this investment?

10. The following table gives the probabilities that a travel agent will sell 0, 1, 2, 3, 4, or 5 vacation trips during one week.

Trips	0	1.	2	3	4	5
Probability	0.03	0.17	0.34	0.25	0.15	0.06

What is the expected number of trips sold per week? Does your answer make any sense? Explain.

11. A decision maker has developed the following payoff table for a problem involving two decision alternatives and three states of nature.

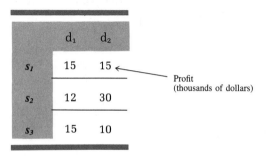

Profit (thousands of dollars)

	d_1	d_2
s_1	15	15
s_2	12	30
s_3	15	10

(a) What is the recommended decision according to the maximax decision criterion?
(b) What is the recommended decision according to the maximin decision criterion?

12. With respect to Exercise 11, what is the decision recommendation according to the expected monetary-value criterion if the probabilities of the states of nature are $s_1 - 0.2$; $s_2 - 0.5$; $s_3 - 0.3$?

TABLES

APPENDIX

Table I. Values of $(1 + i)^n$

n	i = 0.005	i = 0.0075	i = 0.01	i = 0.0125	i = 0.015	i = 0.02
1	1.005000	1.007500	1.010000	1.012500	1.015000	1.020000
2	1.010025	1.015056	1.020100	1.025156	1.030225	1.040400
3	1.015075	1.022669	1.030301	1.037971	1.045678	1.061208
4	1.020150	1.030339	1.040604	1.050945	1.061364	1.082432
5	1.025251	1.038067	1.050110	1.064082	1.077284	1.104081
6	1.030378	1.045852	1.061520	1.077383	1.093443	1.126162
7	1.035529	1.053696	1.072135	1.090850	1.109845	1.148686
8	1.040707	1.061599	1.082857	1.104486	1.126493	1.171659
9	1.045911	1.069561	1.093685	1.118292	1.143390	1.195093
10	1.051140	1.077583	1.104622	1.132271	1.160541	1.218994
11	1.056396	1.085664	1.115668	1.146424	1.177949	1.243374
12	1.061678	1.093807	1.126825	1.160755	1.195618	1.268242
13	1.066986	1.102010	1.138093	1.175264	1.213552	1.293607
14	1.072321	1.110276	1.149474	1.189955	1.231756	1.319479
15	1.077683	1.118603	1.160969	1.204829	1.250232	1.345868
16	1.083071	1.126992	1.172579	1.219890	1.268986	1.372786
17	1.088487	1.135445	1.184304	1.235138	1.288020	1.400241
18	1.093929	1.143960	1.196147	1.250577	1.307341	1.428246
19	1.099399	1.152540	1.208109	1.266210	1.326951	1.456811
20	1.104896	1.161184	1.220190	1.282037	1.346855	1.485947
21	1.110420	1.169893	1.232392	1.298063	1.367058	1.515666
22	1.115972	1.178667	1.244716	1.314288	1.387564	1.545980
23	1.121552	1.187507	1.257163	1.330717	1.408377	1.576899
24	1.127160	1.196414	1.269735	1.347351	1.429503	1.608437
25	1.132796	1.205387	1.282432	1.364193	1.450945	1.640606
26	1.138460	1.214427	1.295256	1.381245	1.472710	1.673418
27	1.144152	1.223535	1.308209	1.398511	1.494800	1.706886
28	1.149873	1.232712	1.321291	1.415992	1.517222	1.741024
29	1.155622	1.241957	1.334504	1.433692	1.539981	1.775845
30	1.161400	1.251272	1.347849	1.451613	1.563080	1.811362
31	1.167207	1.260656	1.361327	1.469759	1.586526	1.847589
32	1.173043	1.270111	1.374941	1.488131	1.610324	1.884541
33	1.178908	1.279637	1.388690	1.506732	1.634479	1.922231
34	1.184803	1.289234	1.402577	1.525566	1.658996	1.960676
35	1.190727	1.298904	1.416603	1.544636	1.683881	1.999890
36	1.196681	1.308645	1.430769	1.563944	1.709140	2.039887
37	1.202664	1.318460	1.445076	1.583493	1.734777	2.080685
38	1.208677	1.328349	1.459527	1.603287	1.760798	2.122299
39	1.214721	1.338311	1.474123	1.623328	1.787210	2.164745
40	1.220794	1.348349	1.488864	1.643619	1.814018	2.208040
41	1.226898	1.358461	1.503752	1.664165	1.841229	2.252200
42	1.233033	1.368650	1.518790	1.684967	1.868847	2.297244
43	1.239198	1.378915	1.533978	1.706029	1.896880	2.343189
44	1.245394	1.389256	1.549318	1.727354	1.925333	2.390053
45	1.251621	1.399676	1.564811	1.748946	1.954213	2.437854
46	1.257879	1.410173	1.580459	1.770808	1.983526	2.486611
47	1.264168	1.420750	1.596263	1.792943	2.013279	2.536344
48	1.270489	1.431405	1.612226	1.815355	2.043478	2.587070
49	1.276842	1.442141	1.628348	1.838047	2.074130	2.638812
50	1.283226	1.452957	1.644632	1.861022	2.105242	2.691588

Table I. Values of $(1 + i)^n$ (Continued)

n	i = 0.03	i = 0.04	i = 0.05	i = 0.06	i = 0.07	i = 0.08
1	1.030000	1.040000	1.050000	1.060000	1.070000	1.080000
2	1.060900	1.081600	1.102500	1.123600	1.144900	1.166400
3	1.092727	1.124864	1.157625	1.191016	1.225043	1.259712
4	1.125509	1.169859	1.215506	1.262477	1.310796	1.360489
5	1.159274	1.216653	1.276282	1.338226	1.402552	1.469328
6	1.194052	1.265319	1.340096	1.418519	1.500730	1.586874
7	1.229874	1.315932	1.407100	1.503630	1.605781	1.713824
8	1.266770	1.368569	1.477455	1.593848	1.718186	1.850930
9	1.304773	1.423312	1.551328	1.689479	1.838459	1.999005
10	1.343916	1.480244	1.628895	1.790848	1.967151	2.158925
11	1.384234	1.539454	1.710339	1.898299	2.104852	2.331639
12	1.425761	1.601032	1.795856	2.012196	2.252192	2.518170
13	1.468534	1.665074	1.885649	2.132928	2.409845	2.719624
14	1.512590	1.731676	1.979932	2.260904	2.578534	2.937194
15	1.557967	1.800944	2.078928	2.396558	2.759032	3.172169
16	1.604706	1.872981	2.182875	2.540352	2.952164	3.425943
17	1.652848	1.947900	2.292018	2.692773	3.158815	3.700018
18	1.702433	2.025817	2.406619	2.854339	3.379932	3.996020
19	1.753506	2.106849	2.526950	3.025600	3.616528	4.315701
20	1.806111	2.191123	2.653298	3.207135	3.869684	4.660957
21	1.860295	2.278768	2.785963	3.399564	4.140562	5.033834
22	1.916103	2.369919	2.925261	3.603537	4.430402	5.436540
23	1.973587	2.464716	3.071524	3.819750	4.740530	5.871464
24	2.032794	2.563304	3.225100	4.048935	5.972367	6.341181
25	2.093778	2.665836	3.386355	4.291871	5.427433	6.848475
26	2.156591	2.772470	3.555673	4.549383	5.807353	7.396353
27	2.221289	2.883369	3.733456	4.822346	6.213868	7.988061
28	2.287928	2.998703	3.920129	5.111687	6.648838	8.627106
29	2.356566	3.118651	4.116136	5.418388	7.114257	9.317275
30	2.427263	3.243398	4.321942	5.743491	7.612255	10.062657
31	2.500080	3.373133	4.538039	6.088101	8.145113	10.867669
32	2.575083	3.508059	4.764941	6.453387	8.715271	11.737083
33	2.652335	3.648381	5.003186	6.840590	9.325340	12.676050
34	2.731905	3.794316	5.253348	7.251025	9.978114	13.690134
35	2.813862	3.946089	5.516015	7.686087	10.676581	14.785344
36	2.898278	4.103933	5.791816	8.147252	11.423942	15.968172
37	2.985227	4.268090	6.081407	8.636087	12.223618	17.245626
38	3.074783	4.438813	6.385477	9.154252	13.079271	18.625276
39	3.167027	4.616366	6.704751	9.703507	13.994820	20.115298
40	3.262038	4.801021	7.039989	10.285718	14.974458	21.724522
41	3.359899	4.993061	7.391988	10.902861	16.022670	23.462483
42	3.460696	5.192784	7.761588	11.557033	17.144258	25.339482
43	3.564517	5.400495	8.149667	12.250455	18.344355	27.366640
44	3.671452	5.616515	8.557150	12.985482	19.628460	29.555972
45	3.781596	5.841176	8.985008	13.764611	21.002452	31.920449
46	3.895044	6.074823	9.434258	14.590487	22.472623	34.474085
47	4.011895	6.317816	9.905971	15.465917	24.045707	37.232012
48	4.132252	6.570528	10.401270	16.393872	25.728907	40.210573
49	4.256219	6.833349	10.921333	17.377504	27.529930	43.427419
50	4.383906	7.106683	11.467400	18.420154	29.457025	46.901613

Table I. Values of $(1 + i)^n$ (Continued)

n	i = 0.09	i = 0.10	i = 0.11	i = 0.12	i = 0.13	i = 0.14
1	1.090000	1.100000	1.110000	1.120000	1.130000	1.140000
2	1.188100	1.210000	1.232100	1.254400	1.276900	1.299600
3	1.295029	1.331000	1.367631	1.404928	1.442897	1.481544
4	1.411582	1.464100	1.518070	1.573519	1.630474	1.688960
5	1.538624	1.610510	1.685058	1.762342	1.842435	1.925415
6	1.677100	1.771561	1.870415	1.973823	2.081952	2.194973
7	1.828039	1.948717	2.076160	2.210681	2.352605	2.502269
8	1.992563	2.143589	2.304538	2.475963	2.658444	2.852586
9	2.171893	2.357948	2.558037	2.773079	3.004042	3.251949
10	2.367364	2.593742	2.839421	3.105848	3.394567	3.707221
11	2.580426	2.853117	3.151757	3.478550	3.835861	4.226232
12	2.812665	3.138428	3.498451	3.895976	4.334523	4.817905
13	3.065805	3.452271	3.883280	4.363493	4.898011	5.492411
14	3.341727	3.797498	4.310441	4.887112	5.534753	6.261349
15	3.642482	4.177248	4.784589	5.473566	6.254270	7.137938
16	3.970306	4.594973	5.310894	6.130394	7.067326	8.137249
17	4.327633	5.054470	5.895093	6.866041	7.986078	9.276464
18	4.717120	5.559917	6.543553	7.689966	9.024268	10.575169
19	5.141661	6.115909	7.263344	8.612762	10.197423	12.055693
20	5.604411	6.727500	8.062312	9.646293	11.523088	13.743490
21	6.108808	7.400250	8.949166	10.803848	13.021089	15.667578
22	6.658600	8.140275	9.933574	12.100310	14.713831	17.861039
23	7.257874	8.954302	11.026267	13.552347	16.626629	20.361585
24	7.911083	9.849733	12.239157	15.178629	18.788091	23.212207
25	8.623081	10.834706	13.585464	17.000064	21.230542	26.461916
26	9.399158	11.918177	15.079865	19.040072	23.990513	30.166584
27	10.245082	13.109994	16.738650	21.324881	27.109279	34.389906
28	11.167140	14.420994	18.579901	23.883866	30.663486	39.204493
29	12.172182	15.863093	20.623691	26.749930	34.615839	44.693122
30	13.267678	17.449402	22.892297	29.959922	39.115898	50.950159
31	14.461770	19.194342	25.410449	33.555113	44.200965	58.083181
32	15.763329	21.113777	28.205599	37.581726	49.947090	66.214826
33	17.182028	23.225154	31.308214	42.091533	56.440212	75.484902
34	18.728411	25.547670	34.752118	47.142517	63.777439	86.052788
35	20.413968	28.102437	38.574851	52.799620	72.068506	98.100178
36	22.251225	30.912681	42.818085	59.135574	81.437412	111.834203
37	24.253835	34.003949	47.528074	66.231843	92.024276	127.490992
38	26.436680	37.404343	52.756162	74.179664	103.987432	145.339731
39	28.815982	41.144778	58.559340	83.081224	117.505798	165.687293
40	31.409420	45.259256	65.000867	93.050970	132.781552	188.883514
41	34.236268	49.785181	72.150963	104.217087	150.043153	215.327206
42	37.317532	54.763699	80.087569	116.723137	169.548763	245.473015
43	40.676110	60.240069	88.897201	130.729914	191.590103	279.839237
44	44.336960	66.264076	98.675893	146.417503	216.496816	319.016730
45	48.327286	72.890484	109.530242	163.987604	244.641402	363.679072
46	52.676742	80.179532	121.578568	183.666116	276.444784	414.594142
47	57.417649	88.197485	134.952211	205.706050	312.382606	472.637322
48	62.585237	97.017234	149.796954	230.390776	352.992345	538.806547
49	68.217908	106.718957	166.274619	258.037669	398.881350	614.239464
50	74.357520	117.390853	184.564827	289.002190	450.735925	700.232988

Table I. Values of $(1 + i)^n$ (Continued)

n	i = 0.15	i = 0.16	i = 0.17	i = 0.18	i = 0.19	i = 0.20
1	1.150000	1.160000	1.170000	1.180000	1.190000	1.200000
2	1.322500	1.345600	1.368900	1.392400	1.416100	1.440000
3	1.520875	1.560896	1.601613	1.643032	1.685159	1.728000
4	1.749006	1.810639	1.873887	1.938778	2.005339	2.073600
5	2.011357	2.100342	2.192448	2.287758	2.386354	2.488320
6	2.313061	2.436396	2.565164	2.699554	2.839761	2.985984
7	2.660020	2.826220	3.001242	3.185474	3.379315	3.583181
8	3.059023	3.278415	3.511453	3.758859	4.021385	4.299817
9	3.517876	3.802961	4.108400	4.435454	4.785449	5.159780
10	4.045558	4.411435	4.806828	5.233836	5.694684	6.191736
11	4.652391	5.117265	5.623989	6.175926	6.776674	7.430084
12	5.350250	5.936027	6.580067	7.287593	8.064242	8.916100
13	6.152788	6.885791	7.698679	8.599359	9.596448	10.699321
14	7.075706	7.987518	9.007454	10.147244	11.419773	12.839185
15	8.137062	9.265521	10.538721	11.973748	13.589530	15.407022
16	9.357621	10.748004	12.330304	14.129023	16.171540	18.488426
17	10.761264	12.467685	14.426456	16.672247	19.244133	22.186111
18	12.375454	14.462514	16.878953	19.673251	22.900518	26.623333
19	14.231772	16.776517	19.748375	23.214436	27.251616	31.948000
20	16.366537	19.460759	23.105599	27.393035	32.429423	38.337600
21	18.821518	22.574481	27.033551	32.323781	38.591014	46.005120
22	21.644746	26.186398	31.629255	38.142061	45.923307	55.206144
23	24.891458	30.376222	37.006228	45.007632	54.648735	66.247373
24	28.625176	35.236417	43.297287	53.109006	65.031994	79.496847
25	32.918953	40.874244	50.657826	62.668627	77.388073	95.396217
26	37.856796	47.414123	59.269656	73.948980	92.091807	114.475460
27	43.535315	55.000382	69.345497	87.259797	109.589251	137.370552
28	50.065612	63.800444	81.134232	102.966560	130.411208	164.844662
29	57.575454	74.008515	94.927051	121.500541	155.189338	197.813595
30	66.211772	85.849877	111.064650	143.370638	184.675312	237.376314
31	76.143538	99.585857	129.945641	169.177353	219.763621	284.851577
32	87.565068	115.519594	152.036399	199.629277	261.518710	341.821892
33	100.699829	134.002729	177.882587	235.562547	311.207264	410.186270
34	115.804803	155.443166	208.122627	277.963805	370.336645	492.223524
35	133.175523	180.314073	243.503474	327.997290	440.700607	590.668229
36	153.151852	209.164324	284.899064	387.036802	524.433722	708.801875
37	176.124630	242.630616	333.331905	456.703427	624.076130	850.562250
38	202.543324	281.451515	389.998329	538.910944	742.650594	1020.674700
39	232.924823	326.483757	456.298045	635.913852	883.754207	1224.809640
40	267.863546	378.721158	533.868713	750.378345	1051.667507	1469.771568
41	308.043078	439.316544	624.626394	885.446447	1251.484333	1763.725882
42	354.249540	509.607191	730.812881	1044.826807	1489.266356	2116.471058
43	407.386971	591.144341	855.051071	1232.895633	1772.226964	2539.765269
44	468.495017	685.727436	1000.409753	1454.816847	2108.950087	3047.718323
45	538.769269	795.443826	1170.479411	1716.683879	2509.650603	3657.261988
46	619.584659	922.714838	1369.460910	2025.686977	2986.484218	4388.714386
47	712.522358	1070.349212	1602.269265	2390.310633	3553.916219	5266.457263
48	819.400712	1241.605086	1874.655040	2820.566547	4229.160301	6319.748715
49	942.310819	1440.261900	2193.346397	3328.268525	5032.700758	7583.698458
50	1083.657442	1670.703804	2566.215284	3927.356860	5988.913902	9100.438150

Table II.
Values of $(1 + i)^{-n}$

n	i = 0.005	i = 0.0075	i = 0.01	i = 0.0125	i = 0.015	i = 0.02
1	0.995025	0.992556	0.990099	0.987654	0.985222	0.980392
2	0.990074	0.985167	0.980296	0.975461	0.970662	0.961169
3	0.985149	0.977833	0.970590	0.963418	0.956317	0.942322
4	0.980248	0.970554	0.960980	0.951524	0.942184	0.923845
5	0.975371	0.963329	0.951466	0.939777	0.928260	0.905731
6	0.970518	0.956158	0.942045	0.928175	0.914542	0.887971
7	0.965690	0.949040	0.932718	0.916716	0.901027	0.870560
8	0.960885	0.941975	0.923483	0.905398	0.887711	0.853490
9	0.956105	0.934963	0.914340	0.894221	0.874592	0.836755
10	0.951348	0.928003	0.905287	0.883181	0.861667	0.820348
11	0.946615	0.921095	0.896324	0.872277	0.848933	0.804263
12	0.941905	0.914238	0.887449	0.861509	0.836387	0.788493
13	0.937219	0.907432	0.878663	0.850873	0.824027	0.773033
14	0.932556	0.900677	0.869963	0.840368	0.811849	0.757875
15	0.927917	0.893973	0.861349	0.829993	0.799852	0.743015
16	0.923300	0.887318	0.852821	0.819746	0.788031	0.728446
17	0.918707	0.880712	0.844377	0.809626	0.776385	0.714163
18	0.914136	0.874156	0.836017	0.799631	0.764912	0.700159
19	0.909588	0.867649	0.827740	0.789759	0.753607	0.686431
20	0.905063	0.861190	0.819544	0.780009	0.742470	0.672971
21	0.900560	0.854779	0.811430	0.770379	0.731498	0.659776
22	0.896080	0.848416	0.803396	0.760868	0.720688	0.646839
23	0.891622	0.842100	0.795442	0.751475	0.710037	0.634156
24	0.887186	0.835831	0.787566	0.742197	0.699544	0.621721
25	0.882772	0.829609	0.779768	0.733034	0.689206	0.609531
26	0.878380	0.823434	0.772048	0.723984	0.679021	0.597579
27	0.874010	0.817304	0.764404	0.715046	0.668986	0.585862
28	0.869662	0.811220	0.756836	0.706219	0.659099	0.574375
29	0.865335	0.805181	0.749342	0.697500	0.649359	0.563112
30	0.861030	0.799187	0.741923	0.688889	0.639762	0.552071
31	0.856746	0.793238	0.734577	0.680384	0.630308	0.541246
32	0.852484	0.787333	0.727304	0.671984	0.620993	0.530633
33	0.848242	0.781472	0.720103	0.663688	0.611816	0.520229
34	0.844022	0.775654	0.712973	0.655494	0.602774	0.510028
35	0.839823	0.769880	0.705914	0.647402	0.593866	0.500028
36	0.835645	0.764149	0.698925	0.639409	0.585090	0.490223
37	0.831487	0.758461	0.692005	0.631515	0.576443	0.480611
38	0.827351	0.752814	0.685153	0.623719	0.567924	0.471187
39	0.823235	0.747210	0.678370	0.616018	0.559531	0.461948
40	0.819139	0.741648	0.671653	0.608413	0.551262	0.452890
41	0.815064	0.736127	0.665003	0.600902	0.543116	0.444010
42	0.811008	0.730647	0.658419	0.593484	0.535089	0.435304
43	0.806974	0.725208	0.651900	0.586157	0.527182	0.426769
44	0.802959	0.719810	0.645445	0.578920	0.519391	0.418401
45	0.798964	0.714451	0.639055	0.571773	0.511715	0.410197
46	0.794989	0.709133	0.632728	0.564714	0.504153	0.402154
47	0.791034	0.703854	0.626463	0.557742	0.496702	0.394268
48	0.787098	0.698614	0.620260	0.550856	0.489362	0.386538
49	0.783182	0.693414	0.614119	0.544056	0.482130	0.378958
50	0.779286	0.688252	0.608039	0.537339	0.475005	0.371528

Table II.
Values of $(1 + i)^{-n}$
(Continued)

n	i = 0.03	i = 0.04	i = 0.05	i = 0.06	i = 0.07	i = 0.08
1	0.970874	0.961538	0.952381	0.943396	0.934579	0.925926
2	0.942596	0.924556	0.907029	0.889996	0.873439	0.857339
3	0.915142	0.888996	0.863838	0.839619	0.816298	0.793832
4	0.888487	0.854804	0.822702	0.792094	0.762895	0.735030
5	0.862609	0.821927	0.783526	0.747258	0.712986	0.680583
6	0.837484	0.790315	0.746215	0.704961	0.666342	0.630170
7	0.813092	0.759918	0.710681	0.665057	0.622750	0.583490
8	0.789409	0.730690	0.676839	0.627412	0.582009	0.540269
9	0.766417	0.702587	0.644609	0.591898	0.543934	0.500249
10	0.744094	0.675564	0.613913	0.558395	0.508349	0.463193
11	0.722421	0.649581	0.584679	0.526788	0.475093	0.428829
12	0.701380	0.624597	0.556837	0.496969	0.444012	0.397114
13	0.680951	0.600574	0.530321	0.468839	0.414964	0.367698
14	0.661118	0.577475	0.505068	0.442301	0.387817	0.340461
15	0.641862	0.555264	0.481017	0.417265	0.362446	0.315242
16	0.623167	0.533908	0.458112	0.393646	0.338735	0.291890
17	0.605016	0.513373	0.436297	0.371364	0.316574	0.270269
18	0.587395	0.493628	0.415521	0.350344	0.295864	0.250249
19	0.570286	0.474642	0.395734	0.330513	0.276508	0.231712
20	0.553676	0.456387	0.376889	0.311805	0.258419	0.214548
21	0.537549	0.438834	0.358942	0.294155	0.241513	0.198656
22	0.521892	0.421955	0.341850	0.277505	0.225713	0.183941
23	0.506692	0.405726	0.325571	0.261797	0.210947	0.170315
24	0.491934	0.390121	0.310068	0.246979	0.197147	0.157699
25	0.477606	0.375117	0.295303	0.232999	0.184249	0.146018
26	0.463695	0.360689	0.281241	0.219810	0.172195	0.135212
27	0.450189	0.346817	0.267848	0.207368	0.160930	0.125187
28	0.437077	0.333477	0.255094	0.195630	0.150402	0.115914
29	0.424346	0.320651	0.242946	0.184557	0.140563	0.107328
30	0.411987	0.308319	0.231377	0.174110	0.131367	0.099377
31	0.399987	0.296460	0.220359	0.164255	0.122773	0.092016
32	0.388337	0.285058	0.209866	0.154957	0.114741	0.085200
33	0.377026	0.274094	0.199873	0.146186	0.107235	0.078889
34	0.366045	0.263552	0.190355	0.137912	0.100219	0.073045
35	0.355383	0.253415	0.181290	0.130105	0.093663	0.067635
36	0.345032	0.243669	0.172657	0.122741	0.087535	0.062625
37	0.334983	0.234297	0.164436	0.115793	0.081809	0.057986
38	0.325226	0.225285	0.156605	0.109239	0.076457	0.053690
39	0.315754	0.216621	0.149148	0.103056	0.071455	0.049713
40	0.306557	0.208289	0.142046	0.097222	0.066780	0.046031
41	0.297628	0.200278	0.135282	0.091719	0.062412	0.042621
42	0.288959	0.192575	0.128840	0.086527	0.058329	0.039464
43	0.280543	0.185168	0.122704	0.081630	0.054513	0.036541
44	0.272372	0.178046	0.116861	0.077009	0.050946	0.033834
45	0.264439	0.171198	0.111297	0.072650	0.047613	0.031328
46	0.256737	0.164614	0.105997	0.068538	0.044499	0.029007
47	0.249259	0.158283	0.100949	0.064658	0.041587	0.026859
48	0.241999	0.152195	0.096142	0.060998	0.038867	0.024869
49	0.234950	0.146341	0.091564	0.057546	0.036324	0.023027
50	0.228107	0.140713	0.087204	0.054288	0.033948	0.021321

Table II.
Values of $(1 + i)^{-n}$
(Continued)

n	i = 0.09	i = 0.10	i = 0.11	i = 0.12	i = 0.13	i = 0.14
1	0.917431	0.909091	0.900901	0.892857	0.884956	0.877193
2	0.841680	0.826446	0.811622	0.797194	0.783147	0.769468
3	0.772183	0.751315	0.731191	0.711780	0.693050	0.674972
4	0.708425	0.683013	0.658731	0.635518	0.613319	0.592080
5	0.649931	0.620921	0.593451	0.567427	0.542760	0.519369
6	0.596267	0.564474	0.534641	0.506631	0.480319	0.455587
7	0.547034	0.513158	0.481658	0.452349	0.425061	0.399637
8	0.501866	0.466507	0.433926	0.403883	0.376160	0.350559
9	0.460428	0.424098	0.390925	0.360610	0.332885	0.307508
10	0.422411	0.385543	0.352184	0.321973	0.294588	0.269744
11	0.387533	0.350494	0.317283	0.287476	0.260698	0.236617
12	0.355535	0.318631	0.285841	0.256675	0.230706	0.207559
13	0.326179	0.289664	0.257514	0.229174	0.204165	0.182069
14	0.299246	0.263331	0.231995	0.204620	0.180677	0.159710
15	0.274538	0.239392	0.209004	0.182696	0.159891	0.140096
16	0.251870	0.217629	0.188292	0.163122	0.141496	0.122892
17	0.231073	0.197845	0.169633	0.145644	0.125218	0.107800
18	0.211994	0.179859	0.152822	0.130040	0.110812	0.094561
19	0.194490	0.163508	0.137678	0.116107	0.098064	0.082948
20	0.178431	0.148644	0.124034	0.103667	0.086782	0.072762
21	0.163698	0.135131	0.111742	0.092560	0.076798	0.063826
22	0.150182	0.122846	0.100669	0.082643	0.067963	0.055988
23	0.137781	0.111678	0.090693	0.073788	0.060144	0.049112
24	0.126405	0.101526	0.081705	0.065882	0.053225	0.043081
25	0.115968	0.092296	0.073608	0.058823	0.047102	0.037790
26	0.106393	0.083905	0.066314	0.052521	0.041683	0.033149
27	0.097608	0.076278	0.059742	0.046894	0.036888	0.029078
28	0.089548	0.069343	0.053822	0.041869	0.032644	0.025507
29	0.082155	0.063039	0.048488	0.037383	0.028889	0.022375
30	0.075371	0.057309	0.043683	0.033378	0.025565	0.019627
31	0.069148	0.052099	0.039354	0.029802	0.022624	0.017217
32	0.063438	0.047362	0.035454	0.026609	0.020021	0.015102
33	0.058200	0.043057	0.031940	0.023758	0.017718	0.013248
34	0.053395	0.039143	0.028775	0.021212	0.015680	0.011621
35	0.048986	0.035584	0.025924	0.018940	0.013876	0.010194
36	0.044941	0.032349	0.023355	0.016910	0.012279	0.008942
37	0.041231	0.029408	0.021040	0.015098	0.010867	0.007844
38	0.037826	0.026735	0.018955	0.013481	0.009617	0.006880
39	0.034703	0.024304	0.017077	0.012036	0.008510	0.006035
40	0.031838	0.022095	0.015384	0.010747	0.007531	0.005294
41	0.029209	0.020086	0.013860	0.009595	0.006665	0.004644
42	0.026797	0.018260	0.012486	0.008567	0.005898	0.004074
43	0.024584	0.016600	0.011249	0.007649	0.005219	0.003573
44	0.022555	0.015091	0.010134	0.006830	0.004619	0.003135
45	0.020692	0.013719	0.009130	0.006098	0.004088	0.002750
46	0.018984	0.012472	0.008225	0.005445	0.003617	0.002412
47	0.017416	0.011338	0.007410	0.004861	0.003201	0.002116
48	0.015978	0.010307	0.006676	0.004340	0.002833	0.001856
49	0.014659	0.009370	0.006014	0.003875	0.002507	0.001628
50	0.013449	0.008519	0.005418	0.003460	0.002219	0.001428

Table II.
Values of $(1 + i)^{-n}$
(Continued)

n	i = 0.15	i = 0.16	i = 0.17	i = 0.18	i = 0.19	i = 0.20
1	0.869565	0.862069	0.854701	0.847458	0.840336	0.833333
2	0.756144	0.743163	0.730514	0.718184	0.706165	0.694444
3	0.657516	0.640658	0.624371	0.608631	0.593416	0.578704
4	0.571753	0.552291	0.533650	0.515789	0.498669	0.482253
5	0.497177	0.476113	0.456111	0.437109	0.419049	0.401878
6	0.432328	0.410442	0.389839	0.370432	0.352142	0.334898
7	0.375937	0.353830	0.333195	0.313925	0.295918	0.279082
8	0.326902	0.305025	0.284782	0.266038	0.248671	0.232568
9	0.284262	0.262953	0.243404	0.225456	0.208967	0.193807
10	0.247185	0.226684	0.208037	0.191064	0.175602	0.161506
11	0.214943	0.195417	0.177810	0.161919	0.147565	0.134588
12	0.186907	0.168463	0.151974	0.137220	0.124004	0.112157
13	0.162528	0.145227	0.129892	0.116288	0.104205	0.093464
14	0.141329	0.125195	0.111019	0.098549	0.087567	0.077887
15	0.122894	0.107927	0.094888	0.083516	0.073586	0.064905
16	0.106865	0.093041	0.081101	0.070776	0.061837	0.054088
17	0.092926	0.080207	0.069317	0.059980	0.051964	0.045073
18	0.080805	0.069144	0.059245	0.050830	0.043667	0.037561
19	0.070265	0.059607	0.050637	0.043077	0.036695	0.031301
20	0.061100	0.051385	0.043280	0.036506	0.030836	0.026084
21	0.053131	0.044298	0.036991	0.030937	0.025913	0.021737
22	0.046201	0.038188	0.031616	0.026218	0.021775	0.018114
23	0.040174	0.032920	0.027022	0.022218	0.018299	0.015095
24	0.034934	0.028380	0.023096	0.018829	0.015377	0.012579
25	0.030378	0.024465	0.019740	0.015957	0.012922	0.010483
26	0.026415	0.021091	0.016872	0.013523	0.010859	0.008735
27	0.022970	0.018182	0.014421	0.011460	0.009125	0.007280
28	0.019974	0.015674	0.012325	0.009712	0.007668	0.006066
29	0.017369	0.013512	0.010534	0.008230	0.006444	0.005055
30	0.015103	0.011648	0.009004	0.006975	0.005415	0.004213
31	0.013133	0.010042	0.007696	0.005911	0.004550	0.003511
32	0.011420	0.008657	0.006577	0.005009	0.003824	0.002926
33	0.009931	0.007463	0.005622	0.004245	0.003213	0.002438
34	0.008635	0.006433	0.004805	0.003598	0.002700	0.002032
35	0.007509	0.005546	0.004107	0.003049	0.002269	0.001693
36	0.006529	0.004781	0.003510	0.002584	0.001907	0.001411
37	0.005678	0.004121	0.003000	0.002190	0.001602	0.001176
38	0.004937	0.003553	0.002564	0.001856	0.001347	0.000980
39	0.004293	0.003063	0.002192	0.001573	0.001132	0.000816
40	0.003733	0.002640	0.001873	0.001333	0.000951	0.000680
41	0.003246	0.002276	0.001601	0.001129	0.000799	0.000567
42	0.002823	0.001962	0.001368	0.000957	0.000671	0.000472
43	0.002455	0.001692	0.001170	0.000811	0.000564	0.000394
44	0.002134	0.001458	0.001000	0.000687	0.000474	0.000328
45	0.001856	0.001257	0.000854	0.000583	0.000398	0.000273
46	0.001614	0.001084	0.000730	0.000494	0.000335	0.000228
47	0.001403	0.000934	0.000624	0.000418	0.000281	0.000190
48	0.001220	0.000805	0.000533	0.000355	0.000236	0.000158
49	0.001061	0.000694	0.000456	0.000300	0.000199	0.000132
50	0.000923	0.000599	0.000390	0.000255	0.000167	0.000110

Table III.
Values of e^x
and e^{-x}

x	e^x	e^{-x}	x	e^x	e^{-x}
0.0	1.000	1.000	2.5	12.18	0.082
0.1	1.105	0.905	2.6	13.46	0.074
0.2	1.221	0.819	2.7	14.88	0.067
0.3	1.350	0.741	2.8	16.44	0.061
0.4	1.492	0.670	2.9	18.17	0.055
0.5	1.649	0.607	3.0	20.09	0.050
0.6	1.822	0.549	3.1	22.20	0.045
0.7	2.014	0.497	3.2	24.53	0.041
0.8	2.226	0.449	3.3	27.11	0.037
0.9	2.460	0.407	3.4	29.96	0.033
1.0	2.718	0.368	3.5	33.12	0.030
1.1	3.004	0.333	3.6	36.60	0.027
1.2	3.320	0.301	3.7	40.45	0.025
1.3	3.669	0.273	3.8	44.70	0.022
1.4	4.055	0.247	3.9	49.40	0.020
1.5	4.482	0.223	4.0	54.60	0.018
1.6	4.953	0.202	4.1	60.34	0.017
1.7	5.474	0.183	4.2	66.69	0.015
1.8	6.050	0.165	4.3	73.70	0.014
1.9	6.686	0.150	4.4	81.45	0.012
2.0	7.389	0.135	4.5	90.02	0.011
2.1	8.166	0.122	4.6	99.48	0.010
2.2	9.025	0.111	4.7	109.95	0.009
2.3	9.974	0.100	4.8	121.51	0.008
2.4	11.023	0.091	4.9	134.29	0.007

Table III.
Values of e^x
and e^{-x}
(Continued)

x	e^x	e^{-x}	x	e^x	e^{-x}
5.0	148.4	0.0067	7.5	1,808.0	0.00055
5.1	164.0	0.0061	7.6	1,998.2	0.00050
5.2	181.3	0.0055	7.7	2,208.3	0.00045
5.3	200.3	0.0050	7.8	2,440.6	0.00041
5.4	221.4	0.0045	7.9	2,697.3	0.00037
5.5	244.7	0.0041	8.0	2,981.0	0.00034
5.6	270.4	0.0037	8.1	3,294.5	0.00030
5.7	298.9	0.0033	8.2	3,641.0	0.00027
5.8	330.3	0.0030	8.3	4,023.9	0.00025
5.9	365.0	0.0027	8.4	4,447.1	0.00022
6.0	403.4	0.0025	8.5	4,914.8	0.00020
6.1	445.9	0.0022	8.6	5,431.7	0.00018
6.2	492.8	0.0020	8.7	6,002.9	0.00017
6.3	544.6	0.0018	8.8	6,634.2	0.00015
6.4	601.8	0.0017	8.9	7,332.0	0.00014
6.5	665.1	0.0015	9.0	8,103.1	0.00012
6.6	735.1	0.0014	9.1	8,955.3	0.00011
6.7	812.4	0.0012	9.2	9,897.1	0.00010
6.8	897.8	0.0011	9.3	10,938.0	0.00009
6.9	992.3	0.0010	9.4	12,088.4	0.00008
7.0	1,096.6	0.0009	9.5	13,359.7	0.00007
7.1	1,212.0	0.0008	9.6	14,764.8	0.00007
7.2	1,339.4	0.0007	9.7	16,317.6	0.00006
7.3	1,480.3	0.0007	9.8	18,033.7	0.00006
7.4	1,636.0	0.0006	9.9	19,930.4	0.00005

Table IV.
Logarithms

N	0	1	2	3	4	5	6	7	8	9
10	0000	0043	0086	0128	0170	0212	0253	0294	0334	0374
11	0414	0453	0492	0531	0569	0607	0645	0682	0719	0755
12	0792	0828	0864	0899	0934	0969	1004	1038	1072	1106
13	1139	1173	1206	1239	1271	1303	1335	1367	1399	1430
14	1461	1492	1523	1553	1584	1614	1644	1673	1703	1732
15	1761	1790	1818	1847	1875	1903	1931	1959	1987	2014
16	2041	2068	2095	2122	2148	2175	2201	2227	2253	2279
17	2304	2330	2355	2380	2405	2430	2455	2480	2504	2529
18	2553	2577	2601	2625	2648	2672	2695	2718	2742	2765
19	2788	2810	2833	2856	2878	2900	2923	2945	2967	2989
20	3010	3032	3054	3075	3096	3118	3139	3160	3181	3201
21	3222	3243	3263	3284	3304	3324	3345	3365	3385	3404
22	3424	3444	3464	3483	3502	3522	3541	3560	3579	3598
23	3617	3636	3655	3674	3692	3711	3729	3747	3766	3784
24	3802	3820	3838	3856	3874	3892	3909	3927	3945	3962
25	3979	3997	4014	4031	4048	4065	4082	4099	4116	4133
26	4150	4166	4183	4200	4216	4232	4249	4265	4281	4298
27	4314	4330	4346	4362	4378	4393	4409	4425	4440	4456
28	4472	4487	4502	4518	4533	4548	4564	4579	4594	4609
29	4624	4639	4654	4669	4683	4698	4713	4728	4742	4757
30	4771	4786	4800	4814	4829	4843	4857	4871	4886	4900
31	4914	4928	4942	4955	4969	4983	4997	5011	5024	5038
32	5051	5065	5079	5092	5105	5119	5132	5145	5159	5172
33	5185	5198	5211	5224	5237	5250	5263	5276	5289	5302
34	5315	5328	5340	5353	5366	5378	5391	5403	5416	5428
35	5441	5453	5465	5478	5490	5502	5514	5527	5539	5551
36	5563	5575	5587	5599	5611	5623	5635	5647	5658	5670
37	5682	5694	5705	5717	5729	5740	5752	5763	5775	5786
38	5798	5809	5821	5832	5843	5855	5866	5877	5888	5899
39	5911	5922	5933	5944	5955	5966	5977	5988	5999	6010
40	6021	6031	6042	6053	6064	6075	6085	6096	6107	6117
41	6128	6138	6149	6160	6170	6180	6191	6201	6212	6222
42	6232	6243	6253	6263	6274	6284	6294	6304	6314	6325
43	6335	6345	6355	6365	6375	6385	6395	6405	6415	6425
44	6435	6444	6454	6464	6474	6484	6493	6503	6513	6522
45	6532	6542	6551	6561	6571	6580	6590	6599	6609	6618
46	6628	6637	6646	6656	6665	6675	6684	6693	6702	6712
47	6721	6730	6739	6749	6758	6767	6776	6785	6794	6803
48	6812	6821	6830	6839	6848	6857	6866	6875	6884	6893
49	6902	6911	6920	6928	6937	6946	6955	6964	6972	6981
50	6990	6998	7007	7016	7024	7033	7042	7050	7059	7067
51	7076	7084	7093	7101	7110	7118	7126	7135	7143	7152
52	7160	7168	7177	7185	7193	7202	7210	7218	7226	7235
53	7243	7251	7259	7267	7275	7284	7292	7300	7308	7316
54	7324	7332	7340	7348	7356	7364	7372	7380	7388	7396

Table IV.
Logarithms
(Continued)

N	0	1	2	3	4	5	6	7	8	9
55	7404	7412	7419	7427	7435	7443	7451	7459	7466	7474
56	7482	7490	7497	7505	7513	7520	7528	7536	7543	7551
57	7559	7566	7574	7582	7589	7597	7604	7612	7619	7627
58	7634	7642	7649	7657	7664	7672	7679	7686	7694	7701
59	7709	7716	7723	7731	7738	7745	7752	7760	7767	7774
60	7782	7789	7796	7803	7810	7818	7825	7832	7839	7846
61	7853	7860	7868	7875	7882	7889	7896	7903	7910	7917
62	7924	7931	7938	7945	7952	7959	7966	7973	7980	7987
63	7993	8000	8007	8014	8021	8028	8035	8041	8048	8055
64	8062	8069	8075	8082	8089	8096	8102	8109	8116	8122
65	8129	8136	8142	8149	8156	8162	8169	8176	8182	8189
66	8195	8202	8209	8215	8222	8228	8235	8241	8248	8254
67	8261	8267	8274	8280	8287	8293	8299	8306	8312	8319
68	8325	8331	8338	8344	8351	8357	8363	8370	8376	8382
69	8388	8395	8401	8407	8414	8420	8426	8432	8439	8445
70	8451	8457	8463	8470	8476	8482	8488	8494	8500	8506
71	8513	8519	8525	8531	8537	8543	8549	8555	8561	8567
72	8573	8579	8585	8591	8597	8603	8609	8615	8621	8627
73	8633	8639	8645	8651	8657	8663	8669	8675	8681	8686
74	8692	8698	8704	8710	8716	8722	8727	8733	8739	8745
75	8751	8756	8762	8768	8774	8779	8785	8791	8797	8802
76	8808	8814	8820	8825	8831	8837	8842	8848	8854	8859
77	8865	8871	8876	8882	8887	8893	8899	8904	8910	8915
78	8921	8927	8932	8938	8943	8949	8954	8960	8965	8971
79	8976	8982	8987	8993	8998	9004	9009	9015	9020	9025
80	9031	9036	9042	9047	9053	9058	9063	9069	9074	9079
81	9085	9090	9096	9101	9106	9112	9117	9122	9128	9133
82	9138	9143	9149	9154	9159	9165	9170	9175	9180	9186
83	9191	9196	9201	9206	9212	9217	9222	9227	9232	9238
84	9243	9248	9253	9258	9263	9269	9274	9279	9284	9289
85	9294	9299	9304	9309	9315	9320	9325	9330	9335	9340
86	9345	9350	9355	9360	9365	9370	9375	9380	9385	9390
87	9395	9400	9405	9410	9415	9420	9425	9430	9435	9440
88	9445	9450	9455	9460	9465	9469	9474	9479	9484	9489
89	9494	9499	9504	9509	9513	9518	9523	9528	9533	9538
90	9542	9547	9552	9557	9562	9566	9571	9576	9581	9586
91	9590	9595	9600	9605	9609	9614	9619	9624	9628	9633
92	9638	9643	9647	9652	9657	9661	9666	9671	9675	9680
93	9685	9689	9694	9699	9703	9708	9713	9717	9722	9727
94	9731	9736	9741	9745	9750	9754	9759	9763	9768	9773
95	9777	9782	9786	9791	9795	9800	9805	9809	9814	9818
96	9823	9827	9832	9836	9841	9845	9850	9854	9859	9863
97	9868	9872	9877	9881	9886	9890	9894	9899	9903	9908
98	9912	9917	9921	9926	9930	9934	9939	9943	9948	9952
99	9956	9961	9965	9969	9974	9978	9983	9987	9991	9996

To find the square root of any positive number rounded to two digits, use the following rule to decide whether to take the entry of the $\sqrt{n}$ or the $\sqrt{10n}$ column.

Move the decimal point an even number of places to the right or to the left until a number greater than or equal to 1 but less than 100 is reached. If the resulting number is less than 10, go to the $\sqrt{n}$ column; if it is 10 or more, go to the $\sqrt{10n}$ column.

Thus to find the square roots of 14,000 or 0.032, we go to the $\sqrt{n}$ column since the decimal point has to be moved four places to the left to give 1.4 or two places to the right to give 3.2, respectively. Similarly, to find the square roots of 2200 or 0.000016, we go to the $\sqrt{10n}$ column since the decimal point has to be moved two places to the left to give 22 or six places to the right to give 16, respectively.

Having found the entry in the appropriate column of Table V, the only thing that remains to be done is to put the decimal point in the right place in the result. To this end we use the following rule.

Having previously moved the decimal point an even number of places to the left or to the right to get a number greater than or equal to 1 but less than 100, the decimal point of the appropriate entry of Table V is moved half as many places in the opposite direction.

For example, to find the square root of 14,000 we first note that the decimal point has to be moved *four places to the left* to give 1.4. We thus take the entry of the $\sqrt{n}$ column corresponding to 1.4, move its decimal point *two places to the right*, and get $\sqrt{14,000} = 118.322$. Similarly, to find the square root of 0.000016 we note that the decimal point has to be moved *six places to the right* to give 16. We thus take the entry of the $\sqrt{10n}$ column corresponding to 1.6, move the decimal point *three places to the left*, and get $\sqrt{0.000016} = 0.004$.

Table V.
Square roots

n	$\sqrt{n}$	$\sqrt{10n}$	n	$\sqrt{n}$	$\sqrt{10n}$
1.0	1.00000	3.16228	3.5	1.87083	5.91608
1.1	1.04881	3.31662	3.6	1.89737	6.00000
1.2	1.09545	3.46410	3.7	1.92354	6.08276
1.3	1.14018	3.60555	3.8	1.94936	6.16441
1.4	1.18322	3.74166	3.9	1.97484	6.24500
1.5	1.22474	3.87298	4.0	2.00000	6.32456
1.6	1.26491	4.00000	4.1	2.02485	6.40312
1.7	1.30384	4.12311	4.2	2.04939	6.48074
1.8	1.34164	4.24264	4.3	2.07364	6.55744
1.9	1.37840	4.35890	4.4	2.09762	6.63325
2.0	1.41421	4.47214	4.5	2.12132	6.70820
2.1	1.44914	4.58258	4.6	2.14476	6.78233
2.2	1.48324	4.69042	4.7	2.16795	6.85565
2.3	1.51658	4.79583	4.8	2.19089	6.92820
2.4	1.54919	4.89898	4.9	2.21359	7.00000
2.5	1.58114	5.00000	5.0	2.23607	7.07107
2.6	1.61245	5.09902	5.1	2.25832	7.14143
2.7	1.64317	5.19615	5.2	2.28035	7.21110
2.8	1.67332	5.29150	5.3	2.30217	7.28011
2.9	1.70294	5.38516	5.4	2.32379	7.34847
3.0	1.73205	5.47723	5.5	2.34521	7.41620
3.1	1.76068	5.56776	5.6	2.36643	7.48331
3.2	1.78885	5.65685	5.7	2.38747	7.54983
3.3	1.81659	5.74456	5.8	2.40832	7.61577
3.4	1.84391	5.83095	5.9	2.42899	7.68115

n	$\sqrt{n}$	$\sqrt{10n}$	n	$\sqrt{n}$	$\sqrt{10n}$
6.0	2.44949	7.74597	8.0	2.82843	8.94427
6.1	2.46982	7.81025	8.1	2.84605	9.00000
6.2	2.48998	7.87401	8.2	2.86356	9.05539
6.3	2.50998	7.93725	8.3	2.88097	9.11043
6.4	2.52982	8.00000	8.4	2.89828	9.16515
6.5	2.54951	8.06226	8.5	2.91548	9.21954
6.6	2.56905	8.12404	8.6	2.93258	9.27362
6.7	2.58844	8.18535	8.7	2.94958	9.32738
6.8	2.60768	8.24621	8.8	2.96648	9.38083
6.9	2.62679	8.30662	8.9	2.98329	9.43398
7.0	2.64575	8.36660	9.0	3.00000	9.48683
7.1	2.66458	8.42615	9.1	3.01662	9.53939
7.2	2.68328	8.48528	9.2	3.03315	9.59166
7.3	2.70185	8.54400	9.3	3.04959	9.64365
7.4	2.72029	8.60233	9.4	3.06594	9.69536
7.5	2.73861	8.66025	9.5	3.08221	9.74679
7.6	2.75681	8.71780	9.6	3.09839	9.79796
7.7	2.77489	8.77496	9.7	3.11448	9.84886
7.8	2.79285	8.83176	9.8	3.13050	9.89949
7.9	2.81069	8.88819	9.9	3.14643	9.94987

Table VI.
Factorials

n	n!	log n!
0	1	0.0000
1	1	0.0000
2	2	0.3010
3	6	0.7782
4	24	1.3802
5	120	2.0792
6	720	2.8573
7	5,040	3.7024
8	40,320	4.6055
9	362,880	5.5598
10	3,628,800	6.5598
11	39,916,800	7.6012
12	479,001,600	8.6803
13	6,227,020,800	9.7943
14	87,178,291,200	10.9404
15	1,307,674,368,000	12.1165

Table VII. Binomial coefficients

n	$\binom{n}{0}$	$\binom{n}{1}$	$\binom{n}{2}$	$\binom{n}{3}$	$\binom{n}{4}$	$\binom{n}{5}$	$\binom{n}{6}$	$\binom{n}{7}$	$\binom{n}{8}$	$\binom{n}{9}$	$\binom{n}{10}$
0	1										
1	1	1									
2	1	2	1								
3	1	3	3	1							
4	1	4	6	4	1						
5	1	5	10	10	5	1					
6	1	6	15	20	15	6	1				
7	1	7	21	35	35	21	7	1			
8	1	8	28	56	70	56	28	8	1		
9	1	9	36	84	126	126	84	36	9	1	
10	1	10	45	120	210	252	210	120	45	10	1
11	1	11	55	165	330	462	462	330	165	55	11
12	1	12	66	220	495	792	924	792	495	220	66
13	1	13	78	286	715	1287	1716	1716	1287	715	286
14	1	14	91	364	1001	2002	3003	3432	3003	2002	1001
15	1	15	105	455	1365	3003	5005	6435	6435	5005	3003
16	1	16	120	560	1820	4368	8008	11440	12870	11440	8008
17	1	17	136	680	2380	6188	12376	19448	24310	24310	19448
18	1	18	153	816	3060	8568	18564	31824	43758	48620	43758
19	1	19	171	969	3876	11628	27132	50388	75582	92378	92378
20	1	20	190	1140	4845	15504	38760	77520	125970	167960	184756

If necessary, use the identity $\binom{n}{k} = \binom{n}{n-k}$.

ANSWERS TO EVEN-NUMBERED EXERCISES

CHAPTER 1

2. (a) false; (b) false; (c) false; (d) false; (e) false; (f) false

4. (a) false; (b) true; (c) false; (d) true; (e) false; (f) false; (g) true; (h) false

6. (a) $B \cup E$ = the set of colleges and universities that grant degrees in business or engineering.
(b) $B \cap P$ = the set of colleges and universities that grant degrees in business and are private.
(c) P' = the set of colleges and universities that are not private.
(d) $B \cap P'$ = the set of colleges and universities that grant degrees in business and are not private.

8. (a) A' = the set of automobiles that have a list price of more than $8,000.
(b) B' = the set of automobiles that do not have front-wheel drive.
(c) $A \cap B$ = the set of automobiles that have a list price of $8,000 or less and have front-wheel drive.
(d) $A \cup B$ = the set of automobiles that have a list price of $8,000 or less or have front-wheel drive.

10. (a) All the houses with 0 or 1 bath; (b) all the houses which do not have 3 bedrooms; (c) all the houses priced at less than $45,000; (d) all the houses less than 3 years old; (e) all the houses with 3 bedrooms and 2 or more baths; (f) all the houses with 2 or more baths priced at $45,000 or more;

12. (a) M' = {Anderson, Sweeney, Jones, Newton}
(b) E' = {Jones, Newton}
(c) $M \cap E$ = {Peters, Tyler}
(d) $M' \cup E$ = {Anderson, Sweeney, Jones, Newton, Peters, Tyler}

14. (a) C', (b) B'; (c) $A \cap B$; (d) $C \cap D$; (e) $A \cap C'$

16. 45

2. (a) $1.7 \cdot 10^{-6}$; (b) $1.3250499 \cdot 10^{7}$; (c) $3.694 \cdot 10^{-3}$

4. (a) 0.000029948; (b) 62,850,000; (c) 0.00000899931

6. (a) 17E−5; (b) 13250499E8; (c) 3694E−2

8. (a) 185,820; (b) -11.29; (c) 0.0000373

10. (a) 1; (b) 2/3; (c) 2

12. (a) 5/9; (b) 36; (c) 243

14. (a) 27; (b) 1/125; (c) 1/7; (d) 3/4

16. $\displaystyle\sum_{i=1}^{8} x_i$

18. $\displaystyle\sum_{i=1}^{15000} x_i$

Section 1.4	**2.** $3x^3 + 7x^2 + 6x + 8$	**12.** $(x - 8)(x + 8)$
	4. $x^2 - 64$	**14.** $x(x - 5)(x + 5)$
	6. $x^2 - 100x^2$	**16.** $x(x + 5)(x + 5)$
	8. $x^3 + 8x^2 + 8x$	**18.** $12(3x + 7)$
	10. $(x + 6)(x + 6)$	

Section 1.5	**2.** $12/25$	**10.** $\dfrac{2x(3x - 5)}{(x + 5)(x - 5)}$
	4. $\dfrac{x - 5}{x + 2}$	**12.** $10/63$
	6. $\dfrac{x + 4}{x - 4}$	**14.** $1/5$
	8. $13/160$	

Section 1.6	**2.** $x = 6$	**14.** $y = \dfrac{35}{18}$
	4. $x = 7.5$	
	6. $x = -8$	**16.** $x = \dfrac{5}{3}$
	8. $y = 23\frac{1}{3}$	**18.** $0.25x + 100$; purchased
	10. $x = 2\frac{1}{3}$	**20.** $40x + 10,000$
	12. $x = 0$	

Supplementary Exercises

2. $O \cap T = \{\text{Cincinnati, Pittsburgh}\}$; $O \cup T =$ the set of cities that have offices, terminal locations, or both

4. (a) $S = \{S - 14, S - 17, S - 20\}$; $P = \{P - 11, P - 13, P - 15, P - 17, P - 20\}$

(b) $A' = \{S - 14, P - 11, P - 13, P - 15\}$ = the set of all boats that do not have a list price of $5000 or more

6. (a) {TV Guide, Life, Look, Time, Newsweek}

(b) {Reader's Digest, McCalls, Ladies Home Journal}

(c) {Reader's Digest, Life, Look, Ladies Home Journal}

(d) {M^{c}Calls}

(e) $\varnothing$

(f) {TV Guide, Time, Newsweek}

(g) {TV Guide, Life, Look, Time, Newsweek, McCalls}

(h) {Reader's Digest, McCalls, Ladies Home Journal, TV Guide, Life, Look, Time, Newsweek}

8. 125

10. (a) $4^2 = 16$; (b) $1/8$; (c) 3; (d) $1/16$; (e) $2^7 \cdot 3^2 = 1152$; (f) $1/9$

12. (a) x^2; (b) $\dfrac{x^6}{8y^3}$; (c) x^3y^2; (d) xy

14. (a) 8; (b) 9; (c) $\dfrac{1}{\sqrt[4]{625^3}} = \dfrac{1}{5^3} = \dfrac{1}{125}$; (d) 32; (e) 2187; (f) $\dfrac{3}{2}$; (g) $\dfrac{5}{2}$

16. (a) 21,466; (b) 0.0181; (c) 147,630; (d) 0.0000035552;
(e) 7,269,000; (f) 0.000099934

18. (a) 0.00258; (b) 26,463; (c) -0.0000075589; (d) 5,353,600;
(e) -5.316; (f) 0.0000646

20. $\displaystyle\sum_{i=1}^{20} R_i$; $\displaystyle\sum_{i=1}^{20} R_i/20$

22. $2x^3 + 9x^2 + 11x + 6$

24. $x^3 + 5x^2 + 6x$

26. $2x^4 + 8x^3 + 21x^2 + 26x + 20$

28. $(x - 9)(x + 9)$

30. $2x(x - 3)(x + 3)$

32. $(x + 5)(x + 5)$

34. $3/5$

36. $\dfrac{2x + 4}{x + 3}$

38. $1/3$

40. $\dfrac{13}{42}$

42. $\dfrac{20}{63}$

44. $\dfrac{x^3 + 4x^2 - x - 4}{2x^2 + 2x}$

46. $x = 6$

48. $y = 4$

50. $x = 10.5$

52. $1400x + 2500$

54. 65,000

56. $325 - [(.017 \cdot 285)x + 285]$

CHAPTER 2

Section 2.2

2. $12 + 3x^2$; (a) 24; (b) 60; (c) 119; (d) 204; (e) 444

4. (a) $d(2) = 2^2 - 20 \cdot 2 + 125 = 89$; (b) $d(5) = 5^2 - 20 \cdot 5 = 50$;
and so forth

6. (a) 7; 3; 1.5
(b) $x = 5$

8. straight line

10. closer and closer to 1

Section 2.3

2. (a) $366,000; (b) $1,476,000; (c) $5000

4. (a) 12; (b) 10; (c) -17; (d) 3

Supplementary Exercises

4. (a) 7; (b) 11; (c) 17; (d) 5; (e) 1; (f) -13

6. (a) 2.4; (b) 2.1; (c) 1.6; (d) 0.9; (e) 0

8. (a) 5; (b) 3; (c) 2; (d) $9/5$; (e) $3/2$; (f) $29/25$

10. (a) 150,000; (b) 120,000; (c) 100,000; (d) 75,000; (e) 62,500;
(f) 60,000

12. (a) $625; $900; $1225; $1600; $2025

16. (a) 2; (b) 37; (c) 4; (d) 5; (e) 37

18. (a) 13; (b) 32; (c) 39; (d) 19; (e) 5; (f) 19

20. (a) $135,000; (b) $170,000; yes

CHAPTER 3

Section 3.1
2. points do lie on a straight line.　　**4.** b, d

6. $y = 4x - 3$; (6, 3) in not on the line; $(-1, -7)$ is on the line

8. 1,500,000 boxes　　　　　　**10.** 125 points

Section 3.2
2. (a) $y = 3x - 1$; (b) $y = -2x - 3$; (c) $y = \frac{1}{2}x + \frac{1}{2}$; (d) $y = \frac{3}{2}x + 3\frac{1}{2}$

4. $y = 30x + 162,000$; sales increase by $9,000

6. $500 + 2x$

8. $10x - 50,000$; $10x - 32,000$

Section 3.3
4. (a) $-\frac{1}{2}$, $1\frac{1}{2}$; (b) 2, -0.75; (c) 1, $-\frac{1}{3}$; (d) -1, $\frac{1}{5}$

6. (a) 2.71, 1.29

8. every 6 months

Supplementary Exercises
2. points do lie on a straight line

4. points do lie on a straight line

6. $y = -2x + 4$

8. $y = 2 + 5x$; (2, 12)-yes; $(-1, -4)$-no

10. $y = 2x - 4$

12. (a) $y = 20,000x + 80,000$; (b) 200,000

14. $y = 0.24x + 2.45$; 1985 − $4.85; 1974 earnings per share

22. 4, −2

24. $35.2 million; yes

CHAPTER 4

Section 4.1
4. $\frac{1}{5}(5)^{-x}$

6. (b) $98,940; $163,080; $268,920; $443,340; and $730,800
(c) $1,205,400

8. (a) 82,875; 91,575; 101,250; 111,900; 123,675; 136,650; 151,050; 166,950, 184,500; and 203,850

10. (a) 36%, 71%, 87%, 98%, 99%

Section 4.2   **6.** (a) 1, 10, 100, 1000

Section 4.3   **2.** (a) $12 = 5^x$; (b) $y = 3^2$; (c) $7 = b^{15}$; (d) $14 = 10^x$; (e) $y = 9^{17}$;
(f) $7 = b^{24}$

4. (a) 6; (c) 2; (e) $-\frac{1}{2}$

6. $-2, -1, 0, 1, 2, 3$

8. (a) $\log D = \log 28.2 - 0.52 \log p$; 1.0867; 0.9302; 0.8386; 0.7736;
0.7233

10. (a) yes; (b) linear; (c) $y = 100 \cdot 2^x$

12. 18,500; 21,800

Supplementary   **2.** 0.0567; 0.2381; 1; 4.2; 17.64; 74.08
Exercises   **4.** $y = 12(1.25)^{-x}$

6. (a) 90.48; 81.87; 74.08; 67.03
(c) 1.5

8. (a) $1,200,000; (b) $82,436; $135,914; $224,084; $369,452;
$609,124; $1,655,772; (c) $1,655,772

10. (a) $x = \log_{10} 81$; (b) $x = \log_e 15$;
(c) $x = \log_2 40$; (d) $x = \log_8 125$

14. (a) 9509; (b) 3082; (c) 1897

CHAPTER 5

Section 5.1   **2.** (a) $2300; (b) $2645; (c) $3041.75

4. (a) .05; (b) .07; (c) .08

6. 5 years

8. 19.56%

10. (a) $9,441.12; (b) $9,563.09; (c) $9,628.24; (d) $9,673.36

12. $12,184.03

14. $13,424.71

16. $12,697.35

Section 5.2   **2.** $1,706,980   **8.** $2783.27

4. 10%   **10.** $8742.18

6. $182.56

Section 5.3   **2.** $15,100.50   **10.** $14.16

4. $8,200.39   **12.** The annuity is worth $3,590.33 more.

6. $127.20   **14.** $591.23

8. $11,434.91   **16.** $10,345.05

2. (a) $100,000; (b) $40,000

4. n = 1, $93,333.33; n = 2, $72,592.59; n = 3, $56,460.91; n = 4, $43,914.04; double-declining balance method is preferable.

6. linear, $160,000; double-declining balance method, $128,000

Supplementary   2. $1210; $1610.51   12. $6995.44
Exercises   4. $13,685.69   14. $158,812.18
                  6. 10.52%   16. $289.22
                  8. 10.52%   18. $3,054.09
                 10. $892.86   20. $3,240

CHAPTER 6

Section 6.2   2. (a) $x_1 = 7$, $x_2 = 3$; (b) $x = 2$, $y = -1$, $z = 3$; (c) $x_1 = 2$, $x_2 = 1$, $x_3 = -1$

4. (a) $x = 2.6$, $y = 0.4$; (b) lines coincide; (c) $x = 2.8333$, $y = 1.3$; (d) parallel; (e) lines coincide; (f) parallel

6. 12 standard, 20 deluxe

8. labor: $3.60/hr.; raw material: $2.40/lb.

10. $x = 0.77$, $y = 0.66$, and $z = 0.80$

Section 6.3   2. (b) 334

4. $4

6. 20 cents

Supplementary   2. $x = 4$, $y = 1$
Exercises   4. (a) $x_1 = 4$, $x_2 = 1$; (b) $x_1 = 2$, $x_2 = -1$; (c) $x_1 = 2$, $x_2 = -3$, $x_3 = 2$
                  6. 5000
                  8. 5
                 10. 4
                 12. (a) -5; (b) 4
                 14. $p_1 = \$1.80$, $p_2 = \$1.20$

CHAPTER 7

Section 7.2   2. $u = -1$, $v = -3$, $w = 3$, $x = 4$, $y = 7$, and $z = -3$.

4. (a) $\begin{pmatrix} 0 & 0 \\ -2 & 1 \end{pmatrix}$ and $\begin{pmatrix} -6 & 4 \\ 6 & 1 \end{pmatrix}$; (b) $(0\ \ 4\ \ 1\ \ 1\ \ 5)$ and $(2\ \ 2\ \ -9\ \ 9\ \ -1)$;

(c) $\begin{pmatrix} 5 & -1 & -5 \\ -3 & 4 & 4 \end{pmatrix}$ and $\begin{pmatrix} -1 & 1 & 1 \\ 1 & 0 & -4 \end{pmatrix}$; (d) do not exist;

(e) $\begin{pmatrix} 3 & 1 & -2 \\ -1 & -1 & 5 \\ 6 & 0 & -1 \\ 0 & 0 & -1 \end{pmatrix}$ and $\begin{pmatrix} -1 & -1 & 4 \\ 1 & 7 & 3 \\ 2 & -2 & -5 \\ 2 & -8 & 5 \end{pmatrix}$

6. (a) $(3 \quad -1)$ (b) $\begin{pmatrix} 0 & 2 & 1 & -6 \\ 3 & -3 & 2 & 1 \\ -1 & 4 & 0 & 1 \\ -5 & 1 & -3 & 2 \end{pmatrix}$ (c) $\begin{pmatrix} 2 \\ -2 \\ 0 \\ 3 \\ 4 \\ 8 \end{pmatrix}$

(d) $(3 \quad 2 \quad -4)$ (e) $\begin{pmatrix} 2 & 4 \\ 5 & 0 \\ -3 & 1 \end{pmatrix}$

8. (a) $\begin{pmatrix} -6 & 4 \\ 4 & 2 \end{pmatrix}$; $\begin{pmatrix} 30 & -20 \\ -40 & 0 \end{pmatrix}$

(b) $(2 \quad 6 \quad -8 \quad 10 \quad 4)$; $(-10 \quad 10 \quad 50 \quad -40 \quad 30)$

(c) $\begin{pmatrix} 4 & 0 & -4 \\ -2 & 4 & 0 \end{pmatrix}$; $\begin{pmatrix} 30 & -10 & -30 \\ -20 & 20 & 40 \end{pmatrix}$

(d) $\begin{pmatrix} 6 \\ 6 \\ -2 \end{pmatrix}$; $\begin{matrix} -10 \\ 20 \\ 20 \\ 20 \end{matrix}$

(e) $\begin{pmatrix} 2 & 0 & 2 \\ 0 & 6 & 8 \\ 8 & -2 & -6 \\ 2 & -8 & 4 \end{pmatrix}$; $\begin{pmatrix} 20 & 10 & -30 \\ -10 & -40 & 10 \\ 20 & 10 & 20 \\ -10 & 40 & -30 \end{pmatrix}$

10. $(19 \quad 62 \quad 19 \quad 2)$

2. (a) (-2); (b) $\begin{pmatrix} 10 & -2 \\ 7 & 19 \end{pmatrix}$; (c) $\begin{pmatrix} 7 & -3 & -2 \\ 8 & 4 & 1 \end{pmatrix}$; (d) $\begin{pmatrix} 1 & 3 & -4 \\ -1 & -3 & 4 \\ 3 & 9 & -12 \end{pmatrix}$;

(e) $\begin{pmatrix} 4 & -4 & 4 & 2 & 2 \\ 6 & 9 & 16 & -12 & 3 \\ 2 & 4 & 6 & -5 & 1 \end{pmatrix}$; (f) $\begin{pmatrix} 2 & 4 & -5 \\ 14 & -13 & 2 \\ 3 & -12 & 9 \end{pmatrix}$.

4. $11.84; **PQ'**

2. (a) $x_1 = 4$ and $x_2 = 1$; (b) $x_1 = 3$ and $x_2 = 5$; (c) $x_1 = -1$ and $x_2 = -3$.

4. (a) $x_1 = 2$, $x_2 = 1$, and $x_3 = -1$; (b) $x_1 = 3$, $x_2 = -1$, and $x_3 = -2$.

6. $x_1 = 2$, $x_2 = -3$, and $x_3 = 2$.

8. $x_1 = 5$, $x_2 = 2$, and $x_3 = -2$

2. original value $= 35$
(a) 105; (b) 140; (c) 35; (d) 35; (e) -35; (f) -35

2. $\begin{pmatrix} -6 & 2 \\ -3 & 12 \end{pmatrix}$

4. $\begin{pmatrix} 13 & 38 \\ -62 & 14 \end{pmatrix}$

6. $\begin{pmatrix} 4 & 10 \\ 3 & -6 \end{pmatrix}$

8. $\begin{pmatrix} 40 & 30 \\ 100 & -60 \end{pmatrix}$

10. $\begin{pmatrix} -8 & 1 & 2 \\ 1 & -2 & 1 \end{pmatrix}$

12. $\begin{pmatrix} 43 & 36 \\ 76 & 59 \end{pmatrix}$

14. $(5 \quad 20 \quad 45)$

16. (350)

18. $432.50

20. $\begin{pmatrix} -\dfrac{12}{94} & \dfrac{10}{94} \\[2ex] \dfrac{14}{94} & \dfrac{4}{94} \end{pmatrix}$

22. $\begin{pmatrix} -\dfrac{1}{6} & \dfrac{5}{6} \\[2ex] \dfrac{2}{6} & -\dfrac{4}{6} \end{pmatrix}$

24. $-1.468;\ 2.213$

26. (a) 1; (b) 1; (c) -47; (d) -54; (e) -1; (f) -4

CHAPTER 8

2. (a) $x > 16$; (b) $x < 15$; (c) $x \geq -3$; (d) $x > 3$; (e) $x \leq -25$.

4. (a) $x > 3$; (b) $x \leq 3$; (c) $x > 17$; (d) $x < 2$; (e) $x \geq 2$; (f) $x < 6$.

6. 13.

8. (a) $|x - 35| \leq 2$; (b) $33 \leq x \leq 37$.

10. (a) $-5 < x < 5$; (b) $2 \leq x \leq 4$; (c) $x \geq 5$ or $x \leq -1/3$; (d) $x > 1$ or $x < -4$.

12. (a) a/c less than b/d; (b) a/c greater than b/d; (c) $a/c = b/d$.

4. (a) $x \geq 10$, $y \geq 0$, $x + y \geq 55$, and $x + y \leq 58$; (b) (12, 44), (15, 40) and (18, 40) are feasible; (11, 42), (8, 49), and (12, 57) are not feasible.

6. (a) $x \geq 0, y \geq 0, 3x + 2y \leq 48,$ and $4x + 5y \leq 92$; (b) only (9, 10) is in the region of feasible solutions.

8. (a) $2,000 - x$, $3,000 - y$, $5,000 - x - y$, and $x + y - 3,000$;
(b) only the first and third points are in the feasible region

10. (a) $x \geq 0$, $y \geq 0$, $z \geq 0$, $x \leq 150$, $y \leq 250$, and $x + y + z \leq 600$
(b) $(150, 250, 200)$

Supplementary
Exercises **2.** (a) true; (b) false; (c) false; (d) true; (e) true; (f) false; (g) true;
(h) true; (i) false

4. (a) $x \leq 8$; (b) $x \geq 5$; (c) $x > 14$

6. $2,800,000 \leq x \leq 3,200,000$

8. $250 \leq x \leq 400$

10. (a) $-2 \leq x \leq 7$; (b) $-10 \leq x \leq 10$; (c) $-4 < x < 4$

16. (a) $x \leq 30$; $y \leq 50$; $x + y + z \leq 120$; $x, y, z \geq 0$

CHAPTER 9

Section 9.1   **2.** (a) $x_1 = 40$, $x_2 = 40$

4. (a) 8 dozen of the first kind; 12 dozen of the second kind
(b) 16 dozen of the first; none of the second

6. for 20 cases of A and 9 cases of B: 4 lbs. of the first supplement and 5 lbs. of the second

8. (a) $x = 150$, $y = 250$, $z = 200$; $1,962.50
(b) $x = 0$, $y = 0$, and $z = 600$; $2,100.00

Section 9.2   **2.** $(0, 0), 0$; $(0, 60), 120$; $(30, 50), 190$; $(40, 40), 200$; $(40, 0), 120$

4. (a) profit is a maximum at $x = 8$ and $y = 12$
(b) profit is a maximum at $x = 16$ and $y = 0$

6. ten cases: maximum at $x = \dfrac{23}{8}$ and $y = \dfrac{15}{8}$

Section 9.3   **2.** max $3x_1 + 2x_2$
s.t.
$$\begin{aligned}
4x_1 + x_2 + s_1 \qquad\qquad &= 200\\
x_1 + x_2 \qquad + s_2 \qquad &= 80\\
\tfrac{1}{3}x_1 + x_2 \qquad\qquad + s_3 &= 60\\
x_1, x_2, s_1, s_2, s_3 &\geq 0
\end{aligned}$$
basic feasible solution: $x_1 = 0$, $x_2 = 0$, $s_1 = 200$, $s_2 = 80$, $s_3 = 60$

4. max $40x_1 + 44x_2$
s.t.
$$\begin{aligned}
3x_1 + 2x_2 + s_1 \qquad\quad &= 48\\
4x_1 + 5x_2 \qquad + s_2 &= 92\\
x_1, x_2, s_1, s_2 &\geq 0
\end{aligned}$$
basic feasible solution: $x_1 = 0$, $x_2 = 0$, $s_1 = 48$, $s_2 = 92$

6. The indicators are 2, 9, 0, 0; the entering variable is x_2; the quotients are 2 and -1; the departing variable is s_1.

8. The indicators are $0, 5/4, -3/4, 0, 0$; the entering variable is x_2; the quotients are 200, 40, 47.27; the departing variable is s_2

10. $x_1 = 1,600$, $x_2 = 1,000$, $s_1 = 0$, and $s_2 = 0$

12. $x_1 = 60$, $x_2 = 0$, $x_3 = 180$, $s_1 = 0$, and $s_2 = 0$

Section 9.4

4. $x_1 = 2$, $x_2 = 4$, $s_1 = 0$, $s_2 = 0$, $a_1 = 0$, and $a_2 = 0$

6. min $1.20\, x_1 + 3.60\, x_2$
s.t.
$$
\begin{aligned}
20\, x_1 + 10\, x_2 - s_1 \quad\quad\quad &= 480 \\
10\, x_1 + 20\, x_2 \quad\quad - s_2 \quad\quad &= 600 \\
10\, x_1 + 60\, x_2 \quad\quad\quad - s_3 &= 1080 \\
x_1, x_2, s_1, s_2, s_3 &\geq 0
\end{aligned}
$$

8. optimal solution: $x_1 = 60$, $x_2 = 0$

10. The indicators are $4, -5, 0, 0, 0$; the entering variable is x_1; the quotients are $12, 4, -2$; the departing variable is s_2.

12. min $5x_1 - 10x_2$
s.t.
$$
\begin{aligned}
x_1 + 3x_2 + s_1 \quad\quad\quad &= 30 \\
2x_1 - x_2 \quad + s_2 \quad\quad &= 20 \\
-x_1 + 10x_2 \quad\quad - s_3 &= 10 \\
x_1, x_2, s_1, s_2, s_3 &\geq 0
\end{aligned}
$$

14. min $2x_1 + 1.5\, x_2$
s.t.
$$
\begin{aligned}
x_1 + x_2 - s_1 \quad\quad &= 1 \\
x_1 + 3x_2 \quad + s_2 &= 3 \\
x_1, x_2, s_1, s_2 &\geq 0
\end{aligned}
$$

Supplementary Exercises

2. $(0, 0)$, 0; $(0, 20)$, 96; $(8, 16)$, 96; $(18, 6)$, 72; $(20, 0)$, 48

4. optimal solution: $(0, 20)$ $(8, 16)$, or any point on the line segment joining these two points

6. $x_1 = 0$, $x_2 = 0$, $x_3 = 5$

8. max $24,000\, x_1 + 30,000\, x_2 + 48,000\, x_3 + 36,000\, x_4$
s.t.
$$
\begin{aligned}
x_1 + x_2 + x_3 + x_4 + s_1 \quad\quad &= 10 \\
2x_1 + x_2 + 4x_3 + x_4 \quad\quad + s_2 &= 20 \\
x_1, x_2, x_3, x_4, s_1, s_2 &\geq 0
\end{aligned}
$$

CHAPTER 10

Section 10.2

2. 10

4. 2

6. (a) 3; (b) 0; (c) limit does not exist because $f(x)$ increases beyond any bound

	8. yes	**10.** not continuous

2. (a) 90; (b) 81; (c) 80.1; (d) 80.01   **8.** 2
4. 6   **10.** 200
6. 11

2. -4 **6.** -34 thousands
4. $-2x$ **8.** (a) yes; (b) yes

2. $f'(x) = -1.5$; -1.5 and -1.5
4. $f'(x) = 2$; 2 and 2
6. $f'(x) = -18 + 15x^4$; -3 and 1,197
8. $f'(x) = 1 - 3/x^2$; $13/16$
10. $f'(x) = -3x^{-4} - 8x^{-5}$; $-5/256$
12. $f'(x) = -72/x^7$; $-9/2048$
14. $f'(x) = 8x^3 - 36x^2 + 40x - 12$; -12
16. $f'(x) = 7x^6 - 18x^5 + 5x^4 - 12x^3$; 0
18. $f'(x) = 2 - 3x^{-2} + 12x^{-3}$; does not exist
20. (a) \$17 million per year; (b) $y = 17x - 32$; \$70 million and \$78 million

2. $5(8x - 1)(3 - x + 4x^2)^4$

4. $\dfrac{-4(3 - 4x)}{(1 + 3x - 2x^2)^5}$

6. $\dfrac{24(x - 2)^2}{(x + 2)^4}$

8. -2

10. (a) $\dfrac{3x^2 + 4}{2y}$; (b) $8/5$ and $-8/5$; (c) $y = -\dfrac{8}{5}x - \dfrac{9}{5}$

14. -31.25

2. 4,700 and 3,008
4. 201 and 0

6. (a) $1/x$; (b) $3/x$; (c) $6x - \dfrac{4 \cdot \ln x}{x}$; (d) $\dfrac{x^2}{\ln 5} + 3x^2(\log_5 x)$;
(e) $\dfrac{1 - \ln x}{x^2}$; (f) $\dfrac{6}{x}(\ln x)^5$; (g) $\dfrac{2 + x}{x(\ln 10)} + \log_{10} x$;

(h) $\dfrac{6x(\log_{10} x) - \dfrac{3x}{\ln 10}}{(\log_{10} x)^2}$

2. $f'(x) = 4x^3 - 6x$ and $f''(x) = 12x^2 - 6$
4. $y' = 5x^4 - 24x^2$ and $y'' = 20x^3 - 48x$
6. $y' = x + 2x(\ln x)$ and $y'' = 3 + 2(\ln x)$

2. $8x + 2$

4. 14

6. 0

8. not continuous

10. continuous

12. 1

14. $-4x$

16. $10x - 8x^{-5}$

18. $\dfrac{(x + 2)(2x + 2) - (x^2 + 2x)(1)}{(x + 2)^2}$

20. -2

22. $-3x^{-4}$

24. $(12x + 18)(2x^2 + 6x)^2$

26. $\frac{1}{2}x^{-\frac{1}{2}}$

28. $\dfrac{2 - y}{x - 1}$

30. $-5e^{-5x}$

32. $2(\ln x)\dfrac{1}{x}$

34. $\dfrac{-2}{x}$

36. (a) profitable; (b) not profitable

38. (a) $8 million per year; (b) $y = -9 + 8x$; when $x = 5$ then $y = 31$; the sales revenue from the tangent line is less.

40. approximately $23,775

CHAPTER 11

2. $x = 3$; yes

4. minimum at $x = -1$, maximum at $x = 2$, minimum at $x = 3$.

6. (a) $x = 0$; maximum; (b) $x = 2$; minimum

8. $D = 41$

10. (b) 5 by 5

12. 16

2. $3x^2 + 2xy^2$, $2yx^2 - 18y^2$, $6x + 2y^2$, and $2x^2 - 36y$

4. $9x^2 - e^y$, $2 - xe^y$, $18x$, and $-xe^y$

6. $\ln y + y/x$, $x/y + \ln x$, $-y/x^2$, and $-x/y^2$

8. -260 and 310

10. Relative minimum at $x = 3$ and $y = -2$

12. Relative maximum at $x = 0$ and $y = 0$

14. (a) $z = 24\left(20 - \dfrac{50}{x} - \dfrac{24}{y}\right) - (3x + 4y)$;

    (b) $x = 20$, $y = 12$, $z = \$264$

Section 11.3   **4.** $x = 2\frac{2}{3}$, $y = 2\frac{2}{3}$

            6. $\$39.35$

Supplementary   **2.** 4
Exercises

            4. 2, minimum; -1, maximum

            6. 2

            8. $\$4,000$ and $\$69,120$

            10. 100

            12. 2 and $.04x_2$

            14. $x = -3$, $y = 3$, and $z = 107$

            16. $x = 12$ thousand and $y = 7$ thousand

            18. $x = \$6666$ and $y = \$3334$

CHAPTER 12

Section 12.4   **2.** (a) $15x + C$; (e) $\frac{3}{5}x^{5/3} + C$

            4. (a) $\frac{1}{3}x^{3/2} - x^{1/2} + C$; (b) $5x - x^3 + x^5 + C$

            6. (a) $6^x/(\ln 6) + C$; (b) $\frac{1}{2}x^2 + 2x + 2(\ln x) + C$; (c) $5 \cdot 3^x/(\ln 3) + C$

            8. $R = 9D - 8\sqrt{D}$; $\$3,440$

            10. (a) $95\frac{5}{9}\%$; (b) 60%

Section 12.5   **2.** $-2/3$

            4. $16\frac{1}{3}$

            6. $\$5,830,780$

Supplementary   **4.** (a) $\frac{1}{4}x^4 + C$; (b) $\frac{4}{7}x^{\frac{7}{4}} + C$; (c) $12x + C$; (d) $2x^{\frac{1}{2}} + C$
Exercises

            6. (a) $\frac{3}{2}x^2 - 5e^x + C$; (b) $x^2 + x + \ln x + C$; (c) $\dfrac{5^x}{\ln 5} + C$;

               (d) $x - e^x + C$; (e) $3x \cdot \dfrac{2^x}{\ln 2} + C$; (f) $15 \cdot \ln x + C$

            8. $R = 3,000D + \dfrac{2,000}{1 + D} - 2,000$; $\$7,500$

            10. (a) $20\frac{2}{3}$; (b) 0.91629; (c) 1.0986

            12. 96%; 16%

CHAPTER 13

Section 13.1
2. (a) 360; (b) 240; (c) 180   **8.** (a) 225; (b) 90; (c) 15
4. 56   **10.** 36
6. (a) 12; (b) 7   **12.** 32

Section 13.3
2. 1,320   **8.** (a) 19,600; (b) 117,600
4. (a) 32,760; (b) 5,040; (c) 3,024   **10.** (a) 455; (b) 105
6. 495

Section 13.4
2. (a) We will choose a house with 3 bedrooms and 1 bath; (b) we will choose a house with 3 baths; (c) we will choose a house with one more bedroom than baths; (d) we will choose a house with the same number of bedrooms and baths.

4. (a) A total of 3 tables are being used; (b) in the larger room 3 tables are being used; (c) a total of 2 tables are being used; (d) at least one of the rooms is empty.

6. (b) (i) (3, 1, 3), (3, 2, 3), and (3, 3, 3), (ii) (1, 2, 2), (1, 2, 3), (1, 3, 2), and (1, 3, 3), (iii) (2, 2, 1), (2, 2, 3), (2, 1, 2), (2, 3, 2), (1, 2, 2), and (3, 2, 2); (c) the first two voters are opposed to the new bond issue; all three voters respond the same way; all three voters respond differently; and the first voter is for the new bond issue.

8. (a) Not mutually exclusive; (b) not mutually exclusive; (c) mutually exclusive; (d) mutually exclusive; (e) mutually exclusive; (f) not mutually exclusive.

10. (a) Not mutually exclusive; (b) mutually exclusive; (c) not mutually exclusive; (d) mutually exclusive; (e) not mutually exclusive; (f) not mutually exclusive; (g) mutually exclusive.

12. (a) 12%; (b) 13%; (c) 87%; (d) 33%; (e) 11%

Supplementary Exercises
2. (a) 49; (b) 42; (c) 27
4. 4,096
6. 2,162,160
8. (c) A is the event that he visits all four of his customers; B is the event that he visits two of his customers on the second day; C is the event that he visits one more customer on the first day then on the second day; D is the event that he visits at least three of his customers on the second day; E is the event that he visits at most two of his customers.

10. (a) Not mutually exclusive; (b) mutually exlusive; (c) mutually exclusive; (d) not mutually exclusive; (e) not mutually exclusive; (f) not mutually exclusive.

12. Should be questioned; figures total 430 instead of 400.

CHAPTER 14

Section 14.1

2. 0.26

4. 0.40

6. 0.75

8. (a) The sum of the probabilities exceeds 1; (b) the sum of the probabilities is less than 1; (c) second probability should exceed the first; (d) second probability should exceed the first; (e) the probability that it will win first or second game exceeds 1; (f) second probability cannot exceed the first; (g) the sum of the three probabilities should be 1.

10. (a) 0.30; (b) 0.79; (c) 0.70

Section 14.2

2. (a) $19.50; (b) $2.50   **6.** 120

4. $5\frac{13}{16}$ **8.** 2.98

Section 14.3

2. (b) continue drilling

4. (a) not take her coat; (b) take her coat; (c) take her coat; (d) take her coat; (e) take her coat

6. (a) continue to drill; (b) stop drilling

Supplementary Exercises

2. 0.12   **8.** $9,900

4. 0.76   **10.** 2.5

6. (a) 0.35; (b) 0.90   **12.** d_2

INDEX

A

Abscissa, 53
Absolute inequality, 214
Absolute value, 215
Algebraic fractions, 28
Amortization, 141
Annuity, 133
  future value of, 133, 135
  present value of, 133, 140
Antidifferentiation, 338
Area under curve, 327
Arithmetic progression, 134
  common difference, 134
Artificial variable, 252
Augmented coefficient matrix,
  192

B

Base of exponential function, 96
Base of exponential notation, 16
Base of logarithmic function, 106
Basic feasible solution, 240
  transformation of, 241
Binomial coefficients, 367
Book value, 144
Break-even analysis, 153
Briggsian logarithms, 120

C

Chain rule of differentiation, 283
Characteristic, 120

Classical probability concept,
  384
Column vector, 173
Combinations, 366
Common logarithms, 108, 120
Complement, 5
Component of vector, 173
Compound depreciation, 144
Compound interest, 124
Compound value, 130
Compounding, 124
  annually, 124
  continuous, 128
  effective rate, 127
  multiple, 126
Constant of integration, 340
Constraint, 230, 253
Continuity, 264
Continuous compounding, 128
Continuous function, 264
  in an interval, 264
Coordinate axes, 51
Coordinates, 52
Curve, slope of, 269

D

Decimal notation, 14
Decision analysis, 384, 395
Decision theory, 384
Definite integral, 334
Degree of polynomial, 23, 89
Delta process, 274
Departing variable, 245
Dependent variable, 50

M

N